LEGAL PERSONALITY IN INTERNATIONAL LAW

Several current international legal issues are related to the concept of legal personality, including the determination of international rights and duties of non-state actors and the legal capacities of transnational institutions. When addressing these issues, different understandings of legal personality are employed. These conceptions consider different entities to be international persons, state different criteria for becoming one and attach different consequences to being one.

Roland Portmann systematizes the different positions on international personality by spelling out the assumptions on which they rest and examining how they were substantiated in legal practice. He puts forward the argument that positions on international personality that strongly emphasize the role of states or effective actors rely on assumptions that have been discarded in present international law. The principal argument is that international law has to be conceived as an open system, in which there is no presumption for or against certain entities enjoying international personality.

ROLAND PORTMANN is a Scientific Collaborator at the Swiss Ministry of Foreign Affairs, Directorate of International Law, Berne, and a Lecturer in Public International Law at the University of St. Gallen, Switzerland.

CAMBRIDGE STUDIES IN INTERNATIONAL AND COMPARATIVE LAW

Established in 1946, this series produces high quality scholarship in the fields of public and private international law and comparative law. Although these are distinct legal sub-disciplines, developments since 1946 confirm their interrelation.

Comparative law is increasingly used as a tool in the making of law at national, regional and international levels. Private international law is now often affected by international conventions, and the issues faced by classical conflicts rules are frequently dealt with by substantive harmonization of law under international auspices. Mixed international arbitrations, especially those involving state economic activity, raise mixed questions of public and private international law, while in many fields (such as the protection of human rights and democratic standards, investment guarantees and international criminal law) international and national systems interact. National constitutional arrangements relating to 'foreign affairs', and to the implementation of international norms, are a focus of attention.

The Board welcomes works of a theoretical or interdisciplinary character, and those focusing on the new approaches to international or comparative law or conflicts of law. Studies of particular institutions or problems are equally welcome, as are translations of the best work published in other languages.

A list of books in the series can be found at the end of this volume.

LEGAL PERSONALITY IN INTERNATIONAL LAW

ROLAND PORTMANN

CAMBRIDGE
UNIVERSITY PRESS

CAMBRIDGE UNIVERSITY PRESS
Cambridge, New York, Melbourne, Madrid, Cape Town,
Singapore, São Paulo, Delhi, Tokyo, Mexico City

Cambridge University Press
The Edinburgh Building, Cambridge CB2 8RU, UK

Published in the United States of America by
Cambridge University Press, New York

www.cambridge.org
Information on this title: www.cambridge.org/9780521768450

First published 2010

A catalogue record for this publication is available from the British Library

Library of Congress cataloguing in publication data
A catalogue record for this publication is available from the British Library
Library of Congress Cataloguing in Publication data
Portmann, Roland, 1977–
Legal personality in international law / Roland Portmann.
p. cm. – (Cambridge studies in international and comparative law ; 70)
Includes bibliographical references.
ISBN 978-0-521-76845-0
1. Persons (International law) I. Title. II. Series.
KZ3910.P67 2010
346.01′2–dc22
2010017818

ISBN 978-0-521-76845-0 Hardback

To Fabia

When convictions have been accepted for a long time in doctrine it is easy to lose sight of their derivation from certain assumptions; they therefore continue to be regarded as truths, even when these assumptions have been discarded.

Roberto Ago, *Positive Law and International Law*, 1957

A study of the history of opinion is a necessary preliminary to the emancipation of the mind. I do not know which makes a man more conservative – to know nothing but the present, or nothing but the past.

John Maynard Keynes, *The End of Laissez-Faire*, 1926

We require to know of each rule of international law how it originated and developed, who first established it, and how it gradually became recognized in practice.

Lassa Oppenheim, *The Science of International Law*, 1908

CONTENTS

FOREWORD

The topic of legal personality in international law is pervasive yet mysterious. What does it add to the modern law of human rights, for example, to affirm or deny that individuals are 'subjects of international law'? The provisions of the human rights treaties, and their implementation mechanisms, continue despite such affirmations or denials. Yet if we say, with Rosalyn Higgins,[1] that the question is not one of formal personality but of actual participation, we may seem to capture an element of the crowded international scene, but at the expense of another; for how far we can participate may well be affected by issues of status – whether one is eligible to chair the drafting committee, or entitled to sit in the delegates' lounge, or none of the above. In practice, issues of status do not go away, even in smoke-filled rooms, and even if the latter are fortunately less common than they used to be.

As Roland Portmann points out in this splendid, lucid work, 'there is little comprehensive literature on legal personality in international law, at least in recent times'. Writers have rather concentrated on statehood or on international organisations, or (for those not fixated on either topic) on denying the value of any concept of legal personality in a 'globalising' legal order. The now substantial body of work on non-governmental organisations, and the (largely distinct) studies concerning international law and 'transnational' corporations, generally fall into this latter category. This work, aiming to offer 'a comprehensive analysis of legal personality in international law', thus fills a real gap.

In a systematic analysis, Roland Portmann spells out the assumptions upon which many conceptions of international legal personality lie. He tests his theory on a broad range of legal scenarios, including the application of treaties to individuals, the rights and duties of non-state actors, and the law of state contracts; effectively arguing that

[1] R. Higgins, *Problems and Process: International Law and How We Use It* (Oxford University Press: 1994), 50.

international law is an open system of legal rules and principles in which no entity is necessarily excluded from participating.

By so clearly tracking the historical and practical development of the individual in international law, this work effectively attacks the myth of the unitary State as *the* actor on the international stage. In place of the myth is an open casting call, in which the legal order assigns roles for states, entities and individuals on the stage based largely on performance, and where status is only a *prima facie* criterion.

James Crawford
Lauterpacht Centre for International Law
14 May 2010

ACKNOWLEDGMENTS

This book is a revised version of a thesis submitted to the University of St. Gallen, Switzerland, in May 2008. The topic and the general approach towards it were mainly elaborated in discussions with my supervisors, Professor Roland Kley of the University of St. Gallen and Professor Robert Kolb of the University of Geneva. In the course of our regular meetings, both of them offered many knowledgeable insights without forcing them upon me, a rare quality in academic teachers and one that I appreciated very much. I especially benefited from their insistence on analytic clarity as well as from their comments on my writing. They also strongly supported my plans for a research stay at the Lauterpacht Centre for International Law at the University of Cambridge.

The Lauterpacht Centre offered an immensely stimulating and congenial atmosphere. I particularly benefited from comments by Professor James Crawford. Interactions with Fellows and other Visiting Fellows were a source of constant learning and inspiration, particularly with Giulio Bartolini, Camille Bergmann, Claudia Cinelli, Ignacio Rodriguez y Alvarez and Michael Waibel. A special source of support throughout and beyond my stay in Cambridge was David S. Berry. He took much time to discuss basic questions of the international legal order and commented on all parts of the manuscript.

I am especially grateful for the advice and support offered by Ralph Weber. He accompanied my endeavour from the first months onwards. Discussions with him not only made me question my own arguments and motivated me to work harder on them, they also revealed the pleasures of academic debate. Professor Kerstin Odendahl took an active interest in my work and offered much appreciated advice and support. Nikolas Stürchler kindly shared his own experiences in turning a thesis into a book. The latter process was much facilitated by the kindness and efficiency I encountered at Cambridge University Press, especially in contacts with Finola O'Sullivan, Nienke van Schaverbeke and Richard Woodham.

Two institutions granted financial support for my research. The Swiss National Science Foundation awarded me a scholarship for my stay in Cambridge. The Janggen-Pöhn Foundation provided me with a grant in order to fully concentrate on finishing my writing in Switzerland. Their support was much appreciated.

Special thanks go to my parents, Marlène and Rolf, as well as to my sister Nadja. This book is dedicated to Fabia, whom I thank most.

Roland Portmann

TABLE OF CASES

ABBREVIATIONS

AJIL	American Journal of International Law
AJIL Supp.	Supplement to the American Journal of International Law: Official Documents
Ann. IDI	Annuaire de l'Institut de Droit International
AöR	Archiv des öffentlichen Rechts
ARSIWA	The ILC's Articles on the Responsibility of States for Internationally Wrongful Acts
ASIL Proc.	Proceedings of the Annual Meeting of the American Society of International Law
ATCA	Alien Tort Claims Act
AVR	Archiv des Völkerrechts
BIS	Bank for International Settlements
BYIL	British Yearbook of International Law
ECHR	European Court of Human Rights
ECJ	European Court of Justice
ECR	European Court Reports
EJIL	European Journal of International Law
EPIL	Encyclopedia of Public International Law
HILJ	Harvard International Law Journal
HLR	Harvard Law Review
IACHR	Inter-American Court of Human Rights
ICC	International Criminal Court
ICJ	International Court of Justice
ICJ Reports	International Court of Justice, Reports of Judgments, Advisory Opinions and Orders
ICLQ	International and Comparative Law Quarterly
ICRC	International Committee of the Red Cross
ICSID	International Centre for Settlement of Investment Disputes
ICSID Reports	Reports of Cases Decided under the Convention on the Settlement of Investment Disputes between States and Nationals of Other States
ICTR	International Criminal Tribunal for Rwanda
ICTY	International Criminal Tribunal for the former Yugoslavia

ILA	International Law Association
ILC	International Law Commission
ILM	International Legal Materials
ILO	International Labour Organization
ILR	International Law Reports
JDI	Journal du Droit International (Clunet)
LNTS	League of Nations Treaty Series
NILR	Netherlands International Law Review
NJIL	Nordic Journal of International Law
PCIJ	Permanent Court of International Justice
RAI	Recueil des Arbitrages Internationaux (de la Pradelle/Politis)
RCADI	Recueil des Cours de l'Académie de Droit International
Rdi	Rivista di diritto internazionale
RDI	Revue de Droit International (de la Pradelle)
RGDIP	Revue Générale de Droit International Public
UNC	Charter of the United Nations
UNTS	United Nations Treaty Series
VCCR	Vienna Convention on Consular Relations
VCLT	Vienna Convention on the Law of Treaties
YILC	Yearbook of the International Law Commission
YLJ	Yale Law Journal
ZaöRV	Zeitschrift für ausländisches öffentliches Recht und Völkerrecht
ZöR	Zeitschrift für öffentliches Recht

Introduction

Legal personality is a concept present in international law. It is principally employed to distinguish between those social entities relevant to the international legal system and those excluded from it. There is almost universal agreement that states are international persons. But it is unresolved whether and according to what criteria entities other than states – individuals, international and non-governmental organizations, private corporations – can become international persons and what consequences such international legal status entails. In this sense, it still holds true that, as the International Court of Justice put it in *Reparation for Injuries*, international personality is a concept 'giv[ing] rise to controversy'.[1]

Despite (or perhaps because of) its controversial nature, there is little comprehensive literature on legal personality in international law, at least in recent times. Certainly, most textbooks contain chapters on international personality or on the subjects of international law, the two expressions mostly used as synonyms.[2] And equally true, there is a large number of scholarly contributions focusing on one particular aspect of international personality, for example on the international legal status of individuals or on the international capacities of international and non-governmental organizations. But there are very few general treatments of the topic and, to the extent they exist, they tend to be brief and observational in nature[3] or more

[1] *Reparation for Injuries Suffered in the Service of the United Nations* (Advisory Opinion), 1949 ICJ Reports 174, at 178.

[2] The latter holds true throughout this work. Likewise, the terms 'personality', 'legal personality' and 'international personality' will be used interchangeably.

[3] Important examples include Barberis, Julio A., 'Nouvelles Questions Conçernant la Personnalité Juridique Internationale', RCADI, 179 (1983–I), 145–304; Menon, P. K., 'The Subjects of Modern International Law', *Hague Yearbook of International Law*, 3 (1990), 30–86; Kolb, Robert, 'Une observation sur la détermination de la subjectivité internationale', ZöR, 52 (1997), 115–25; Kolb, Robert, 'Nouvelle observation sur la

concerned with historical and biographical rather than with legal analysis.[4]

This book aims to offer a comprehensive analysis of legal personality in international law. Deliberately, it combines theoretical and practical aspects of the concept. Starting from the observation that different positions on personality (here called conceptions) are present in contemporary international legal argument, these conceptions are organized and examined with regard to their intellectual origins as well as their manifestations in legal practice. Such engagement with the existing body of international legal argument allows examination of the basic assumptions on which the different conceptions of international personality rest and scrutinization of their application as well as substantiation – in the form of presumptions for and consequences of legal personality – in the case law. It is then possible to determine which assumptions underlying the different conceptions are still to be considered legally sound and which ones have been discarded in international law over time. Correspondingly, it can be established whether presumptions for certain entities being international persons and whether certain consequences attached to this legal status conform with the basic premises of the contemporary international legal order.

Five different conceptions on international personality are identified as being present in international legal argument: the 'states-only conception', the 'recognition conception', the 'individualistic conception', the 'formal conception' and the 'actor conception'. These conceptions consider different entities to be international persons, contain different mechanisms in order to become one and attach different consequences to being one. The main argument of this book is that it is not tenable anymore to consider states the only natural persons of international

détermination de la personnalité juridique internationale', ZöR, 57 (2002), 229–41; Klabbers, Jan, '(I Can't Get No) Recognition: Subjects Doctrine and the Emergence of Non-State Actors' in Jarna Petman and Jan Klabbers (eds.), *Nordic Cosmopolitanism: Essays in International Law for Martti Koskenniemi* (Leiden: Brill, 2003), 351–69; and Cosnard, Michel, 'Rapport Introductif' in Société Française pour le Droit International (ed.), *Colloque du Mans: Le Sujet en Droit International* (Paris: Éditions A. Pedone, 2005), 13–53, all of them not intending to represent a comprehensive treatment. A more general work is Arangio-Ruiz, Gaetano, *Diritto Internazionale e Personalità Giuridica* (Bologna: Cooperativa Libraria Universitaria, 1972), which is, however, very different in general outlook from the present study and somewhat outdated.

4 See Nijman, Janne Elisabeth, *The Concept of International Legal Personality: An Inquiry Into the History and Theory of International Law* (The Hague: T. M. C. Asser Press, 2004), which is a very useful study in terms of the historical and biographical context in which the concept has developed, but which mostly refrains from actual legal analysis.

law possessing free discretion to allocate personality to other entities; moreover, it cannot be a question of effective actor-quality in international relations that allows one to acquire international legal status. The assumptions underlying these conceptions have been progressively discarded in international law. It is submitted that international personality has to be administered according to a set of legal principles informed by the formal and individualistic conceptions. Accordingly, with the exception of individuals in certain situations, there are no a priori international persons: personality is acquired in international law whenever an international norm is addressed at a particular entity, without there being a presumption for or against certain units. The sole consequence of being an international person in this framework is to be able to invoke international responsibility and to be held internationally responsible as far as applicable secondary rules exist. In particular, it is argued that it is not a direct consequence of international personality to have the capacity to create international law.

Two aspects related to the relevance of the concept of international personality have to be addressed at once. First, the term 'international personality' has often been avoided in legal doctrine in recent years. A group of scholars, most notably perhaps Rosalyn Higgins, prefers to speak of 'actors' or 'participants' rather than international persons.[5] As the categorization into the five conceptions suggests, in this book the actor approach is understood as representing an additional conception of international personality. For it concerns the same function of determining the entities relevant for the international legal system. Of course, this is not to deny that the actor conception contains certain innovative aspects distinguishing it from more traditional approaches; but such aspects will be considered as part of the general investigation into the conceptions of international personality. Second, it has to be admitted that the concept of international personality is only rarely directly addressed in international practice. However, this does not mean that it is irrelevant for determining legal issues. This book makes the case that predispositions about international personality influence legal outcomes in several areas, namely the direct application of treaties to individuals, the capacities of international organizations, the rights and duties of non-state actors under customary international law, and the legal nature of state contracts. More specifically, it is demonstrated – by relating the

[5] Higgins, Rosalyn, *Problems and Process: International Law and How we Use it* (Oxford: Clarendon Press, 1994), esp. 50.

legal reasoning in practical instances to the assumptions underlying different conceptions – which conception of personality was manifested in particular authoritative statements on these topics. In this way, the practical relevance and the consequences of applying a particular view of personality become more tangible.

The structure of this book is as follows. Part I seeks to demonstrate that the concept and the conceptions of international personality are present in international legal argument and that the choice of a particular conception is significant to specific international legal issues. Part II sketches the broader history of the concept before investigating, as the main contribution of the book, the intellectual origins and the practical manifestations of the five conceptions present in international law today. Part III finally evaluates the legal constructions elucidated in the preceding part and formulates a viable legal framework for personality in international law.

PART I

The concept of personality in international law

In analogy to municipal law, the notion of personality is used in international law to distinguish between those social actors the international legal system takes account of and those being excluded from it. But owing to the peculiarities of the international legal system, there is no clearly established international law of persons. As a result, there are different positions on exactly which entities count as persons in international law, under what criteria personality is acquired and what specific consequences this status entails. This lack of clarity is disconcerting in itself. But it also influences the outcome in particular legal situations. In order to substantiate these claims, Part I of this book will first outline the presence and function of personality in international legal argument (1). It will then identify the different substantive positions on the concept and how one has to deal with them (2). Finally, the case will be made for the significance of the concept in legal practice even when personality is not directly addressed (3).

1

Notion

Legal personality is a controversial concept of international law. But it is, of course, not a concept confined to the international legal system. It represents one of the pillars of municipal law as well. In order to approach the meaning of the notion, it is therefore convenient to review the function of personality in municipal private law. A private law analogy might help to develop an understanding of the role of the concept in international law. Yet, at the same time, it is important to note the peculiarities of international personality. It is because of them that the concept poses much more difficult legal issues in international law than in municipal law. These differences are also the reason why a private law analogy can only help to demonstrate the problem, but not to find a solution for the controversial concept of personality in international law.

A legal system has to determine whom it endows with the rights and duties contained in it and whose actions it takes account of by attaching legal consequences to them. To this effect, municipal law usually includes a law of persons. Historically, this law of persons was concerned with marking several distinctions in the legal personality of individuals. It comprised classes like nobles, clerics, serfs or slaves to which it allocated different degrees of personality in law.[1] Most of these distinctions vanished from the private law of persons in the nineteenth century. Yet, it did not become obsolete. As an effect of the emerging right to form groups and associations in most countries, new categories of legal personality, in this case of corporate nature, were introduced into the private law of persons. For the purposes of law, these recognized groups and associations were regarded as distinct entities from the individuals composing them. One could then not only have legal relationships with other human beings under municipal private law, but also with such groups

[1] See also Maitland, Frederic William, 'Moral Personality and Legal Personality (Sidgwick Lecture)', *Journal of the Society of Comparative Legislation*, 6 (1905), 192–200, at 198.

and associations being acknowledged persons of the legal system. As a result of this process, individuals (distinguished only according to age and mental condition) and various forms of corporations are today considered legal persons of most municipal private laws. In general, these entities are clearly specified, either through provisions in civil codes or through other authoritative statements of the private law of persons. As legal persons, these entities have rights and duties and can act in a legally relevant way, that is, can enter into contracts or commit torts, the consequences of both acts being determined by the legal system. The private law of persons therefore establishes which entities are legally relevant for a specific municipal legal system.

In international law, it also has to be determined which entities have rights and duties and act in legally relevant ways. The notion of legal personality is traditionally employed to this end, and accordingly called international personality. In principle, international law makes use of the concept of legal personality in the way municipal law does and textbooks[2] or General Courses[3] on international law failing to address the concept are very rare. However, two peculiarities distinguish personality in international law from that in municipal law.

The first peculiarity often stated is that international personality not only denotes the quality of having rights and duties as well as certain capacities under the law, but that it also includes the *competence to create the law*.[4] This association of international personality with law-creation is an effect of there being no centralized legislator in the international legal system as opposed to municipal private law where the creation of

[2] A selection of contemporary textbooks dealing with the concept of international personality includes: Brownlie, Ian, *Principles of Public International Law*, 6th edition (Oxford University Press, 2003), 57–67; Ipsen, Knut, *Völkerrecht*, 5th edition (Munich: C. H. Beck, 2004), 55–111; Shaw, Malcolm N., *International Law*, 6th edition (Cambridge University Press, 2008), 195–264; Verhoeven, Joe, *Droit International Public* (Brussels: Larcier, 2000), 47–316; Jennings, Robert Y. and Arthur Watts, *Oppenheim's International Law Volume I: Peace*, 9th edition (London: Longman, 1992), 117–329; Müller, Jörg Paul and Luzius Wildhaber, *Praxis des Völkerrechts*, 3rd edition (Berne: Stämpfli, 2001), 209–315; Rousseau, Charles, *Droit International Public (Tome II): Les sujets de droit* (Paris: Edition Sirey, 1974), (whole volume); Cassese, Antonio, *International Law* (Oxford University Press, 2001), 46–85; Daillier, Patrick and Alain Pellet, *Droit International Public*, 5th edition (Paris: L. G. D. J., 1994), 547–684; Doehring, Karl, *Völkerrecht*, 2nd edition (Heidelberg: C. F. Müller, 2004), 24–120.

[3] See the overview provided by Kolb, Robert, *Les Cours Généraux de Droit International Public de l'Académie de La Haye* (Brussels: Bruylant, 2003), which shows that most General Courses since 1929 have addressed the concept of international personality.

[4] See e.g. Brownlie, *Principles*, 57.

law lies in the competence of centralized state power (and consequently is not exercised by the legal persons of private law). International law, on the contrary, is thought to emanate from the will of states in the first place: the states composing the international system enact international law themselves through different modes of explicit and implicit coordination.[5] As states are considered the quintessential international persons – indeed at times statehood and international personality were regarded as synonymous – it is not disputed that at least international personality of states includes the capacity to create law apart from being subject to this very law. What is disputed is whether this is a necessary attribute of an international person more generally or whether there also can be international persons lacking the competence to create law. The merits of these differing views will be considered more closely in the remainder of this book.

The second peculiarity is that there is *no centralized law of persons* in the international legal system. There is neither a pertinent treaty nor are there established rules of customary international law that comprehensively determine matters of personality.[6] In contrast to the law of treaties or international responsibility, the law of persons has also never been selected for codification by the International Law Commission, although this was suggested in 1949.[7] The closest international law gets to an authoritative statement on international personality is the well-known definition articulated by the ICJ in the *Reparation for Injuries* opinion:

> an international person . . . is . . . capable of possessing international rights and duties, and . . . has capacity to maintain its rights by bringing international claims.[8]

[5] This view is reflected in Article 38 ICJ Statute. This well-known provision, though technically only stating the law to be applied by the ICJ, is generally considered to represent the authoritative statement on the sources of international law. However, it has to be admitted that the existence of Article 38 ICJ Statute has not solved the issue of sources of international law completely and there are still ongoing doctrinal discussions, especially on the nature of international custom and the general principles of law.

[6] It is widely agreed that Article 34(1) of the ICJ Statute giving standing only to states does not reflect a statement on international personality more broadly. This is in contrast to the importance Article 38 of the same Statute enjoys in determining the sources of international law.

[7] *Survey of International Law in Relation to the Work of Codification of the International Law Commission: Preparatory work within the purview of article 18, paragraph 1, of the Statute of the International Law Commission*, Memorandum submitted by the Secretary-General, UN Doc. A/CN.4/1/Rev.1, at 19–22.

[8] *Reparation for Injuries Suffered in the Service of the United Nations* (Advisory Opinion), 1949 ICJ Reports 174, 179.

In the absence of other authoritative statements, these lines are often referred to when dealing with international personality.[9] Unfortunately, the definition is not very illuminating for it neither addresses which entities actually are international persons nor does it state comprehensive criteria according to which personality is attributed. The latter aspect is further obscured by the somewhat tautological nature of the definition.[10] In the absence of an established international law of persons, it is mostly from general considerations of the nature of the international legal system that guidelines on personality in international law are inferred: theoretical positions on the function of law in international affairs, the role of the state and the place of the individual play an important part in international legal argument where the concept of international personality is concerned. Personality in international law therefore tends to be a relatively philosophical and at times abstract topic. It is a concept closely related to the nature and purpose of international law in general.

Developments in international practice (both state practice and practice of international tribunals) are, however, taken into account when dealing with the concept. The problem is that these developments can be interpreted in different ways depending from what theoretical positions one starts.[11] For example, the fact that private investors regularly claim rights contained in bilateral investment treaties on the international scene, as in the context of ICSID arbitrations,[12] can be understood either

9 See e.g. Daillier and Pellet, *Droit International* (5th edition), 393; Herdegen, Matthias, *Völkerrecht*, 3rd edition (Munich: C. H. Beck, 2004), 62; Ipsen, *Völkerrecht*, 55; Menon, 'Subjects', at 31; Rousseau, *Droit International Public*, 8; Schwarzenberger, Georg, *A Manual of International Law*, 6th edition (London: Professional Books, 1976), 42; Brownlie, *Principles*, 57.

10 Critical examinations of the definition, particularly of its circularity, can be found in Brownlie, *Principles*, 57; Bowett, Derek William, *The Law of International Institutions*, 4th edition (London: Stevens, 1982), 336–7; Clapham, Andrew, *Human Rights Obligations of Non-State Actors* (Oxford University Press, 2006), 64; Cosnard, 'Rapport', at 16 and 30; Crawford, James R., *The Creation of States in International Law*, 2nd edition (Oxford University Press, 2006), 28 (by implication); Currie, John, *Public International Law* (Toronto: Irwin Law, 2001), 19; Klabbers, 'Subjects Doctrine', at 367–8; Klabbers, Jan, 'The Concept of Legal Personality', *Ius Gentium*, 11 (2005), 35–66, at 39–41; Kolb, 'Observation', at 117; Tomuschat, Christian, 'International Law: Ensuring the Survival of Mankind on the Eve of a New Century: General Course on Public International Law', RCADI, 281 (1999), at 127.

11 A similar point is made by Verzijl, Jan Hendrik Willem, *International Law in Historical Perspective Volume 2: International Persons* (Leyden: A. Sijthoff, 1969), 1.

12 The International Centre for Settlement of Investment Disputes (ICSID) was established under the Washington Convention on the Settlement of Investment Disputes between States and Nationals of Other States, 18 March 1965, 575 UNTS 160.

as an incident in which private persons are direct holders of international rights and as such are international persons or, inversely, as a reinforcement of the *Mavrommatis* formula[13] according to which the investors are only beneficiaries of rights actually held by their home state.[14] A similar problem arises in the context of international human rights law when it is asserted that individuals actually are the holders of international rights without being international persons, a view which might have repercussions for the secondary obligation.[15] In addition to these different readings of general developments in international law, there is often no agreement on the interpretation of specific pronouncements by international courts thought to be related to international personality. For example, it is disputed whether the ICJ's affirmation of individual rights (in addition to state rights) outside the human rights context in the *LaGrand*[16] and *Avena*[17] judgments implies international personality of the individual or, as has been suggested, by analogy even of other non-state entities.[18] Another well-known, though somewhat aged, example is

13 *The Mavrommatis Palestine Concessions* (Greece v. UK), Jurisdiction, 1924 PCIJ Series A No. 2, at 12.

14 Compare Dumberry, Patrick, 'L'Entreprise, Sujet de Droit International? Retour sur la Question à la Lumière des Développements Récents du Droit International des Investissements', RGDIP, CVIII (2004), 103–21, at 114–9, as well as Spiermann, Ole, 'Individual Rights, State Interests and the Power to Waive ICSID Jurisdiction under Bilateral Investment Treaties', *Arbitration International*, 20 (2004), 179–211, at 183–6, with the balanced view held by Crawford, James R., 'The ILC's Articles on Responsibility of States for Internationally Wrongful Acts: A Retrospect', AJIL, 96 (2002), 874–90, at 887–8.

15 Compare Caflisch, Lucius and Antonio Augusto Cançado Trindade, 'Les Conventions Américaine et Européenne des Droits de l'Homme et le Droit International Général', RGDIP, CVIII (2004), 5–62, at 33, as well as Wildhaber, Luzius, 'The European Convention on Human Rights and International Law', ICLQ, 56 (2007), 217–31, at 227 (both affirming international personality of individuals in the context of human rights regimes), with Orakhelashvili, Alexander, 'The Position of the Individual in International Law', *California Western International Law Journal*, 31 (2001), 241–76, at 254–5 (refusing to do so). On the consequences for the secondary obligation see Pisillo-Mazzeschi, Riccardo, 'International Obligations to Provide for Reparation Claims?' in Albrecht Randelzhofer and Christian Tomuschat (eds.), *State Responsibility and the Individual* (The Hague: Martinus Nijhoff, 1999), 149–72, at 165–71.

16 *LaGrand Case* (Germany v. United States), Judgment, 2001 ICJ Reports 466, at 494 (para. 77).

17 *Case Concerning Avena and Other Mexican Nationals* (Mexico v. United States), 2004 ICJ Reports 12, at 27 (para. 40).

18 Compare the enthusiastic statement by Gaja, Giorgio (Special Rapporteur), *First Report on Responsibility of International Organizations*, ILC 2003, UN Doc. A/CN.4/532, para. 17 ('The Court stated in the *LaGrand* case that individuals are also subjects of international law. This approach may lead the Court to assert the legal personality even of

the PCIJ's opinion in *Jurisdiction of the Courts of Danzig* with its rather inconclusive reasoning on direct treaty rights of individuals.[19] Not surprisingly, the opinion has been interpreted controversially and has been used to foster different theoretical positions on international personality.[20] And even when international personality was more directly addressed, as was of course the case in *Reparation for Injuries* with regard to international organizations, interpretations of the criteria to be fulfilled for an international organization to become an international person differed widely.[21] Thus, case law and practice are constantly taken into account in the debate on international personality, but their interpretation is strongly related to differing theoretical positions. Consequently, there is often no consensus on the implications of these practical developments.

non-governmental organizations.') with the sceptical remarks by Crawford, 'The ILC's Articles on Responsibility of States', at 887–8. See also the unfavourable comment on the dual nature of the international right by Jennings, Robert Y., 'The LaGrand Case', *The Law and Practice of International Courts and Tribunals*, 1 (2002), 13–54, at 47–9. Arguably, the ILC, too, could not reach final consensus on the meaning of *LaGrand* and *Avena* and formulated a deliberately indecisive Article 1 in its Draft Articles on Diplomatic Protection commenting that it is 'formulated in such a way as to leave open the question whether the State exercising diplomatic protection does so in its own right or that of its national – or both'. See *Draft Articles on Diplomatic Protection with commentaries*, ILC 2006, UN Doc. A/61/10, para. 50 (p. 26).

19 *Jurisdiction of the Courts of Danzig* (Advisory Opinion), 1928 PCIJ Series B No. 15, at 17–18.

20 See the opposing interpretations as put forward by Schwarzenberger, Georg, *International Law Volume I: International Law as Applied by International Courts and Tribunals*, 2nd edition (London: Stevens and Sons, 1949), 77, and by Lauterpacht, Hersch, *The Development of International Law by the Permanent Court of International Justice* (London: Longmans, Green and Co., 1934), 51–3.

21 Compare the views by Seyersted, Finn, *Objective International Personality of Intergovernmental Organisations: Do Their Capacities Really Depend upon Their Constitutions?* (Copenhagen s.n., 1963), 9, Seidl-Hohenveldern, Ignaz, 'Die völkerrechtliche Haftung für Handlungen internationaler Organisationen im Verhältnis zu Nichtmitgliedstaaten', *Österreichische Zeitschrift für Öffentliches Recht*, XI (Neue Folge) (1961), 497–506, at 498, and by Schwarzenberger, Georg, *International Law Volume I: International Law as Applied by International Courts and Tribunals*, 3rd edition (London: Stevens, 1957), 138. See also the short summary of the debate provided by Akande, Dapo, 'International Organizations' in Malcolm D. Evans (ed.), *International Law*, 2nd edition (Oxford University Press, 2006), 277–305, at 282.

2

Conceptions

The picture emerges that the concept of personality is present in international law but there are different substantial views on it. Five main positions can be distinguished:

(1) *States-only*: The first position reserves international personality exclusively to states. There are no conditions for international personality other than having acquired statehood. The corollaries of personality are synonymous with those of being a state. This position is today very rarely, if at all, explicitly advocated. But it is important in historical context and is at times still relevant for legal issues today.
(2) *Recognition*: The second position conceives of states as the original or primary persons of international law. However, other entities can also acquire international personality, often called derivative or secondary international persons. The mechanism through which this is possible is explicit or implicit recognition by states. Being an international person in principle entails certain fundamental international rights, duties and capacities analogous to those of states.
(3) *Individualistic*: The third position states a presumption for the individual as an international person in the field of so-called fundamental norms of international law. In addition, states and various other entities can be international persons if there are international norms addressing them. The consequence of personality is international responsibility. Individuals become internationally responsible for violations of fundamental international norms irrespective of whether they act in a public or private function.
(4) *Formal*: The fourth position declares international law an open system. There is no presumption as to whom is a legal person. International personality becomes an a posteriori concept: every entity is an international person that according to general principles of interpretation is the addressee of the norms of international law.

Basically, there are no consequences attached to being an international person.

(5) *Actor*: The fifth position, rejecting the concept of international personality as traditionally understood, stipulates a presumption that all effective actors of international relations are relevant for the international legal system. The specific rights and duties held by particular actors are determined in an international decision-making process in which the actors themselves participate depending on their effective power.

These five positions are those mainly invoked in international legal argument, that is, in doctrinal debates and in international practice. As presented here, they are condensed into what may be called 'ideal types'. It follows that there are various modifications of these positions present in international legal reasoning. In general, however, such modifications will share – although often without explicit reference – a common basis with the pure forms as presented in this book. Thus, by examining the 'ideal types', there will also be new insights into the original assumptions on which the modified positions rest. Of course, these five positions to a certain extent represent different stages in the history of international law. However, notwithstanding their different historical origins, they all form part of the body of international legal argument applied today and as such are relevant in contemporary doctrine and practice.

The situation with five different substantive positions on international personality can be grasped by the distinction between a concept and various conceptions thereof. 'International personality' is the overall concept and the five positions are conceptions of it. The distinction between concept and conceptions was initially articulated by W. B. Gallie in a prominent paper on 'essentially contested concepts' and was later introduced into legal philosophy by H. L. A. Hart, Ronald Dworkin and John Rawls.[1] Put briefly, the idea is that there are certain concepts, for example 'fairness' or 'justice', the basic purpose of which might be agreed on but where there is no consensus on

[1] Gallie, W. B., 'Essentially Contested Concepts', *Proceedings of the Aristotelian Society*, 56 (1956), 167–98, at 176–7; Hart, H. L. A., *The Concept of Law* (Oxford: Clarendon Press, 1961), 156; Rawls, John, *A Theory of Justice*, revised edition (Oxford University Press, 1999), 5–6; Dworkin, Ronald, *Taking Rights Seriously* (London: Duckworth, 1977), 103–5 and 134–5. It has to be noted that by making use of the distinction, it is not suggested that the concept of international personality is *essentially* contested in Gallie's sense; it is rather advocated with Dworkin and Rawls that though there presently are different conceptions of the concept of international personality, there can still be an overall convincing formulation of the concept.

what they specifically entail: there are often social and indeed legal situations in which most participants agree that the concepts of 'fairness' or 'justice' are relevant, but where there are many different views on what exactly represents a 'fair' or 'just' solution. This seems to fit well with the present case of international personality. It is agreed that the concept's purpose is to determine which social entities the international legal system takes account of, but there is no consensus on what these entities are and under what conditions they do become relevant. To a certain extent, such different views may be theoretically unavoidable in a topic of fundamental significance. But from a legal perspective, the variety of theoretical positions and the diverse statements in jurisprudence related to them are disturbing for they threaten the coherence and the unity of the international legal system. Therefore, although it might be too much to ask for the one 'correct' view, it seems to be worthwhile to strive for greater agreement and consistency on matters of international personality.

To achieve greater consistency, one might be tempted to avoid altogether the five conceptions of personality present in international law today and to formulate an entirely new legal framework, presumably by focusing on the so-called facts of international life and on what actually happens in international practice. One could then give up the somewhat aged and seemingly unproductive discussions on international personality in legal scholarship and offer a new and coherent legal structure. Yet such an approach, though perhaps not without merit, encounters two main difficulties. First, it has already been noted that one would not be the first to interpret practical developments related to international personality, and the sole focus on them would only lead to one more interpretation of specific practical incidents without much new insight. Second, such an approach would misunderstand the nature of international legal argument more profoundly.[2] International law being a system of law, comprehensive

[2] The term 'international legal argument' was perhaps most influentially coined by Martti Koskenniemi when studying the structure of modern international law from a critical perspective (Koskenniemi, Martti, *From Apology to Utopia: The Structure of International Legal Argument. Reissue with New Epilogue*, 2nd edition (Cambridge University Press, 2005) (originally published 1989), esp. 58–70). Koskenniemi's main thesis was that international legal argument is essentially indeterminate for it is based on contradictory premises (e.g. sovereignty and bindingness of treaties). A similar point had been made earlier, and in even more abstract terms, by David Kennedy (Kennedy, David, 'Theses about International Law Discourse', *German Yearbook of International Law*, 23 (1980), 353–91, esp. at 375–6). Though the discussion on international personality with its seemingly irreconcilable propositions at times appears to reflect parts of the indeterminacy thesis, this is not the argument put forward in this book. In the present context, the

professional reasoning regularly has recourse to the existing body of legal material. Particularly in the absence of pertinent customary and treaty rules, international legal argument is most persuasive when one is able to show how existing jurisprudence and doctrine – that is, statements and interpretations of the law – support a particular view in a legal situation. As the five identified conceptions are present in the body of existing legal material, international lawyers will be confronted with them whenever making a professional legal argument related to matters of international personality. It will be very difficult to ignore them entirely and still be convincing in professional discourse; and if neglected by one party they will most certainly be invoked as counter-arguments by the other.[3] For this reason, it is submitted that one has to engage with, rather than ignore, the existing body of conceptions of international personality as they appear in international legal theory and practice. For these conceptions are simply part of the existing body of international legal argument. It is then primarily through engagement with them that one can strive to elucidate a more coherent legal framework for personality in international law.

In this book, to engage with the five different conceptions of international personality means to examine from what basic propositions these positions start and from what assumptions they are derived. Through time these conceptions have so often been reiterated without their presuppositions having been explained anew that it is difficult to see the legal premises from which they actually start. In this sense, the intellectual origins of the five conceptions have to be analysed. Such analysis, then, enables one to look at incidents in international practice and to relate them to particular assumptions inherent in the different conceptions. Accordingly, it can be shown – significantly better, it is thought, than with a sole focus on legal practice – in which incidents a particular conception of international personality was manifested and how specific assumptions were substantiated therein. With this comprehensive picture of the conceptions' legal presuppositions

term 'international legal argument' is only used to describe what international lawyers do in order to live through the difficulties international law poses in daily practice. In so doing, they aim to find legally determinable answers in the conditions of the international legal system.

3 For example, if one argues that international law is directly applicable to a matter concerning a private person and a state without engaging further with existing views on international personality, one will most certainly be confronted with the counter-argument that in doctrine and practice a private person is generally not considered an international person and therefore international law cannot be directly applicable, but, if at all, only apply by analogy. The relevance of the latter distinction will be addressed in the next chapter.

and their manifestations in legal practice it becomes possible to show contradictions and potential for complementarities among the conceptions and to evaluate which positions are still to be considered legally sound and which have been discarded in international law over time.[4] From this examination, a more coherent legal framework for international personality can be constructed which is at the same time firmly grounded in existing international legal argument.

It follows that this book is concerned with what can be called – with certain qualifications to be enunciated – the 'intellectual history' of the conceptions of personality in international law. The term 'intellectual history' (as well as the similar expression 'conceptual history') has at times given rise to controversy, especially in the field of political philosophy where such approaches have chiefly been pursued.[5] Put briefly, the main issue has been to what extent there can be intellectual history at all.[6] There is no need to enter this debate for present purposes, particularly because it seems to be largely settled – in accordance with common sense, it appears – that intellectual history of a concept is possible as long as one carefully considers the socio-political context in which specific intellectual positions arose and were used to achieve certain ends.[7] In this book,

[4] The line is taken from Ago, Roberto, 'Positive Law and International Law', AJIL, 51 (1957), 691–733, at 701.

[5] For useful overviews of the debate see Richter, Melvin, 'Reconstructing the History of Political Languages: Pocock, Skinner, and Geschichtliche Grundbegriffe', *History and Theory*, 29 (1990), 38–70, at 63–70, and Palonen, Kari, 'The History of Concepts as a Style of Political Theorizing: Quentin Skinner's and Reinhart Koselleck's Subversion of Normative Political Theory', *European Journal of Political Theory*, 1 (2002), 91–106, at 102.

[6] The debate was mainly started by Skinner, Quentin, 'Meaning and Understanding in the History of Ideas', *History and Theory*, 8 (1969), 3–53, at 48–53, apparently arguing that there can be no such thing as intellectual history for 'there simply are no perennial problems . . .: there are only individual answers to individual questions'. Skinner's primary targets were Lovejoy, Arthur O., *The Great Chain of Being: A Study of the History of an Idea (The William James Lectures Delivered at Harvard University, 1933)*, 14th edition (Cambridge, Mass: Harvard University Press, 1978), 3–23, as well as possibly Strauss, Leo, *What Is Political Philosophy?* (New York: The Free Press, 1968), 16.

[7] See Skinner, Quentin, *Visions of Politics I: Regarding Method* (Cambridge University Press, 2002), 177–8. For similar views see also Collingwood, R. G., *An Autobiography* (Oxford University Press, 1939), 111–15; Pocock, J. G. A., 'Theory in History: Problems of Context and Narrative' in John S. Dryzek, Bonnie Honig and Anne Phillips (eds.), *The Oxford Handbook of Political Theory* (Oxford University Press, 2006), 163–174, *passim*; Koselleck, Reinhart, 'Begriffsgeschichte und Sozialgeschichte' in Reinhart Koselleck (ed.), *Historische Semantik und Begriffsgeschichte* (Stuttgart: Klett-Cotta, 1978), 19–36, at 21–5; Palonen, Kari, *Quentin Skinner: History, Politics, Rhetoric* (Cambridge: Polity Press, 2003), 29–60 and 133–72; Berlin, Isaiah, 'Does Political Theory Still Exist?' in Henry

the historical context will be examined as far as it helps to understand the legal and philosophical constructions inherent in a particular conception. But the main focus of this book lies on the juridical analysis. Without failing to acknowledge the historical conditions of particular ideas, the book examines legal arguments and how they were theoretically derived as well as practically substantiated. In consequence, it is an attempt to go beyond the merely historical and biographical.[8] Historical analysis is then, in this book, not an end in itself but rather a means to arrive at *legal* conclusions in the matter of personality in international law.

Hardy and Roger Hausherr (eds.), *The Proper Study of Mankind: An Anthology of Essays* (New York: Farrar, Strauss and Giroux, 2000), 59–90, at 89. In international law, such an approach has also been advocated by Koskenniemi, Martti, 'Why History of International Law Today?' *Rechtsgeschichte*, 4 (2004), 61–6, at 64–5. More generally, the pursuance of intellectual history as part of research in international law had already been called for by Oppenheim, Lassa, 'The Science of International Law', AJIL, 2 (1908), 313–56, at 316.

8 This is the main difference from the primarily context-oriented work by Nijman, *Concept of International Legal Personality*, which follows a strict contextualist methodology and refrains from any legal-technical and practical analysis of the concept. The study is, however, very useful in terms of the biographical and the socio-political history of the concept of international personality.

3

Significance

On a general level, the significance of personality in international law is straightforward. In analogy to the use of personality in municipal law, it is to distinguish those social actors belonging to the international legal system from those being excluded from it. International persons can claim direct protection by international law or are subjected to obligations determined by it whereas entities not having that status generally cannot do so for they do not directly exist for the international legal system. On a more specific level, however, it is more difficult to detect the significance of international personality. The topic, as has been noted, often looms in the background of legal argument and is rarely directly addressed in legal practice. But this does not mean that it is not relevant for legal outcomes. One's conception of international personality, it is submitted, significantly influences international legal issues. In particular, it often determines the starting point of legal analysis and eventually its outcome. In the following, this is illustrated by means of four legal situations in which the choice of a particular conception of international personality has important legal effects: (a) the direct application of treaties to individuals, (b) responsibility of international organizations, (c) the rights and duties of non-state actors under customary international law, and (d) the applicable law to so-called state contracts.

(a) The direct effect of international treaties on individuals is a long-standing issue in international law.[1] But before entering the topic, it is necessary to distinguish the matter in international law from how it is

[1] See e.g. the controversial discussion in the ILC on proposed Article 66 of the Law of Treaties ('Where a treaty provides for obligations or rights which are to be performed or enjoyed by individuals . . . such obligations or rights are applicable to the individuals . . . in question') in YILC 1964-I, at 114–19. As a result of the controversy, the proposed Article was withdrawn without substantial replacement, leaving the question of direct effect of treaties on individuals unanswered.

dealt with in national law.[2] For most national legal systems contain their own legal principles according to which the legal effect of international treaties is determined.[3] These principles reflect a particular view on the relationship between municipal and international law. Typically, there are rules as to whether a treaty needs incorporation into the domestic legal system (dualist systems) or not (monist systems). In the latter case, there are often additional legal principles on whether a specific treaty provision is directly applicable to individuals (self-executing character). All these determinations are entirely a matter of domestic law; the concept of international personality is thus of no immediate relevance to them, even though in more indirect terms the general theories of dualism and monism are related to different conceptions of international personality.

In the present context, however, it is obviously as a matter of international law that the determination of a treaty's direct effect on individuals is of interest. And in this case, the concept of international personality is relevant though it is only very seldom directly addressed in legal practice in this respect. In general, an international treaty norm will not itself establish its addressees in expressive terms; and even if the norm mentions a right of individuals, it is still open to doubt whether this implies a truly direct international right of the individual or only an obligation of the state (owed towards the other state parties to the treaty) to incorporate this right into the domestic legal system.[4] In this situation, it is relevant what conception of international personality is applied.

[2] For the distinction (with a focus on the situation in US law) see also the analysis by Vazquez, Carlos M., 'Treaty-Based Rights and Remedies of Individuals', *Columbia Law Review*, 92 (1992), 1082–163, esp. at 1093–7 and 1161.

[3] See e.g. the overview in Brownlie, *Principles*, 31–3 and 41–8.

[4] This issue has repeatedly arisen in the context of Article 36(1) of the Vienna Convention on Consular Relations of 1963. The ICJ dealt with the matter in the *LaGrand Case* (Germany v. United States), Judgment, 2001 ICJ Reports 466, and in the *Case Concerning Avena and Other Mexican Nationals* (Mexico v. United States), 2004 ICJ Reports 12. Slightly earlier, a somewhat different view on the same Article 36(1) of the Vienna Convention had been enunciated by the Inter-American Court of Human Rights in *Right to Information on Consular Assistance in the Framework of the Guarantees of the Due Process of Law* (Advisory Opinion OC-16/99), 1999 IACHR Series A No. 16. With respect to an entirely different treaty, namely the *Beamtenabkommen* between Poland and the Free City of Danzig of 1921, the same legal issue had been memorably addressed by the PCIJ in *Jurisdiction of the Courts of Danzig* (Advisory Opinion), 1928 PCIJ Series B No. 15. All these authoritative pronouncements and the particular views on international personality manifested therein will be dealt with in more detail in the course of this study. For the moment, the direct effect of treaties on individuals and the significance of international personality for this topic is treated in more general terms without going into the specifics of a particular case.

If one starts from the presumption that primarily states are international persons and individuals only exceptionally have such international status, it will be difficult to rebut this general presumption through a single treaty provision mentioning an individual right in some form. The focus of legal analysis will then not only rest on the interpretation of the text of the provision, but also on signs indicating that states have granted legal status to individuals in the area of interest more generally. Such signs, though, may prove very difficult to find.[5] If, on the contrary, one regards international personality as an essentially open concept without a presumption for or against individuals, the direct effect of treaties will be dealt with according to normal rules of treaty interpretation. There will be no search for additional indications granting individuals an international status. As a third option, if one starts from the presumption that individuals are international persons when international norms of fundamental importance are concerned, the main legal argument will be about the status of the treaty rule in question: it will be argued, for example, that the relevant norm has to be considered a fundamental human right or a peremptory norm. The number of direct effects of treaties on individuals is then limited to those norms enjoying a higher legal status. In sum, depending on the position one takes with regard to international personality of individuals, the focus of the investigation and the outcome of the analysis may vary considerably when dealing with the direct effect of treaties on individuals as a matter of international law.[6] In this sense, the concept of international personality may be significant although not often directly addressed. It is only through examination of the starting point of legal analysis that one can detect which conception of international personality was applied.

[5] Employing this conception and nevertheless intending to make a treaty directly applicable, a solution present in European Community law is to declare the treaty not to form part of the normal international legal system, but to represent a new kind of legal order; such separation then entails intended and possibly unintended consequences of fragmentation in international law, especially concerning the applicable rules of treaty interpretation. See *Van Gend en Loos* v. *Netherlands Inland Revenue Administration*, Case 26/62, 1963 ECR 1, at 12; and Spiermann, Ole, 'The Other Side of the Story: An Unpopular Essay on the Making of the European Community Legal Order', EJIL, 10 (1999), 763–89, esp. at 766. On the consequences of fragmentation see Report of the Study Group (Finalized by Martti Koskenniemi), *Fragmentation of International Law: Difficulties Arising from the Diversification and Expansion of International Law*, ILC 2006, UN Doc. A/CN.4/L.682.

[6] See also the similar argument by Spiermann, Ole, 'The LaGrand Case and the Individual as a Subject of International Law', ZöR, 58 (2003), 197–221, esp. at 208–11.

(b) Since the *Reparation for Injuries* opinion it is settled that international organizations can be international persons.[7] The mechanism through which international organizations may acquire personality in international law and the consequences this status entails are, however, questions that have been less well clarified.[8] The matter becomes especially relevant in the context of international organizations invoking international responsibility – that is, bringing international claims against another international person for wrongful conduct – and being held internationally responsible.[9] In both cases, the main issue is whether the organization's status as a legal person is opposable to non-members. The question arose prominently in the *Legality of Use of Force* cases concerning responsibility of NATO member states for the use of force against the former Yugoslavia in the Kosovo military campaign[10] and, though in the fairly special circumstances of English domestic law and with private creditors, in the *International Tin Council* (ITC) cases.[11] *Reparation for Injuries* certainly settled the question in the affirmative for

[7] *Reparation for Injuries Suffered in the Service of the United Nations* (Advisory Opinion), 1949 ICJ Reports 174, at 179.

[8] See e.g. Akande, 'International Organizations', at 281–2; Schermers, Henry G. and Niels M. Blokker, *International Institutional Law: Unity within Diversity*, 3rd revised edition (The Hague: Martinus Nijhoff, 1995), §§1565–9 (pp. 978–81); and Rama-Montaldo, Manuel, 'International Legal Personality and Implied Powers of International Organizations', BYIL, 44 (1970), 111–55, esp. at 112–22.

[9] See also Gaja, Giorgio (Special Rapporteur), *First Report on Responsibility of International Organizations*, ILC 2003, UN Doc. A/CN.4/532, para. 15.

[10] *Legality of Use of Force* (Preliminary Objections, Judgment), 2004 ICJ Reports 279 (and various pages). See in particular the Preliminary Objections of the French Republic, 5 July 2000, at 28–9, Preliminary Objections of the Italian Republic, 3 July 2000, at 19, and Preliminary Objections of the Portuguese Republic, 5 July 2000, paras 130–41. The case was subsequently dismissed by the Court for lack of jurisdiction. See also Stein, Torsten, 'Kosovo and the International Community. The Attribution of Possible Internationally Wrongful Acts: Responsibility of NATO or of its Member States' in Christian Tomuschat (ed.), *Kosovo and the International Community: A Legal Assessment* (The Hague: Kluwer Law International, 2002), 181–92, esp. at 192. A similar argument was put forward by the French government in *Bankovic and Others* v. *Belgium and Others* (Grand Chamber, Decision on Admissibility), ECHR 2001-XII, para. 32.

[11] *Maclaine Watson & Co. Ltd* v. *International Tin Council* (House of Lords, 1989), 29 ILM 670, esp. at 672–5 (Lord Templeman). The case is relevant notwithstanding its private-law character because the relations between the member states and the organization established by them are governed by international law. See also *Maclaine Watson & Company Limited* v. *Council and Commission of the European Communities* (Advocate-General's Opinion), 1990 ECR I-01797, paras. 134–7, and *Arab Organization for Industrialization* (AOI), *Arab British Helicopter Company and Arab Republic of Egypt* v. *Westland Helicopters Ltd., United Arab Emirates, Kingdom of Saudi Arabia and State of Qatar* (Swiss Federal Court, 1988), 80 ILR 622, esp. at 658.

the United Nations,[12] but for other organizations the answer depends on which conception of international personality is applied.

If one considers international organizations as international persons only when states have recognized them, the organization's personality is relative and only opposable to those having expressly or tacitly granted recognition.[13] The organization can then not bring an international claim against a state not having recognized its international personality; conversely, such states cannot hold the organization accountable (although its members may possibly be held accountable). On the other hand, if one starts from an actor conception of international personality, every international organization with effective institutional bodies is regarded as an objective international person.[14] Accordingly, the organization can bring claims against other international persons and it (but not the member states) can be held responsible by them. As a third option, finally, if one adheres to an implied powers view of personality of international organizations, whether an organization can bring an international claim and whether it can be held accountable in the place of its member states depends on the particular competences contained in its constitution.[15] The conception of international personality applied thus influences the legal outcome in matters of international responsibility of international organizations.

(c) It is increasingly acknowledged that different forms of non-state actors apart from international organizations – NGOs, multinational corporations, private military organizations – exercise influence in international relations.[16] In this context, the question has been asked whether these entities are directly subject to rules of customary international law, that is, to those basic norms regularly observed by states when acting in

[12] *Reparation for Injuries*, at 185.

[13] E.g. Schwarzenberger, Georg, 'The Fundamental Principles of International Law', RCADI, 87 (1955-I), 195–385, at 252; Bowett, *International Institutions*, 342–3.

[14] E.g. Seyersted, *Objective International Personality*, esp. 9; Higgins, Rosalyn, 'International Law and the Avoidance, Containment and Resolution of Disputes: General Course on Public International Law', RCADI, 230 (1991-V), 9–342, at 78: 'It is not a matter of recognition. It is a matter of objective reality.'

[15] E.g. Kelsen, Hans, *The Law of the United Nations: A Critical Analysis of Its Fundamental Problems* (London: Stevens, 1950), 329.

[16] Two examples among many include Nye, Joseph S. Jr, *Understanding International Conflicts: An Introduction to Theory and History* in *Longman Classics in Political Science* 4th edition (New York: Longman, 2003), 245–9, and Willetts, Peter, 'Transnational Actors and International Organizations in Global Politics' in John Baylis and Steve Smith (eds.), *The Globalization of World Politics: An Introduction to International Relations*, 2nd edition (Oxford University Press, 2001), 356–83, esp. at 359–64.

the international sphere.[17] In terms of rights, at issue is whether certain privileges customarily granted to states in international relations are pertinent for non-state entities acting in this realm as well.[18] In terms of obligations, it is primarily debated whether non-state actors are responsible for violations of customary norms of international law.[19] The position taken on these matters is predicated on the conception of international personality employed.

By definition, non-state actors will be considered bound by customary international law if one adheres to an actor conception of international personality. In this case, it follows from the observation alone that a certain entity exercises influence in international relations, that it enjoys rights and bears duties under customary international law. Non-state actors are consequently subject to customary international rules whenever they are regarded as international actors. The result is different if one starts from the presumption that primarily states are international persons and as such holders of customary rights and duties. Non-state

[17] As far as treaty norms are concerned, this is primarily a matter of the familiar direct effect of treaties.

[18] In this context the international right of the International Committee of the Red Cross (ICRC) to confidentiality might be situated. The topic has been dealt with in *Prosecutor* v. *Simic et al.* (Decision on the Prosecution Motion under Rule 73 for a Ruling concerning the Testimony of a Witness), ICTY Trial Chamber, 27 July 1999.

[19] See e.g. Vazquez, Carlos M., 'Direct vs. Indirect Obligations of Corporations Under International Law', *Columbia Journal of Transnational Law*, 43 (2005), 927–59, Ratner, Stephen R., 'Corporations and Human Rights: A Theory of Legal Responsibility', YLJ, 111 (2001), 443–545, and Seibert-Fohr, Anja and Rüdiger Wolfrum, 'Die einzelstaatliche Durchsetzung völkerrechtlicher Mindeststandards gegenüber transnationalen Unternehmen', AVR, 43 (2005), 153–86, all of them focusing on multinational corporations. Clapham, *Non-State Actors*, esp. 25–83, and Thürer, Daniel, 'The Emergence of Non-Governmental Organizations and Transnational Enterprises in International Law and the Changing Role of the State' in Rainer Hofmann (ed.), *Non-State Actors as New Subjects of International Law* (Berlin: Duncker and Humblot, 1998), 37–58, concentrate on human rights obligations of non-state actors more generally. A general though very short overview of the topic is also provided by Crawford, James R. and Simon Olleson, 'The Nature and Forms of International Responsibility' in Malcolm D. Evans (ed.), *International Law*, 2nd edition (Oxford University Press, 2006), 451–77, at 452–4. The matter has primarily been dealt with by domestic courts, particularly in the United States in the context of the Alien Tort Claims Act (ATCA). The most well-known case is probably *Kadic* v. *Karadzic II* (US Court of Appeals, Second Circuit, 1995) (Chief Judge Newman), 104 ILR 135, wherein it was held that the leader of the non-state military organization of the Bosnian Serbs, Radovan Karadzic, was responsible for violations of international law committed in the Bosnian civil war. The case will be discussed as a manifestation of the individualistic conception of international personality in Part II of this study.

actors can then only be regarded as addressees of customary international law when recognized by states as international persons. Though such recognition will often be difficult to prove, if it can be established, certain customary rights and duties are thought to automatically follow from it; if they lack recognition, however, there will be no customary rights and duties for non-state actors. This is in contrast to a conception not stating a presumption as regards the addressees of customary international law. In this case, every entity, be it a state or a non-state actor, can be subject to customary international law whenever the rule in question so declares. However, customary rules being the result of the practice of states in their respective intercourse, the rule itself will in general not include compelling signals for being pertinent for non-state entities as well. As a result, it might be difficult to establish convincingly that a specific customary norm is applicable to non-state actors on account of the norm alone. Finally, if one starts from a presumption that individuals are international persons in the field of fundamental norms of customary international law, this produces different results again. At least in this restricted area, the focus of legal analysis will then be on relating the role of non-state actors to the one exercised by individuals, for example by showing that individual responsibility for torture by analogy means that there can also be corporate responsibility for committing such international crime. As a general consequence, it follows that the choice of a particular conception of international personality has significant influence on whether non-state actors have rights and duties under customary international law.

(d) The applicable law to so-called state contracts is another longstanding issue in international law related to international personality.[20]

[20] Classic studies on the topic (and its relation to international personality) include Jennings, Robert Y., 'State Contracts in International Law', BYIL, 37 (1961), 156–82, at 156 and 164; McNair, Arnold, 'The General Principles of Law Recognized by Civilized Nations', BYIL, 33 (1957), 1–19, at 19, by implication; Verdross, Alfred, 'Die Sicherung von ausländischen Privatrechten aus Abkommen zur wirtschaftlichen Entwicklung mit Schiedsklauseln', ZaöRV, 18 (1957), 635–51, at 638; Mann, F. A., 'The Proper Law of Contracts Concluded by International Persons', BYIL, 35 (1959), 34–57, at 34; Mann, F. A., 'State Contracts and State Responsibility', AJIL, 54 (1960), 572–91, at 572, by implication; Mosler, Hermann, 'Die Erweiterung des Kreises der Völkerrechtssubjekte', ZaöRV, 22 (1962), 1–48, at 40–5; Lalive, Jean-Flavien, 'Contrats entre états ou entreprises étatiques et personnes privées: développements récents', RCADI, 181 (1983-III), 13–283, at 28–32, by implication; Bowett, Derek William, 'State Contracts with Aliens: Contemporary Developments on Compensation for Termination or Breach', BYIL, 59 (1988), 49–74, at 54; Leben, Charles, 'La Théorie du Contrat d'État et l'Évolution du Droit International des Investissements', RCADI, 302 (2003), 197–386, at 302–10; Barberis, 'Personnalité Juridique', at 173, 179–80 and 189–206.

The term 'state contract' is normally employed to denote a contractual relationship between a state and a private party of foreign nationality. A classic example of a state contract is an agreement in which a state confers rights onto a foreign corporation to exploit natural resources based on its soil in exchange for royalties ('concessionary contract'); other prominent instances include agreements on the construction of large infrastructure projects or the issue of state bonds. Such contracts regulating particular investments between a state and a private party have to be distinguished from bilateral investment treaties (BITs) entered into by two states. Avoiding the uncertainties of customary international law regarding the protection of foreign investment, states agree in BITs on certain standards concerning investments in their respective territories, including principles on fair and equitable treatment, national treatment, and expropriation. As an effect, investments of a private party are protected by treaty standards whenever the state of nationality has entered into a BIT with the host state. In case of alleged breach, BITs often confer a direct right of recourse to international arbitration on the investor, thereby replacing the rules of diplomatic protection. Thus, when dealing with BITs, issues of international personality are significant only in terms of the familiar question of direct effect of treaties.[21] When state contracts are concerned, however, the notion of international personality becomes pertinent in a different sense, namely whether public international law can become the proper law of a contract that is precisely not an international treaty.

The main legal question with state contracts is hence whether and under what conditions such contracts are subject to rules of public international law. The matter becomes particularly relevant when the state, after having entered into the contractual relationship, legislates in such a way as to unilaterally alter, annul or terminate the contract. The legal consequences of such action depend on what is considered to be the proper law of contract: if the municipal law of the state party is the legal system in which the contract has to be situated, the alteration, annulment or termination of the contract by legislation is within that law and there is, in the strict sense of the term, no breach of contract;[22] if, on the other

[21] See also Seidl-Hohenveldern, Ignaz, *International Economic Law*, 3rd revised edition (The Hague: Kluwer Law International, 1999), 9–11, Spiermann, 'Individual Rights', at 183–5, and Dumberry, 'L'Entreprise, Sujet du Droit International?' at 114–19.

[22] A distinct question is then whether this action amounts to an unlawful expropriation or denial of justice as a matter of customary international law or an applicable BIT.

hand, international law provides the proper law of contract, national legislation is no justification for the non-performance of contractual obligations and there is hence a breach of contract possibly entailing state responsibility under international law.[23]

When determining the proper law of a state contract, there is a fundamental difference between the actor conception and all other conceptions of international personality. If one adheres to the actor conception, international law may be imposed automatically as the proper law of a state contract, for both states and corporations can be considered effective actors on the international scene and thus subject to international norms; in fact, in this case international law might even be imposed against the express choice by the parties of municipal law.[24] With all other conceptions of international personality, such automatic application of international law is intolerable. There, the starting point is that an agreement between a state and a private party is not a treaty automatically governed by international law: lacking international personality of the private party, the contract is presumably governed by municipal law.[25] International law can then only become relevant if either international law (alone or in connection with a municipal law) is chosen by the parties as the proper law of contract; disputes regarding the contract are referred to an international arbitration tribunal authorized by statute to apply international law;[26] or, a so-called umbrella clause is included in an applicable BIT, presumably transforming the contract claim into a treaty claim.[27] Even if one of these conditions is

[23] Articles 26 and 27 VCLT, Articles 3 and 32 ARSIWA. On a general level, see for the distinction also Crawford and Olleson, 'International Responsibility', at 455.

[24] See *Sandline International Inc.* v. *Papua New Guinea* (Interim Award, 1998), 117 ILR 552, para. 10.1: '[A]n agreement between a private party and a state is an international, not a domestic, contract. This Tribunal is an international, not a domestic, arbitral tribunal and is bound to apply the rules of international law.' In the particular circumstances of the case, international law was declared applicable despite the fact that the parties had chosen English law as the proper law of contract. The case will be discussed in depth as a manifestation of the actor conception of international personality in Part II of this study.

[25] See the seminal statement in *CAA and Vivendi Universal* v. *Argentina* (Decision on Annulment, 2002), 6 ICSID Reports 340, para. 96 (p. 365).

[26] E.g. Article 42(1) ICSID Convention: 'The Tribunal shall decide a dispute in accordance with such rules of law as may be agreed by the parties. In the absence of such agreement, the Tribunal shall apply the law of the Contracting State party to the dispute (including its rules on the conflict of laws) and such rules of international law as may be applicable.'

[27] Umbrella clauses generally stipulate that the parties to a BIT observe any obligations entered into with investors of the other state. The purpose is to create an international obligation of the host state to observe state contracts. This international obligation

fulfilled, the concrete relevance of international law still depends on what particular conception of international personality is applied. If states are considered as having free discretion to recognize a private entity as an international person, the choice of international law as the proper law or the inclusion of an umbrella clause will be interpreted as bestowing the investor with international personality for the purposes of the contract.[28] In consequence, international law will be directly and fully applied to regulate all matters involving the contractual relationship. On the other hand, if private entities cannot become international persons by mere recognition of one state, the status of the investor is not regarded as having been altered at all by its having agreed to one of the three instruments; by implication, international law is applied only by mere analogy and in a restrictive and narrow manner.[29] The furthest one is then prepared to go is to acknowledge that there exists a third system of law, namely *quasi*-international law, to which state contracts are subjected.[30] In conclusion, such different approaches when applying international law might exercise considerable influence on legal outcomes.

stemming from a treaty is enforceable by the investor where the BIT confers a direct right of recourse to arbitration. In this case, international law becomes relevant for determining the legal consequences of a breach of state contract, although the contract was originally governed by some municipal law. The extent to which international law is applicable is, however, very controversial. For the origins and the purpose of umbrella clauses see Sinclair, Anthony C., 'The Origins of the Umbrella Clause in the International Law of Investment Protection', *Arbitration International*, 20 (2004), 411–34, esp. at 411–18.

28 See e.g. Schwarzenberger, Georg, *Foreign Investments and International Law* (London: Stevens and Sons, 1969, 5–6 (choices of law) and 116–17 (umbrella clauses), Barberis, 'Personnalité Juridique', at 206, and Garcia-Amador, F. V. (Special Rapporteur), *Fourth Report on State Responsibility*, UN Doc. A/CN.4/119, YILC (1959-II), para. 129 (p. 32). Somewhat ambiguously: Mosler, 'Völkerrechtssubjekte', at 44.

29 See e.g. Bowett, 'State Contracts', at 54; Brownlie, *Principles*, 525.

30 Verdross, 'Sicherung von ausländischen Privatrechten', at 639.

PART II

The conceptions of personality in international law: their origins and legal manifestations

In this second Part, the five conceptions of international personality present in international legal argument today – 'states-only', 'recognition', 'individualistic', 'formal' and 'actor' – are examined with respect to their origins as well as to their manifestations in legal practice. It is argued that these immediately relevant conceptions have formed since the late nineteenth century.[1] Earlier doctrine and practice on matters of international personality are thus not considered to directly inform current international law discourse. Such earlier developments can, however, enlighten the understanding of the five relevant conceptions by outlining the wider historical background of the personal scope of international law. Therefore, before exploring the conceptions still present in legal argument today, an introductory chapter will sketch the broader historical context. Thereafter, as the main object of Part II, the five conceptions of international personality present in today's international law will be examined in terms of doctrinal as well as practical developments.

[1] By postulating a split between international law in the nineteenth century and earlier periods, this study is partly in disagreement with the conventional division of international legal history into a pre-modern (up to 1500), modern (1500–1919) and twentieth-century (1919 onwards) period (see Grewe, Wilhelm G., *Epochen der Völkerrechtsgeschichte*, 2nd edition (Baden-Baden: Nomos, 1988), esp. 23–5, and Preiser, Wolfgang, *Die Völkerrechtsgeschichte: Ihre Aufgabe und ihre Methode* (Wiesbaden: Franz Steiner Verlag, 1964), 65–6). This study in effect disputes that the nineteenth century, at least in terms of the ideas surrounding legal personality, was a mere prolongation of the modern international-law period. In a more general sense, this point has been forcefully advocated by Koskenniemi, Martti, *The Gentle Civilizer of Nations: The Rise and Fall of International Law 1870–1960* (Cambridge University Press, 2001), esp. 3–4 and 19–24. A similar argument can be found in Kennedy, David, 'International Law and the Nineteenth Century: History of an Illusion', NJIL, 65 (1996), 385–420, esp. at 388–9.

4

Early doctrine and practice

It is with Emer de Vattel's textbook of 1758 that international law came to be conclusively shaped as a law between states.[1] According to Vattel, international law was applicable to states and to a certain extent, though not exclusively, created by states. Before Vattel, international law had been a fusion of pre-existing rules, complemented to a certain degree by human-made law, being applicable to rulers of nations, to corps of citizens and to private individuals. After Vattel's treatise, until the end of the nineteenth century, international law was in principle, though not exclusively, regarded as inter-state law, the debate mostly focusing on the means of creation of international law and its status as law. In what follows, approaches regarding the personal scope of international law preceding Vattel will be reviewed first. Subsequently, Vattel's conception of international law as inter-state law and the broader origins of this view will be outlined. Finally, the doctrinal and practical developments with respect to the personal scope of international law taking place after Vattel until the mid nineteenth century will be explored.

[1] Vattel, Emer de, *Le Droit des Gens, ou Principes de la Loi Naturelle, appliqués à la Conduite aux Affaires des Nations et des Souverains*, 'The Classics of International Law' (James Brown Scott, ed.) (The Carnegie Institute of Washington, 1916) (originally published 1758), Préliminaires §3 (p. 1). See Jouannet, Emmanuelle, *Emer de Vattel et l'Émergence Doctrinale du Droit International Classique* (Paris: A. Pedone, 1998), esp. 9; Beaulac, Stéphane, *The Power of Language in the Making of International Law: The Word Sovereignty in Bodin and Vattel and the Myth of Westphalia* (Leiden/Boston: Martinus Nijhoff, 2004), 142; Lapradelle, Albert de, 'Introduction' in James Brown Scott (ed.), *Le Droit des Gens, ou Principes de la Loi Naturelle, appliqués à la Conduite aux Affaires des Nations et des Souverains* (The Carnegie Institute of Washington, 1916), iii–lix, at x; Remec, Peter Pavel, *The Position of the Individual in International Law according to Grotius and Vattel* (The Hague: Martinus Nijhoff, 1960), esp. 158. See also Verdross, Alfred and Bruno Simma, *Universelles Völkerrecht: Theorie und Praxis*, 3rd edition (Berlin: Duncker und Humblot, 1984), §12 (p. 9). The etymological origin of the term 'international law', however, is generally credited to Jeremy Bentham (see Bentham, Jeremy, *An Introduction to the Principles of Morals and Legislation* (Kitchener: Batoche Books, 2000) (originally published 1781), Ch. XVII §2 no. XXV (p. 236)).

Before Vattel: international law as an all-embracing web of laws

One of the first to describe international law as a law between 'nations' was Hugo Grotius in his *De Jure Bellis ac Pacis* in 1625.[2] By using the term 'law of nations', however, Grotius did not envisage a law between states. He regarded the state as an 'association of free men',[3] being a mere summation of individuals under the personal leadership of the ruler without any separate identity.[4] Grotius' 'law of nations' was in effect a law primarily between the rulers of nations and, to some extent, between the corps of citizens or between private individuals.[5] It was not an inter-state law. In this respect, Grotius had followed medieval and scholastic thought by emphasizing the role of the ruler and, in some incidents, the role of the corps of citizens and private individuals in 'international law'.[6]

Medieval and scholastic thought on the personal scope of international law was essentially all-embracing. Reminiscent of the Roman *ius gentium* – the law in principle applying to all human beings as opposed to the *ius civile*, which only took effect among Roman citizens[7] – medieval international law applied between rulers as well as among private individuals.[8] This all-embracing European legal system was closely linked to

[2] See Grotius, Hugo, *De Jure Belli ac Pacis. Libri Tre*, 'The Classics of International Law' (James Brown Scott, ed.) (Oxford: The Clarendon Press, 1925) (originally published 1625), prolegomena para. 17 (p. 15). See also Neff, Stephen C., 'A Short History of International Law' in Malcolm D. Evans (ed.), *International Law*, 2nd edition (Oxford University Press, 2006), 29–55, at 35.

[3] Grotius, *De Jure Belli*, I, I, XIV (p. 44).

[4] See Haggenmacher, Peter, *Grotius et la Doctrine de la Guerre Juste* (Paris: Presses Universitaires de France, 1983), 539–41. See also: Jouannet, *Vattel*, 261–4.

[5] Haggenmacher, *Grotius*, 541–3; Jouannet, *Vattel*, 263 and 361. See also Crawford, James R., *International Law as an Open System: Selected Essays* (London: Cameron May, 2002), 19. For cases in which private matters between individuals are addressed by Grotius see e.g. Grotius, *De Jure Belli*, II, III, VI (p. 208) (on ownership by children or insane persons); II, XII, XXVI (p. 360) (on equality of private contracts); II, XX, XIV (p. 485) (on punishment executed by Christians). Suggestions that Grotius in effect thought of the state as a separate person can be found in Remec, *The Position of the Individual*, 72–4. Nevertheless, the role of the individual in Grotian thought is also acknowledged by the latter, at 59–63 and 81.

[6] Haggenmacher, *Grotius*, 543. Emphasizing the general scholastic heritage of Grotian thought: Kolb, Robert, *Réfléxions de Philosophie du Droit International: Problèmes Fondamentaux du Droit International Public, Théorie et Philosophie du Droit International* (Brussels: Bruylant, 2003), 15, and Nussbaum, Arthur, *A Concise History of the Law of Nations*, 2nd edition (New York: The Macmillan Company, 1954), 108. This is not to deny, though, that Grotius was an extremely original thinker in other aspects of international law.

[7] See Haggenmacher, *Grotius*, esp. 320, and Kolb, *Réfléxions*, 8.

[8] See e.g. Neff, 'Short History', 32–3.

the idea of a religious, political and cultural unity in the medieval European *respublica christiana* under the leadership of the Pope and the Emperor.[9] International law in this sense was a European supranational law regulating matters between private individuals as well as between rulers of entities on the basis of a complex fusion of Roman law, canon law and feudal law. Contracts between princes and contracts between private individuals were thus regulated by the same pre-existing legal rules of the *respublica christiana*.[10] Accordingly, agreements between princes did not in the first place constitute an autonomous source for international law in the supranational European legal order: there were only few elements of law-creation in a contract between princes.[11]

The system of the *respublica christiana* collapsed in the early sixteenth century with the loss of supremacy by the Pope and the Emperor and with the corresponding gain of external sovereignty by the princes in Europe.[12] There was no authoritative supranational law left as the religious and political authorities were rejected by at least part of Europe. Canon law and feudal law, accordingly, did not constitute an authoritative basis for a European legal order any more. Out of this crisis of the medieval European order, a somewhat more horizontal international legal system gradually emerged. Starting with Francisco de Vitoria and later accentuated by Francisco Suarez, Alberico Gentili and finally Hugo Grotius,[13] the sources of this law were believed to be, on the one hand,

[9] See Grewe, *Völkerrechtsgeschichte*, esp. 91–3; Kolb, *Réflexions*, 9; Lesaffer, Randall, 'The Grotian Tradition Revisited: Change and Continuity in the History of International Law', BYIL, 73 (2002), 103–39, at 112. It has to be emphasized that the supremacy of the Emperor, and to a lesser extent of the Pope, was not much more than an ideal which was only partly reflected in actual political power. This ideal was, however, important for the juridical and political process.

[10] Lesaffer, 'Grotian Tradition Revisited', at 113.

[11] See Lesaffer, Randall, 'The Medieval Canon Law of Contract and Early Modern Treaty Law', *Journal of the History of International Law*, 2 (2000), 178–98, at 180 and 195, and Lesaffer, 'Grotian Tradition Revisited', at 113. A rather different view is put forward by Grewe, *Völkerrechtsgeschichte*, 115–17.

[12] Grewe, *Völkerrechtsgeschichte*, 168–9.

[13] It should be pointed out, as occasionally seems to be forgotten, that these so-called founders of international law did not intend to establish a system of international law in the first place. With the possible exception of Suarez, they were concerned rather with one or more practical issues that could not be dealt with exclusively by reference to national law (Vitoria primarily with the relations between the Spanish and the American Indians; Gentili with the immunity of the Spanish ambassador to England, the latter having been involved in a conspiracy to overthrow Queen Elizabeth I, and with the laws of war; Grotius initially with counselling the Dutch East India Company in a prize case

prevailing natural and divine law principles and, on the other hand, tacit or explicit agreements between the newly sovereign princes, the latter being the human law of nations.[14] International law was thus to an increasing degree created by the princes themselves and was no longer only a set of pre-existing rules. In some instances, the princes thereby authorized other entities, especially the well-known trading companies, to conclude treaties with foreign sovereigns.[15] To what extent such companies, originally formed by individuals and engaged primarily in economic ventures, constituted independent actors in international law is disputed, however, and it is difficult to distinguish between them in representing their domestic sovereign and in striving for private economic gains.[16] In any event, law-creation by the princes or other authorized entities could not contradict the prevailing overarching natural and divine principles as considered inherent in the international community; human-made law was in effect not independent and separate from divine and natural law in the tradition of Vitoria, Suarez, Gentili and Grotius, but rather a different form of law in a greater system.[17]

Importantly, this complex system of natural and man-made international law rules applied to rulers of nations as well as to private

and later on with the laws of war, too). To solve these specific problems, these famous authors turned to existing rules and principles they associated with 'international law'.

[14] Vitoria, Francisco de, *Political Writings*, 'Cambridge History of Political Thought' (Anthony Pagden and Jeremy Lawrence, eds.) (Cambridge University Press, 1991) (originally published 1539), Relectio De Indis Question 3 Art. 1 para. 4 (pp. 280–1), Relectio De Potestate Civili Question 3 Art. 1 paras 15–17 (pp. 32–6); Suarez, Francisco, *Selections from Three Works of Francisco Suarez*, 'The Classics of International Law' (James Brown Scott, ed.) (Oxford: The Clarendon Press, 1944) (originally published 1612–1621), De Legibus book I ch. XIX (pp. 341–7); Gentili, Alberico, *De Iure Belli Libri Tres*, 'The Classics of International Law' (James Brown Scott, ed.) (Oxford: The Clarendon Press, 1933) (1598), 8 and 360–6; Grotius, *De Jure Belli*, I, I, XIV (p. 44). See also Lesaffer, 'Grotian Tradition Revisited', at 123–4 (primarily focusing on Vitoria but proclaiming the wider acceptance of Vitorian thought by his successors). While Vitoria's and Suarez' doctrines relied heavily on divine law, the protestants Gentili and Grotius regarded law principles determined by reason as the main sources of natural law.

[15] See Verzijl, *International Law in Historical Perspective (II)*, 39–43, and Grewe, *Völkerrechtsgeschichte*, 347–50.

[16] Sole Arbitrator Max Huber argued in the *Island of Palmas* arbitration case in 1928 that such contracts between a Chartered Company and a foreign sovereign were no proper international law treaties but had an indirect effect on international law situations (see 4 ILR 108, 109). For a rather different view, emphasizing the role of trading companies in international law at the time, see Grewe, *Völkerrechtsgeschichte*, 350–3.

[17] Kennedy, David, 'Primitive Legal Scholarship', HILJ, 27 (1986), 1–98, at 16–7 (Vitoria), 42–5 (Suarez), 62–5 (Gentili) and 81–3 (Grotius). See also Koskenniemi, *Apology to Utopia*, 98–9, Nussbaum, *Concise History*, 86–7 and 108–9, and Lesaffer, 'Medieval Canon Law of Contract', at 181.

individuals.[18] Though adapting to the new political and social circumstances, international law in the tradition from Vitoria to Grotius was still conceived as an overarching law of all men including rulers and private individuals. The medieval and scholastic tradition did not disappear with the collapse of the *respublica christiana* in the sixteenth century. Its all-embracing character prevailed in doctrine and practice.[19] Only after Grotius, in the second half of the seventeenth and the first half of the eighteenth centuries, did international law begin to be regarded as an inter-state law. This development would culminate in the mid eighteenth century with Emer de Vattel's treatise on the law of nations.

Vattel: international law as an inter-state law

In his widely circulated treatise[20] *Le Droit des Gens, ou Principes de la Loi Naturelle, appliqués à la Conduite aux Affaires des Nations et des Souverains* of 1758, Vattel defined international law as

> ... la science du droit qui a lieu entre les Nations, ou États, et des obligations qui répondent à ce droit.[21]

Vattel regarded international law as an inter-state law.[22] It was not the ruler of a state or its citizens who were international legal persons, but the state itself. Crucially, Vattel conceived the state as a separate body with its own will as distinguished from the individual wills of its members or of

[18] Kennedy, 'Primitive Legal Scholarship', at 8; Lesaffer, 'Grotian Tradition Revisited', at 124.

[19] See also Koskenniemi, *Apology to Utopia*, 97–8.

[20] See the statistics regarding citations of Vattel's treatise in pleadings and court decisions in Dickinson, Edwin D., 'Changing Concepts and the Doctrine of Incorporation', AJIL, 26 (1932), 239–60, at 259 nr. 132. On the relevance of Vattel's book for international legal practice see also Nussbaum, *Concise History*, 161–2, Remec, *The Position of the Individual*, 56, and Jouannet, *Vattel*, 14–15. The relevance in doctrinal discourse is highlighted by Koskenniemi, *Apology to Utopia*, 124. Neff, 'Short History', at 36, claims that Vattel's book can be considered the 'greatest international-law textbook ever written' and further acknowledges its wide usage.

[21] Vattel, *Le Droit des Gens*, Préliminaires §3 (p. 1). This definition is very similar, though not identical, to the definition of the law of nations by Wolff, Christian, *Jus Gentium Methodo Scientifica Pertractatum*, 'The Classics of International Law' (James Brown Scott, ed.) (Oxford: The Clarendon Press, 1934) (originally published 1740–1748), prelogomena §1 (p. 9). However, Vattel's overall conception of the personal scope of international law differed in important respects from Wolff's, as will be pointed out in this section.

[22] The terms 'nations' and 'states' were used interchangeably by Vattel (see Beaulac, *Making of International Law*, 135, and Remec, *The Position of the Individual*, 172).

its ruler:[23] '[L'État] devient une personne morale, qui a son entendement et sa volonté propre, et qui est capable d'obligations et de droits.'[24] According to Vattel, a state was the result of a voluntary contractual agreement between a group of individuals.[25] The purpose of states was to promote the mutual welfare and security of their members. In order to achieve these goals, the state was empowered with sovereignty, meaning the public authority to govern. This authority could not be alienated; its exercise could only be delegated to a person (monarchy), a group of persons (aristocracy) or to the people itself (democracy), depending on the relevant constitutional provisions. Sovereignty itself rested in the state. Inalienable sovereignty was the prerequisite for the separate personality and will of the state: it was because of the voluntary subordination of all individuals under the authority of the state and the inalienability of this sovereignty that the latter was thought of as being a distinctive person with a separate will.[26] With this conception of a separate personality and will of the state, the state, as opposed to the person or group of persons being authorized by the constitution to exercise public power, was the entity that acted in international affairs. The international scene, according to Vattel, was thus characterized by the interaction of independent and equal states; international law, then, was the law between states.[27]

Vattel's conception of the legal scope of international law marked the end of a wider intellectual development emerging from the mid seventeenth century onwards. Thomas Hobbes, Samuel Pufendorf and Christian Wolff had elaborated on contractual theories of the state as a separate person and had profoundly influenced Vattel's understanding.[28] Hobbes had introduced the concept of an 'artificial personality' into political philosophy.[29] However, in Hobbes's conception the state

[23] See Jouannet, *Vattel*, esp. 319, Beaulac, *Making of International Law*, 138, 143–9, and Remec, *The Position of the Individual*, 160–2.

[24] Vattel, *Le Droit des Gens*, Préliminaires, §2 (p. 1).

[25] See for this and the following ibid., (Livre I, Chap. I) §§1–3 (pp. 17–18).

[26] See Jouannet, *Vattel*, 321.

[27] Vattel, *Le Droit des Gens*, Livre I, Introduction §11 (p. 21) and Livre II, Chap. XVIII §346 (p. 533). See also: Beaulac, *Making of International Law*, 148–9, and Jouannet, *Vattel*, 403–9.

[28] See Vattel, *Le Droit des Gens*, (Préface) x–xx. Jouannet, *Vattel*, discusses the preceding doctrines and influences on Vattel at length at 259–318. See also Beaulac, *Making of International Law*, 138–41.

[29] Hobbes, Thomas, *Leviathan*, 'Cambridge Texts in the History of Political Thought' (Richard Tuck, ed.) (Cambridge University Press, 1996) (originally published 1651), part II, ch. XVII (pp. 120–1). See also Boucher, David and Paul Kelly, 'The Social

remained closely attached to the person of the ruler.[30] Pufendorf had elaborated on Hobbes's ideas and ascribed to the state a personality not only distinct from its citizens, but also from its ruler.[31] Nevertheless, Pufendorf did not – at least not unambiguously – ascribe sovereignty to the state, but rather to the organs ruling the state.[32] It was in Christian Wolff's writings that the artificial person of the state acquired sovereignty.[33] But still, according to Wolff, this sovereignty could be passed on, in terms of exercising power or substantively, to the person ruling the state. In effect, the prince thus became not only the executor of sovereignty, but the possessor of it. It is only with Vattel that sovereignty was tied to the artificial person of the state and could not substantively be passed on to another organ. With Vattel's *Droit des Gens*, states came to be thought of as being the only public authorities and thus also the only actors on the international stage.

As a consequence of the separate personality of the state, according to Vattel, states were also the creators of human-made international law. As the highest public authority, it was the state and not the ruler or another organ exercising sovereignty that entered into international agreements.[34] This view corresponded with international practice where increasingly the state instead of princes was mentioned as a party to a treaty.[35] Vattel distinguished three forms of human-made international law: conventional, customary and voluntary international law.[36] Conventional international law was the result of the express will, customary law of the implicit will of the states. The third form, voluntary law, was in effect closely linked to the natural law part of Vattel's

Contract and its Critics: An Overview' in David Boucher and Paul Kelly (eds.), *The social contract from Hobbes to Rawls* (London/New York: Routledge, 1994), 1–34, at 15.

30 Hobbes, *Leviathan*, part II, ch. XVII (p. 121). See also Jouannet, *Vattel*, 269–83. This view is not shared by Skinner, Quentin, 'The state' in Terence Ball, James Farr and Russell L. Hanson (eds.), *Political Innovation and Conceptual Change* (Cambridge University Press, 1989), 90–131, at 90–1 and 121.

31 Pufendorf, Samuel, *De Jure Naturae et Gentium Libri Octo*, 'The Classics of International Law' (James Brown Scott, ed.) (Oxford: The Clarendon Press, 1934) (originally published 1688), Book VII, Ch. II, paras 5–6 (pp. 971–4). See also Boucher and Kelly, 'Social Contract', 15, and Beaulac, *Making of International Law*, 140.

32 Pufendorf, *De Jure Naturae et Gentium*, Book VII, Ch. VI, paras 7–8 (pp. 1063–6). See also Jouannet, *Vattel*, 295–9.

33 Wolff, *Jus Gentium*, ch. 4, para. 368 (p. 191). See also Jouannet, *Vattel*, 316.

34 Vattel, *Le Droit des Gens*, Préliminaires §24 (p. 13).

35 Lesaffer, 'Grotian Tradition Revisited', at 130–1.

36 Vattel, *Le Droit des Gens*, Préliminaires §27 (p. 15). Again, Vattel's conception in this respect is clearly reminiscent of, but not identical to, Wolff's definition of the different forms of law. See Wolff, *Jus Gentium*, prolegomena §4 (p. 10) and §§22–5 (pp. 17–19).

international legal theory:[37] it was the law that was presumed to reflect the will of the states in order to preserve basic principles of the international community. Alongside these forms of human-made law, Vattel also regarded fundamental principles of natural law, properly adapted, as part of the law of nations.[38] In consequence, Vattel proclaimed a hierarchy of norms in international law, according to which state-made law could not contradict 'voluntary' law or proper natural law principles.[39] The will of states in law-creation was thus still, if not as restrictively as in Vitorian and Grotian thought,[40] constrained by fundamental principles of the international community. In accepting a 'positive' law of nations, Vattel disagreed with Hobbes and Pufendorf, both of whom had rejected any human-made international law.[41] In Vattel's theory, states could create international law, but they were restricted by natural law principles.

In Vattelian doctrine, hence, international law was applicable to the separate personality of the state. It was not applicable to the ruler of a state, to its body of citizens or to private individuals. In so far as international law was human-made, it was the will of the state, and not the person or group of persons executing this will, determining the human-made international law. All of these cornerstones of Vattelian thought were generally agreed on by subsequent doctrine and practice. More controversial, however, proved Vattel's acceptance of fundamental natural-law principles transcending the will of states in law-creation.

After Vattel: pragmatic law-application, unresolved law-creation

In international legal doctrine and practice from the late eighteenth until the mid nineteenth century, it was generally agreed that international law was applicable to states as separate legal persons.[42] The state, understood as the outcome of a contract between individuals, was the starting point

37 Jouannet, *Vattel*, 92–3 and 100–103; Koskenniemi, *Apology to Utopia*, 113–14.

38 Vattel, *Le Droit des Gens*, Préliminaires §7 (p. 4) and §§27–8 (pp. 15–16). Vattel calls these natural-law principles 'necessary law of nations'.

39 Ibid., Préliminaires §§21–2 (pp. 11–13). See also Jouannet, *Vattel*, 93.

40 On the complex constraints on positive law in Grotian thought see Jouannet, *Vattel*, 68, and Kennedy, 'Primitive Legal Scholarship', at 82.

41 Pufendorf, *De Jure Naturae et Gentium*, Book II, Ch. III, para. 23 (p. 226). Hobbes, *Leviathan*, part II, ch. XXVI (183–4).

42 See Martens, Georg Friedrich von, *Précis du Droit des Gens Moderne de l'Europe (Tome 1-2)*, (M. Ch. Vergé, ed.) (Paris: Guillaumin Libraries, 1858 (originally published 1788)), (the whole treatise being a compilation of the law as applied in diplomatic practice and in

for international law.[43] In principle, there were no private matters between individuals or other private entities dealt with in public international law. International law was perceived to be that system of law that was relevant to the relations between states, while relations between individuals or other private entities were usually regarded as being exclusively regulated by the applicable municipal legal system. However, in some special cases, international law was seen as applicable to non-state entities. For example, in the early nineteenth century, treaties between European states and indigenous chiefs and peoples were commonly regarded as treaties governed by international law, notwithstanding the lack of statehood of the latter party to the treaty.[44] Furthermore, it was generally accepted in the early nineteenth century that international law contained norms prohibiting piracy and was in this respect directly binding upon individuals.[45] Finally, in special circumstances, international arbitration could take place between a formally private company and a semi-sovereign state as happened in the Suez Canal arbitration of 1864.[46] These examples show that there was some scope for other entities than states in the application of international law in the late eighteenth and early nineteenth centuries. Still, these were exceptions to the generally accepted rule that international law applied to the separate legal person of the state. Vattel's doctrine,

arbitration to the relations between states); Klueber, Johann Ludwig, *Droit des Gens Moderne de l'Europe*, (M. A. Ott, ed.) (Paris: Librairíe de Guillaumin, 1861) (originally published 1818), esp. §1 (pp. 1–3); Bluntschli, Johan Caspar, *Das moderne Völkerrecht der civilisierten Staaten: als Rechtsbuch dargestellt*, 3rd revised edition (Nördlingen: C. H. Beck, 1878), pp. 53–4 and 63–7, Wheaton, Henry, *Elements of International Law*, 'The Classics of International Law' (James Brown Scott, ed.) (Oxford: The Clarendon Press, 1936) (originally published 1836), §1 (p. 3) and §§16–19 (pp. 25–7); Manning, William Oke, *Commentaries on the Law of Nations*, revised edition by Amos Sheldon (London: H. Sweet, 1875) (originally published 1839), p. 3; Phillimore, Robert, *Commentaries Upon International Law*, 3rd edition (London: Butterworths, 1879, para. LXI (p. 79); Fiore, Pasquale, *Trattato di Diritto Internazionale Pubblico*, 3rd edition (Turin: Unione Tipografico-Editrice, 1887), para. 286 (p. 185).

43 See e.g. Martens, *Précis du droit des gens*, §2 (p. 34), and Klueber, *Droit des gens*, §1 (p. 1) and §20 (p. 25). See also Koskenniemi, *Gentle Civilizer*, 20–22.

44 See McNair, Arnold D., *The Law of Treaties*, 2nd edition (Oxford: The Clarendon Press, 1961), 53–4 (arguing that at least American courts regarded contracts with native chiefs as treaties until the Indian Appropriations Act of 1871), and Brownlie, Ian, *Treaties and Indigenous Peoples: The Robb Lectures 1991* (Oxford: The Clarendon Press, 1992), 8–9.

45 See e.g. *United States* v. *Smith*, 18 U.S. 153 (US Supreme Court, 1820), wherein it was confirmed – by extensive recourse to doctrine, including Grotius and Vattel – that international law contained a definition of the crime of piracy. See also Kennedy, 'History of an Illusion', at 407.

46 See *Compagnie du Canal du Suez* v. *Egypte* in RAI II (1856–1872), 344–86.

having itself been the outcome of a wider intellectual and practical development, was thus usually adhered to in the early nineteenth century, though not in a strictly dogmatic, but rather a pragmatic, sense: it was not entirely ruled out, though clearly marked as exceptional, that entities other than states could be subject to international law rules.

With regard to international law-creation, Vattel's proclaimed coexistence of state-made international law and principles of natural law was present in the writings of the professional mainstream, too.[47] It was generally felt in the early nineteenth century that the substance of international law could not only depend on the will of the states as represented in express and tacit agreements, but had to a certain degree to be founded in natural law principles.[48] There were, however, some variations in the respective importance positive and natural law elements acquired. This was partly due to national differences in the academic treatment of international law in the early nineteenth century: while international law in France was normally taught as part of natural law, in Germany it was normally considered as a division of public law and in Britain, lacking formal legal university education at the time, as a subject of moral philosophy.[49] While French and British traditions were thus more inclined to highlight the natural law aspects of international law, German thought was slightly more formal and focused more on actual state practice without totally neglecting natural law.[50] Notwithstanding the general consensus in the early nineteenth century that natural law and state-made law coexisted as sources of international law, the

[47] See Martens, *Précis du Droit des Gens*, §§1–2 (pp. 29–36) and §46 (p. 148); Klueber, *Droit des Gens*, §§3–5 (pp. 4–6); Bluntschli, *Das moderne Völkerrecht*, 53–61; Wheaton, *Elements*, §§14–15 (pp. 20–25); Manning, *Commentaries*, 66–77; Phillimore, *International Law*, para. XXIII (pp. 15–16) and XL (p. 38); Fiore, *Diritto Internazionale*, para. 170 (p. 115).

[48] Ago, 'Positive Law', at 694; Koskenniemi, *Apology to Utopia*, 131–3; Neff, 'Short History', at 38; Nussbaum, *Concise History*, 236–9; Koskenniemi, *Gentle Civilizer*, 28–35; Sylvest, Casper, 'International Law in Nineteenth-Century Britain', BYIL, 75 (2004), 9–70, at 12 and 37–46 (with respect to British international legal thought).

[49] See Grewe, *Völkerrechtsgeschichte*, 594–7; Koskenniemi, *Gentle Civilizer*, 33; Sylvest, 'International Law in Nineteenth-Century Britain', at 19 (for Britain); Stolleis, Michael, *Geschichte des öffentlichen Rechts in Deutschland 2. Band: Staatsrechtslehre und Verwaltungswissenschaft 1800–1914* (Munich: C. H. Beck, 1992), 52 (English translation: Stolleis, Michael, *Public Law in Germany 1800–1914* (New York and Oxford: Berghahn Books, 2001) (for Germany)).

[50] See e.g. the very important role Manning, *Commentaries*, 66–87, ascribes to natural law in relation to positive law as opposed to Martens, *Précis du Droit des Gens*, §§1–2 (pp. 29–30, 34).

variations in their respective significance indicate that law-creation was not a settled topic at the time. It rather represented an unresolved question that also threatened international law's acceptance as a legal science. Accordingly, most scholarly writing at the time felt the need to defend itself against the claim, most famously put forward by John Austin in 1832,[51] that international law was no law properly so called because of its natural law elements.[52] No respected writer, though, completely disregarded natural law elements as sources of international law until the mid nineteenth century. International law remained to varying degrees a law created by the will of states and by natural law.

In sum, international law from the mid eighteenth century to the later decades of the nineteenth century was characterized by its application to the relations between states and by the coexistence of state-made and natural law as its sources. In terms of international law application, this basic idea was, however, employed pragmatically: in specific circumstances considered international in character, international law was nevertheless applied even without the participation of states. With respect to the sources of international law, there existed a variety of different approaches as to the significance attributed to natural and positive international law. The question of international law-creation was still considered problematic, especially in view of the criticisms put forward against international law from the standpoint of legal positivism in the Austinian sense. Ideas evolving from German and Italian thought on public law would eventually offer an answer to the problem of international law-creation and thereby put strict restraints on the hitherto pragmatic application of international law.

[51] Austin, John, *The Province of Jurisprudence Determined*, 'Cambridge Texts in the History of Political Thought' (Wilfrid D. Rumble, ed.) (Cambridge University Press, 1995) (originally published 1832), 171 (Lecture VI).

[52] See e.g. Manning, *Commentaries*, 5–7, and, for the general argument, Sylvest, 'International Law in Nineteenth-Century Britain', at 18. Without reference to Austin, but generally defending international law's status as law, Bluntschli, *Das moderne Völkerrecht*, 2–10.

5

The states-only conception

The states-only conception of international personality restricts the personal scope of international law to relations between states exclusively: only states are international legal persons. Individuals and other entities only fully exist as nationals of a state and are therefore not directly relevant for international law. This conception of international personality was mainly formulated by Heinrich Triepel, Lassa Oppenheim and Dionisio Anzilotti. It is argued that the origins of this conception lie mainly in German public law thought of the later decades of the nineteenth century. It was in the specific German socio-political and legal context that the reduction of international law to relations among states originally arose and that particularly relevant ideas about the position of the individual within a state were advocated. The states-only conception, though never unchallenged, was widely adopted in international law doctrine afterwards.[1] Some of its most important manifestations in legal practice are the *Mavrommatis*-formula, the *Serbian Loans* statement regarding state contracts, the ECJ's *Van Gend en Loos* decision as well as, arguably, the *Jurisdiction of Courts of Danzig* Advisory Opinion. All of these manifestations, as will be shown, are still relevant for legal issues today. On a more general level, and therefore not explicitly addressed in this section, the states-only conception was encapsulated in the well-known *Lotus* dictum on international law 'govern[ing] relations between independent States'.[2]

[1] For a very early, but perhaps not as influential a view, see Heilborn, Paul, *Das System des Völkerrechts entwickelt aus den völkerrechtlichen Begriffen* (Berlin: Verlag von Julius Springer, 1896), 58–83, esp. 82, basically reiterated in Heilborn, Paul, 'Les Sources du Droit International', RCADI, 11 (1926-I), 1–63, esp. at 9. For more recent and slightly modified versions see, e.g., Quadri, Rolando, 'Cours Général de Droit International Public', RCADI, 113 (1964-III), 245–483, at 433, or Weil, Prosper, 'Cours Général de Droit International Public: le Droit International en Quéte de son Identité', RCADI, 237 (1992-VI), 9–370, at 100–4.

[2] *Case of the SS Lotus* (Judgment), 1927 PCIJ Series A No. 10, at 18. The whole dictum reads: 'International law governs relations between independent States. The rules of law binding upon States therefore emanate from their own free will as expressed in

Basic propositions

In this conception, only states are international legal persons; statehood and international personality are regarded as synonymous:

> S'il y a un droit international, il ne peut s'appliquer qu'aux rapports entre États coordonnées.[3] Le droit international public règle des rapports entre des États et seulement entre des États parfaitement égaux.[4]

> Tutti i gruppi sociali fra cui intercedono accordi . . . sono dunque destinatari di norme internazionali, subietti dell'ordine giuridico internazionale. Se a questi gruppi sociali vogliamo dare il nome di Stati, la conclusione a cui siamo giunti si può anche esprimere dicendo che gli Stati sono i soggetti del diritto internazionale.[5]

> The conception of International Persons is derived from the conception of the Law of Nations. As this law is the body of rules which the civilised States consider legally binding in their intercourse, every State which belongs to the civilised States, and is, therefore, a member of the Family of Nations, is an International Person. Sovereign States exclusively are International Persons – i.e. subjects of International Law.[6]

The international system is regarded as a community consisting of states.[7] A state's participation in this community depends on recognition by the existing members.[8] As there is no superior entity above state level,

conventions or by usages generally accepted as expressing principles of law and established in order to regulate the relations between the co-existing independent communities or with a view to the achievement of common aims. Restrictions upon the independence of States cannot therefore be presumed.'

[3] Triepel, Heinrich, *Droit International et Droit Interne*, 'Bibliothèque Française de Droit des Gens de la Fondation Carnegie' (A. de Lapradelle, ed.) (Paris: A. Pedone, 1920), 20.

[4] Triepel, Heinrich, 'Les Rapports entre le Droit Interne et le Droit International', RCADI, 1 (1923-I), 77–121, at 81.

[5] Anzilotti, Dionisio, 'Corso di Diritto Internazionale' in Società Italiana per l'Organizzazione Internazionale (ed.), *Opere di Dionisio Anzilotti* (Padova: Cedam, 1955) (originally published 1928), at 112.

[6] Oppenheim, Lassa, *International Law: A Treatise*, 1st edition (London: Longmans, Green, and Co, 1905), §63 (p. 99).

[7] Triepel, *Droit International et Interne*, 18; Anzilotti, 'Corso', at 39–42; Oppenheim, *International Law* (1st edn.), §7 (pp. 11–13) and §12 (p. 16). In what follows, references are given to what is understood to be a key part of the conception. Of course, the whole chapter on this conception relies on the writings of Triepel, Anzilotti and Oppenheim.

[8] Two important aspects have to be specified with respect to the constitutive role of recognition in this conception. First, by recognizing a state as part of the international system, such a state automatically becomes an international person. Recognition does not therefore concern international personality as such; personality is the automatic effect of being a recognized state in this conception. Consequently, the focus for the purposes of

international law can only be a law emanating from the will of the states constituting the international community.[9] This law, in turn, is only applicable to states because they are the only components of the international system; individuals, or other entities recognized as persons by a national legal system, are not part of the international community.[10] Individuals are only a constitutive element of the state of which they are a national. International law thus contrasts with national law in the foregoing two *interrelated* aspects: the two legal orders have different sources and different subjects.[11] The international and the national legal order are thus two separate systems of law, or, as Triepel famously put it, two circles touching each other but never overlapping.[12] The relationship between international and national law is hence envisaged as dualist.

According to this dualist conception, the source of national law is the individual will of one state. International law, on the other hand, emanates from the common will of a number of states.[13] By implication, international law is not a mere external public law (and thus part of national law) that one state can lawfully create and change according to its own will.[14] There must be a common will of several states to establish or to change international rules. Moreover, international law cannot be based on natural law elements.[15] Only the common will of states creates international law. This common will can be express or tacit: if it is

this study is to explain why only (recognized) statehood qualifies for being an international person, not why this statehood has to be recognized in the first place. Second, the existence of a state does not depend on recognition in this conception. A state exists per se; only its relevance for the international system depends on recognition. For especially clear statements see Oppenheim, *International Law* (1st edn.), §71 (p. 108). See also Anzilotti, 'Corso', at 154.

9 Triepel, *Droit International et Interne*, 28; Anzilotti, 'Corso', at 66–7; Oppenheim, *International Law* (1st edn.), §5 (p. 8) and §16 (pp. 21–2).

10 Triepel, *Droit International et Interne*, 15–16; Anzilotti, Dionisio, 'Il diritto internazionale nei giudizi interni' in Società Italiana per l'Organizzazione Internazionale (ed.), *Opere di Dionisio Anzilotti: Scritti di diritto internazionale pubblico* (Padova: Cedam, 1955) (originally published 1905), 281–539, at 321; Oppenheim, *International Law* (1st edn.), §12 (p. 16).

11 See Triepel, *Droit International et Interne*, 9; Triepel, 'Rapports', at 80–3; Anzilotti, 'Giudizi interni', at 319–20 (especially emphasizing the strict interrelation of the two aspects); Anzilotti, 'Corso', at 61 (by implication); Oppenheim, *International Law* (1st edn.), §20 (pp. 25–6).

12 Triepel, 'Rapports', at 83.

13 Triepel, *Droit International et Interne*, 32 and 49–61; Triepel, 'Rapports', 82–3; Anzilotti, 'Giudizi interniv, 319–20; Oppenheim, *International Law* (1st edn.), §20 (p. 25).

14 Triepel, *Droit International et Interne*, 75–80; Anzilotti, 'Corso', 51–2.

15 Triepel, *Droit International et Interne*, 30–1; Triepel, 'Rapports', at 88–9 and 100; Anzilotti, Dionisio, 'Teoria Generale della Responsibilità dello Stato nel Diritto

express, the international rules are laid down in a law-making treaty; if it is tacit, the rules are part of international custom.[16] The expressly or tacitly created international rules only establish international law for those states having consented to them, i.e. for the very states that were part of the common will forming the rule. Therefore, there is only particular international law.[17] General international law can only exist if all states of the international community express their common will to create a specific international rule, which is thought a rare incident.

The question arises why international law understood along these lines is binding. Triepel (and the early Anzilotti) conceive the express or tacit agreement between several states as a *Vereinbarung* (*accordo*, law-making agreement) that in itself is binding.[18] According to their reasoning, such a law-making agreement differs from a mere contract (*Vertrag, contratto*) in that the wills of the states concerned are identical in the former case while they are only complementary in the latter.[19] A contract cannot create law but only respective contractual rights and obligations, the validity of which is determined by an existing legal system. A law-making agreement, conversely, can stipulate binding law because the wills establishing the law are identical and – though consisting of the individual wills of the states – are to a certain degree distinct from the particular state wills. Thus, they cannot be altered by an individual state will. International law emanating from a law-making agreement is therefore binding on the individual states as they themselves cannot change this law on their own.[20] Anzilotti later modified his view and accepted the basic norm *pacta sunt servanda* rather than the theory of the *Vereinbarung* as the foundation for the binding nature of

Internazionale', in Società Italiana per l'Organizzazione Internazionale (ed.), *Opere di Dionisio Anzilotti: Scritti di diritto internazionale pubblico* (Padova: Cedam, 1955) (originally published 1902), 1–147, at 26 and 61; Oppenheim, 'Science of International Law', at 328–30; Oppenheim, *International Law* (1st edn.), §16 (p. 22).

[16] Triepel, *Droit International et Interne*, 49–61 and 99–102; Triepel, 'Rapports', at 83; Anzilotti, 'Responsibilità', at 38–42; Anzilotti, 'Corsov, at 67; Oppenheim, *International Law* (1st edn.), §16–18 (pp. 21–4).

[17] Triepel, *Droit International et Interne*, 82–3; Anzilotti, 'Corso', at 68–9 and 73 (by implication for custom); Oppenheim, *International Law* (1st edn.), §18 (pp. 23–4).

[18] Triepel, *Droit International et Interne*, 49–61; Triepel, 'Rapports', at 82–3; Anzilotti, 'Responsibilità', at 38–42.

[19] Triepel, *Droit International et Interne*, 69–71; Anzilotti, 'Responsibilità', at 39–40.

[20] It has to be noted, however, that Triepel admitted in his course at The Hague in 1923 that international law's binding nature in the end depended on ethical and psychological elements that were not part of the legal realm (Triepel, 'Rapports', at 87).

international law as created by the common will of states.[21] Oppenheim, too, drew a distinction between law-making treaties and mere contracts,[22] but regarded the common will of states as binding law because state practice showed that states regarded themselves bound by international law.[23] Though there is evidently some variation as to why international law is binding, the source of this law is always conceived to be the common will of states.

With regard to the social relations the two different systems of law regulate, national law, on the one hand, applies to the relations between individuals as well as between the state and individuals. International law, on the other hand, regulates the relations between the recognized states that have consented to the international norms in question.[24] By implication, international law cannot be applicable to individuals in general as international norms are only pertinent for the particular states that have consented to them.[25] In addition, according to this conception, even if a particular state has consented to a specific international norm and this norm contains provisions affecting individuals, these provisions are not regarded as being directly applicable to the nationals of the consenting state.[26] Individuals are not envisaged as part of the international community in this conception. They are only constitutive members of the state they belong to. In consequence, law-making agreements that contain provisions concerning individuals are only to be interpreted as obligations of the consenting states to grant rights or to impose obligations onto individuals in their national legal system. Individuals or other private entities are only objects, but never subjects of international law.[27] Hence, international law only applies to states; states have to transform their international obligations into national law in order to

[21] Anzilotti, 'Corso', at 67. [22] Oppenheim, *International Law* (1st edn.), §18 (p. 23).

[23] Ibid., §10 (pp. 13–14): 'The fact is that theorists only are divided concerning the character of the Law of Nations as real law. In practice International Law is constantly recognized as law. The Governments and Parliaments of the different States are of the opinion that they are legally, not morally only, bound by the Law of Nations . . .'

[24] Triepel, *Droit International et Interne*, 18–19 and 82–3; Anzilotti, 'Corso', at 112, 68–9 and 73 (by implication for custom); Oppenheim, *International Law* (1st edn.), §18 (pp. 23–4).

[25] Triepel, 'Rapports', at 88–9; Anzilotti, 'Corso', at 120–1; Oppenheim, *International Law* (1st edn.), §292 (p. 346).

[26] See for this and the following statements Triepel, 'Rapports', at 81; Anzilotti, 'Corso', at 121–2; Oppenheim, *International Law* (1st edn.), §289 (pp. 341–4).

[27] Triepel, 'Rapports', at 81; Oppenheim, *International Law* (1st edn.), §290 (p. 344).

grant rights or impose duties onto the legal persons of their national legal system.

In conclusion, this conception can be encapsulated in two basic propositions.

(1) The international community consists only of states. No other entities form part of the international realm. Individuals do not exist as independent entities outside the borders of their state of nationality.
(2) International law solely emanates from common state will. International law is created only by states and applies alone to those states having consented to it. It cannot apply to an entity not having consented to the rule in question. Thus, only states can be bound by international law, since only they can consent to it. This represents the link between sources and personal application of international law, that is, of sources and legal personality.

The first proposition relates to the understanding of the state and the role of the individual in it. The second proposition articulates a particular view on the sources of law. In order to understand and subsequently assess the significance of these propositions, it is necessary to turn to their origins. Hence, it will be examined what assumptions about the state and its relationship to the individual lead to the first proposition and what suppositions explain the exclusive concern with state will as a source of international law in the second proposition.

Origins of the basic propositions

The origins of the basic propositions of the states-only conception of international legal personality, it is argued, rest in the view of the state as a historical fact entirely absorbing individuals and in the notion of law as an expression of state will. These origins are rooted in the German socio-political and intellectual context of the nineteenth century. Particularly relevant is German public law thought emerging in that environment. In the German context, because of its late unification, public law typically had to deal with relationships between states rather than within a state. International law was hence regarded as a branch of public law.[28]

[28] See Stolleis, Michael, *Geschichte des öffentlichen Rechts in Deutschland 3. Band: Staats- und Verwaltungsrechtswissenschaft in Republik und Diktatur 1914–1945* (Munich: C. H. Beck, 1999), 88–9 (English Translation: Stolleis, Michael, *A History of Public Law in Germany 1914–1945* (Oxford University Press, 2004)), and Koskenniemi, *Gentle Civilizer*, 210–11.

The problem of German (and Italian) statehood

The states-only conception of international personality is closely linked to the German socio-political context of the nineteenth century. The relevance of this context is not surprising with regard to Triepel. He spent all his personal and professional life as a public lawyer in late-nineteenth and early-twentieth century Germany.[29] At least in his work in international law, Triepel is considered one of the leading protagonists of German legal positivism,[30] to which he gave a forceful articulation in his widely read study *Völkerrecht und Landesrecht* in 1899. The relevance of the German context, however, requires further explanation for Oppenheim and Anzilotti before the German historical background can be briefly examined.

Lassa Oppenheim was of German origin.[31] Born near Frankfurt-am-Main in 1858, he studied and taught in Germany and Switzerland before moving to Great Britain in 1895. Having specialized in criminal law in continental Europe, he chose international law as his new subject of study upon arrival in London. After teaching at the London School of Economics and publishing the first edition of his *International Law* in 1905–06, he became the fourth Whewell Professor of International Law at the University of Cambridge in 1908, holding the chair until his death in 1919. While Oppenheim's career in international law thus started and progressed in Great Britain, his legal education and his early academic work had taken place in Germany. Oppenheim had been a pupil of Karl Binding in Leipzig, a bond he shared with Heinrich Triepel,[32] and had also studied in Berlin. His work in international law reveals a close attachment to the positivist approach dominating German legal thought

[29] For biographical information on Triepel and his deep involvement in German public law see Gassner, Ulrich M., *Heinrich Triepel: Leben und Werk* (Berlin: Duncker und Humblot, 1999), 202–445.

[30] For Triepel distancing himself somewhat from legal positivism in later years in his work on German constitutional law see Stolleis, *Geschichte des öffentlichen Rechts (III)*, 172–3.

[31] For biographical information on Oppenheim see Schmoeckel, Mathias, 'The Internationalist as a Scientist and Herald: Lassa Oppenheim', EJIL, 11 (2000), 699–712, esp. 699–701, Schmoeckel, Mathias, 'Lassa Oppenheim (1858–1919)' in Jack Beatson and Reinhard Zimmermann (eds.), *Jurists Uprooted: German-Speaking Emigré Lawyers in Twentieth Century Britain* (Oxford University Press, 2004), 583–599, esp. 590–8, and Kingsbury, Benedict, 'Legal Positivism as Normative Politics: International Society, Balance of Power and Lassa Oppenheim's Positive International Law', EJIL, 13 (2002), 401–36, at 404–5.

[32] Gassner, *Triepel*, 220.

around 1900.[33] Oppenheim introduced German conceptions of the state and legal methodology to Britain that were alien to the British international law tradition.[34] Oppenheim's general legal methodology and his understanding of concepts like statehood, personality or the sources of law have thus to be located in the German intellectual and socio-political context of the later decades of the nineteenth century.

In the case of Anzilotti, the relevance of the German context is not directly traceable to personal experiences in Germany. Born in 1867 into the final stages of the Italian *Risorgimento*, Anzilotti taught at various Italian universities from 1892 onwards, continuing to do so after his election as a Judge to the Permanent Court of International Justice in 1921.[35] Apart from his tenure in The Hague, Anzilotti spent his working life in Italy and was primarily influenced by evolutions in the Italian intellectual and socio-political context. However, there are two main reasons for the relevance of the German context for Anzilotti's conception of international personality. The first, more general, reason is that after Italy's unity had finally been achieved in 1871 there was a widely felt need in Italy to legitimize the new state.[36] Italian scholars were thus looking for a proper philosophical and legal basis for the new state. Such a basis was considered to be provided by the Hegelian philosophy of the

[33] See Schmoeckel, 'Internationalist as a Scientist', at 708–9, and Kingsbury, 'Lassa Oppenheim's Positive International Law', at 406.

[34] See Carty, Anthony, 'Why Theory? – The Implications for International Law Teaching' in Philip Allott, Anthony Carty, Martti Koskenniemi and Colin Warbrick (eds.), *Theory and International Law: An Introduction* (London: British Institute of International and Comparative Law, 1991), 75–104, at 77 and 81; Kingsbury, 'Lassa Oppenheim's Positive International Law', at 406; Schmoeckel, 'Internationalist as a Scientist', at 709–10. Carty goes on arguing that Oppenheim 'killed off' theory in British international law by introducing German concepts. This claim is not part of the argument put forward here. It is only argued here that Oppenheim brought legal conceptions related to his German training to international law in Britain (see for a critique of Carty's latter claim Crawford, James R., 'Public International Law in Twentieth-Century England' in Jack Beatson and Reinhard Zimmermann (eds.), *Jurists Uprooted: German-Speaking Emigré Lawyers in Twentieth Century Britain* (Oxford University Press, 2004), 681–707, at 699–700).

[35] Anzilotti served as the President of the Court from 1928 until 1930 and was re-elected as a Judge to a second term of nine years in 1930. He held a chair at the University of Rome until his retirement in 1937. For biographical information on Anzilotti see Tanca, Antonio, 'Dionisio Anzilotti (1867–1950): Biographical Note with Bibliography', EJIL, 3 (1992), 156–62, esp. 156–7.

[36] Sereni, Angelo Piero, *The Italian Conception of International Law* (New York: Columbia University Press, 1943), 202–3.

state.[37] Accordingly, Italian philosophers and lawyers were drawn to German thought on statehood, the latter abounding at the time as Germany, too, had not become a state until 1871. As a second reason for the relevance of the German context for Anzilotti, specific methodological issues led Italian international lawyers to closely study German (public) law doctrine. Coming from a codified municipal law system where resort to the enacted law was regarded as sufficient to solve any legal problem, Italian international lawyers were inclined to focus on written rules as the only source of international law.[38] General principles deduced from sources other than the legislative will of the state could not be considered as sources of law in the Italian legal context. A similar legal tradition, for reasons explained below, had been emerging in Germany during the nineteenth century. As Italian international lawyers lacked a proper international law tradition themselves, they turned to these existing German (public) law writings in order to address international law issues.[39] French and, to a lesser extent, Anglo-Saxon international law were characterized by a strong influence of natural law, an influence that Italian lawyers could generally not accept in their legal system; they thus rejected it in international law, too, as natural law undermined the power of the state. Anzilotti's work, representing the foundation of the Italian positivist school in international law, particularly reveals the strong influence German (public) law thought had on Italian international law doctrine.[40]

The German socio-political context of the nineteenth century is distinguished by its concern for unification. In contrast to the established nation states of France, Spain or Great Britain at the time, there was no German state at the turn of the nineteenth century.[41] The German territories in Central Europe, reaching from powerful Prussia and Austria to smaller monarchies and free cities, had only been loosely bound together in the complex structure of the Holy Roman Empire of the German Nation (*Heiliges Römisches Reich Deutscher Nation*) since the Middle Ages. Though the Empire symbolized a common German institution, its actual powers had become rather limited since the regional

[37] Ibid., 202. In short, Hegel conceived the state not as the simple outcome of a social contract, but as a realization of the highest moral idea. The Hegelian conception will be further outlined below.

[38] See ibid., 207–10. [39] Ibid., 212.

[40] See Gaja, Giorgio, 'Positivism and Dualism in Dionisio Anzilotti', EJIL, 3 (1992), 123–38, at 127 and 138, and Sereni, *Italian Conception*, 225.

[41] For a general overview of statehood in European history see Schulze, Hagen, *Staat und Nation in der europäischen Geschichte*, 2nd edition (Munich: C. H. Beck, 2004), esp. 239.

kings had acquired quasi-full sovereignty in the Peace Treaties of Westphalia in 1648.[42] Accordingly, when the Empire finally ceased to exist in the wake of the Napoleonic wars in 1806, there was more symbolic than factual relevance to it.[43] After the defeat of Napoleon, at the Congress of Vienna in 1815, the European statesmen rejected the formation of a potentially powerful German state in Central Europe and left the German territories sovereign.[44] To prevent too much fragmentation, however, the German Confederation (*Deutscher Bund*) was formed according to the Confederation Treaty of 1815 (*Bundesakte*) and Article 1 of the Final Act of Vienna. The German Confederation was intended to serve as a coordination organ for the 39 sovereign German states constituting it.

It was only in 1866 that the German Confederation was dissolved in the wake of the Prussian–Austrian war, a war deliberately initiated by the Prussian Chancellor Otto von Bismarck in order to achieve a unified German state under the leadership of Prussia. Bismarck finally achieved his goal after two more wars against Denmark and France: Germany at last became a state in 1871. The German Empire (*Deutsches Kaiserreich*) now encompassed all German-speaking monarchies and city republics of Central Europe in one state, with the notable exception of Austria. The great European powers, France, Great Britain and Russia, carefully watched the newly constituted *Reich*. The German state thus saw its existence endangered by the outside.[45] At the same time, the German state was a rather fragile construction internally. The functioning of the political system was heavily dependent on the charismatic leadership of Chancellor Bismarck.[46] After the dismissal of Bismarck in 1890, no one,

[42] Questioning the extent to which the powers of the Empire diminished in relation to the competences of the individual states as a result of the Peace of Westphalia: Stolleis, Michael, *Geschichte des öffentlichen Rechts in Deutschland 1. Band: Reichspublizistik und Policeywissenschaft 1600–1800* (Munich: C. H. Beck, 1988), 228. However, independently of its causes, it is not disputed that the powers of the Empire continuously diminished in the seventeenth and eighteenth centuries.

[43] Winkler, Heinrich August, *Deutsche Geschichte vom Ende des Alten Reiches bis zum Untergang der Weimarer Republik* (Bonn: Bundeszentrale für politische Bildung, 2000), 51.

[44] See for this and the following Wehler, Hans-Ulrich, *Deutsche Gesellschaftsgeschichte 2. Band: Von der Reformära bis zur industriellen und politischen 'Deutschen Doppelrevolution' 1815–1845/49* (Munich: C. H. Beck, 1987), 325–8.

[45] Wehler, Hans-Ulrich, *Deutsche Gesellschaftsgeschichte 3. Band: Von der deutschen Doppelrevolution bis zum Beginn des Ersten Weltkrieges 1849–1914* (Munich: C. H. Beck, 1995), 966–77 and 1145–52.

[46] See for the description of this type of leadership Weber, Max, 'Politik als Beruf', in Horst Baier et al. (eds.), *Max Weber Gesamtausgabe* (Tübingen: J. C. B. Mohr, 1992) (originally published 1919), 156–252, at 160–2. For an extensive discussion of Bismarck as an

including the monarchy, could actually fill the leadership vacuum left by Bismarck's departure. As a result, there was a constant degree of political instability in the *Reich* as different centres of powers emerged and competed with each other in what has been called a polycratic system.[47] Hence, German statehood, though achieved in a formal sense in 1871, was still regarded as fragile at the end of the nineteenth century.

The state as a historical fact absorbing individuals

From the end of the Holy Roman Empire to the creation of the German state and its immediate aftermath, statehood and its (legal) prerequisites and implications were persistent issues in German public law.[48] In this context, a historical and organic view of the state dominated. Social contract theories were rejected. Individuals were perceived to come into full existence only by being part of the state. They did not have a separate identity apart from being nationals of the state. The states-only conception of international personality as formulated by Triepel, Anzilotti and Oppenheim has to be related to this view of the state, a view that emerged in the particular circumstances of the Holy Roman Empire and was subsequently elaborated by Georg Friedrich Wilhelm Hegel as well as by the leading German public lawyers of the late nineteenth century.

In the last two centuries of the Holy Roman Empire, German public law, called *Reichspublizistik* at the time, emerged as a new field of study.[49] Its purpose was to legally analyse constitutional issues regarding the relationship between the Empire and its constitutive members. One of the most pressing issues for this all-German public law was the legal status of the *Reich* as opposed to the legal nature of its members.[50] In order to allocate competences to the organs of the Empire or to its individual members, it was necessary to decide the legal status of these

example of charismatic leadership in the sense of Max Weber see Wehler, *Deutsche Gesellschaftsgeschichte (III)*, 368–76. Weber himself, writing after Bismarck's chancellorship, may indeed have envisaged Bismarck as a paradigmatic example of charismatic leadership in his typology of legitimate political leadership.

47 Wehler, *Deutsche Gesellschaftsgeschichte (III)*, 1000.

48 See also Stolleis, *Geschichte des öffentlichen Rechts (II)*, 121, and Koskenniemi, *Gentle Civilizer*, 181.

49 See Stolleis, *Geschichte des öffentlichen Rechts (I)*, 141–6.

50 See Randelzhofer, Albrecht, *Völkerrechtliche Aspekte des Heiligen Römischen Reiches nach 1648* (Berlin: Duncker und Humblot, 1967), 67, and Stolleis, *Geschichte des öffentlichen Rechts (I)*, 182. While Randelzhofer claims that the discussion was most pressing after the Peace of Westphalia, Stolleis considers the decades before 1648 as particularly relevant.

respective entities. Was the *Reich* itself a sovereign state? If not, what kind of entity was it? And, depending on the answers to the former questions, what legal status did the member territories of the *Reich* possess? There was considerable debate about these issues in German public law in the seventeenth and eighteenth centuries.[51] In one of the more influential contributions,[52] Samuel Pufendorf argued in 1667 that the Holy Roman Empire was neither a sovereign state nor a mere federation: it was an irregular construction escaping both categories and was therefore to be characterized as a hybrid state-like entity.[53] This approach of viewing the *Reich* as something very similar, though not identical to, a state was shared by most *Reichspublizisten* until the later decades of the eighteenth century.[54] Importantly, starting from the premise that the Holy Roman Empire was a state-like entity, statehood could not be regarded as the outcome of a social contract between free individuals, the latter voluntarily subjecting themselves to a public power and legal order so as to be protected from interferences by other individuals. The *Reich* was far too complex a system, deeply characterized by its historical development, as to be legitimized by a social contract theory. Accordingly, statehood was rather understood as an organically and historically rooted social fact by the *Reichspublizisten*.[55] It was only by thinking of the state as a historically developed social system that the *Reich* could be understood as at least something reminiscent of a state whose constitutional order could then be analysed in legal terms. German public lawyers were hence sceptical of the contractual theory of the state dominating in the rest of Europe at the end of the eighteenth century.

With the end of the Holy Roman Empire in 1806 and the subsequent creation of the German Confederation (*Deutscher Bund*) as a loose

[51] See the overviews by Randelzhofer, *Völkerrechtliche Aspekte*, 68–91, and Stolleis, *Geschichte des öffentlichen Rechts (I)*, 174–84.

[52] See the appraisals by Randelzhofer, *Völkerrechtliche Aspekte*, 81 and Stolleis, *Geschichte des öffentlichen Rechts (I)*, 234.

[53] Pufendorf, Samuel, *Über die Verfassung des deutschen Reiches* (Berlin: Reimar Hobbing, 1922) (originally published 1667), Chapter 6, §§1–9 (pp. 85–95), esp. §9 (pp. 94–5). The book was originally published under the name Severinus de Monzambano, a fictitious Italian writing down his observations about the Holy Roman Empire while travelling in it.

[54] See Stolleis, *Geschichte des öffentlichen Rechts (I)*, 228 and 234–5. In general, most *Reichspublizisten* might thereby have had a more favourable opinion of the Holy Roman Empire than the one Pufendorf had put forward in his rather critical study (see Pufendorf, *Verfassung des deutschen Reiches*, esp. Chapter 7, §§7–10 (pp. 105–10)).

[55] Stolleis, *Geschichte des öffentlichen Rechts (II)*, 124.

organization of sovereign states, the *Reichspublizistik* lost its object of study. Its intellectual traditions, however, remained present in German public law.[56] Though there was general agreement that the newly created German Confederation was not a state, German public law continued to reflect on statehood.[57] The tradition of the *Reichspublizistik* to regard the state as something historically rooted rather than formally constructed by a social contract was thereby further reinforced.[58] After the French Revolution and its excesses, anti-rationalistic and anti-individualistic tendencies developed in the German intellectual context.[59] This general tendency can be encapsulated by reviewing Georg Friedrich Wilhelm Hegel's conception of the state and its subsequent treatment in German public law.[60] For Hegel, in contrast to social contract theories, individual freedom and statehood were not contradicting but rather corresponding objects: '[Der Staat] hat aber ein ganz anderes Verhältnis zum Individuum; indem er objektiver Geist ist, so hat das Individuum selbst nur Objektivität, Wahrheit und Sittlichkeit als es ein Glied desselben ist.'[61]

The individual, accordingly, only came to its full existence and moral standing as part of the state. The state preceded the individual and the latter only objectively existed in the former. The individual hence did not give up any of its freedom by becoming part of a state; on the contrary,

[56] Ibid., 48. [57] Ibid., 96–7 and 123–30.

[58] Thought about the state was thereby termed 'General Theory of the State' (*Allgemeine Staatslehre*). For the close relationship between public law and the *Allgemeine Staatslehre* see ibid., 122–3.

[59] See ibid., 126–30.

[60] Hegel's anti-individualistic and anti-rationalistic tendencies are sometimes disputed (for a balanced account see Taylor, Charles, 'Hegel's Ambiguous Legacy for Modern Liberalism', *Cardozo Law Review*, 10 (1989), 857–70, esp. at 869–70, and for an argument for considering Hegel as a liberal, Westphal, Kenneth, 'The basic context and structure of Hegel's Philosophy of Right' in Frederick C. Beiser (ed.), *The Cambridge Companion to Hegel* (Cambridge University Press, 1993), 234–69, esp. at 236–7). In the context of the present study, however, it is more important to focus on how Hegel's philosophy was used in German public law and international law rather than what the original intentions of Hegel had been. It therefore suffices to review his ideas broadly and to examine the usage of Hegel in the relevant German legal context.

[61] Hegel, Georg Friedrich Wilhelm, *Grundlinien der Philosophie des Rechts*, 'Georg Friedrich Wilhelm Hegel: Sämtliche Werke' (Georg Lasson, ed.) (Leipzig: Felix Meiner, 1930) (originally published 1821), §258 (pp. 195–6). The relationship between the state and the indvidual is also presented by Hegel in Hegel, Georg Friedrich Wilhelm, *Vorlesungen über die Philosophie der Weltgeschichte*, 'Georg Friedrich Wilhelm Hegel: Sämtliche Werke' (Georg Lasson, ed.) (Leipzig: Felix Meiner, 1930) (originally published 1830), 90–1 and 94–5.

the individual only existed as a free person by taking part in a state community.

The reconciliation of individual freedom and statehood was possible according to Hegel because the state itself was the realization of a moral idea.[62] For Hegel, the state was not the result of a social contract entered into by free individuals in order to protect their own, possibly contradicting, personal interests.[63] The French Revolution and its excesses had shown that a community built on this abstract idea of a seemingly rational social compact was bound to end in miserable conditions: arbitrariness, violence and the destruction of all existing social institutions had been the devastating result of this social experiment in France.[64] In contrast, Hegel conceived the state as the outcome of a historical process. For him, the state was an objective spirit, i.e. an idea manifesting itself in reality. This manifestation was the result of a historical process starting with the social institutions of the family and the civil society and culminating in modern statehood. The state was thus thought of not as an abstract entity created by a formal contract of individuals, but as an institution marking the high end of a historical development.[65] Hegel understood the state as an organism, a system resembling the human body and able to organize itself, to preserve itself and to develop according to changing social needs in the course of history.[66]

62 Hegel, *Philosophie des Rechts*, §257 (p. 195).

63 See also Haddock, Bruce, 'Hegel's Critique of the Theory of Social Contract' in David Boucher and Paul Kelly (eds.), *The Social Contract from Hobbes to Rawls* (London/New York: Routledge, 1994), 147–63, at 147–8. Though not questioning that Hegel generally rejected the theory of social contract, Haddock sees some remaining contractual aspects in Hegel's language that nevertheless do not contradict the general argument.

64 Hegel, *Philosophie des Rechts*, §258 (p. 197). Though Hegel does not mention the French Revolution explicitly in this passage, it becomes clear by implication.

65 See ibid., §§341–60 (pp. 271–9), esp. §349 (p. 274), as well as Hegel, *Philosophie der Weltgeschichte*, e.g. 93–4. It is interesting to note that Hegel, in an early study on the Holy Roman Empire in 1801, had denied its statehood despite the fact that the constitution of the Reich was formally still in force at the time (Hegel, Georg Friedrich Wilhelm, *Die Verfassung des deutschen Reiches: Eine politische Flugschrift*, (Georg Mollat, ed.) (Stuttgart: Frommanns, 1935) (originally published 1801), 1–2 and 12–13). This underlines the point that Hegel had a more factual and historic understanding of the state and did not regard a formal contract or constitution as a basis for statehood.

66 Hegel, *Philosophie des Rechts*, §269 (pp. 206–7). See also Wolff, Michael, 'Hegels staatstheoretischer Organizismus: Zum Begriff und zur Methode der Hegelschen Staatswissenschaft', *Hegel-Studien*, 19 (1984), 147–77, esp. at 159 and 164.

Hegel's theory of the state, though certainly not agreed upon in all its different and sometimes ambiguous aspects, was highly influential in German public law discourse in the mid nineteenth century.[67] This can be seen in the works of Carl Friedrich Gerber and Paul Laband, the dominant figures in German public law at the time. For Gerber, too, the state was defined as a moral organism existing as a social fact:

> Die Staatsgewalt ist die Willensmacht eines persönlich gedachten sittlichen Organismus. Sie ist nicht eine künstliche und mechanische Zusammenfassung vieler Einzelwillen, sondern die sittliche Gesamtkraft des selbstbewussten Volkes. Ihre Existenz und Natur beruht nicht auf einer willkürlichen Bestimmung und überlegten Schöpfung, sondern sie ist eine Naturkraft, welche im Staate, als der wichtigsten Sozialform der Menschheit, ursprünglich enthalten ist.[68]

The individual entered the picture in Gerber's public law as the subject (*Untertan*) of this state. However, reminiscent of Hegel, this subjection of the individual to the state was not seen as problematic, but rather as liberating: 'Es ist aber die eigentümliche Natur dieses Gewaltverhältnisses, dass die Unterwerfung nicht als eine Minderung des Rechts, sondern als eine Wohltat empfunden wird; denn der ganze Zweck desselben ist die Gewährleistung einer gedeihlichen Existenz in der Volksgemeinschaft.'[69] Individual freedom, in Gerber's view, was thus not endangered by being subjected to the state, but rather guaranteed by being part of it. The individual again was only fully existent as part of the state, not as an independent entity on its own. In Laband's treatise on German public law, written after the creation of the German *Kaiserreich* in 1871, and soon the work of reference for a whole generation of German public lawyers, statehood was the result of the historical process in which the German *Kaiserreich* had arisen in 1871.[70] The individual, again, was only existent as an object of state power (*Herrschaftsobjekt*); there was no separate existence of the individual for the purposes of public law than that as a national of the state.[71]

[67] The same elements, though not so much related to Hegel himself, are put forward by Stolleis, *Geschichte des öffentlichen Rechts (II)*, 123–6, 156–8, 176–7 and 184–5.

[68] Gerber, Carl Friedrich von, *Grundzüge des deutschen Staatsrechts*, 3rd edition (Leipzig: Bernhard Tauchnitz, 1880), §7 (pp. 19–21, spelling modernized).

[69] Ibid., §17 (p. 50, spelling modernized).

[70] Laband, Paul, *Das Staatsrecht des deutschen Reiches*, 'Handbuch des öffentlichen Rechts der Gegenwart in Monographien' (Heinrich Marquardten, ed.) (Freiburg i.B. and Tübingen: J. C. B. Mohr (Paul Siebeck), 1883), §1 (pp. 6–14).

[71] Ibid., §4 (pp. 29–36).

Georg Jellinek skilfully synthesized and elaborated the foregoing developments at the end of the nineteenth century.[72] Jellinek, too, started from the premise that the state was a historical fact:

> [In der Wirklichkeit der Gesellschaft] wogen die historischen Kräfte, die das An-sich der Staaten bilden und zerstören, das jenseits aller juristischen Konstruktion besteht. Von diesem An-sich gilt, was mit einem genialen Worte der vielverlästerte deutsche Denker [i.e. Hegel[73]] ausgesprochen hat: Für das Werden, Sein und Vergehen der Staaten gibt es kein anderes Forum als die Weltgeschichte, die das Weltgericht bildet.[74]

The state was hence conceived as a social fact (*An-sich des Staates*) resulting from historical developments. Modifying terminology, Jellinek did not use the organism metaphor any more because German society had become too heterogeneous and strained in times of polycratic government after the departure of Bismarck for suggesting a frictionless body.[75] However, Jellinek still proceeded from the idea of an objectively existent state. He postulated two possible perspectives from which this state could be scientifically investigated. On the one hand, the pre-existing state could be examined from a sociological perspective; on the other hand, the state could be analysed in legal terms.[76] While the sociological perspective focused on social relationships and actual powers within a state, the legal perspective examined the formal constitutional structure, i.e. the competences of its different organs or the organization of administrative proceedings. This was the famous two-sided theory of the state (*Zwei-Seiten-Theorie*). Importantly, the state still existed *per se*: the scientific perspectives did not determine the object of observation, but rather presumed its (the state's) existence.

[72] For considering Jellinek's work a synthetical rather than original work encapsulating nineteenth-century German thought on the state, see Stolleis, *Geschichte des öffentlichen Rechts (II)*, 450 and 454, and Koskenniemi, *Gentle Civilizer*, 198.

[73] See also Kersten, Jens, *Georg Jellinek und die klassische Staatslehre* (Tübingen: Mohr Siebeck, 2000), 150 and 162. In a general sense, Jellinek's relationship with Hegelian philosophy was rather ambiguous and far from being all-positive. For a one-sided view, considering Jellinek's overall conception as strongly Hegelian without paying attention to any ambiguities, see Duguit, Léon, 'The Law and the State', HLR, 31 (1917), 1–185, at 125–6.

[74] Jellinek, Georg, *Allgemeine Staatslehre*, 3rd edition (Berlin: Julius Springer, 1921) (originally published 1900), 125.

[75] See also Kersten, *Georg Jellinek*, 152, and Stolleis, *Geschichte des öffentlichen Rechts (II)*, 454–5.

[76] Jellinek, *Allgemeine Staatslehre*, 63. Jellinek was not entirely original in promoting the *Zwei-Seiten-Lehre*. Gerber, *Deutsches Staatsrecht*, §1 (pp. 1–3) had already made a similar distinction.

Individuals, from a sociological as well as from a legal perspective, entered the picture in Jellinek's theory as one of the constitutive elements of a state (*Staatsvolk* or *sesshafte Menschen*).[77] By being constitutive elements, individuals were, in Jellinek's terminology, at the same time subjects and objects of the state. As subjects, they constituted the state and had legal entitlements of a different nature vis-à-vis the state. As objects, individuals had to defer to state power as expressed by state will. By regarding the individual simultaneously as a subject and as an object, Jellinek modified the view held by Gerber and Laband that the individual was only a passive object of state power. In Jellinek's theory of the state, individuals had a much more active role in constituting and administering the state.[78] However, this modification did not imply that Jellinek had a very different view from his predecessors regarding the relationship between individual freedom and the state. For Jellinek, too, individual freedom was best preserved in the state. In the state community, individuals would accept the necessity of state power for the greater interest and thus for their individual good.[79] Though individuals played an active role in the state as one of its constitutive subjects, they were still not regarded as independent entities by Jellinek. Whatever active role and legal entitlements individuals had, these were based on their being members of the state and not on their individuality as such.

Jellinek's view on statehood marked the end of a broader intellectual development in German public law, starting with the *Reichspublizistik* and proceeding with Hegel, Gerber and Laband. In this intellectual tradition, the state was regarded as a historical fact enabling individuals to come to their full existence. This idea was in stark contrast to social contract theories which started from naturally free individuals and saw the state as the result of these individuals entering into a contract, thereby renouncing some parts of their freedom. In the dominant German theory, conversely, it was only when a state was present as a result of historical forces that the individual achieved its freedom and full existence. It is this latter view on statehood and its relation to individuality, for reasons stated earlier, to which the states-only conception of international personality has to be related. When Triepel, Anzilotti and

[77] The other two elements of state, according to Jellinek's famous three-elements-theory (*Drei-Elementen-Lehre*), were state territory (*Staatsgebiet*) and state power (*Staatsgewalt*).

[78] See also Kersten, *Georg Jellinek*, 291.

[79] Jellinek, *Allgemeine Staatslehre*, 220–9. See also Kersten, *Georg Jellinek*, 158).

Oppenheim postulate in their first proposition that the international community consists only of states and that there is no entity above state level, this can be understood as viewing the state as a historical fact, being the highest social institution. The state, in this view, exists independently of legal provisions. Statehood was conceived as a social fact from which legal analysis departed; it was not a legal question whether a state existed or not. The proposition that international law does not directly apply to individuals has to be related to the predominant doctrine in German public law that individuals fully exist only as nationals of the state. Individuals, in this view, were not conceived as independent entities, but only existed as constitutive members of the state. Individuals hence did not have a separate identity according to which international law could directly address them. By terming the individual an object of international law as opposed to the state's role as a subject, Triepel, Anzilotti and Oppenheim used the same terminology Jellinek had used to describe the dual role of the individual inside the state. However, in international law, the individual was only a passive object while the more active part of a subject exclusively belonged to the state's internal law.

Law as an expression of state will

Triepel's, Anzilotti's and Oppenheim's exclusive focus on the common will of states as the source of international law has to be related to the emerging legal positivism in nineteenth-century German public law. Particularly after the unsuccessful liberal-national revolution of 1845–9, German public lawyers concentrated on existing positive law to avoid (liberal) political statements that would have been reminiscent of the French Revolution and the failed German revolution. Moreover, this general tendency to avoid liberal and individualistic natural law principles was strongly reinforced by the view of the state as a historical fact preceding the law. Hence, as the highest social institution existing per se, only the state was competent to create law. This emerging German legal positivism was introduced into international law by Carl Bergbohm, Georg Jellinek and, to some extent, Karl Binding. The states-only conception of international personality built on this notion of law as an expression of state will. By implication, this restriction of law-creation led to the very limited application of international law to those (state) parties having created the legal rule in question. This represented the link between the sources of law and law-application.

In the Holy Roman Empire, German public lawyers had analysed the constitutional structure of the *Reich*. After the dissolution of the Empire, this tradition was continued by German public lawyers in the loose setting of the *Deutscher Bund*, even though there was no single constitution to be analysed any more. The different constitutional systems of the German states and city republics were compared in order to find aspects of a general German public law in the tradition of the *Reichspublizistik*. This not only meant a comparison of the written constitutional provisions (there were only very few in some cases), but the incorporation of general natural law principles (not yet of a liberal and individualistic character) dictated by reason, too.[80] Natural law aspects were thus used to fill the lacunae of a potentially all-German public law. Apart from the intellectual legacy of the *Reichspublizistik*, an additional rationale for this all-German view and the subsequent use of natural law was the contemporary political situation. Most public lawyers were proponents of a liberal nationalism in Germany.[81] They supported in their vast majority a unified German state based on the political system of a constitutional monarchy. The unification of Germany was thus in the first place a liberal project for them, aimed at bringing to an end the often absolutist regimes in the German states and replacing them with a liberal constitutional monarchy on the national level. By postulating the idea of a common German public law, German public lawyers provided a legal framework for a unified Germany. However, this link between the public law profession and a national-liberal political agenda came to a close after the unsuccessful liberal revolutions of 1845–9.[82] The analysis of all-German public law principles on the basis of natural law was too much associated with revolution, liberalism and individualism, all being concepts reminiscent of the French Revolution and its Jacobin excesses. This was politically not suitable in the still more or less absolutist German states of the mid nineteenth century. Hence, for these political reasons, German public law rejected natural law and started to become focused on positive law in order to separate public law from politics from around 1850 onwards.[83]

[80] Stolleis, *Geschichte des öffentlichen Rechts (II)*, 96.

[81] See for a description of German liberal nationalism, which has to be distinguished from post-1871 *Reichs*nationalism, Wehler, *Deutsche Gesellschaftsgeschichte (III)*, 941–4. For the association of most German public lawyers with the former movement see Stolleis, *Geschichte des öffentlichen Rechts (II)*, 96–7, 119–20 and 184–5.

[82] See Stolleis, *Geschichte des öffentlichen Rechts (II)*, 274–8 and 122–3.

[83] Apart from these specific reasons in German public law for the turn to positivism, there are also two other factors to be mentioned: first, the turn to positivism has to be seen in the context of the broader developments in science in the aftermath of Auguste Comte

This turn to the exclusive analysis of positive law was further reinforced by developments in the theory of the state. Conceiving the state as a social fact that existed independently of legal provisions, law was regarded as solely emanating from this pre-existing state will. Because the state was viewed as the highest social institution, there was no source of law other than the will of the state. The state preceded the law. Gerber and Laband, two proponents of this historical view of the state, formulated this strictly positivist doctrine in German public law. Gerber conceived law solely as the result of an expression of state will as there was no higher social institution than the state.[84] Public lawyers had only to take into account different manifestations of state will in order to analyse the law; no other source was accepted. For Laband, too, starting from the state as a social fact, the only source of law was an expression of will in a certain form by the competent state organ.[85] Accordingly, all public lawyers had to do was to organize and systematize the expressions of state will.

This so-called *Gerber-Laband Gesetzespositivismus*, skilfully encapsulating socio-political and intellectual developments in nineteenth-century Germany, was quickly taken up in German international law doctrine. In a widely read study, Carl Bergbohm applied a radical legal positivism to international law in 1877.[86] Bergbohm argued that, as in public law, only the express or implicit will of states could create international law.[87] Accordingly, international law existed as far as there were treaties or agreements stating the law. Thus, international law was treaty law binding on those states that consented to it.[88] By implication, Bergbohm strongly rejected any theories that accepted natural law as a source of international

(see Truyol y Serra, Antonio, 'Doctrines Contemporaines du Droit des Gens', RGDIP, XXI–XXII (1950–1), 369–416, 23–40, 199–236, at 403 (XXI)), and second, the earlier turn to positivism in German private law has to be taken into account (see Stolleis, *Geschichte des öffentlichen Rechts (II)*, 276).

84 See Gerber, *Deutsches Staatsrecht*, §2 (p. 3), §§3–4 (pp. 6–8) and §6 (pp. 12–18).

85 See Laband, *Staatsrecht*, §2 (p. 16) and esp. §10 (pp. 69–73).

86 Regarding the reception of Bergbohm's study and the broader background of his strict positivism (as well as a comparison with August Blumerincq's form of legal positivism) see Mälksoo, Lauri, 'The Science of International Law and the Concept of Politics: The Arguments and Lives of the International Law Professors at the University of Dorpat/Iur'ev/Tartu 1855–1985', BYIL, 76 (2005), 383–501, at 419–37.

87 Bergbohm, Carl, *Staatsverträge und Gesetze als Quellen des Völkerrechts* (Dorpat: C. Mattiesen, 1877), esp. 40–3.

88 Ibid., 77–91. Bergbohm distinguished between particular and general treaty law, whereby general treaty law also only bound those states that had consented to it. The difference lay only in the fact that almost all states had somehow consented to a general treaty, while only few states were party to a particular law treaty. General international law in Bergbohm's terms did thus not imply law applying to states not having consented to it.

law, thereby criticizing international legal scholarship of the nineteenth century for still doing so.[89] On the other hand, he opposed the view that there was no international law at all.[90] Bergbohm thus challenged both natural law theories as well as theories denying international law.[91] In his view, international law existed in the expressions of state will. Bergbohm's radical legal positivism in international law was acclaimed and further developed by Georg Jellinek.[92] Jellinek, with explicit reference to Hegel, strongly agreed with Bergbohm that international law could only be based on state will.[93] Jellinek, too, was concerned with constructing international law as a positive legal science and erasing any natural law elements from it.[94] But why would international law exclusively based on state will be binding? In Jellinek's view, Bergbohm had not addressed this issue.[95] To solve it, Jellinek had to return to the nature of the state. The primary purpose of the state, understood as a social fact, was to preserve its own existence.[96] As was the case in public law in general, the state could bind itself as long as this was not contrary to its interests. It was in the interests of states to interact with each other and to establish binding rules in order to preserve their own statehood. Treaties concluded by states to regulate their interactions with each other were thus generally binding.[97] This was the so-called theory of auto-limitation of the state (*Selbstbindungslehre*). The only exception to this general rule was the *clausula rebus sic stantibus*: a state could not be bound by an expression of will if it was contrary to its duty of self-preservation.[98]

[89] Ibid., 6–8. [90] Ibid., 5 and 9–12.

[91] Bergbohm was primarily concerned with opposing Johan Caspar Bluntschtli's doctrine accepting natural law elements (see ibid., 8) as well as challenging Adolf Lasson's external public law theory (see Bergbohm, *Staatsverträge*, 10). See also Mälksoo, 'Concept of Politics', at 425–30.

[92] Jellinek, Georg, *Die rechtliche Natur der Staatenverträge: Ein Beitrag zur juristischen Construction des Völkerrechts* (Vienna: Alfred Hölder, 1880), III, 5 and 45. For Jellinek's significance see Stolleis, *Geschichte des öffentlichen Rechts (II)*, 450 and 454.

[93] See Jellinek, *Staatenverträge*, 3. Hegel's argument, to which Jellinek refers, is presented in Hegel, *Philosophie des Rechts*, §333 (p. 268). See also Bernstorff, Jochen von, 'Georg Jellinek – Völkerrecht als modernes öffentliches Recht im fin de siècle' in Stanley L. Paulson and Martin Schulte (eds.), *Georg Jellinek: Beiträge zu Leben und Werk* (Tübingen: Mohr Siebeck, 2000), 183–206, at 187, and Hall, Stephen, 'The Persistent Spectre: Natural Law, International Order and the Limits of Legal Positivism', EJIL, 12 (2001), 269–307, at 282.

[94] Jellinek, *Staatenverträge*, 1 and 4. [95] Ibid., 5–6. [96] Ibid., 41.

[97] Ibid., 44–5. See also Bernstorff, 'Völkerrecht als modernes öffentliches Recht', at 195.

[98] Jellinek, *Staatenverträge*, 62. See also Truyol y Serra, 'Doctrines du Droit des Gens', at 407, and Bernstorff, 'Völkerrecht als modernes öffentliches Recht', at 195.

The theory of auto-limitation was finally altered, by the criminal and public lawyer Karl Binding, to a theory of the distinctive common will of states (*Vereinbarungslehre*).[99] Analysing in hindsight the foundation of the Northern German Confederation (*Norddeutscher Bund*) after the dissolution of the *Deutscher Bund* in 1866, Binding declared that the northern German states had been able to commit themselves to the new confederation by entering into a law-making agreement (*Vereinbarung*) as opposed to concluding a mere contract (*Vertrag*). While the intentions of the parties to a contract had only to be complementary, in the case of a *Vereinbarung* they had to be identical.[100] In the latter case, there was a distinctive common will of the parties as distinguished from their individual wills. As a consequence, the *Vereinbarung* could not be changed by an individual will of one state and the *Norddeutscher Bund* was thus existent even if individual states subsequently changed their minds. Only the same common will that had established the confederation could also change or dismiss it. In contrast to Jellinek, Binding thus distinguished different forms of state will in order to declare the binding nature of their expressions.

It is obviously this latter *Vereinbarungslehre* that is inherent in Triepel's and the early Anzilotti's view on the binding nature of a strictly positive international law. With this theory, it was possible to think of international law as binding even if only based on state will. Moreover, relating the states-only conception of international personality to the strict legal positivism as put forward by Bergbohm, Jellinek and Binding in the German context, it is now possible to understand more profoundly the reasons for its exclusive concern with expressions of state will as a source of international law. First, this concern and the accompanying rejection of natural law principles as a source of law can be interpreted as a way to escape any political statement. International law, like law in general, had to be erased from any political, and hence unstable, influences in the German socio-political context of the nineteenth century.[101] Natural law principles were associated with the chaotic political circumstances of the French Revolution and were hence rejected at least by the ruling classes. Legal science only had to focus on the law enacted by the competent state will. That also held true for international law. Second,

[99] Binding, Karl, 'Die Gründung des Norddeutschen Bundes' in Leipziger Juristenfakultät (ed.), *Festgabe für Dr. Bernhard Windscheid* (Leipzig: Duncker und Humblot, 1888), 3–72, at 5, 7–11 and 69–72.

[100] Ibid., at 70. [101] See also Mälksoo, 'Concept of Politics', at 435.

the exclusive concern with state will as a source of international law was related to the view of the state as the highest social institution. As there was no entity higher than the state and there could be no law that was contrary to the state's interest – because a state had a duty to preserve itself – there could only be (international) law in accordance with state will. This concern with law not being contradictory to state interests reflected the still fragile construction of the German (or Italian) state at the end of the nineteenth century. It was felt that international law rules could only be accepted if these obligations did not run contrary to the states' interests.

For these reasons, the states-only conception of international personality as formulated by Triepel, Anzilotti and Oppenheim rejected any sources of international law apart from those embodying a state will. By doing so, they broke with the view predominant in international law until late in the nineteenth century according to which natural law principles had been accepted as at least complementary sources of international law. This restriction regarding sources had repercussions for the international law of persons. With international legal provisions only existing for the parties having consented to them, there was no more room for general international law principles relevant for all members of the international community. Even if a separate existence of individuals or other entities as part of the international realm were accepted – which was, of course, not the case in this conception of international personality – there could be no application of international law to entities which had not expressly or tacitly consented to a particular rule. International law application was hence limited to consenting state parties by restricting international law-creation to the expression of state will. There could be no more application of international law to non-state entities as they could not take part in law-creation.

Main manifestations in legal practice

The view of the state as the sole international legal person has been manifested in legal practice. The most important manifestations are, it is argued, the *Mavrommatis*-formula, the *Jurisdiction of the Courts of Danzig* Advisory Opinion, the *Serbian Loans* statement regarding state contracts and the ECJ's decision in *Van Gend en Loos*. These expressions of the states-only conception of international personality have acquired a status transcending the actual case and have become regularly invoked principles in international legal argument. After reviewing the cases and arguing why they are manifestations of the states-only conception of international personality, the relevance of the concept for current international law issues will be examined.

The Mavrommatis-*formula*

The *Mavrommatis*-formula asserts that the individual has no direct rights in the international legal system, but that a state can invoke its own international rights to protect a national's interest.[102] This corresponds with the states-only conception of international legal personality: only states are international right holders and the individual is only relevant for international law as a national of a state, not as an independent entity. The formula has been affirmed in several leading cases and, to a certain extent, is still present in the ILC's work on diplomatic protection today.

The *Mavrommatis* case arose out of a dispute between Mr Mavrommatis, a Greek national, and the British government. Prior to World War I, Mavrommatis had been granted concessions by the then ruling Ottoman government to construct public works in Palestine. After the creation of the British mandate over Palestine, the British government, Mavrommatis claimed, had failed to fully recognize his concessionary rights, thereby allegedly violating Article 9 of Protocol XII of the Lausanne Peace Treaty between Turkey and the Allied Powers,[103] the latter including Greece and Great Britain. Greece subsequently took up Mavrommatis's claim and brought it before the PCIJ. The British government contested the jurisdiction of the Court on the grounds that the conditions for jurisdiction as contained in Article 26 of the Mandate for Palestine[104] were not fulfilled. Though the key question for the Court when applying Article 26 was to decide whether the dispute was related to the 'interpretation or the application of the provisions of the Mandate', it first had to deal with the condition whether the dispute arose between

[102] *The Mavrommatis Palestine Concessions* (Greece v. UK), Jurisdiction, 1924 PCIJ Series A No. 2, at 12. It has to be admitted that the formula does not expressly exclude direct individual rights; it only declares that by exercising diplomatic protection a state is asserting its own rights and not those of the individual concerned. This has mostly been interpreted in the sense that the individual has no direct rights, although the dual nature of rights may not be entirely excluded by the formula.

[103] 28 LNTS 13.

[104] Mandate for the Administration of the Former Turkish Territory of Palestine, conferred upon his Britannic Majesty, confirmed and defined by the League of Nations, 24 July 1922, available at http://domino.un.org/unispal.nsf.

the 'Mandatory and another Member of the League of Nations', i.e. between Great Britain and another state being a member of the League. In this latter respect, the Court argued:

> In the case of the Mavrommatis Concessions it is true that the dispute was at first between a private person and a State – i.e. between M. Mavrommatis and Great Britain. Subsequently, the Greek Government took up the case. The dispute then entered upon a new phase; it entered the domain of international law, and became a dispute between two States. ... By taking up the case of one of its subjects and by resorting to diplomatic action or international juridical proceedings on his behalf, a State is in reality asserting its own rights. ... The question, therefore, whether the present dispute originates in an injury to a private interest, which in point of fact is the case in many international disputes, is irrelevant from this standpoint. Once a State has taken up a case on behalf of one of its subjects before an international tribunal, in the eyes of the latter the State is sole claimant.[105]

This statement has become the *Mavrommatis*-formula and represents the classic formulation of diplomatic protection in international law.[106] According to the formula, the ill-treatment of a foreign national affects the international rights of the national's home state, not the rights of the individual. Hence, the alleged failure of the British government to recognize Mavrommatis's concessionary rights affected the international rights of Greece, not the rights of Mavrommatis. Starting from a private interest, according to the Court, international law becomes relevant only when the home state of a private party takes up the case and invokes its own international rights opposite other states. The invocation of these rights may have as its underlying rationale the protection of a private interest, but it remains the right of the state, not the right of the individual.

The *Mavrommatis*-formula corresponds with the states-only conception of international legal personality. Though some aspects of the formula, as is often claimed, can be traced back to Vattel's *Droit des Gens*,[107] the wording and the basic elements of the *Mavrommatis*-formula clearly

105 *The Mavrommatis Palestine Concessions*, at 12.

106 See also Dugard, John R. (Special Rapporteur), *First Report on Diplomatic Protection*, ILC 2000, UN Doc. A/CN.4/506, para. 62.

107 See e.g. Dugard, *First Report*, para. 62. The correct reference for Vattel's idea of diplomatic protection is Vattel, *Le Droit des Gens*, Livre II Chapitre VI §71 (p. 309): 'Quiconque maltraite un Citoyen offende indirectement l'État, qui doit protéger ce Citoyen.' Vattel was, as the quote indicates, primarily concerned with the attribution of acts of citizens.

mark it as a manifestation of the states-only conception of international personality – not least because Anzilotti was one of the drafters of the judgment.[108] According to the *Mavrommatis*-formula, only states have rights in the international legal system and the individual is not regarded as a separate entity in the international realm, but only exists as a national of a particular state. Article 9 of Protocol XII of the Lausanne Peace Treaty can therefore, according to the judgment, only apply to Greece as one of the consenting states to this particular rule, but it cannot directly apply to Mavrommatis. This proclaimed predominance of the state and the non-existence of the individual in the international realm, apart from being a national of a state, correspond with the basic propositions of the states-only conception of international personality. As in the states-only conception, the *Mavrommatis*-formula accepts solely states as international law subjects and sees no independent role for individuals in the international legal system apart from being a national of a state. Starting from this conception of international personality, diplomatic protection, as formulated in *Mavrommatis*, can only mean the enforcement of a right of the state itself, not of a right held by the individual because there are no such individual rights in this conception.

The *Mavrommatis*-formula and its assertion that diplomatic protection means the invocation of a state's own right and not the enforcement by the state of a right held by the individual has often been challenged in doctrine.[109] However, the formula was reaffirmed by the PCIJ in the *Panevezys-Saldutiskis Railway Case*[110] and by the ICJ in the *Nottebohm* case.[111] Similarly, the ICJ declared in *Barcelona Traction* that by

[108] For Anzilotti's involvement in drafting the judgment see Spiermann, Ole, *International Legal Argument in the Permanent Court of International Justice: The Rise of the International Judiciary* (Cambridge University Press, 2005), 191–206. Anzilotti's view on diplomatic protection, clearly applying his and Triepel's conception of international legal personality, can be seen in Anzilotti, Dionisio, 'Notion et Fondement de la Responsabilité Internationale des États à Raison des Dommages Soufferts par des Étrangers' in Società Italiana per l'Organizzazione Internazionale (ed.), *Opere di Dionisio Anzilotti: Scritti di diritto internazionale pubblico* (Padua: Cedam, 1956) (originally published 1906), 149–207, at 151–3.

[109] For overviews see Dugard, *First Report*, paras 65–7, and García-Amador, F.V. (Special Rapporteur), *First Report on International Responsibility*, ILC 1956, UN Doc. A/CN.4/96, paras 98–105.

[110] *The Panevezys-Saldutiskis Railway Case* (Estonia v. Lithuania), Judgment, 1939 PCIJ Series A/B No. 76, p. 16.

[111] *Nottebohm Case* (Liechtenstein v. Guatemala), Second Phase (Judgment), 1955 ICJ Reports 4, at 24.

exercising diplomatic protection on behalf of shareholders, 'it is its own right that the State is asserting'.[112] Even more current developments in international human rights and investor protection law can be interpreted as applications of the *Mavrommatis*-formula, for the rights concerned are dependent on the rights of states.[113] In the ILC's project on diplomatic protection, moreover, the *Mavrommatis*-formula, though to a certain extent put into historical perspective, has been partly endorsed by adopting Draft Articles 1 and 2 which are deliberately neutral on whether diplomatic protection is the invocation of a state's own right or the right of the national.[114] The *Mavrommatis*-formula, though often challenged in doctrine, evidently is still present in international legal practice. By upholding the formula, the basic propositions of the states-only conception of international personality, in particular that the individual has no independent existence in the international realm and exists only as a national of a state, is (tacitly) accepted.

The Jurisdiction of the Courts of Danzig *Advisory Opinion*

The *Jurisdiction of the Courts of Danzig* opinion has been the subject of controversy.[115] Some commentators, including Anzilotti, consider the opinion as a strict manifestation of the states-only conception of international personality. Others regard it as an example of the direct applicability of international law to individuals, if the parties so intend, and hence for a broadening of the notion of international personality. It is argued here that the *Jurisdiction of the Courts of Danzig* opinion principally manifested the states-only conception, but applied it in such a way as to partly open the (back) door for involving the individual in international law.

The case arose out of the rather special circumstances of the city of Danzig in the interwar period. Pursuant to Articles 100 and 102 of the Treaty of Versailles, Danzig had been ceded by Germany and established

[112] *Case Concerning the Barcelona Traction, Light and Power Company, Limited* (Belgium v. Spain), Second Phase (Merits), 1970 ICJ Reports 3, at para. 78. See also Dugard, John R. (Special Rapporteur), *Fourth Report on Diplomatic Protection*, ILC 2003, UN Doc. A/CN.4/530, paras 3–27.

[113] See, e.g., Crawford, 'The ILC's Articles on Responsibility of States', at 887–8, who, however, states merely the possibility of such an interpretation, but does not endorse it.

[114] *Draft Articles on Diplomatic Protection with commentaries*, ILC 2006, UN Doc. A/61/10, para. 50 (pp. 24–30). See also Dugard, *First Report*, para. 73.

[115] See, e.g., Waldock, Humphrey (Special Rapporteur), *Third Report on the Law of Treaties*, ILC 1964, UN Doc. A/CN.4/167, 1964-II, YILC p. 46.

as a Free City in 1919. The status of a Free City was intended to ensure Poland's access to the sea while protecting the city's German-speaking population. Having prerequisites of a state for the purposes of international law,[116] the Free City of Danzig, in accordance with Article 104 of the Versailles Peace Treaty, entered into an agreement with Poland according to which the Danzig railways were to be administered by Poland.[117] Additionally, the two parties concluded the 'Definitive Agreement Regarding Officials'[118] (*endgültiges Beamtenabkommen*) to regulate the entry of the Danzig railway workers into Polish employment. Several former Danzig railway officials subsequently brought employment-law cases against the Polish Railway Administration before the courts of Danzig founding pecuniary claims on the *Beamtenabkommen*. These proceedings were brought to the attention of the High Commissioner of the League of Nations at Danzig who decided that the claims could not be based on the *Beamtenabkommen*. The Free City of Danzig appealed against this decision to the Council of the League of Nations, the latter requesting an advisory opinion of the PCIJ on this issue. The Court was confronted with the question whether the *Beamtenabkommen* was applicable to individual railway workers. The Polish government contended that the agreement, being an international treaty, was only applicable to the parties to the treaty, not to individuals. The Court replied:

> It may be readily admitted that, according to a well established principle of international law, the *Beamtenabkommen*, being an international agreement, cannot, as such, create direct rights and obligations for private individuals. But it cannot be disputed that the very object of an international agreement, according to the intention of the contracting Parties, may be the adoption by the Parties of some definite rules creating individual rights and obligations and enforceable by the national courts. That there is such an intention in the present case can be established by reference to the terms of the *Beamtenabkommen*.[119]

There is some controversy as to what the Court actually said in this paragraph. Hersch Lauterpacht has interpreted the second and third

[116] Crawford, *Creation of States*, 240.
[117] Convention between Poland and the Free City of Danzig, 9 November 1920, 6 LNTS 160, Article 21.
[118] Endgültiges Beamtenabkommen, 22 October 1921, reproduced in 1928 PCIJ Series B No. 15, at 37–43.
[119] *Jurisdiction of the Courts of Danzig* (Advisory Opinion), 1928 PCIJ Series B No. 15, at 17–18.

sentences as an acknowledgment by the Court that treaties, if the parties so intend, can directly apply to individuals.[120] Though it might be admitted that the wording of the paragraph is not entirely clear, this seems to be an overstatement. Anzilotti, the then president of the Court and one of the drafters of the opinion, as well as others, have more convincingly argued that the Court simply declared in this statement that a treaty could not create individual rights, but could obligate the parties to incorporate rules, the content of which being defined in the treaty itself, that subsequently created individual rights in the municipal system.[121] In other words, the Court saw nothing to prevent states from defining specific rules benefitting individuals in an international treaty; these rules, however, had then to be adopted by the parties in their municipal legal system in order to make them applicable to individuals. This is what the Court meant by admitting, after having stated that international treaties could not directly apply to individuals, that 'the very *object* of an international agreement . . . may be the *adoption* by the parties of some definite rules creating individual rights and obligations'.[122]

The confusion surrounding the Court's statement might be related to the way the Court proceeded from this statement of principle. Without examining whether the parties had actually adopted the rules laid down in the *Beamtenabkommen* in their municipal system, the Court came to the conclusion that:

> . . . in the intention of the contracting Parties, the relations between the Polish Railways Administration and the Danzig officials should be governed by the *Beamtenabkommen*, the provisions of which constitute part

[120] Lauterpacht, *Development*, 51–3, and Lauterpacht, Hersch, *Oppenheim's International Law: A Treatise*, 8th edition (New York: David McKay Company, 1955), §13a (p. 21). See also McCorquodale, Robert, 'The Individual and the International Legal System' in Malcolm D. Evans (ed.), *International Law*, 2nd edition (Oxford University Press, 2006), 307–32, at 312. Not explicitly focusing on the wording in this paragraph but more on the opinion in general, Spiermann, 'LaGrand Case', at 209, and Crawford, 'The ILC's Articles on Responsibility of States', at 887. Also in this direction Crawford, *Open System*, 27.

[121] See Anzilotti, 'Corso', at 339–40 n. 24. For Anzilotti being one of the drafters of the opinion, as well as for this statement being a manifestation of the states-only conception, see Spiermann, *International Legal Argument in the PCIJ*, 271. For similar interpretations see Beckett, W. E., 'Decisions of the Permanent Court of International Justice on Points of Law and Procedure of General Application', BYIL, 11 (1930), 1–54, at 4; McNair, *Law of Treaties*, 337–9; and Friedmann, Wolfgang, *The Changing Structure of International Law* (London: Stevens & Sons, 1964), 239 n. 17.

[122] *Jurisdiction of the Courts of Danzig*, at 17–18 (emphasis added).

> of what the High Commissioner calls the 'contract of service', and that, consequently, the Danzig officials have, in accordance with the first part of the Decision, a right of action against the Polish Railways Administration for the recovery of pecuniary claims based on the *Beamtenabkommen*.[123]

It is this conclusion, when related to the principle stated before, that offers space for controversy. By not examining whether the *Beamtenabkommen* had been incorporated into the municipal legal system of Poland and nevertheless declaring the agreement directly relevant for the employment relationship between the Danzig officials and the Polish Railway Administration, the Court seemed to embrace the view that an international agreement could directly create individual rights, a view that was logically inconsistent with the principle previously stated. Anzilotti explained in his textbook:

> Se, nel caso specifico [*Jurisdiction of the Courts of Danzig*], la Corte non ha creduto necessario esaminare se le norme formulate nell' accordo erano state effetivamente adottate, ciò è stato perchè essa ha ritenuto la parte la quale si era impegnata ad adottare le dette norme non poteva in alcun caso avvalersi del fatto di non aver adempiuto quest' obbligo per sottrarsi ai doveri, che l'accordo le imponeva, verso l'altra parte contraente.[124]

With this explanation, Anzilotti referred to the last paragraph of the opinion where the Court had declared that Poland could not rely on not having adopted the rules defined in the *Beamtenabkommen* in order to challenge the jurisdiction of the courts of Danzig.[125] The fact that Poland was under obligation, pursuant to the *Beamtenabkommen*, to incorporate these rights into the employment contracts with the Danzig railway officials sufficed for the Court to regard them as applicable to individual claims. Otherwise Poland would benefit from non-fulfilment of an international obligation which, by implication, would be against the principle of good faith, namely the maxim that nobody can profit from his own wrong.[126] Therefore, the Court deemed it unnecessary to examine if the rights agreed on in the *Beamtenabkommen* had actually been adopted by Poland into the 'contracts of service' with the Danzig railway officials. It

[123] Ibid., at 21. [124] Anzilotti, 'Corso', at 340, no. 24.

[125] *Jurisdiction of the Courts of Danzig*, at 26–7. See also Spiermann, *International Legal Argument in the PCIJ*, 271–2.

[126] See Kolb, Robert, *La Bonne Foi en Droit International Public: Contribution à l'Étude des Principes Généraux de Droit* (Paris: Presses Universitaires de France, 2000), 487–99, esp. 495.

was sufficient that Poland was obligated, according to the agreement, to incorporate these rights into the contracts.

Interpreting the *Jurisdiction of the Courts of Danzig* opinion in this way, it seems fair to say that the principle stated by the Court at the beginning of the opinion is a manifestation of the states-only conception of international personality. According to the first part of the principle stated by the Court, an international agreement cannot directly apply to individuals, but applies only to states. This is clearly a manifestation of the view that only states are international legal persons and that individuals exist only as nationals of a state, but not as independent entities in the international realm. According to the second part of the principle, the object of an international agreement can be the regulation of matters involving individuals, but such provisions cannot directly apply to individuals and consequently merely constitute an obligation of the parties to incorporate them into their municipal system. In content and wording, this is a manifestation of the view put forward by the states-only conception that the individual can be the object, but not the subject, of international law. In Anzilotti's view, the Court subsequently applied the states-only conception in a strict sense, the only diversion from it being the irrelevance attached to the non-incorporation of the *Beamtenabkommen* into Polish law. This diversion was justified according to the last paragraph of the Court's opinion because otherwise Poland would have profited from its own wrong. In a favourable reading, it might be argued that the Court applied the states-only conception of international personality in the opinion as a whole. However, this might be an overstatement, too. It has to be admitted that, in result, the *Jurisdiction of the Courts of Danzig* opinion leaves the door partly open for involvement of the individual in international law. In the end, the Court admits, though for special reasons, that the Danzig railway officials have direct rights arising from the *Beamtenabkommen*. However, only the back door to the international legal system partly opened with this result. The front door, the principle, was closed for individuals. On balance, there was no application of another conception of international personality – namely the one postulating that the direct application of treaties to individuals was only dependent on the intention of the parties, as some observers have claimed[127] – but rather a somehow special

[127] See, e.g., Spiermann, 'LaGrand Case', at 209; Crawford, 'The ILC's Articles on Responsibility of States', at 887; Brownlie, Ian, 'The Place of the Individual in International Law', *Virginia Law Review*, 50 (1964), 435–62, at 440 (though very clearly

application of the states-only conception. This does not imply that the reasoning of the Court in the *Jurisdiction of the Courts of Danzig* opinion was necessarily logically and legally sound; it means only that the Court, in its original intention, tried to apply sensibly the states-only conception of international personality.

The *Jurisdiction of the Courts of Danzig* opinion and the issue of international treaties' direct effect upon individuals continued to preoccupy international lawyers.[128] In the same year, 1928, the Upper Silesian Arbitral Tribunal, established under the German–Polish Convention of 1922, decided in *Steiner and Gross* v. *Polish State* that the Convention directly conferred jurisdiction on the Tribunal to hear cases brought by Polish nationals.[129] In its award, the Tribunal stressed the 'unequivocal terms' and the 'clear wording' of the Convention which could therefore not be interpreted differently.[130] This can be read as an indication that a less clear provision would have been interpreted as not being directly applicable.[131] Nevertheless, this decision cast doubt on the states-only conception of international personality.[132]

The Serbian Loans *statement on state contracts*

In the *Serbian Loans* case, the PCIJ was concerned, inter alia, with determining the law governing contracts between a state and individuals,

marking this as an exception). On the whole, Spiermann also puts this argument forward in Spiermann, 'Other Side of the Story', at 768–9.

128 International courts, however, had had to consider the application of international treaties towards individuals before *Jurisdiction of the Courts of Danzig*. In 1909, the Central American Court of Justice doubted a treaty's direct effect upon individuals in *Dr. Pedro Andres Fornos Diaz* v. *The Government of the Republic of Guatemala*, 3 AJIL 1909, 737, at 742. In *Certain Questions relating to Settlers of German Origin in the Territory ceded by Germany to Poland* (Advisory Opinion), 1923 PCIJ Series B No. 6, at 25, the PCIJ had dealt with the direct effect of the Polish Minorities Treaty, hinting at such a possibility. See also *Questions concerning Acquisition of Polish Nationality* (Advisory Opinion), 1923 PCIJ Series B No. 7, at 16.

129 *Steiner and Gross* v. *Polish State* (Upper Silesian Arbitral Tribunal, 30 March 1928), 4 Annual Digest of Public International Law Cases (ILR) 291, at 291–2.

130 Ibid., at 292. 131 See also Spiermann, 'Other Side of the Story', at 769–70.

132 Later, however, the ILC could not agree on including the proposed Article 66 concerning the application of treaties to individuals in its draft on the law of treaties (see the discussion in YILC 1964-I, at 114–19, especially the statements by Roberto Ago revealing a state-centric conception of personality; as a result of the discussion, the article was subsequently withdrawn by Special Rapporteur Waldock). In a sense, this failure was again a manifestation of the states-only conception of international personality.

i.e. the law determining the validity, binding nature and consequences of breach of a state contract. The Court declared that the law governing such contracts could only be national law, presumably the law of the contracting state.[133] By implication, it was excluded that the proper law of contract could be international law. This exclusion corresponds with the states-only conception of international personality. The *Serbian Loans* principle has subsequently been altered to varying degrees in international practice. In some instances, other conceptions of international personality were employed and international law was hence directly applied to state contracts. Others have proved more faithful to the *Serbian Loans* precedent and the states-only conception of personality. In this latter sense, international law can only be applied restrictively to state contracts by analogy since a private party is not an international person.

The *Serbian Loans* case originally arose out of a dispute between French holders of bonds issued by the Kingdom of the Serbs, Croats and Slovenes. The main issue was on which monetary base the interest of these bonds had to be serviced. By special agreement, the French state and the Kingdom of the Serbs, Croats and Slovenes referred the case to the PCIJ. The Court first dealt with its jurisdiction because contrary to the *Mavrommatis*-formula, France did not claim that its own international rights had been breached; there were only rights and obligations between the Serbian state and its private bondholders involved, matters 'which are, within themselves, in the domain of municipal law'.[134] However, as the Court observed, after France had acted in the interest of its nationals and diplomatic negotiations between the two governments had taken place, there existed a 'difference of opinion' of international character between the two governments on which the Court regarded itself competent.[135] Having thus established jurisdiction, the PCIJ, after interpreting the contractual obligations between the Serbian state and the French bondholders, went on to determine the applicable law by which the validity and the consequences of these contractual

[133] *Case Concerning the Payments of Various Serbian Loans Issued in France* (Judgment), 1929 PCIJ Series A No. 20, at 41–2.

[134] Ibid., at 17–18.

[135] See the dissenting opinions of Judge Pessôa, at 62–5, and Judge *ad hoc* Novacovitch, at 76–80, both strongly denying jurisdiction of the Court on the grounds that, contrary to *Mavrommatis*, there were no international rights and obligations of states involved in *Serbian Loans*.

obligations were to be judged. It was in this part of the judgment that the Court elaborated on the presumption stated earlier, namely that such contracts could only be governed by municipal law:

> Any contract which is not a contract between States in their capacity as subjects of international law is based on the municipal law of some country. The question as to which this law is forms the subject of that branch of law which is at the present day usually described as private international law or the doctrine of the conflict of laws. The rules thereof may be common to several States and may even be established by international conventions and custom, and in the latter case may possess the character of true international law governing the relations between States. But apart from this, it has to be considered that these rules form part of municipal law.[136]

The Court made it clear that international law only applied to contracts between states as the subjects of international law, i.e. that only such agreements could be based on the general rules of international law regarding validity, binding nature or consequences of the contractual relationship. A contract between a state and a private party, on the contrary, could only be based on the municipal law of some state, the specific legal system being determined by the rules of private international law, which itself forms part of municipal law. With these principles in mind, the Court finally decided that, in the present case, the applicable law was, on balance, Serbian law.

By applying international law exclusively to agreements concluded by states and excluding contracts between states and a private party entirely from the domain of international law, the Court manifested the states-only conception of international personality. The Court made clear that only states as subjects of international law could enter into agreements the legal status of which was determined by international law. Any matters between a state and a private party, according to the *Serbian Loans* statement, were left in the domain of municipal law. Private individuals again only existed in the national, and not in the international realm. The international scene, and hence also the law regulating the social relations therein, was exclusively reserved for states.

In the decades following the *Serbian Loans* case, various tribunals have been concerned with determining the law applicable to state contracts. Whereas the ICJ reaffirmed the *Serbian Loans* statement to a certain

136 *Case Concerning the Payments of Various Serbian Loans Issued in France*, at 41.

extent in the *Anglo-Iranian Oil Co. Case*,[137] an arbitral tribunal had already applied international law to state contracts in 1930 in the *Lena Goldfields* v. *Soviet Union* award.[138] There followed numerous awards in which international law was applied, thereby modifying the *Serbian Loans* statement. However, the conditions, the extent and the consequences attached to the application of international law to state contracts proved different. Some of these differences can be explained by the employment of different conceptions of international personality. In some instances, a limited personality of the private party to the state contract was, expressly or by implication, accepted and international law consequently directly applied.[139] These legal manifestations will be more closely examined in the following chapters. In the more prevalent view, however, international law was applied to state contracts by upholding the states-only conception of international personality as expressed in *Serbian Loans.* In this view, international law can never automatically impose itself on state contracts, but can only apply by analogy provided that either the parties have chosen international law as the proper law of contract, or the tribunal concerned is authorized by an overriding statutory or treaty provision to apply international law. Importantly, in both cases the status of the private party is not believed to be altered at all: it is still *not* an international person. In consequence, international law is only applied by analogy in a restrained and cautious manner, merely supplementing or correcting the municipal law primarily governing the

[137] *Anglo-Iranian Oil Co. Case* (United Kingdom v. Iran), Jurisdiction, 1952 ICJ Reports 93, at 112. It has to be said, though, that in this case the question was not primarily the law applicable to the concessionary contract between the British company and Iran, but whether this contract could create international rights the British government could invoke against Iran. The Court held that the contract created no international rights and obligations whatsoever.

[138] *Lena Goldfields* v. *Soviet Union* (Lena Goldfields Arbitration, 1930), 5 Annual Digest of Public International Law Cases (ILR) 3 and 426, at 3–4 and 426–8. See also Veeder, V.V., 'The Lena Goldfields Arbitration: The Historical Roots of Three Ideas', ICLQ, 47 (1998), 747–92, esp. at 750–1.

[139] Most famously, this has been done, using different conceptions of personality, in *Texaco Overseas Petroleum Company and California Asiatic Oil Company* v. *The Government of the Libyan Arab Republic* (Award on the Merits, Sole Arbitrator Dupuy, 1977), 53 ILR 422, paras 46–8 (pp. 457–9); *Sapphire International Petroleums Ltd.* v. *National Iranian Oil Company*, 35 ILR 136 (1963), at 175–6 (Sole Arbitrator Cavin); and, by implication, *Sandline* v. *Papua New Guinea*, 117 ILR 552 (1998), para. 10.1. See also Garcia Amador, F.V. (Special Rapporteur), *Fourth Report on State Responsibility*, ILC 1959, UN Doc. A/CN.4/119, para. 129.

contract.[140] International law, in this view, is not directly applicable to the contract because the contractual relationship between the private party and the state is thought to be unequal for the private entity lacks international personality.[141] A state contract is therefore to be strictly separated from a treaty, the latter being concluded between two international persons and genuinely governed by international law while the former is not entered into by two international persons and is in principle governed by municipal law.[142] Accordingly, this view only slightly modifies the *Serbian Loans* statement.

The direct effect of European Community law

In *Van Gend en Loos v. Netherlands Inland Revenue Administration*, the ECJ declared that Article 12 of the EEC Treaty[143] was directly applicable to individuals.[144] To arrive at this conclusion, however, the ECJ argued that the European Community represented a new legal order of international law. This made it possible, in contrast to regular international law as understood by the Court, that not only states but also individuals were the subjects of this order. By proclaiming a new international legal order as a precondition for the direct effect of the EEC Treaty, this decision, paradoxically, represents a manifestation of the states-only conception of international personality.[145]

[140] See e.g. *Klöckner Industrie-Anlagen GmbH and Others* v. *Republic of Cameroon* (Decision on Annulment, 1985), 2 ICSID Reports 95, at para. 69, and *Amco Asia Corporation and Others* v. *The Republic of Indonesia* (Decision on Annulment, 1986), 1 ICSID Reports 509, at paras 18–28. Both awards were handed down in the context of an ICSID arbitration and were mostly concerned with interpreting Article 42(1) ICSID.

[141] See Bowett, 'State Contracts', at 54: 'In fact, however, the claimed analogy is no analogy at all. The investment contract between a State and a private entity not only is not a treaty but cannot even be regarded as analogous to a treaty. For there is a world of difference between an agreement under international law between two equal, sovereign States and a contract between a State and a private party governed prima facie by the State's own law.'

[142] See for especially clear statements in this respect *CAA and Vivendi Universal* v. *Argentina* (Decision on Annulment, 2002), 6 ICSID Reports 340, paras 96–8, and *Société Générale de Surveillance (SGS)* v. *Pakistan* (Decision on Objections to Jurisdiction, 2004), 8 ICSID Reports 406, paras 146–8.

[143] Treaty Establishing the European Economic Community, 25 March 1957, 298 UNTS 11.

[144] Case 26/62, *Van Gend en Loos* v. *Netherlands Inland Revenue Administration*, 1963 ECR 1, at 12.

[145] The whole argument put forward in this section draws heavily on Spiermann, 'Other Side of the Story', esp. at 765–75. See also Weiler, J.H.H., 'The Transformation of

The Dutch company Van Gend en Loos had imported chemicals from Germany and had been charged tariffs by the Dutch authorities that were, in the view of the company, in violation of Article 12 of the EEC Treaty. The company therefore brought an action against the Dutch custom authorities based on Article 12 of the EEC Treaty. The matter was then referred to the ECJ, the main question being whether Article 12 was directly applicable to nationals of an EEC member state, in this case Van Gend en Loos. The Court replied:

> To ascertain whether the provisions of an international Treaty extend so far in their effects it is necessary to consider the spirit, the general scheme and the wording of those provisions. . . . The conclusion to be drawn from this is that the Community constitutes a new legal order of international law for the benefit of which the states have limited their sovereign rights, albeit within limited fields, and the subjects of which comprise not only Member States but also their nationals. . . . It follows [that] Article 12 must be interpreted as producing direct effects and creating individual rights which national courts must protect.[146]

In this passage, the ECJ linked two elements: the view of the Community as a new legal order of international law and the direct applicability of Community law towards nationals of member states.[147] The Court apparently found it impossible to directly apply Article 12 under traditional international law. Individuals could only be subjects of European Community law if this legal order was regarded as different from international law. International law, consequently, was conceived by the ECJ as only applying to states, and not to individuals.

Paradoxically, the direct effect of European Community law was hence based in part on the states-only conception of international personality.[148] The ECJ apparently conceived regular international law as a law that could not directly apply to individuals. In general international law, according to the ECJ, individuals were only relevant as nationals of their states. This view corresponds with the states-only conception of international personality. Because the ECJ started from this conception, it had to separate the European Community from general international law in order to declare Community law directly applicable to individuals. This

Europe', YLJ, 100 (1991), 2403–83, at 2413–14, and Jennings and Watts, *Oppenheim's International Law*, 70–3.

146 *Van Gend en Loos* v. *Netherlands Inland Revenue Administration*, at 12.

147 See for the interrelation also Spiermann, 'Other Side of the Story', at 765, and Weiler, 'Transformation', at 2413.

148 See also Spiermann, 'Other Side of the Story', at 766.

was the first step, accentuated by the Court one year later in *Costa* v. *ENEL*,[149] in regarding the European Community legal system as a constitutional rather than an international legal order. Even more specific is the 1991 opinion on the European Economic Area Agreement[150] wherein the ECJ, by referring to *Van Gend en Loos*, drew a very clear distinction between the EEA Agreement as a regular international treaty which 'merely creates rights and obligations as between the Contracting Parties' and the EEC Treaty constituting 'the constitutional charter of a Community' being directly applicable to individuals.[151] Again, the Court conceived regular international law as law exclusively applicable to states while the European Community law was a new constitutional legal order applying to individuals. The European Community as a new legal system hence had its origins in the states-only conception of personality.

149 Case 6/64, *Flaminio Costa* v. *Ente Nazionale per l'Energia Elletrica (ENEL)*, 1964 ECR 585, at 593.
150 Agreement on the European Economic Area, 2 May 1992, 1793 UNTS 4.
151 Opinion 1/91, *Draft Agreement Relating to the Creation of the European Economic Area*, 1991 ECR I-6079, paras 20–1 (I-6102).

6

The recognition conception

The recognition conception is a modification of the states-only conception. Whereas it still stipulates the primacy of the state in international law, it accepts that states can recognize other entities as international persons. The origins of this conception lie mainly in the works of Karl Strupp, Arrigo Cavaglieri and Georg Schwarzenberger, all of them paying strict attention to what they perceived as state practice regarding personality.[1] This conception has been widely accepted in doctrine ever since and there might be some merit to the view that it represents the dominant conception of international personality today.[2] One of its most important legal manifestations, though with certain ambiguous aspects, is the *Reparation for Injuries* Advisory Opinion of the ICJ dealing with the personality of the United Nations. The creation of international organizations in general and the legal issues related to it, as well as the partly direct role of individuals in investment law treaties, can be regarded as manifestations of this conception.

Basic propositions

According to this conception, states are the 'normal' persons of international law but are free to recognize other entities as international legal persons:

[1] The conception was advocated in a similar way in the same context by Manfredi Siotto-Pintor at his course at The Hague in 1932. However, important as his contribution is, Siotto-Pintor seems rather to have systematized and applied existing ideas (like the ones put forward by Cavaglieri and Strupp) than formulated original ones (see Siotto-Pintor, Manfredi, 'Les Sujets du Droit International autres que les États', RCADI, 41 (1932-III), 245–360, esp. at 258–9, 281, 286, and 299).

[2] For various modern versions, see Daillier and Pellet, *Droit International* (5th edn.), 395 and 551; Ipsen, *Völkerrecht*, 57–8; Kolb, 'Observation', at 120–1; Kolb, 'Nouvelle Observation', at 230–1; Mosler, Hermann, 'Subjects of International Law', EPIL, 4 (2000), 710–27, at 712–13 and 717–18 (but with some ambiguity at 726); Mosler, 'Völkerrechtssubjekte', at 25–6; Arangio-Ruiz, *Personalità Giuridica*, 16–19 (by implication); Rousseau, *Droit International Public*, 10; Tomuschat, 'General Course', at 160. Also in this direction: Brownlie, *Principles*, 57–8.

> Es ist nicht zutreffend, wenn viele, z.B. Anzilotti, Corso 69, aus dem Begriffe des Völkerrechts ... die alleinige Völkerrechtssubjektivität der Staaten herleiten. Denn derselbe Gemeinwille der Staaten, der bislang die Staaten (aber auch als kriegsführende Partei anerkannte Insurgenten!) als Rechtssubjekte anerkannt hat, kann jederzeit auch anderen Subjekten Persönlichkeit im Rechtssinne verleihen.[3]

> ... il n'y a aucun doute, à notre avis, que la personnalité internationale a été reconnue à des collectivités qui ne sont pas des États et qui, néanmoins, tirent directement du droit international des prétentions et des obligations. ... Les États sont les sujets ordinaires du droit international et leur activité, à moins de développement d'accords particuliers, est soumise tout de suite et entièrement aux règles du droit général. Les autres collectivités, au contraire, ou même les individus, – à supposer (ce qui, à notre avis, n'est pas encore arrivé), qu'une capacité d'avoir des droits et des devoirs internationaux leur fût reconnue – ne trouvent pas dans la société juridique des États le milieu naturel de leur activité et voient dans le droit international un système de règles, dont la plupart leur sont inapplicables. Par conséquent, la portée de leur personnalité internationale est très limitée.[4]

> The original subjects of international law are sovereign States. ... Nonetheless, it is a mistake to deduce from this state of affairs that sovereign States alone are eligible to be subjects of international law. This is a matter within the discretion of each of the existing subjects of international law. States which are members of an international institution may agree to treat such an international institution as a subject of international law for limited purposes. Non-members, however, may choose completely to ignore the existence of an international institution, as happened in the case of the League of Nations. ... Every State is free to grant or to refuse to grant such recognition. It follows that a certain entity may have international personality in relation to one or several existing subjects of international law, but may lack such status in relation to others. ... There is no inherent impossibility in granting international personality to individuals.[5]

It follows that international personality is acquired through recognition by states in this conception. This holds true for new states and, as a modification of the states-only conception of international personality,

[3] Strupp, Karl, *Das völkerrechtliche Delikt*, 'Handbuch des Völkerrechts' (Fritz Stier-Somlo, ed.) (Berlin et al.: W. Kohlhammer, 1920), 22 n. 1.

[4] Cavaglieri, Arrigo, 'Règles Générales du Droit de la Paix', RCADI, 26 (1929-I), 315–585, at 319–20.

[5] Schwarzenberger, Georg, *A Manual of International Law*, 1st edition, (London: Stevens & Sons, 1947), 25, 27 and 35.

also for non-state entities. Regarding new states, they first have to be recognized as an international person before being able to act in international law.[6] Once recognized, sovereign states are international persons with full capacity and as such administer the acquisition of international personality through the process of recognition.[7] In exercising this competence, states can also recognize non-state entities as international persons. There are, however, some peculiarities regarding the mode, scope and effects of recognizing the international personality of non-state entities as opposed to the recognition of states in this conception.

In case of recognition of new states as international persons, the mode of recognition, according to this conception, is an express or tacit unilateral act by existing states.[8] Existing states have complete discretion in granting recognition and the scope thereof is relative, i.e. only opposable to those states having exercised the act; most states will, however, recognize a new state because of practical necessities.[9] The effect of recognition for a new state is unlimited personality.

In the event of recognition of non-state entities as international persons, the mode of recognition cannot be a unilateral act if the entity in question is subject to one particular state power (e.g. individuals or minority groups). In this case, recognition has to be exercised by at least two states, one of them being the home state of these entities.[10] Because the presumption with such non-state entities is that they naturally belong to the municipal, and not to the international, legal order, the act of recognition as an international person has to be in more unequivocal terms than is the case with the recognition of states.[11] It tends therefore to be explicit or by clear implication. The scope of personality of non-state entities is strictly limited to the recognizing states and states have full discretion whether to recognize or

[6] Cavaglieri, Arrigo, 'I soggetti del diritto internazionale', Rdi, 20 (1925), 18–32, 169–87, at 176; Strupp, Karl, *Grundzüge des positiven Völkerrechts*, 4th edition (Bonn: Ludwig Röhrscheid, 1928), 25; Schwarzenberger, *Manual*, 28–9.

[7] Cavaglieri, 'Soggetti', at 177; Strupp, *Grundzüge*, 22; Schwarzenberger, *Manual*, 28.

[8] Cavaglieri, 'Soggetti', at 184; Strupp, Karl, 'Les Règles Générales du Droit de la Paix', RCADI, 47 (1934-I), 263–593, at 448; Schwarzenberger, *Manual*, 27–8.

[9] Cavaglieri, 'Soggetti', at 183; Strupp, 'Règles Générales', at 421 and 448 (by implication); Schwarzenberger, *Manual*, 28, and Schwarzenberger, 'Fundamental Principles', at 251–2.

[10] Cavaglieri, 'Soggetti', at 185. In this direction Strupp, 'Règles Générales', at 466 in the case of individuals, but underlining the generally unilateral character of recognition at 467–8. Schwarzenberger, *Manual*, 35, seems to endorse the view that in the case of individuals there must be several states, including the home state, granting personality through a treaty or custom but he does not state this explicitly either.

[11] Cavaglieri, 'Soggetti', at 182–3; Strupp, 'Règles Générales', at 419 and 466 (by implication); Schwarzenberger, *Manual*, 25–6.

not. The effect of recognition is a limited personality existing in accordance with the parameters defined in the act of recognition.[12] In general, the effect of international personality of non-state actors has to be interpreted restrictively.

The limited and exceptional personality of non-state entities contrasts with the full personality of states, including their competence to administer the acquisition of international personality in this conception. This supremacy of the state is explained by historical facts. States have come into existence as the result of purely factual developments leading to the establishment of public authorities on a defined territory with a specific population.[13] States are the highest public authorities in the international system. It follows that international law can only emanate from collective state will. The binding nature of this will is not primarily seen as a legal issue; international practice, according to this conception, supports the view that international law is generally considered binding.[14] The sources of international law are therefore treaties and custom:[15] in treaties, states explicitly create law whereas customary rules are established through state practice which is accepted as law.[16] Regarding the scope of the rules created by states, treaty law is clearly only pertinent for those states having consented to it; in principle, the same holds true for customary law, though state practice can prove the general acceptance of fundamental rules thereof.[17] The creation and scope of international law is hence strictly attached to the will of states and there can be no international entitlement or obligation for a state not having consented (in a treaty or through state practice) to such a rule. States being the sole international legislators in this conception, they alone are consequently competent to recognize international persons. As with the creation of substantive rules, such recognition is only binding for the states that have

[12] Cavaglieri, 'Soggetti', at 182–3; Strupp, 'Règles Générales', at 421; Schwarzenberger, *Manual*, 28 and 34–5.

[13] Cavaglieri, 'Règles Générales', at 321; Strupp, 'Règles Générales', at 422 (pointing out the similarities of such a definition of statehood with Article 1 of the Montevideo Convention on the Rights and Duties of States of 26 December 1933, 165 LNTS 19); Schwarzenberger, *Manual*, 31.

[14] Strupp, 'Règles Générales', at 300.

[15] General principles of law are, in this conception, mostly regarded as part of customary law (see e.g. Schwarzenberger, *Manual*, 13–14).

[16] Cavaglieri, 'Règles Générales', at 321 and 322–7; Strupp, *Grundzüge*, 11, and Strupp, 'Règles Générales', at 420; Schwarzenberger, *Manual*, 12–13.

[17] Cavaglieri, 'Règles Générales', at 324–7; Strupp, *Grundzüge*, 14–15; Schwarzenberger, 'Fundamental Principles', at 207–12.

granted it. Recognition then follows the same logic as law-creation in general: it is in the competence of states to grant recognition and it is only opposable to those states that have granted it. Both international law-creation and the assignment of personality in the thus created legal system lie in the competence of states because they are the highest public authorities in international relations.

To summarize, the recognition conception of international personality is based on three main propositions:

(1) States are, as a matter of historical fact, the highest authorities in international relations. Individuals and entities created by national law are represented by their home state in the international realm.
(2) States being the highest authorities in the international realm, international law can only emanate from state will and is only binding on those states having consented to it. In their function as international legislators, states can recognize, at their full discretion, the entities taking part in the international legal system.
(3) There is a presumption that only states are international persons. However, states can overcome this presumption by (creating and) recognizing non-state entities as limited international persons. In the case of non-state entities being subject to the sovereign power of one particular state (e.g. individuals), they can only acquire international personality with the consent of the state of nationality.

By turning to the origins of these propositions, their significance and concrete substance will be examined.

Origins of the basic propositions

The recognition conception was formulated in the German and Italian context after World War I. There were now a variety of new approaches to statehood, law-creation and legal method, most of them severely questioning the traditional legal positivism associated with Triepel, Anzilotti and Oppenheim. The recognition conception to a large extent resisted such fundamental changes to the existing framework of international law. It did not intend to change the theoretical framework of the states-only conception in any meaningful sense by recognizing other legal persons apart from states:

> Dal punto di vista della costruzione dommatica del diritto internazionale, si può osservare che il riconoscimento di una certa personalità giuridica

internazionale ad enti diversi dagli Stati, finché rimanga contenuto nei limitati confini finora accertati, non sembra colpire radicalmente la concezione dottrinale prevalente, purché certi concetti e principii fondamentali vengano temperati nella loro espressione troppo rigida e intransigente.[18]

While upholding the basic legal framework of the states-only conception, the recognition conception grounded this framework in its social conditions in order to alleviate certain dogmatic exaggerations. Consequently, the origins of the first and second above-mentioned propositions of the recognition conception lie in rejecting new approaches to statehood and law-creation and upholding the traditional notions. The third proposition is to be regarded as a corrective measure. Its origins rest in the view that legal analysis has to take into account the social conditions of law. Such a sociological view had been formulated by Georg Jellinek, Max Huber and Santi Romano in the German and Italian context. Importantly, in this intellectual tradition, sociological examination was only meant to complement positivist legal analysis, not to exclude it. The intention of this approach was to be a corrective measure in case legal analysis distanced itself too far from social reality. In light of newly emerging actors on the international scene like international organizations at the time, the states-only conception of international personality in particular seemed to be in need of such a corrective. Strupp, Cavaglieri and Schwarzenberger therefore accentuated sociological elements, i.e. effective state practice, in their recognition conception of international personality in order to complement the framework of the states-only conception and reconcile it with social reality.[19]

[18] Cavaglieri, 'Soggetti', at 185. It is also interesting to note in this respect that Strupp dedicated his 1920 book on international responsibility, in which he first contested the states-only conception of international personality and in particular Anzilotti's view on it, to 'Herrn Dr. Dionisio Anzilotti und Herrn Geh. Rat Dr. Heinrich Triepel, den Vorkämpfern der positiven Völkerrechtswissenschaft' (Strupp, *Delikt*, VII).

[19] As regards their general approach to international law and the reconciliation of positivism with social practice in it see Link, Sandra, *Ein Realist mit Idealen – Der Völkerrechtler Karl Strupp (1886–1940)* (Baden-Baden: Nomos Verlagsgesellschaft, 2003), 342–3 (on Strupp being a positivist while favouring the study of social developments over legal logic); Truyol y Serra, 'Doctrines du Droit des Gens', at 414, and Kolb, *Les Cours Généraux*, 21–2 (on Cavaglieri being a positivist though subordinating legal logic to effective state practice); Crawford, 'International Law in Twentieth-Century England', at 682 (on Schwarzenberger being 'strongly positivist and realist in tendency') and Steinle, Stephanie, *Völkerrecht und Machtpolitik: Georg Schwarzenberger (1908–1991)*, 'Studien zur Geschichte des Völkerrechts' (Michael Stolleis, ed.) (Baden-Baden:

Germany and Italy transformed

It might be useful to start with some biographical information. Karl Strupp studied law and history in Germany and was introduced to international law by his teacher Georg Jellinek.[20] Strupp subsequently taught and practised public law with special emphasis on international law at the University of Frankfurt am Main. Like many of his colleagues of Jewish origins, Strupp lost his chair in 1933 as a consequence of the infamous Article 3 of the *Gesetz zur Wiederherstellung des Berufsbeamtentums.* He left Germany and subsequently taught in Istanbul before moving to Denmark and finally Paris. Arrigo Cavaglieri was educated in his native Italy and held the international law chair at the University of Naples from 1924 onwards. Cavaglieri was also heavily involved in practice as an advisor to the Italian Foreign Ministry on matters of international law. His understanding of international law had been strongly influenced by the towering figure of Dionisio Anzilotti. In addition, like most Italian scholars, Cavaglieri remained particularly interested in the work of the German legal profession and made regular references to its ideas and developments.[21] As an indication of Cavaglieri's high standing in the international legal profession at large, it might be added that he gave the first General Course at The Hague Academy in 1929.[22] Georg Schwarzenberger, finally, was of German origin, and received his legal education and spent his early academic career in Germany.[23] Schwarzenberger published four major studies on international law in Germany in the early 1930s, one of them dealing with the legal personality of the Bank for International Settlements.[24] After the regime change of 1933, for the same reasons as Strupp, he had to leave his native country. Schwarzenberger emigrated to Great Britain in 1934 where he subsequently held positions at the University of London. Though spending most of his academic career outside Germany, Schwarzenberger's thought

Nomos, 2000), 13 (on Schwarzenberger's roots in positivism in the tradition of Bergbohm) and 94 (on Schwarzenberger using a sociologist methodology).

[20] On Strupp's life see Link, *Realist mit Idealen*, 20–2 and 166–74.

[21] See e.g. the references and thorough analysis of the works of Jellinek, Triepel, Heilborn and others in Cavaglieri, Arrigo, 'La Conception Positive de la Société Internationale', RGDIP, XVIII (1911), 259–92, esp. at 267–76, or in Cavaglieri, 'Règles Générales', e.g. at 321–39.

[22] See Kolb, *Les Cours Généraux*, 6.

[23] See Steinle, *Völkerrecht und Machtpolitik*, 5–35.

[24] Schwarzenberger, Georg, *Die internationalen Banken für Zahlungsausgleich und Agrarkredite*, 'Wirtschaftsprobleme der Gegenwart' (Adolf Weber, ed.) (Berlin: Junker und Dünnhaupt, 1932), esp. 51–8. The Bank for International Settlements had been established in 1930 in the context of the Young Plan in order to deal with reparations imposed on Germany in the Peace Treaties of Versailles.

was nevertheless firmly rooted in the German intellectual tradition and the specific context of his German experience.[25]

In light of this biographical information, the relevant contexts for analysing the origins of the recognition conception's basic propositions are the German and the German-related Italian, as well as the wider international, context of the interwar period up until the mid 1930s. The question arises: what had changed in this environment in relation to the similar context in which the states-only conception of international personality had been formulated two decades earlier?

The socio-political environment in Germany was different after World War I. The German *Kaiserreich* had been defeated in the war, punished (unfairly, in the opinion of most Germans at the time) at Versailles, and finally replaced by the Weimar Republic in the chaotic circumstances after the capitulation. It is a commonplace to note that the Weimar constitution was inherently unstable.[26] In Italy, the changes in the socio-political environment were more gradual, but no less severe. Italy had entered the war late on the side of the Entente. Though consequently being present at Versailles as one of the victorious powers, Italy was nevertheless forced, in accordance with the principle of self-determination, to let the mostly Slavic Dalmatia become part of Yugoslavia (it gained, however, the formerly Austrian province of South Tyrol). This led to widespread disappointment in Italy and fostered nationalist feelings. There were also serious economic problems favouring the ever stronger socialist party. In these circumstances, the fascist movement around Benito Mussolini, combining nationalist and anti-socialist ideas, could form a coalition government in 1922 and impose a dictatorship in 1925. The fascist government subsequently introduced extensive modifications and amendments to the existing Italian codes.[27]

[25] Steinle, Stephanie, 'Georg Schwarzenberger (1908–1991)' in Jack Beatson and Reinhard Zimmermann (eds.), *Jurists Uprooted: German-Speaking Emigré Lawyers in Twentieth-Century Britain* (Oxford University Press, 2004), 663–80, at 670.

[26] Two of the main reasons for instabilities were that the executive power was divided between the government and the exceptionally strong *Reichspräsident* and the party system was too fragmented to provide governments with the majorities necessary to govern effectively. See e.g. Wehler, Hans-Ulrich, *Deutsche Gesellschaftsgeschichte 4. Band: Von Beginn des Ersten Weltkrieges bis zur Gründung der beiden deutschen Staaten 1914–1949* (Munich: C. H. Beck, 2003), 349.

[27] See Torrazza, Eugenio and Stefano Di Iorio, *Storia del Diritto Italiano* (Napoli: Edizioni Simone, 1998), 188–9.

In this unstable socio-political environment, a variety of new approaches to public law were put forward, leading to the so-called *Methoden- und Richtungsstreit* in German, and to a somewhat lesser extent, Italian public law.[28] It is useful for present purposes to distinguish three interrelated debates taking place: about the nature of statehood, about the sources of law and about legal method.[29] With regard to statehood, the new political institutions in Germany and Italy seemed artificially imposed and fragile.[30] The view of the state as deeply rooted in historical facts was consequently challenged. New approaches to statehood included the view of the state as a mere construct of legal norms.[31] Concerning the sources of law, state will as the only source of law was being questioned. Approaches favouring natural law principles found their way back into professional discourse.[32] As regards legal method, i.e. the concrete reasoning in a given system of sources of law, the predominant method with its focus on organizing and systematizing legal norms was criticized as either too abstract (not taking notice of social and philosophical elements) or, conversely, as still too metaphysical and hence not purely legal.[33]

[28] For Germany see Friedrich, Manfred, 'Der Methoden- und Richtungsstreit: Zur Grundlagendiskussion der Weimarer Staatsrechtslehre', AöR, 102 (1977), 161–209, and Stolleis, *Geschichte des öffentlichen Rechts (III)*, 153–8. For Italy see Torrazza and Di Iorio, *Diritto Italiano*, 189, and Bobbio, Norberto, 'Trends in Italian Legal Theory', *American Journal of Comparative Law*, 8 (1959), 329–40, at 336.

[29] A similar distinction between statehood and legal method is made in broad terms by Friedrich, 'Methoden- und Richtungsstreit', at 162, and by Bobbio, 'Italian Legal Theory', at 336. As for the distinction between sources and legal method (the latter describing the way of legal reasoning in a given system of sources), it has to be acknowledged that it was certainly not consciously present at the time of the *Methoden- und Richtungsstreit*; it is rather an analytical distinction convenient for present purposes.

[30] Stolleis, *Geschichte des öffentlichen Rechts (III)*, 101–9.

[31] Kelsen, Hans, *Der soziologische und der juristische Staatsbegriff: Kritische Untersuchung des Verhältnisses von Staat und Recht* (Tübingen: J. C. B. Mohr (Paul Siebeck), 1922), esp. 86–91.

[32] See for such an approach Kaufmann, Erich, 'Die Gleichheit vor dem Gesetz im Sinne des Art. 109 der Reichsverfassung' in Vereinigung der Deutschen Staatsrechtslehrer (ed.), *Veröffentlichungen der Vereinigung der Deutschen Staatsrechtslehrer* (Berlin and Leipzig: Walter de Gruyter & Co., 1927), 2–62, esp. at 5–6. Kaufmann argued in this memorable statement that the legal principle of equality had its legal source not in enactment by parliament but in general morality.

[33] For the former, see Romano, Santi, *L'Ordinamento Giuridico* (Florence: Sansoni, 1951) (originally published 1918), esp. 25–8, and Smend, Rudolf, *Verfassung und Verfassungsrecht* (Munich and Leipzig: Duncker und Humblot, 1928), esp. 128–38. For the latter see Kelsen, Hans, *Reine Rechtslehre: Einleitung in die rechtswissenschaftliche Problematik* (Leipzig and Vienna: Franz Deuticke, 1934), esp. 19–21.

The *Methoden- und Richtungsstreit* affected international legal scholarship in Germany and Italy. The obvious reason for this influence was that international law was still primarily treated as a branch of public law in German and Italian legal scholarship.[34] Cross-fertilization thus came naturally. An additional reason was the widely perceived unfairness of the Peace Treaty of Versailles in Germany and Italy (particularly its assertion of fault in Article 231 and the imposed burden of reparation on Germany as well as the refusal of Italian rule over Dalmatia).[35] Questions about the foundation of a treaty allegedly contradicting basic elements of justice were raised and partly answered by applying natural law elements re-developed in the *Methoden- und Richtungsstreit*.[36]

These specific German and Italian international law topics were pursued in the broader international context. On the international scene, too, considerable transformations had taken place after World War I. Most importantly perhaps, the League of Nations and other international organizations had been created. These posed difficult questions of legal personality. It was widely discussed, but never really settled, whether the League of Nations was an international person.[37] As another example, the legal status of the Bank for International Settlements, created in 1930 in the context of the Young Plan to deal with reparations imposed on Germany, was far from clear.[38] The issue of international personality was also present in minority treaties concluded after the disintegration of empires in Europe and the creation of new states. Were the minorities or their individual members, respectively, international persons? Here, too, fundamental questions arose in doctrinal debate as well as in the practice of the newly created Permanent Court of International Justice,[39] and the parties were far from reaching

[34] Stolleis, *Geschichte des öffentlichen Rechts (III)*, 89. For Italy, Santi Romano's treatises in constitutional, administrative and international law might serve as an indication.

[35] See for these debates ibid., 86–9, with particular reference to Strupp's work on international responsibility (88).

[36] See e.g. Kaufmann, 'Gleichheit vor dem Gesetz', at 14.

[37] See the remarks by Brierly, James Leslie, 'The Covenant and the Charter', BYIL, 23 (1946), 83–94, at 85, and Crawford, *Creation of States*, 29 (with references).

[38] See Williams, John Fischer, 'The Legal Character of the Bank for International Settlements', AJIL, 24 (1930), 665–73, and Schwarzenberger, *Internationale Banken*, 51–8.

[39] The question was e.g. present, by implication, in *Certain Questions relating to Settlers of German Origin in the Territory ceded by Germany to Poland* (Advisory Opinion), 1923 PCIJ Series B No. 6, at 25, and in *Questions concerning Acquisition of Polish Nationality* (Advisory Opinion), 1923 PCIJ Series B No. 7, at 16.

consensus on the matter. In this environment, engaging doctrinal debates took place. Hersch Lauterpacht stressed the function of general principles for international law and started to question the dominant ideas of statehood, personality and sources.[40] Georges Scelle envisioned his international solidarity and denounced the state as a fiction proclaiming individuals as the only international persons.[41] Max Huber accentuated the social conditions of international law.[42] Dualism and its strict separation of the national and international legal order was questioned and replaced with monist approaches by Hans Kelsen and Alfred Verdross.[43]

In sum, the hitherto dominant views on statehood, the sources of law and legal method were challenged in the specific German and Italian contexts as well as in international law in general. The criticism of this dominant view was primarily associated with traditional legal positivism as displayed in the states-only conception of international personality. In this socio-political and intellectual environment, Strupp, Cavaglieri and Schwarzenberger formulated the recognition conception of international personality.[44]

The framework of the states-only conception confirmed

The recognition conception responded to the criticism against the traditional notions of statehood and law-creation by defending through slight

[40] An early and concise formulation of these ideas can be found in Lauterpacht, Hersch, 'Westlake and Present Day International Law', *Economica*, 15 (1925), 307–25, esp. at 309–22.

[41] See e.g. Scelle, Georges, 'Règles Générales du Droit de la Paix', RCADI, 46 (1933-IV), 327–703, at 343.

[42] Huber, Max, *Die soziologischen Grundlagen des Völkerrechts*, 'Internationalrechtliche Abhandlungen' (Peter Klein and Herbert Kraus, eds.) (Berlin: Walter Rothschild, 1928) (originally published 1910), esp. 8–14.

[43] See Kelsen, Hans, *Das Problem der Souveränität und die Theorie des Völkerrechts: Beitrag zu einer Reinen Rechtslehre*, 2nd edition (Tübingen: J. C. B Mohr (Paul Siebeck, 1928) (originally published 1920), 120–44; Verdross, Alfred, *Die Verfassung der Völkerrechtsgemeinschaft* (Vienna and Berlin: Julius Springer, 1926), 34–42. See also Scelle, 'Règles Générales', at 353.

[44] While all three were obviously actively involved in international law in the described context and thus generally affected by the domestic *Methoden- and Richtungsstreit*, only Strupp was specifically participating in domestic discussions of the latter (see e.g. Strupp, Karl, 'Das Ausnahmerecht der Länder nach Art. 48 IV der Reichsverfassung', AöR, 5 (1923), 182–205, wherein Strupp examines the emergency rights of German states according to the federal constitution).

amendments the historical view of the state absorbing individuals and of law as emanating solely from state will. New approaches to statehood and law-creation were rejected and the basic framework of the states-only conception confirmed.

As regards statehood, the recognition conception rejected the newly emerging formal approach towards statehood as devised by Hans Kelsen and his *Reine Rechtslehre*.[45] It was also at odds with approaches mainly associated with Georges Scelle calling the state a legal fiction.[46] All these approaches, according to the recognition conception, stemmed from purely logical or philosophical reasoning that did not take into account the social reality according to which states existed simply as a result of historical forces. Legal analysis had to start from this social fact. Accordingly, the state was still conceived as a historical fact preceding the law:

> Pour nous, l'État est un phénomène social, avant d'être un phénomène juridique; il est une formation historique, à laquelle le droit se rattache, mais qu'il est incapable de créer par ses règles. Ce n'est pas l'État qui est le produit du droit, mais le contraire. Par conséquent . . . notre pensée . . . n'est pas favorable aux constructions purement logiques de la *reine Rechtslehre*.[47]

This understanding of the state resembles similar formulas articulated in the states-only conception. Strupp, Cavaglieri and Schwarzenberger adhered to the historical idea of the state – Cavaglieri by explicitly referring to Jellinek[48] – that had evolved in nineteenth-century German public law and had been incorporated into the states-only conception. The state was not just a contract entered into by individuals or a legal fiction consisting only of acting individuals; it was a social reality, deeply rooted in historical developments. In accordance with the states-only conception, the state was then the highest public authority in international life: there was no institution above state level.[49]

With this understanding of the state, the individual was still confined to a domestic role. The basic separation between the national and the

[45] See Strupp, 'Règles Générales', at 423; Cavaglieri, 'Règles Générales', at 321. Kunz, Josef L., *Die Anerkennung von Staaten und Regierungen im Völkerrecht*, 'Handbuch des Völkerrechts' (Fritz Stier-Somlo, ed.) (Stuttgart: W. Kohlhammer, 1928), 18, one of Kelsen's pupils, explicitly mentions Strupp and Cavaglieri as the contemporary opponents of the formal approach of the *reine Rechtslehre* towards statehood.

[46] Cavaglieri, 'Règles Générales', at 320 (by clear implication).

[47] Ibid., at 321. See also Strupp, 'Règles Générales', at 422; Schwarzenberger, *Manual*, 25.

[48] Cavaglieri, 'Règles Générales', at 340.

[49] Strupp, *Grundzüge*, 2; Cavaglieri, 'Règles Générales', at 321–2; Schwarzenberger, *Manual*, 25.

international legal order was upheld. Newly emerging monist approaches were rejected:

> Das Völkerrecht bricht nicht ipso iure Landesrecht, der sog. 'Primat' (Vorrang) des Völkerrechts (Kelsen, Verdross) ist nur Postulat, wie umgekehrt kein 'Primat des Landesrechts' besteht ... Vielmehr sind Völkerrecht und Landesrecht völlig getrennte Rechtskreise (so nach dem Vorgange Triepels die italienische Schule, besonders Anzilotti, Cavaglieri, Diena [dualistische Theorie]). Gegen die Einheitslehre in der einen oder anderen Form spricht vor allem die Verschiedenheit der Normadressaten (im Völkerrecht die Völkerrechtssubjekte, im Landesrecht die Staatsangehörigen ...) wie die Tatsache, dass die Völkerrechtswidrigkeit eines landesrechtlichen Aktes dessen staatsrechtliche Gültigkeit nicht berührt.[50]

In consequence, the dualist approach of the states-only conception was affirmed by the recognition conception: individuals were still only constitutive parts of the state, but not of the international realm. Individuals were, in principle, only objects, not subjects, of international law.[51] In the exceptional circumstances in which they could become international persons, they depended on the consent of their state of nationality. As a general rule, the state absorbed the individual.

As regards the sources of international law, new approaches bringing back natural law were vehemently rejected by the recognition conception. It was warned that the return of natural law – a tendency particularly acute in Germany according to Strupp – would question the status of international law as legal science.[52] As states were the supreme authorities in the international realm, the only source of international law could be state will: 'l'origine des règles juridiques internationales est dans la volonté des États manifestée par des traités et des coutumes uniforme. ... la sphère d'application de chaque règle du droit international se mesure au nombre des États qui la reconnaisse ouvertement.'[53]

The quotation reveals that the recognition conception affirmed the states-only conception's restrictive view of sources in international law:

[50] Strupp, *Grundzüge*, 16. See also Cavaglieri, 'Règles Générales', at 319; Schwarzenberger, *Manual*, 36–7.

[51] Schwarzenberger, *Manual*, 25. Consequently, Schwarzenberger also rejected the interpretation of *Jurisdiction of the Courts of Danzig* as proof of the individual as the subject of international law (Schwarzenberger, *International Law* (2nd edn.), 77).

[52] Strupp, *Grundzüge*, 13; Schwarzenberger, Georg, 'The Inductive Approach to International Law', HLR, 60 (1947), 539–70, at 540–9 (apart from early naturalist approaches particularly criticizing Lauterpacht's approach).

[53] Cavaglieri, 'Conception Positive', at 260 and 263.

as in the states-only conception, only states could create international law and it was only binding on those states having consented to it. However, there were two small modifications. First, the foundation of international law was not seen in a *Vereinbarung* anymore. Triepel and the early Anzilotti were criticized that their *Vereinbarungslehre* and the corresponding common will presupposed a new legal person that in fact did not exist.[54] The foundation of international law could therefore only rest in state practice accepting international law as binding.[55] Second, Strupp, Cavaglieri and Schwarzenberger accepted general rules of international law as opposed to only particular international law. However, these general rules were based on universal acceptance in state practice and the general framework on sources of international law was therefore not contradicted.[56] As part of this familiar theory of sources in international law, states were also competent to administer legal personality. In principle, this is reminiscent of the states-only conception too, as according to the latter, existing states had to recognize a new state before the latter could take part in the international legal system. This principle was, however, taken further by the recognition conception in that non-state entities could now be accepted as international persons through the process of recognition.

In result, the recognition conception of international personality defended the general legal framework of the states-only conception against new approaches to statehood and the sources of law. In the recognition conception as in the states-only conception, the state was a historical fact preceding the law and the supreme authority in international relations; the individual was confined to the boundaries of the state; and state will was the only source of international law.

Supplementation with a sociological perspective

The recognition conception's third proposition, declaring the presumption of the states-only conception rebuttable through evidence of state

[54] Strupp, *Grundzüge*, 4–5 (declaring that he had originally followed Triepel and Anzilotti, but had subsequently abandoned the *Vereinbarungslehre* under the influence of Cavaglieri).

[55] See also Cavaglieri, 'Conception Positive', at 263–4, and Schwarzenberger, Georg, *Machtpolitik* (Tübingen: J.C.B. Mohr, 1955), 130–1 (by implication). This was also the view held by Oppenheim, *International Law* (1st edn.), §10 (pp. 13–14).

[56] Strupp, *Grundzüge*, 14–15; Cavaglieri, 'Conception Positive', at 271–5, and Cavaglieri, 'Règles Générales', at 323–7; Schwarzenberger, 'Fundamental Principles', at 201–2.

practice to the contrary, has to be related to the view of law as grounded in its social conditions. This view was understood as a corrective measure, not a fundamental critique, of the basic framework of nineteenth-century positivism. It was influentially articulated by Georg Jellinek, Max Huber and Santi Romano (the latter's institutionalism being its most radical version) at the beginning of the twentieth century. Their sociological view gained currency in the unstable socio-political context in Germany and Italy after World War I. By favouring examinations of social reality over abstract legal reasoning, it was assured that legal analysis would not be irreconcilable with contemporary social developments. In international law, the need for such reconciliation was particularly felt in questions involving international personality because of the emergence of international organizations. The recognition conception's third proposition can be understood as an attempt to reconcile the states-only conception's legal framework with the increasing role of international organizations in international affairs.

In the tradition of the Gerber–Laband *Gesetzespositivismus*, the dominant legal method in Germany and Italy at the beginning of the twentieth century was abstract and formalistic.[57] According to this convention, the sole task for lawyers was to make logical deductions in a system of existing legal texts. This sole focus on organizing and systematizing legal norms was called *Begriffsjurisprudenz.* However, such *Begriffsjurisprudenz* had previously been criticized without questioning legal positivism itself.[58] One example is Georg Jellinek, clearly not an opponent of legal positivism in principle. In his two-sided theory of the state, he had already accentuated the sociological component of statehood as opposed to its legal form. In the same study of 1900, Jellinek also offered his views on the foundation of law, concluding that law could only have obligatory force when in conformity with social practice.[59] According to Jellinek, social facts themselves contained normative power ('*normative Kraft des Faktischen*').[60] Law could therefore not distance itself too much from social practice as it would be incompatible with the

[57] Stolleis, *Geschichte des öffentlichen Rechts (III)*, 171 (by implication). As was noted in the previous chapter, Italian legal thought was heavily influenced by German law at the end of the nineteenth and during the first decades of the twentieth century. The Gerber–Laband *Gesetzespositivismus* was therefore also dominant in Italy at the time. See also Torrazza and Di Iorio, *Diritto Italiano*, 189.

[58] Stolleis, *Geschichte des öffentlichen Rechts (III)*, 171–2.

[59] Jellinek, *Allgemeine Staatslehre*, 332–60. [60] Ibid., 339–41.

latter's normative power and consequently cease to be regarded as law.[61] In consequence, although Jellinek did of course not question the framework of legal positivism itself, he put emphasis on its social conditions.

Restricted to international law, Max Huber, the Swiss arbitrator as well as Judge and President at the Permanent Court of International Justice, made a similar argument in an article published in 1910.[62] Huber argued that international law in particular could not depend on formal legal logic alone, but had to reflect the realities of international relations.[63] After all, international law was based on the will of its subjects, i.e. sovereign states. An abstract *Begriffsjurisprudenz*, according to Huber, would harm international law because it would distance law too far from what states as international legislators actually considered to be the law.[64] International legal analysis therefore had to take into account the realities of international life. The significance Huber ascribed to such factual relations can also be detected from his well-known award in *Island of Palmas* wherein Huber favoured effective display of sovereignty over legal title.[65] Essentially, however, Huber did not question the framework of traditional legal positivism. He agreed with its basic assumptions about the state and law-creation. As is the case with Jellinek, Huber still conceived the state as the most powerful and all-consuming form of social organization:

> Soweit wir das Leben der Völker zu überblicken vermögen, ist die Organisation, die wir trotz ihrer endlosen gesellschaftlichen und rechtlichen Wandlungen immer als Staat bezeichnen, der mächtigste Faktor alles sozialen Lebens. ... Alle Verhältnisse des menschlichen Zusammenlebens sind vom Staat unmittelbar oder mittelbar beeinflusst, wenn nicht geradezu bestimmt. ... Der Staat der Gegenwart mit seiner zwar formell gebundenen, inhaltlich aber schrankenlosen Gesetzgebungsgewalt, seinen nach dem 'Gesetz der wachsenden Staatstätigkeit' unaufhörlich sich mehrenden materiellen und geistigen Aufgaben ...[66]

[61] Ibid., 341–2.
[62] On Huber's life and legal approach in general see Diggelmann, Oliver, *Anfänge der Völkerrechtssoziologie: Die Völkerrechtskonzeptionen von Max Huber und Georges Scelle im Vergleich* (Zürich: Schulthess, 2000), 61–146.
[63] Huber, *Soziologische Grundlagen*, 9. [64] Ibid., 9–10.
[65] *Island of Palmas Arbitration Case* (Sole Arbitrator Huber), 4 Annual Digest of Public International Law Cases (ILR) 3 (1928), at 104–6. See also Khan, Daniel-Erasmus, 'Max Huber as Arbitrator: The Palmas (Miangas) Case and Other Arbitrations', EJIL, 18 (2007), 145–70, at 169.
[66] Huber, *Soziologische Grundlagen*, 1.

Huber's statement that the state also contained spiritual aspects is reminiscent of Hegel's ethical and organic view of the state.[67] In line with this tradition, it was only the state that created law. In result, Huber merely criticized certain exaggerations of purely logical legal reasoning, and not the fundamentals of legal positivism in the German intellectual tradition. For Huber, taking social realities into account in legal reasoning was thus merely a corrective measure.

In a similar sense, in Italy, Santi Romano formulated an empiricist version of social institutionalism with the aim of basing law in its social substructure.[68] Though Romano's institutionalism went further in several respects than Jellinek's and Huber's sociological approaches, he nevertheless shared the basic criticism of law understood as abstract *Begriffsjurisprudenz* and supported the intent to make the examination of the social environment part of legal analysis while at the same time preserving the traditional positivist framework.[69] In essence, Romano argued that as a result of social realities, there was a set of fundamental principles in international law composing the international constitution.[70] As a particular feature, by focusing on the institutions of social life contributing to the international constitution, Romano dealt with questions of legal personality. Institutions, according to Romano, were empirically observable realities of social life.[71] Examples were the family, the church, and the state. These institutions were all normative orders themselves, as every social setting naturally led to rules (*ubi societas,*

[67] Ibid., 99. See also Diggelmann, *Völkerrechtssoziologie*, 91–2.

[68] Romano, *Ordinamento Giuridico*, 10–14 and 24–8. See Stone, Julius, *Social Dimensions of Law and Justice* (London: Stevens, 1966), 519–22, for considering Romano's work as a positivist version of institutionalism (519). Maurice Hauriou articulated a natural law version of institutionalism in France. In Germany, Carl Schmitt's *Konkretes Ordnungsdenken* and his justification of Hitler's dictatorship can be considered as institutionalist. For Hauriou and Schmitt see Fikentscher, Wolfgang, *Methoden des Rechts in vergleichender Darstellung Band I: Frühe und Religiöse Rechte, Romanischer Rechtskreis* (Tübingen: J. C. B. Mohr, 1975), 504–26.

[69] See also Truyol y Serra, 'Doctrines du Droit des Gens', at 214.

[70] Kolb, *Bonne Foi*, 65–6, and Kolb, *Réfléxions*, 23. It is important to distinguish Romano's approach towards international constitutionalism from the constitutional theory advocated by the Austrian Alfred Verdross in the same period. Whereas Romano focuses on social realities composing the international constitution, Verdross concentrates on basic moral principles having the same effect. Verdross's theory is discussed as part of the origins of the individualistic conception of international personality.

[71] Romano, *Ordinamento Giuridico*, 35: 'Per istituzione noi intendiamo ogni ente o corpo sociale.'

ibi ius).[72] Accordingly, for every normative order, there was a necessary institution without which the order would not exist. For example, the existence of a state was a precondition for there being a particular national legal order. The necessary institution of one particular order was then the basic legal person of this order.[73] However, such institutions were not necessarily legal persons of another legal order: they would have to be recognized by another legal system in order to become a legal person of that system.[74] For instance, the church, though a person of its own normative order, only acquired personality in the state's legal system through recognition by the latter. In turn, such recognition could only be granted to institutions, that is, to empirically observable social entities. Romano hence linked law to its underlying social institutions and, as a specific feature, formulated a theory as to how such social institutions acquired legal personality in one particular legal order.

Jellinek's, Huber's and Romano's sociological approach and the latter's specific institutional theory on legal personality became particularly relevant in matters of international personality. With the emergence of international organizations, the shortcomings of applying the propositions of the states-only conception became apparent when dealing with the legal status of these new entities. Corrective measures as articulated in the sociological approach by Jellinek, Huber and Romano were needed. Guido Fusinato's expert opinion of 1914 on the International Institute of Agriculture, one of the earliest opinions on the legal nature of an international organization, exemplified this view.[75]

The International Institute of Agriculture had been set up in 1905 through a convention signed by 54 states and was located in Rome. Fusinato began his opinion by recalling the fundamental principle that the national and international legal order were essentially separated and that only states were international persons.[76] He proceeded by stating that social and economic necessities had, however, pushed states to create non-state entities such as the Institute which themselves had an

[72] Ibid., 27: 'Ogni ordinamento giuridico è un'istituzione, e viceversa ogni istituzione è un ordinamento giuridico.'

[73] Ibid., 78. [74] Ibid., 79.

[75] See Fusinato, Guido, 'La Personalità Giuridica dell'Istituto Internazionale d'Agricoltura', Rdi, 8 (1914), 149–55, as well as Cavaglieri, 'Soggetti', at 170–1, and Schwarzenberger, *Internationale Banken*, 52.

[76] Fusinato, 'Istituto Internazionale d'Agricoltura', at 149 (the text of the opinion, contrary to its title, is in French as this was the language the opinion was delivered in).

international character.[77] With their international character, such institutions could not be legal persons of one national legal order.[78] But did they qualify as international persons? Established doctrine prohibited the acceptance of other international persons apart from states and Fusinato hence proposed to conceive the Institute as a new category of international personality, a 'civil international person'.[79] Such 'civil international persons', in contrast to states as the normal persons of international law, were only subject to the rules enacted for them by the creating states; there were no other international norms pertinent to them.

Fusinato's opinion indicated the difficulties of adhering to strictly logical deductions within the states-only conception of international personality while at the same time dealing with an essentially international entity. By strictly following logical deductions in the framework of the states-only conception, Fusinato in essence advocated a new legal system with only one legal person, the International Institute of Agriculture. This was precisely a case in which formal legal reasoning distanced law too far from social realities: there could not be a new legal system with only one legal person. Among others, Cavaglieri and Schwarzenberger therefore took issue with the approach chosen by Fusinato.[80] They declared that Fusinato's approach did not conform to reality. States as international legislators had the power to create a new international person if they intended to do so; by adhering to strictly logical deductions, this reality could not be grasped. In light of this evidence, the states-only conception had to be adjusted in this respect.[81] This led to the third proposition declaring the state-only conception rebuttable in light of social practice to the contrary.

Thus, the third proposition in the recognition conception must be related to the sociological approaches formulated by Jellinek, Huber and Romano.[82] These approaches were understood in their context as a

[77] Ibid., at 149–50. [78] Ibid., at 151. [79] Ibid., at 150 and 152–4.

[80] Cavaglieri, 'Soggetti', at 170–1; Schwarzenberger, *Internationale Banken*, 52.

[81] Cavaglieri, 'Soggetti', at 173 (formulating his theory of personality); Schwarzenberger, *Internationale Banken*, 54–5 (applying it to the issue of the Bank of International Settlements).

[82] For their general impact see Link, *Realist mit Idealen*, 343 (for Jellinek's influence, in particular his line 'normative Kraft des Faktischen', on Strupp); Kolb, *Les Cours Généraux*, 23 (for Romano's considerable influence on Italian scholarship and Cavaglieri); Steinle, *Völkerrecht und Machtpolitik*, 94–103, and Schwarzenberger, *International Law* (2nd edn.), 4–7 (for Huber's influence on Schwarzenberger, in particular through the *Island of Palmas* award).

corrective measure in case legal deductions distanced law too far from social reality. It was not directed against the existing international legal framework with its idea of statehood and sources in principle; it merely aimed to reconcile it with changing social realities. This aim became particularly relevant in the field of international personality. As the states-only conception of international personality seemed increasingly out of touch with developments on the international scene, in particular with the increasing role of international organizations, the recognition conception included the third proposition as a corrective measure to counter dogmatic exaggerations of the states-only conception. While the latter's basic framework was accepted and states were regarded as the original or necessary persons of international law, there could be other persons if social practice showed that states had recognized them as such.

Main manifestations in legal practice

In legal practice, the recognition conception is mostly used when dealing with entities that effectively play a role in international relations like the UN, the ICRC, the Holy See or transnational corporations. As these entities are not states and therefore not international persons as such (original international personality of acknowledged states), they have to be admitted by states to the international legal system (derivative international personality of non-state entities). The main difficulty lies in convincingly rebutting the presumption that only states enjoy international legal status. There is rarely express recognition and the debate unfolds as to how tacit recognition can be established. This leaves a considerable degree of uncertainty when dealing with the international legal status of non-state entities in accordance with the recognition conception of international personality.

The Reparation for Injuries *Advisory Opinion*

In the *Reparation for Injuries* opinion, the ICJ declared the UN an international person.[83] There have been controversial interpretations as to how the Court actually arrived at this conclusion. In the present book, it is submitted that the logical structure of the Advisory Opinion and in particular the sociological observations put forward in it indicate

[83] *Reparation for Injuries Suffered in the Service of the United Nations* (Advisory Opinion), 1949 ICJ Reports 174, at 179.

that *Reparation for Injuries* is a manifestation of the recognition conception of international personality. The Court basically aimed at opening up the international legal system to a non-state entity without questioning the basic international legal framework and the accompanying presumption for states. The *Reparation for Injuries* opinion has been adopted widely in subsequent practice dealing with the legal status of international organizations and there certainly is some merit to the view that it is the landmark decision concerning international personality in general.

The incident leading to the Advisory Opinion in *Reparation for Injuries* was the assassination of Count Bernadotte, the UN Secretary-General's envoy to Palestine/Israel, by paramilitary units in Jerusalem in 1948. The question arose whether the UN could bring an international claim against Israel in order to obtain reparation for the damage caused to the UN and to the victim or to persons entitled through the latter.[84] The General Assembly referred the question in general terms to the ICJ. In its Advisory Opinion, the Court first defined the capacity to bring an international claim. It meant the 'customary methods recognized by international law for the establishment, the presentation and the settlement of claims'.[85] These customary methods included 'protest, request for an enquiry, negotiation, and request for submission to an arbitral tribunal or to the Court in so far as this may be authorized by the Statute'.[86] Such instruments for bringing international claims could certainly be employed by states according to the ICJ. For the case of the UN, the Court held:

> But, in the international sphere, has the Organization [the UN] such a nature as involves the capacity to bring an international claim? In order to answer this question, the Court must first enquire whether the Charter has given the Organization such a position that it possesses, in regard to its Members, rights which it is entitled to ask them to respect. In other words, does the Organization possess international personality? This is no doubt a doctrinal expression, which has sometimes given rise to controversy. But it will be used here to mean that if the Organization is recognized as having that personality, it is an entity capable of availing itself of obligations incumbent upon its Members.[87]

The Court thus deemed it necessary to enquire whether the UN was recognized as an international person in order to make a decision on its capacity to bring international claims.

[84] Ibid., at 176–7. [85] Ibid., at 177. [86] Ibid., at 177. [87] Ibid., at 178.

The ICJ then observed that the UN Charter did not settle the issue of international personality in explicit terms: 'To answer this question [whether the UN is an international person], which is not settled by the actual terms of the Charter, we must consider what characteristics it was intended thereby to give to the Organization.'[88] The Court then proceeded with its often-quoted statements about international personality in general and the UN's in particular:

> The subjects of law in any legal system are not necessarily identical in their nature or in the extent of their rights, and their nature depends upon the needs of the community. Throughout its history, the development of international law has been influenced by the requirements of international life, and the progressive increase in the collective activities of States has already given rise to instances of action upon the international plane by certain entities which are not States. This development culminated in the establishment in June 1945 of an international organization whose purposes and principles are specified in the Charter of the United Nations. But to achieve these ends the attribution of international personality is indispensable.[89]

> Accordingly, the Court has come to the conclusion that the Organization is an international person. That is not the same thing as saying that it is a State, which it is certainly not, or that its legal personality and rights and duties are the same as those of a State. Still less is it the same thing as saying that it is 'a super-State', whatever that expression may mean. It does not even imply that all its rights and duties must be upon the international plane, any more than all the rights and duties of a State must be upon that plane. What it does mean is that it is a subject of international law and capable of possessing international rights and duties, and that it has capacity to maintain its rights by bringing international claims.[90]

> Whereas a State possesses the totality of international rights and duties recognized by international law, the rights and duties of an entity such as the Organization must depend upon its purposes and functions as specified or implied in its constituent documents and developed in practice.[91]

Having labelled the UN an international person in the sense identified above, the Court had one more obstacle to overcome: Israel was not a member state of the UN at the time. The issue arose as to whether the UN's international personality was also opposable towards states not having ratified the Charter. On this point, the Court declared in rather unequivocal terms:

> . . . the Court's opinion is that fifty States, representing the vast majority of the members of the international community, had the power, in

[88] Ibid., at 178. [89] Ibid., at 178. [90] Ibid., at 179. [91] Ibid., at 180.

> conformity with international law, to bring into being an entity possessing objective international personality, and not merely personality recognized by them alone, together with capacity to bring international claims.[92]

In effect, the ICJ declared the UN an objective international person capable of bringing international claims; the Court was, however, careful to distinguish the UN's limited international personality in contrast to the full international personality of states.

There is considerable disagreement in doctrine as to which conception of international personality the Court actually applied when establishing the UN as an international person in the *Reparation for Injuries* opinion.[93] According to the systematization of international personality employed in the present book, the debate includes three different conceptions: the actor conception, the formal conception and the recognition conception.[94] Angelo Piero Sereni, Finn Seyersted and Manuel Rama-Montaldo have advocated that *Reparation for Injuries* has to be understood as a manifestation of the actor conception of international personality.[95] They contend that the UN's international personality did not depend on the Charter or on the intention of member states but on the UN fulfilling certain objective preconditions comprised in customary international law. In contrast, Ignaz Seidl-Hohenveldern and others have interpreted the Court's Advisory Opinion as being closely attached to the Charter and the enumerated rights, duties and capacities therein.[96] In this view, the Court is thought to have applied the formal conception of international personality. Accordingly, the UN's capacity to bring

[92] Ibid., at 185.

[93] See also Akande, 'International Organizations', at 282, and Mosler, 'Völkerrechtssubjekte', at 19. Jan Klabbers has argued that the reason for this disagreement is that the Court endlessly shifted between different conceptions of international personality (Klabbers, 'Legal Personality', esp. at 39–41). This view is, however, unconvincing as will be contended below.

[94] For the actor conception see Chapter 9, and for the formal conception Chapter 8.

[95] Sereni, Angelo Piero, *Diritto Internazionale (II/2)* (Milan: Guiffré, 1960), 843–50; Seyersted, Finn, 'United Nations Forces: Some Legal Problems', BYIL, 37 (1961), 351–475, esp. at 454–5; Seyersted, *Objective International Personality*, esp. 9; Rama-Montaldo, 'International Legal Personality', at 124–9. In the same direction, Fitzmaurice, Gerald, 'The Law and Procedure of the International Court of Justice: International Organizations and Tribunals', BYIL, 29 (1952), 1–62, at 3, Akande, 'International Organizations', at 282, as well as Brownlie, *Principles*, 649.

[96] See Seidl-Hohenveldern, 'Handlungen internationaler Organisationen', at 498. In this direction also Arangio-Ruiz, *Personalità Giuridica*, 257–8, n. 1. This approach is mainly associated with Kelsen, *Law of the United Nations*, 329–30.

international claims is understood as a right drawn from the Charter by implication. Finally, the *Reparation for Injuries* opinion has been understood, by Schwarzenberger among others, as a manifestation of the recognition conception of international personality.[97] In this view, the Court examined whether member states had recognized the UN as an international person by implication. The only diversion from a proper application of the recognition conception was that the Court regarded the international personality of the UN as opposable to a non-member without examining whether the latter had recognized the UN.[98]

Unlike the systematization presented here, in most doctrinal analyses of the *Reparation for Injuries* opinion, the formal conception and the recognition conception are merged into a so-called 'implied powers doctrine'.[99] Though there are certainly similarities between the two conceptions – especially when it comes to 'implied powers' and 'implied recognition' – one has to be careful not to overlook their basic differences. Where the formal conception is applied, the constitution of the UN is analysed in order to derive from it explicitly or implicitly enumerated rights, duties or capacities; these powers in turn determine the organization's international personality.[100] In the case of the recognition conception, however, the UN Charter is examined with the aim of inferring from it whether the parties had intended to recognize the organization as an international person; this recognized personality then leads to certain legal consequences, e.g. the capacity to bring an international claim. Such capacities are not implied powers deduced from the analysis of the constitution, but legal consequences attached to being a recognized international person. Accordingly, in the recognition conception, the intention of the parties to vest the organization with

[97] Schwarzenberger, *International Law* (3rd edn.), 138. See also Reuter, Paul, *Institutions Internationales* (Paris: Presses Universitaires, 1955), 316–8, and Bindschedler, Rudolf L., 'Die Anerkennung im Völkerrecht', ARV, 9 (1961–1962), 377–97, at 387–8. Also in this direction Schermers and Blokker, *International Institutional Law*, §1566 (979), and Kolb, 'Nouvelle Observation', at 231–2, n. 10 (by implication).

[98] Schwarzenberger, 'Fundamental Principles', at 252; Schwarzenberger, *International Law* (3rd edn.), 128–9; Bindschedler, 'Anerkennung', at 388.

[99] See e.g. Schermers and Blokker, *International Institutional Law*, §1565 (978–9); Akande, 'International Organizations', at 281–2; Seyersted, *Objective International Personality*, 15–17.

[100] This is the implied powers doctrine properly so called and generally associated with Hans Kelsen's study of the UN. See Kelsen, *Law of the United Nations*, 329: 'The constituent treaty need not expressly confer upon the international community juridical personality. The latter is – or is not – implied in the substantial provisions of the constituent treaty.'

international personality is crucial, whereas in the formal conception, crucial is whether a particular capacity can be deduced from the Charter. Although it has to be admitted that the sometimes ambiguous wording of the Court's opinion in *Reparation for Injuries* did not help to clarify this distinction, for present purposes, it is important to uphold it. Therefore, the actor conception has not only to be contrasted with an 'implied powers doctrine', but also with the formal, as well as with the recognition, conception of international personality.

Taking into account all three conceptions, it is submitted that a careful reading of the *Reparation for Injuries* opinion reveals it as predominantly a manifestation of the recognition conception of international personality. Whereas the wording of the Advisory Opinion is to some extent ambiguous, the logical structure of the opinion hints that, and the general statements on international personality strongly indicate that, the recognition conception was applied. The latter finding only becomes clear when the origins of the recognition conception, in particular its use of sociological elements as a corrective measure, are related to how the Court used the invocation of social developments in its reasoning. As in the recognition conception, the Court apparently used factual changes on the international scene in order to open up the possibility of including non-state entities into international law. With regard to international personality, the *Reparation for Injuries* opinion is therefore not to be understood as a manifestation of the formal conception (or implied powers doctrine properly so called):[101] the doctrine of implied powers was not applied with regard to the question of the UN's status as an international person; it only became pertinent in the opinion after international personality had been established so as to induce concrete rights, duties and capacities out of the Charter not derived from personality.[102] Nor is the Advisory Opinion to be interpreted as a manifestation of the actor conception of international personality: the characteristics of

[101] Judge Hackworth's dissenting opinion anticipates that the majority opinion is not a manifestation of the formal conception of international personality (see *Reparation for Injuries*, at 196–204, Dissenting Opinion by Judge Hackworth). Though Judge Hackworth concurs in the result that the UN has capacity to bring international claims and is an international person to this extent, he disagrees with the reasoning leading to this result and with the further implications drawn from it. Hackworth therefore contends that the majority opinion is not a proper application of the implied powers doctrine (formal conception).

[102] The argument that 'implied powers' became relevant in *Reparation for Injuries* only after personality had been established is shared by Rama-Montaldo, 'International Legal Personality', at 129–31. However, as regards the establishment of international

the UN did not in themselves determine it an international person, but in the opinion of the Court only indicated that member states had intended to vest it with such a status. It is hence the recognition conception that was predominantly applied in *Reparation for Injuries.*

As regards the logical structure of the opinion, the Court's point of departure was that the text of the UN Charter did not settle the issue of international personality ('To answer this question, which is not settled by the actual terms of the Charter . . .').[103] Lacking explicit recognition, the Court proceeded by examining whether the UN's international personality had been recognized by implication. It is important to highlight that the Court thereby did not merely examine which characteristics the UN had, but which ones member states had intended it to possess ('. . . we must consider what characteristics it was intended thereby to give to the Organization'). In order to detect the intention of member states, the Court analysed the Charter and the functions and powers contained therein. It came to the conclusion that the states, having created the UN, must have recognized its personality by implication because it was necessary to achieve the ends of the organization ('to achieve these ends the attribution of international personality is indispensable'). Furthermore, hinting most clearly at the application of the recognition conception while at the same time going beyond it, the Court did not regard the UN's international personality as only a relative one recognized by its 50 member states ('not merely personality recognized by them alone'), but opposable to all states ('an entity possessing objective international personality'). In result, the ICJ argued that the UN had been recognized by its member states as an objective international person by implication because this personality was indispensable for the organization to fulfil its various functions and powers; as one consequence of being a recognized international person, the UN had the capacity to bring international claims against non-member states.[104]

Apart from the logical structure, the general statements on international personality and the use of sociological observations strongly indicate that the *Reparation for Injuries* opinion is a manifestation of the recognition

personality, Rama-Montaldo interprets the Advisory Opinion as a manifestation of the actor conception (ibid., at 125 6).

[103] Article 104 UNC vests the UN with only (functionally limited) personality in the municipal law of member states.

[104] As regards this consequence following from international personality, see also Lauterpacht, Hersch, *The Development of International Law by the International Court*, (revised edition of 'The Development of International Law by the Permanent Court of International Justice (1934)') (London: Stevens, 1958), 178.

conception. The first statement on the subjects of law emphasized that international personality could vary ('The subjects of law in any legal system are not necessarily identical in their nature or in the extent of their rights'). That is in conformity with the recognition conception's approach, which introduces the idea of a limited and derivative international personality of non-state entities as opposed to the full and original personality of states. Accordingly, the Court underlined the differences between state and non-state actors in international law ('Whereas a State possesses the totality of international rights and duties recognized by international law, the rights and duties of an entity such as the Organization must depend upon its purposes and functions'). Thus, the Court regarded states as the highest authorities in international law. The Court then used sociological language to explain why and to what extent entities other than states could become international persons ('their nature depends upon the needs of the community').[105] As in the recognition conception, this has to be understood as grounding law in its social environment ('Throughout its history, the development of international law has been influenced by the requirements of international life'). By emphasizing the social developments in international life, it was possible for the ICJ, as it had been for the proponents of the recognition conception, to overcome the dogma that only states could be international persons – without mentioning radically new ideas of statehood, sovereignty or law-creation. It is important to note in this respect that the jurisprudence of the PCIJ had principally adhered to the states-only conception of international personality.[106] In order to overcome this, the ICJ tellingly did not employ a fundamentally different legal framework, but made mention of social developments that had to be taken into account by international law. The Court therefore highlighted social developments that had led to actions by non-state entities in the international realm ('the progressive increase in the collective activities of States has already given rise to instances of action upon the international plane by certain entities which are not States'). As in the recognition conception, these social developments opened up the possibility that non-state entities could become limited international persons; they did not in themselves lead to the international personality of the UN. It still depended on the will of states

[105] See also Judge Alvarez's individual opinion which emphasizes social developments as one of the main factors influencing the decision (*Reparation for Injuries*, at 190, Opinion Individuelle de M. Alvarez).

[106] See e.g. *Case Concerning the Payments of Various Serbian Loans Issued in France* (Judgment), 1929 PCIJ Series A No. 20, at 41.

whether and to what extent non-state entities could acquire international personality ('the intentions of its founders'). Factual changes were hence only used as a corrective measure against the old dogma – as is the case in the recognition conception. Opening up the possibility for non-state entities to become international persons, it was a matter for state practice to overcome the presumption for states. In consequence, the *Reparation for Injuries* opinion has to be read as an instance of the recognition conception: it makes use of similar sociological language in order to introduce the possibility of non-state entities becoming international persons and reaffirms that the intention of states in the end determines the international personality of a non-state entity.

It remains to be addressed that the Court declared the UN an 'objective international person', a fact that is obviously at odds with the recognition conception as formulated by Strupp, Cavaglieri and Schwarzenberger. The latter consequently labelled this proposition as 'somewhat novel'[107] and complained that the Court had not 'attempted to underpin this extra-ordinary thesis by argument'.[108] However, it has to be said that the Court confined its statement to the UN. Hence, it was argued that the special character of the UN as the 'supreme type of international organization'[109] permitted the conclusion that the personality recognized by its member states should also be opposable to non-members. True, this is not fully in accordance with the recognition conception. But the way in which the objective international personality of the UN was established does not indicate that the Court employed a different conception of personality or that it fundamentally altered the recognition conception. The Court, after having established the UN's international personality according to the recognition conception, merely went one step further in the special case of the UN. The proposition of the UN's objective international personality hence does not imply that the Court applied an objective actor conception. It was only an adjustment of the recognition conception in the specific situation of the UN.

It is beyond doubt that the *Reparation for Injuries* opinion is the landmark decision concerning personality of international organizations in international law.[110] However, there are preceding opinions dealing

[107] Schwarzenberger, *International Law* (3rd edn.), 128.
[108] Schwarzenberger, 'Fundamental Principles', at 252.
[109] *Reparation for Injuries*, at 179.
[110] See e.g. Klabbers, Jan, 'The Life and Times of the Law of International Organizations', NJIL, 70 (2001), 287–317, at 302.

with international institutions that had to some extent paved the way for the ICJ's opinion of 1949. The PCIJ had been requested early in its tenure to deliver Advisory Opinions on the constitutional provisions of the International Labour Organization (ILO) and on matters involving competences of the League of Nations. Whereas the Court approached these issues in 1922 and 1923 merely as questions of treaty interpretation and was not indicating that international institutions demanded any additional considerations,[111] it was already foreshadowing the implied powers doctrine in yet another opinion on the ILO in 1926.[112] The latter opinion was subsequently quoted by the ICJ in *Reparation for Injuries* when dealing with specific competences of the UN.[113] Importantly, the ILO opinion had not touched upon the question of personality when introducing the implied powers doctrine. It was one year later in the *Jurisdiction of the European Commission of the Danube* opinion that the PCIJ went one step further and vaguely hinted at the possibility of international institutions being bestowed with functionally limited international personality.[114] The ICJ, however, did not quote the opinion in *Reparation for Injuries* and the latter is clearly the first case in which the Court unequivocally declared an international organization a person of international law.

[111] For the opinions concerning the ILO see *Designation of the Workers' Delegate for the Netherlands at the Third Session of the International Labour Conference* (Advisory Opinion), 1922 PCIJ Series B No. 1, esp. at 22–3; *Competence of the ILO in regard to International Regulation of the Conditions of the Labour of Persons Employed in Agriculture* (Advisory Opinion), 1922 PCIJ Series B No. 2, esp. at 23; *Competence of the ILO to Examine Proposal for the Organization and Development of the Methods of Agricultural Production* (Advisory Opinion), 1922 PCIJ Series B No. 3, esp. at 54–5. For matters involving competences of the League of Nations see *Status of Eastern Carelia* (Advisory Opinion), 1923 Series B No. 5, at 27–8, wherein the Court memorably denied the power of the Council of the League of Nations to request an Advisory Opinion in the particular circumstances of lacking Russian consent, and *Questions concerning the Acquisition of Polish Nationality* (Advisory Opinion), 1923 PCIJ Series B No. 7, at 12–13, wherein the Court focused on rules of treaty interpretation in order to decide on a particular competence of the League. See also Spiermann, *International Legal Argument in the PCIJ*, 148 and 160–1, and Klabbers, 'Law of International Organizations', at 295.

[112] *Competence of the ILO to Regulate Incidentally the Personal Work of the Employer* (Advisory Opinion), 1926 PCIJ Series B No. 13, at 18.

[113] *Reparation for Injuries*, at 182–3.

[114] *Jurisdiction of the European Commission of the Danube between Galatz and Braila* (Advisory Opinion), 1927 PCIJ Series B No. 14, at 63–4. See also Spiermann, *International Legal Argument in the PCIJ*, 267; Rama-Montaldo, 'International Legal Personality', at 141; and Klabbers, 'Law of International Organizations', at 296.

After the *Reparation for Injuries* opinion, it was settled that international organizations could be international persons. Correspondingly, the ICJ did not spend much effort on further establishing international personality of international organizations in its subsequent jurisprudence. In the *Interpretation of the Agreement between WHO and Egypt* opinion, the Court, having referred to *Reparation for Injuries*, straightforwardly declared: 'International organizations are subjects of international law and, as such, are bound by any obligations incumbent upon them under general rules of international law, under their constitutions or under international agreements to which they are parties.'[115] In a further Advisory Opinion on the *Legality of the Use of Nuclear Weapons by a State in Armed Conflict*, the Court even found it 'need hardly point out that international organizations are subjects of international law which do not, unlike states, possess a general competence'.[116] The main task for the ICJ was not to establish personality, but to state the specific powers an international organization possessed.[117] As regards the legal consequences of international personality, the Court rather unobtrusively remarked at the end of the *Cumuraswamy* opinion that such personality also entailed the responsibility of international organizations.[118] It therefore seems that personality of international organizations and the legal consequences thereof were regarded as settled issues in the jurisprudence of the ICJ following *Reparation for Injuries*; the Court no longer deemed it necessary to explore these matters in depth anymore.

115 *Interpretation of the Agreement of 25 March 1951 between the WHO and Egypt* (Advisory Opinion), 1980 ICJ Reports 73, at 89–90 (para. 37).

116 *Legality of the Use of Nuclear Weapons by a State in Armed Conflict* (Advisory Opinion), 1996 ICJ Reports 66, at 78 (para. 25).

117 In this respect, the implied powers doctrine was regularly reaffirmed. See *Legality of the Use of Nuclear Weapons by a State in Armed Conflict*, at 79 (para. 25). See also *Certain Expenses of the United Nations* (Advisory Opinion), 1962 ICJ Reports 151, at 167. The *Certain Expenses* opinion is sometimes understood as reflecting a particular conception of international personality (see e.g. Seyersted, 'United Nations Forces', at 460). This seems to be mistaken. The Court only affirmed that in order to decide whether certain expenses were 'expenses of the organization', one had to take an implied powers view of the functions of the UN (see also Rama-Montaldo, 'International Legal Personality', at 121–2). The concept of international personality was not employed by the Court.

118 *Difference relating to Immunity from Legal Process of a Special Rapporteur of the Commission on Human Rights* (Advisory Opinion), 1999 ICJ Reports 62, at 88–9 (para. 66). See also Gaja (Special Rapporteur), *First Report on responsibility of international organizations*, ILC 2003, UN Doc. A/CN.4/532, at 19 (para. 35).

Yet, it has to be said that the Court has not in recent times dealt substantially with those cases wherein the legal status of international organizations posed more fundamental questions of law. The memorable *Tin Council* case, for example, was decided by municipal English courts.[119] Questions surrounding the international legal status of the European Union were mostly struggled with in policy and academic circles. And the *Legality of Use of Force* cases – comprising the crucial issue whether NATO's international personality was opposable to Yugoslavia – were dismissed by the Court due to lack of jurisdiction.[120] The legal views put forward in these instances were partly contrary to what the ICJ had argued in *Reparation for Injuries* according to the interpretation submitted in this book. Consequently, these latter legal manifestations are dealt with in the later chapter presenting the actor conception of international personality.

Finally, it has to be acknowledged that the influence of the *Reparation for Injuries* opinion was not only confined to the legal status of international organizations. The general observations on international personality articulated in the opinion inspired theory and practice of international law more generally. It has already been said that most textbooks start their chapter on the subjects of international law by quoting the *Reparation for Injuries* opinion. In international practice, the Advisory Opinion has sometimes been referred to in investment arbitration proceedings based on alleged breaches of state contracts.[121] The findings of the ICJ have then been used to declare the private party of the contract an international person of limited scope. Such instances will be dealt with in the present chapter. In general, the main argument put forward here is that such wider applications of the *Reparation for Injuries* opinion imply the recognition conception of international personality.

The international legal status of the ICRC

The International Committee of the Red Cross (ICRC) is a private association established under Swiss law. Notwithstanding its essentially private legal character, legal doctrine has long regarded the ICRC as an

[119] *Maclaine Watson & Co. Ltd* v. *International Tin Council* (House of Lords 1989), 29 ILM 670, esp. at 672–5 (Lord Templeman).

[120] *Legality of Use of Force* cases (Preliminary Objections, Judgment), 2004 ICJ Reports (various pages).

[121] See e.g. *Texaco Overseas Petroleum Company and California Asiatic Oil Company* v. *The Government of the Libyan Arab Republic* (Award on the Merits, Sole Arbitrator Dupuy, 1977), 53 ILR 422, paras 44–8.

international person. In *Prosecutor* v. *Simic et al.*, the Trial Chamber of the International Criminal Tribunal for the former Yugoslavia (ICTY) confirmed this view when attributing to the ICRC an international right to confidentiality.[122] The reasoning in the decision as well as in legal doctrine represents a manifestation of the recognition conception of international personality.

The main source of concern when dealing with the ICRC's international personality is that it is not an international organization created by states. Inspired by Henry Dunant and his book *Un souvenir de Solférino*, Swiss private individuals founded the ICRC in 1863. It is a private association within the meaning of Articles 60 and following of the Swiss Civil Code and consists of a maximum of 25 members, all of whom have to be Swiss citizens.[123] The goals of the association include to provide victims of war with practical assistance and to protect them through codification of the law of armed conflict.[124] From its early days, the ICRC offered services for wounded and sick military personnel, prisoners of war, civilian war victims and refugees and initiated codification attempts for the law of armed conflict. In the latter respect, an early sign of progress was the adoption of the Geneva Convention of 1864 by sixteen states at a diplomatic conference organized by the Swiss government at the request of the ICRC.[125] After several adaptations, the growing number of humanitarian Conventions were revised and expanded after World War II, leading to the four Geneva Conventions of 1949 that are still in force today for 194 states.[126] Two Additional Protocols were added to the Conventions in 1977 and one was adopted in 2005.[127] The four Geneva Conventions of 1949 and the two

[122] *Prosecutor* v. *Simic et al.* (Decision on the Prosecution Motion under Rule 73 for a Ruling concerning the Testimony of a Witness), ICTY Trial Chamber 27 July 1999, para. 46 n. 9.

[123] Articles 2 and 7(1) ICRC Statute.

[124] See for this and the following historical information Bindschedler-Robert, Denise, 'Red Cross', EPIL, 4 (2003), 56–63, at 57–8.

[125] Convention for the Amelioration of the Condition of the Wounded in Armies in the Field. Geneva, 22 August 1864 (available at www.icrc.org).

[126] Convention (I) for the Amelioration of the Condition of the Wounded and Sick in Armed Forces in the Field, 75 UNTS 32; Convention (II) for the Amelioration of the Condition of Wounded, Sick and Shipwrecked Members of Armed Forces at Sea, 75 UNTS 86; Convention (III) relative to the Treatment of Prisoners of War, 75 UNTS 136; Convention (IV) relative to the Protection of Civilian Persons in Time of War, 75 UNTS 288. All signed at Geneva, 12 August 1949.

[127] Protocol additional to the Geneva Conventions of 12 August 1949, and relating to the Protection of Victims of International Armed Conflicts (Protocol I), 8 June 1977, 1125 UNTS 4; Protocol Additional to the Geneva Conventions of 12 August 1949, and

Additional Protocols of 1977 contain specific responsibilities of the ICRC in armed conflict, including the tasks of visiting prisoners of war and maintaining an International Tracing Agency. 'In consideration of the special role and mandates conferred upon it by the Geneva Conventions of 12 August 1949', the ICRC was granted permanent observer status to the General Assembly of the UN in 1990.[128] The ICRC has also entered into more than fifty headquarters agreements with states regulating the status of its delegations and their staff. Its relationship with Switzerland was specified in an agreement concluded on 19 March 1993 in which 'the international juridical personality and the legal capacity' of the ICRC was recognized by Switzerland.

Faced with an essentially private entity, which nevertheless plays an important role in armed conflict and is vested with certain responsibilities in international treaties, legal doctrine, though sceptical in the beginning,[129] has come to regard the ICRC as an international person:

> Les capacités essentielles qui sont les attributs de la personnalité juridique internationale sont donc, à nos yeux, reconnues au CICR, par une attitude des États qui est allée se consolidant et se précisant au cours des dernières décennies. ... Reconnaître au CICR les capacités caractéristiques des sujets du droit international, c'est admettre implicitement qu'il est revêtu de cette qualité.[130]

The quotation indicates that in order to arrive at this conclusion, implicit recognition of the ICRC's personality by states was significant. The argument in legal doctrine therefore is that the ICRC possesses international personality because states have tacitly recognized it as an international person.[131] It was not the ICRC's effective influence in international

relating to the Protection of Victims of Non-International Armed Conflicts (Protocol II), 8 June 1977, 1125 UNTS 610.

[128] GA Resolution 45/6 of 16 October 1990 (adopted by consensus).

[129] See Reuter, Paul, 'La Personnalité Juridique Internationale du Comité International de la Croix-Rouge' in Christophe Swinarski (ed.), *Études et Essais sur le Droit International Humanitaire et sur les Principes de la Croix-Rouge en l'Honneur de Jean Pictet* (Geneva and La Haye: Martinus Nijhoff, 1984), 783–91, at 786.

[130] Dominicé, Christian, 'La Personnalité Juridique Internationale du CICR' in Christophe Swinarski (ed.), *Études et Essais sur le Droit International Humanitaire et sur les Principes de la Croix-Rouge en l'Honneur de Jean Pictet* (Geneva and The Hague: Martinus Nijhoff, 1984), 663–73, at 672.

[131] See also Bugnion, François, *Le Comité International de la Croix-Rouge et la Protection des Victimes de la Guerre*, 2nd edition (Geneva: Comité International de la Croix-Rouge, 2000), 1121–8; Crawford, *Creation of States*, 43–4; Ipsen, *Völkerrecht*, 104 (by implication); and Reuter, 'Comité International de la Croix-Rouge', at 786 (by implication and with some ambiguous aspects).

relations that was decisive, but rather that the relevant provisions of the Geneva Conventions and the agreements concluded by the ICRC indicated that states must have recognized the ICRC as an international person by implication. This view rests on the recognition conception of international personality, for it emphasizes the role of states as the administrators of international personality through the process of recognition.

These doctrinal views on the ICRC's legal status became relevant in practice when a former ICRC interpreter volunteered to give evidence before the ICTY in *Prosecutor* v. *Simic et al.* on behalf of the Prosecutor's Office. After the ICRC had voiced its concern about such disclosure of information obtained by virtue of working for the ICRC, the Prosecutor filed an *ex parte* motion pursuant to Article 73 of the ICTY Rules of Procedure and Evidence and requested the Trial Chamber to rule on whether the former ICRC employee could be called as a witness. The ICRC was granted permission to appear before the Chamber and to make submissions as *amicus curiae* pursuant to Article 74 of the ICTY Rules. In its submission and the attached expert opinions, the ICRC in essence argued that it had a right under international law to confidentiality which entitled it to prevent disclosure of information by former employees.[132] The Prosecutor disputed that such an international right of the ICRC existed.[133]

In order to rule on this dispute, the ICTY Trial Chamber first found it necessary to address the legal status of the ICRC, which was, however, not disputed by the parties. It declared: 'It is widely acknowledged that the ICRC, an independent humanitarian organization, enjoys a special status in international law, based on the mandate conferred upon it by the international community. The Trial Chamber notes that the functions and tasks of the ICRC are directly derived from international law, that is, the Geneva Conventions and Additional Protocols.'[134] In a footnote to this statement, the Chamber specified: 'It is generally acknowledged that the ICRC, although a private organization under Swiss law, has an international legal personality ...'[135] By implication, it followed for the

[132] *Prosecutor* v. *Simic et al.*, paras 44–5. The submission of the ICRC is presented in more detail by Jeannet, Stéphane, 'Recognition of the ICRC's Long-standing Rule of Confidentiality – An Important Decision by the International Criminal Tribunal for the Former Yugoslavia', *International Review of the Red Cross* (2000), 403–25, at 406–8.
[133] *Prosecutor v. Simic et al.*, para. 45. [134] Ibid., para. 46. [135] Ibid., para. 46 n. 9.

Chamber that the ICRC, as an international person, was capable of possessing international rights.[136] The question was then whether there existed an international rule that entitled the ICRC to prevent disclosure of information. The Chamber argued that a functional interpretation of the relevant provisions of the Geneva Conventions and the Additional Protocols led to the conclusion that there existed such a conventional obligation for the parties to the agreements and a corresponding right of the ICRC opposable towards these parties.[137] Observing that at the time 188 states had ratified the Geneva Conventions, and analysing state practice towards the ICRC more widely, the Chamber concluded that 'the ICRC has a right under customary international law to non-disclosure of the Information'.[138] Accordingly, the Trial Chamber ruled that the Prosecutor of the ICTY was not to be permitted to call the former ICRC employee as a witness.

The Trial Chamber established the ICRC's international personality without much elaboration. But its recourse to the general consensus in doctrine and the consequences it attached to personality sufficiently indicate that it applied the recognition conception of international personality. As regards the recourse to the doctrinal consensus, it has already been pointed out by writers that legal doctrine widely understood the ICRC as an international person because, in their opinion, it had been recognized as such by states. In essence, this was also the argument put forward in the submission by the ICRC.[139] Concerning the consequences the Chamber derived from personality, it conceived the ICRC capable of possessing direct international rights because of its status as an international person: the Chamber first established the ICRC's personality in international law before examining whether it had the specific international right to confidentiality. This is in conformity with the recognition conception, which understands international personality as a precondition for having international rights.

[136] This can be inferred to some extent from ibid., para. 72. In general, it follows from the logical structure of the decision.

[137] Ibid., paras 72–3.

[138] Ibid., para. 74. Interestingly, Article 73 of the ICC Rules of Procedure and Evidence adopted in 2002 declares information obtained by the ICRC as privileged, except where the ICRC does not object to disclosure after a consultation process or has otherwise waived its privilege. This provision might be a consequence of the ICTY decision in *Prosecutor* v. *Simic et al.*

[139] See Jeannet, 'ICRC's Long-standing Rule of Confidentiality', at 410 n. 10.

The Holy See and the Order of Malta as international persons

In most modern international law textbooks, the Holy See and the Sovereign Order of Malta are considered established subjects of international law.[140] There usually is not much further elaboration on the topic. But international personality of these two non-state entities has not always been certain. In particular with regard to the Holy See, there has been some debate and indeed controversy about its exact international legal status, especially in the period between 1870 and 1929 when there was no papal state.[141] It has only gradually been established in practice and in doctrine that the Holy See is an international person in its own right, that is, has an international legal status apart from being the permanent government of a state. The reasoning thereby applied corresponds with the recognition conception of international personality. In a similar vein, the international personality of the Sovereign Order of Malta is today accepted in doctrine and practice.

The Holy See is the central organ of the Catholic Church consisting of the Pope, the College of Cardinals and administrative departments.[142] Until 1870, the Pope had also been the monarch of the Papal States, independent states including Rome in the centre of a disunited Italy. Being the permanent head of state of an acknowledged international person, the Pope had received and sent diplomatic envoys, had participated at conferences, entered into treaties and had generally been treated in international affairs like any other monarch of a European state. The Holy See's international status therefore was not an issue. Yet, in the final stages of the *Risorgimento*, the Papal States including Rome were occupied by Italian troops and annexed by the now unifying state of Italy. The Papal States consequently ceased to exist in 1870. With regard to the Pope's position, the Italian government declared in an official statement of 18 October 1870, aimed at appeasing the other Catholic powers of Europe, that it would respect the Holy See's special status and grant it immunities and privileges; to this end, Italy enacted the so-called Law of Guarantees of 13 May 1871. However, such domestic law provisions could not conceal that the Pope had lost his temporal powers and subsequently could only exercise spiritual leadership. The Pope thus opposed such treatment by the Italian authorities and considered himself

[140] See e.g. Brownlie, *Principles*, 63–4; Ipsen, *Völkerrecht*, 101–5.

[141] See Verzijl, *International Law in Historical Perspective (II)*, 299, and the overview provided by Crawford, *Creation of States*, 221 n. 89.

[142] For convenience, the Holy See and the Pope are hereafter treated as synonyms.

a prisoner in the Vatican for the following 60 years.[143] A settlement of the so-called 'Roman Question' was finally achieved in 1929 with the conclusion of the Lateran Treaty between the Holy See and Italy.[144] According to the treaty, Italy acknowledged the sovereignty of the Holy See in international relations[145] and recognized the State of the Vatican City of which the Pope was the sovereign.[146] As a consequence of the Lateran Treaty, the Holy See again became the permanent government of a state in 1929; that Vatican City is a state in international law and as such an international person was acknowledged early on and is the dominant view today, despite certain peculiarities of Vatican City concerning size of population and territory as well as type of government.[147]

The major issue when dealing with the Holy See's international personality is whether it possesses international legal status apart from being the government of a state (Papal States until 1870, Vatican City since 1929). Of course, the matter was especially relevant in the period between 1870 and 1929 when there was no state of which the Pope was the sovereign. But the issue remains pertinent even today whenever international actions of the Pope have to be dealt with: have such actions to be attributed to Vatican City or to the Holy See itself? When the question of separate international legal status of the Holy See first arose between

[143] See e.g. Giacometti, Zaccharia, 'Zur Lösung der Römischen Frage', *Zeitschrift für die gesamte Staatswissenschaft*, 90 (1931), 8–50, at 19.

[144] Treaty between the Vatican and Italy, 11 February 1929, AJIL Supp., 23 (1929), 187–195.

[145] Article 2: 'Italy recognizes the sovereignty of the Holy See in the field of international relations as an attribute that pertains to the very nature of the Holy See, in conformity with its traditions and with the demands of its mission in the world.'

[146] Article 26: 'Italy . . . recognizes the State of the Vatican under the sovereignty of the Supreme Pontiff.' In turn, the Holy See recognized Italy and declared the 'Roman Question' settled: 'The Holy See declares the "Roman Question" definitively and irrevocably settled and, therefore, eliminated; and recognizes the Kingdom of Italy under the dynasty of the House of Savoy with Rome as the Capital of the Italian State.'

[147] Anzilotti, Dionisio, 'La condizione giuridica internazionale della Santa Sede in seguito agli accordi del Laterano', Rdi, 9 (1929), 165–76, at 168; Diena, Giulio, 'La Sante Sede e il diritto internazionale dopo gli accordi Lateranensi dell'11 febbraio 1929', Rdi, 9 (1929), 177–87, at 180; v.d. Heydte, Friedrich August Freiherr, 'Die Stellung und Funktion des Heiligen Stuhls im heutigen Völkerrecht', *Österreichische ZöR*, II (1950), 572–86, at 572; Kunz, Josef L., 'The Status of the Holy See in International Law', AJIL, 46 (1952), 308–14, at 309. See more recently Crawford, *Creation of States*, 225; Jennings and Watts, *Oppenheim's International Law*, 328; Verzijl, *International Law in Historical Perspective (II)*, 300; Ipsen, *Völkerrecht*, 102. Doubtful: Brownlie, *Principles*, 63–4. Against: Quadri, Rolando, *Diritto Internazionale Pubblico*, 4th edition (Palermo: Priulla, 1963), 430; Giacometti, 'Römische Frage', at 38–42; Rousseau, *Droit International Public*, 364–5.

1870 and 1929, the issue was mainly debated along the lines of the states-only and the recognition conception of international personality: whereas Oppenheim did not consider the Holy See an international person but only assigned 'a *quasi*-international position' to it,[148] Strupp affirmed the Holy See's international personality because in his opinion several states had tacitly recognized the Pope as a subject of international law through continuing diplomatic relations even after the Papal States had ceased to exist.[149] The latter view, adjusted to the fact that now again there is a papal state, is the position held in doctrine today and is cautiously summarized by Ian Brownlie:

> . . . difficult to solve is the question of the personality of the Holy See as a religious organ apart from its territorial base in the Vatican City. It would seem that the personality of political and religious institutions of this type can only be relative to those states prepared to enter into relationships with such institutions on the international plane.[150]

In this dominant line of reasoning, it is argued that states have recognized the Holy See as a separate international person by entering into a variety of multilateral or bilateral treaties with it (and not with Vatican City),[151] and through other incidents of diplomatic interaction. Strictly following the recognition conception, the Holy See's international personality is then only relative, that is only opposable to those states that have recognized the Pope as an international person.[152]

148 Oppenheim, Lassa, *International Law: A Treatise*, 3rd edition (London: Longmans, Green, and Co., 1920), §106 (p. 185, esp. n. 1). See also Heilborn, *System des Völkerrechts*, 194–211, esp. 201.

149 Strupp, *Grundzüge*, 25. Ambiguous: Cavaglieri, 'Soggetti', at 29–30. Interestingly, even Anzilotti came round (when adjusting his conception of international personality more widely) to regard the Holy See as an international person (see Anzilotti, Dionisio, *Lehrbuch des Völkerrechts*, translation of the 3rd edition (Berlin and Leipzig: Walter de Gruyter, 1929), 112).

150 Brownlie, *Principles*, 64. See also Rousseau, *Droit International Public*, 357; Crawford, *Creation of States*, 227. For earlier articulations see Kunz, 'Status of the Holy See', at 309–13; Giacometti, 'Römische Frage', at 42; v.d. Heydte, 'Stellung des Heiligen Stuhls', at 584–5 (though with unusual reasoning); Anzilotti, *Völkerrecht*, 111–12; Anzilotti, 'Santa Sede', at 167–8 (by implication); Diena, 'Santa Sede', at 187; Quadri, *Diritto Internazionale*, 429–30 (albeit with ambiguous reasoning concerning the role of recognition). Against a separate personality: Jennings and Watts, *Oppenheim's International Law*, 328; Verzijl, *International Law in Historical Perspective (II)*, 299–300. For separate personality, but applying the actor conception: Balladore Pallieri, Giorgio, *Diritto Internazionale Pubblico*, 5th edition, (Milan: Giuffré, 1948), 86–7.

151 See an overview of such treaties in Crawford, *Creation of States*, 227–9.

152 See also Brownlie, *Principles*, 64.

According to doctrine, there hence exist two international persons today: the state of Vatican City and the Holy See as a religious entity. Depending on the particular purposes the Pope pursues in a certain international legal context, he acts as the head of government of Vatican City or as the religious leader of the Holy See.[153] This view of dual personality also found resonance in practice when the Supreme Court of the Philippines, although rather evasively, declared in a case concerning sovereign immunity:

> Some writers even suggested that the [Lateran] treaty created two international persons – The Holy See and Vatican City. . . . Inasmuch as the Pope prefers to conduct foreign relations and enter into transactions as The Holy See and not in the name of Vatican City, one can conclude that in the Pope's own view, it is The Holy See that is the international person. The Republic of Indonesia has accorded The Holy See the status of a foreign sovereign. The Holy See, through its Ambassador . . . has had diplomatic representations with the Philippine Government since 1957. This appears to be the universal practice in international relations.[154]

The Holy See's status as an international person in its own right is therefore established as far as it is recognized by states through incidents of diplomatic contact. This is a manifestation of the recognition conception of international personality: the Holy See is an international person in its own right because it is recognized as such by states.

In a similar context, the Sovereign Order of St John of Jerusalem, of Rhodes and of Malta (known as the Order of Malta) is generally accepted as possessing international personality.[155] Admitted by the Pope as a religious order in 1113, the Order of Malta initially supported crusaders and pilgrims to Palestine.[156] Subsequently, the Order exercised sovereignty over the islands of Rhodes (1310–1522) and Malta (1530–1798). After having been coerced to cede sovereignty over Malta to Napoleon in 1798, the Order took refuge in Rome where it has been officially seated

[153] However, it is doubtful whether the practice of the Holy See is consistent in this respect (see Crawford, *Creation of States*, 228). In any event, it seems that the Pope has a high degree of discretion in determining whether he acts on behalf of Vatican City or on behalf of the Holy See.

[154] *The Holy See* v. *Starbright Sales Enterprises Inc.* (Philippines Supreme Court, 1994), 102 ILR 163, at 169–70.

[155] Ipsen, *Völkerrecht*, 105; Jennings and Watts, *Oppenheim's International Law*, 329 n. 7, and Crawford, *Creation of States*, 231.

[156] See for general and historical information Breycha-Vauthier, Arthur C. and Michael Potulicki, 'The Order of St. John in International Law: A Forerunner of the Red Cross', AJIL, 48 (1954), 554–63, at 554–6.

since 1834. Like the Holy See, the Order of Malta is granted special status in Italy by virtue of Italian laws of 1884 and 1929. Today the Order is mainly dedicated to providing medical services in its function as a relief organization. Since 1994, it has had observer status at the General Assembly of the UN.[157] Notwithstanding its loss of territorial sovereignty, the Order of Malta is still regarded as an international person. The reason put forward is that the Order of Malta 'exchanges envoys with, or is otherwise recognized by, more than eighty states'.[158] This view has been confirmed by Italian courts having had to deal with the legal nature of the Order in various cases: 'As the jurisprudence of this Supreme Court has consistently held in a settled series of cases, the Sovereign Military Order of Malta is a sovereign subject of international law, recognized as such by the other subjects of the international community . . .'[159] Such statements correspond with the recognition conception of international personality: the Order of Malta is an international person – despite it clearly not being a state or the sovereign of a state – because states have recognized it as such.

The Texaco/Calasiatic v. Libya *award*

In *Texaco/Calasiatic v. Libya*, sole arbitrator René-Jean Dupuy declared two American companies international persons for the purposes of oil concession contracts concluded with Libya.[160] The reasoning applied in the memorable award represents a manifestation of the recognition conception of international personality. The case is regularly invoked today in matters concerning the role of private entities in international law.[161] However, in particular the statements on international personality have attracted strong criticism in doctrine and the award's

157 GA Resolution 48/265 of 24 August 1994.

158 Crawford, *Creation of States*, 231. See also Jennings and Watts, *Oppenheim's International Law*, 329 n. 7; Breycha-Vauthier and Potulicki, 'Order of St. John', at 558.

159 *Ministry of Finance* v. *Association of Italian Knights of the Order of Malta* (Italy, Court of Cassation, 1978), 65 ILR 320, at 323. See also *Nanni and Others* v. *Pace and the Sovereign Order of Malta* (Italy, Court of Cassation, 1935), 8 Annual Digest and Reports of Public International Law Cases (ILR) 2, at 4–6.

160 *Texaco Overseas Petroleum Company and California Asiatic Oil Company* v. *The Government of the Libyan Arab Republic* (Award on the Merits, Sole Arbitrator Dupuy, 1977), 53 ILR 422, paras 46–8 (pp. 457–9). The original French version of the award was published in JDI, 104 (1977), 350–389.

161 See e.g. Spiermann, *International Legal Argument in the PCIJ*, 79 n. 1, and Orakhelashvili, 'Position of the Individual', at 259.

reasoning certainly does not represent the dominant position in international law today.[162]

The case arose out of the nationalization by the Libyan government of certain assets held by Texaco Overseas Petroleum Company ('Texaco') and California Asiatic Oil Company ('Calasiatic'). The assets were related to oil concessions concluded between the two American companies and Libya from 1955 to 1968. The concessions stated that 'the contractual rights expressly created by this concession shall not be altered except by mutual consent of the parties'.[163] Notwithstanding this provision, in September 1973 the Libyan Revolutionary Command Council enacted Law No. 66 according to which 51 per cent of Texaco's and Calasiatic's assets relating to the concessions were nationalized. The two companies promptly notified the Libyan authorities that they intended to submit the dispute to arbitration pursuant to Clause 28 of the concessions. The Libyan government, however, did not respond to the notice and, with yet another Decree of Nationalization in February 1974, nationalized the remaining assets relating to the oil concessions. As Libya continued to ignore Texaco's and Calasiatic's efforts to seek arbitration on both incidents of nationalization, the President of the ICJ, at the request of the two companies and in accordance with Clause 28 of the concessions, finally appointed Professor René-Jean Dupuy as the sole arbitrator to consider the two disputes. The Libyan government refused to take part in the proceedings except to raise jurisdictional objections in a letter to the President of the ICJ. Sole arbitrator Dupuy considered these objections in a preliminary award and concluded that he had jurisdiction to hear and to decide the matter.[164]

On the merits, the sole arbitrator first ruled that the concessions concluded between the parties between 1955 and 1968 were indeed contracts.[165] He then turned to the question of the law applicable to these contracts. In Clause 28 of the concessions, the parties had stated the following choice of law: 'This concession shall be governed by and interpreted in accordance with the principles of the law of Libya common to the principles of international law and in the absence of such common principles by and in accordance with the general principles of

[162] See e.g. Brownlie, *Principles*, 65 and 524–5.

[163] *Texaco/Calasiatic* v. *Libya* (Merits), para. 3 (p. 423).

[164] *Texaco/Calasiatic* v. *Libya* (Preliminary Award on Jurisdiction, Sole Arbitrator Dupuy, 1975), 53 ILR 389.

[165] *Texaco/Calasiatic* v. *Libya* (Merits), paras 19–21 (pp. 438–41).

law, including such of those principles as may have been applied by international tribunals.'[166] Sole arbitrator Dupuy scrutinized two aspects with regard to this choice of law clause: first, he examined whether the parties had the right to choose the law that was to govern their contract; second, after declaring the choice of law permissible, he turned to the meaning of the clause itself. As concerns the suitability of a choice of law clause in a state contract, Professor Dupuy declared that the legal basis on which such an examination had to be based was international law itself because this was the legal order from which the contract derived its binding force (which was to be distinguished from the legal order governing the contract).[167] According to the sole arbitrator, international law supported the principle of autonomy of the will and the parties were therefore free to choose the law governing the contract.[168] In his view, this finding was not put into serious doubt by the *Serbian Loans* dictum when the PCIJ had declared that 'any contract which is not a contract between States in their capacity as subjects of international law is based on the municipal law of some country'.[169] According to Dupuy, the statement was sufficiently open-ended so as not to preclude the freedom of the parties to choose the proper law of a state contract; and in any event, in the sole arbitrator's view international law had evolved considerably since the *Serbian Loans* case and the principle of the autonomy of the will was now firmly established in doctrine and practice.[170] He thus concluded that the choice of law clause was permissible.

Professor Dupuy then proceeded to interpret the choice of law clause in order to decide which legal system actually governed the contract.[171] His interpretation involved several aspects not directly addressed in the clause itself. In this sense, three factors were examined which led to the application of international law: first, the reference to general principles of law;[172] second, the submission of disputes arising out of the contractual relations to international arbitration;[173] and third, the fact that the contracts represented 'economic development agreements'.[174] This approach has attracted considerable criticism in doctrine because it was believed to neglect the intention of the parties as regards the

[166] Ibid., para. 23 (p. 442). [167] Ibid., para. 26 (pp. 442–3). [168] Ibid., para. 35 (p. 450).

[169] *Case Concerning the Payments of Various Serbian Loans Issued in France* (Judgment), 1929 PCIJ Series A No. 20, at 41. See the analysis of the statement in the section dealing with legal manifestations of the states-only conception of international personality.

[170] *Texaco/Calasiatic* v. *Libya* (Merits), paras 27–9 (pp. 443–5).

[171] Ibid., para. 36 (p. 450). [172] Ibid., paras 41–3 (pp. 452–4).

[173] Ibid., para. 44 (pp. 454–5). [174] Ibid., para. 45 (pp. 455–7).

applicable law.[175] However, a careful reading of the award seems to suggest that the sole arbitrator merely used these factors to interpret the rather complex choice of law clause and did not consider them as determining the applicable law independently of the intention of the parties.[176] In any event, for the present purposes it is important that Dupuy arrived at the conclusion that international law was to a considerable extent the proper law of contract.

Having established international law as the proper law of contract, the sole arbitrator continued by examining the consequences and exact scope of this finding.[177] It was in this context that Professor Dupuy found it necessary to refer to the concept of international personality. By referring to the ICJ's Advisory Opinion in *Reparation for Injuries* and paraphrasing it for the purposes of a state contract, he declared:

> In other words, stating that a contract between a State and a private person falls within the international legal order means that for the purposes of interpretation and performance of the contract, it should be recognized that a private contracting party has specific international capacities. But, unlike a State, the private person has only a limited capacity and his quality as a subject of international law does enable him only to invoke, in the field of international law, the rights which he derives from the contract.[178]

In the sole arbitrator's view, then, the choice of international law as the proper law of contract indicated that Texaco and Calasiatic were bestowed with limited international personality for the purposes of the contract. For it was 'established today that legal international capacity is not solely attributable to a State' and that although states were the 'original subjects of the international legal order' other subjects of international law could exist as 'assigned to specific purposes'.[179] Professor Dupuy further emphasized these statements by quoting from an article by Ignaz Seidl-Hohenveldern ('why should a State be prevented from

[175] See Rigaux, François, 'Des Dieux et des Héros: Réflexions sur une Sentence Arbitrale', *Revue Critique du Droit International Privé*, 67 (1978), 435–59, at 456–8, and Fatouros, A. A., 'International Law and the Internationalized Contract', AJIL, 74 (1980), 134–41, at 135–6. But see Lalive, Jean-Flavien, 'Un Grand Arbitrage Pétrolier Entre un Gouvernement et Deux Sociétés Privées Étrangères', JDI, 104 (1977), 319–49, at 337–8, who seems not to regard Dupuy's reasoning in determining the applicable law extraordinary at all.

[176] This also seems to be the position taken by Greenwood, Christopher, 'State Contracts in International Law – The Libyan Oil Arbitrations', BYIL, 53 (1982), 27–81, at 53.

[177] *Texaco/Calasiatic* v. *Libya* (Merits), para. 46 (p. 457).

[178] Ibid., para. 47 (p. 458).

[179] Ibid., para 47 (pp. 457–8).

recognizing its partner to such a contract as a subject of international law?')[180] and from F. V. Garcìa Amador's Fourth report on State responsibility ('In the matter of contracts, the international personality of the individual depends on the recognition granted to them by the State in its legal relations with him').[181] The sole arbitrator thus considered Texaco and Calasiatic as international persons for the purposes of the contract because they were recognized as such by Libya. Importantly, though not expressly stated, it followed for Dupuy that the applicable principles of public international law were to be directly applied to the state contract, as opposed to an application by mere analogy.[182] Though Texaco and Calasiatic were not states and the contract not a treaty, as he readily clarified,[183] there nevertheless existed for the purposes of the contract a relationship between international persons. In consequence, the sole arbitrator relied heavily on international law,[184] in particular on the principle *pacta sunt servanda*, when subsequently examining whether Libya had breached the concession contracts and whether there was any accepted justification for such a breach.[185] Sole arbitrator Dupuy finally concluded that Libya had breached the concessions without sufficient justification in international law and ordered *restitutio in integrum* on behalf of the two American companies.[186]

The reasoning employed in *Texaco/Calasiatic* v. *Libya* represents a considered manifestation of the recognition conception of international personality. Sole arbitrator Dupuy recalled the conception's essential principle, in part by referring to the *Reparation for Injuries* Advisory Opinion, that states were the original persons in international law competent to assign personality to other entities. Applying this principle, he interpreted the fact that Libya had entered into a contractual relationship with American companies and had designated international law as the proper law of contract as an act of recognition by Libya of Texaco's and Calasiatic's international personality. It therefore seems to be settled – also in light of the references used by the sole arbitrator – that the award

180 Ibid., para. 48 (p. 458). 181 Ibid., para. 48 (p. 459).

182 See also Von Mehren, Robert B. and Nicholas Kourides, 'International Arbitrations between States and Foreign Private Parties: The Libyan Nationalization Cases', AJIL, 75 (1981), 476–552, at 511–12, and Greenwood, 'Libyan Oil Arbitrations', at 44–5. For the distinction in general see Schwarzenberger, *Foreign Investments*, 5–6.

183 *Texaco/Calasiatic* v. *Libya* (Merits), para. 46 (p. 457).

184 See also Greenwood, 'Libyan Oil Arbitrations', at 47.

185 *Texaco/Calasiatic* v. *Libya* (Merits), para. 51 (pp. 461–2) and para. 53 (pp. 462–3) as well as the ensuing in-depth discussion at paras 54–91 (pp. 463–95).

186 Ibid., paras 97–109 (pp. 497–508).

intended to apply the recognition conception.[187] What is more doubtful is whether this was done in a consistent manner. For even if one accepts the possibility inherent in the recognition conception that the state party to an international contract can recognize the private party as a limited international person, there must be strong evidence for such an intention of the particular state. The presumption is always that there was no such recognition and that international law would only apply by analogy.[188] As had been the case with the applicable law, Dupuy has therefore been criticized for not having paid enough attention to the actual intentions of Libya.[189] This might be true. But at a level of principle, the sole arbitrator still intended to apply the recognition conception, although perhaps did not do so not in an entirely consistent manner.

The *Texaco/Calasiatic* v. *Libya* award has attracted much doctrinal comment, most of it critical.[190] Similarly, subsequent practice has in general followed neither Professor Dupuy's statements on international personality nor the direct application of international law to a state contract.[191] On the contrary, some more recent awards have stressed the basic difference between treaties (concluded among states as international persons and directly regulated by international law) and state contracts (concluded between a state and a private party and regulated by municipal law and possibly international law by way of analogy).[192] Yet the carefully written award by sole arbitrator Dupuy certainly has to be considered as one of the more important international legal texts inspiring the debate on the limits of international law in personal terms and settling certain other issues concerning state contracts. For example, the award, though not the first to mention it, definitely confirmed the

[187] By implication, this is also argued by Rigaux, 'Sentence arbitrale', at 444; Greenwood, 'Libyan Oil Arbitrations', at 44; Von Mehren and Kourides, 'Libyan Nationalization Cases', at 512.

[188] See the very clear statements by Schwarzenberger, *Foreign Investments*, 5–6, in this respect.

[189] See Greenwood, 'Libyan Oil Arbitrations', at 49. In a similar direction Rigaux, 'Sentence arbitrale', at 445, though the latter seems to reject the recognition conception itself, not its particular application by Dupuy.

[190] In addition to comments already cited, see also Brownlie, Ian, 'Legal Status of Natural Resources in International Law (Some Aspects)', RCADI, 162 (1979-I), 245–318, at 309, and Barberis, 'Personnalité Juridique', at 203.

[191] An exception is *Revere Copper and Brass, Inc.* v. *Overseas Private Investment Corporation* (Award, 1978), 56 ILR 258, at 271–2 and at 274–5 (with explicit reference to the reasoning of Sole Arbitrator Dupuy in *Texaco/Calsiatic* v. *Libya*).

[192] See e.g. *CAA and Vivendi Universal* v. *Argentina* (Decision on Annulment, 2002), 6 ICSID Reports 340, paras 96–8.

possibility of choice of international law as the law governing a state contract. However, unlike the reasoning employed by Professor Dupuy, subsequent practice has not regarded recognition of the private party's international personality as a necessary or even possible corollary of such a choice. In this respect, *Texaco/Calasiatic* v. *Libya* has not been followed in the context of subsequent international commercial arbitration.

7

The individualistic conception

The individualistic conception of international personality asserts that, as a matter of fundamental legal principle, the individual human being is an international person and, as such, has certain basic international rights and duties. The conception as presented here was forcefully put forward by Hersch Lauterpacht before and immediately after World War II.[1] However, Lauterpacht was neither the only nor the first advocate of an individualistic conception of international personality in the twentieth century. Various forms of this conception had been formulated earlier in the interwar period by distinguished international lawyers, including Georges Scelle,[2] Hugo Krabbe,[3] James Leslie Brierly,[4] Nicolas Politis,[5] Maurice Bourquin[6] and Alejandro Alvarez.[7] The common denominator of all these theories is that the status of the individual as a subject of international law does not depend on explicit or implicit expression of state will to that effect, but exists a priori. The lines of reasoning employed to arrive at this conclusion are, however, rather

[1] See e.g. Lauterpacht, Hersch, 'The Subjects of the Law of Nations' in Elihu Lauterpacht (ed.), *International Law: Being the Collected Papers of Hersch Lauterpacht* (Cambridge University Press, 1975) (originally published 1947), 487–533, at 520–1 and 526–7.

[2] Scelle, Georges, *Précis de Droit des Gens* (Paris: Recueil Sirey, 1932), 42 ('les individus seuls sont sujets de droit en droit international public').

[3] Krabbe, Hugo, *Die moderne Staatsidee*, 2nd edition (The Hague: Martinus Nijhoff, 1919), 275–6 ('Subjekte des internationalen Rechts sind die Menschen').

[4] Brierly, James Leslie, 'Règles Générales du Droit de la Paix', RCADI, 58 (1936-IV), 1–242, at 47 ('en dernière analyse, seuls les individus sont susceptibles d'être sujets de ce droit-là [droit international]').

[5] Politis, Nicolas, *Les Nouvelles Tendances du Droit International* (Paris: Librarie Hachette, 1927), 55–93 (on the emergence of international righs) and 94–137 (on international criminal law).

[6] Bourquin, Maurice, 'Règles Générales du Droit de la Paix', RCADI, 35 (1931-I), 5–232, at 42–7 (forcefully denouncing the states-only proposition).

[7] Alvarez, Alejandro, *La Codification du Droit International: Ses Tendances – Ses Bases* (Paris: A. Pedone, 1912), 83–4 (cautiously affirming individual rights).

diverse, making use of sociological,[8] psychological[9] and natural law[10] approaches, as are the consequences attached to the individualistic presumption, with some, most notably Scelle, arguing that states do not exist and that only individuals can be international persons.[11] It was then Hersch Lauterpacht, it is submitted, who encapsulated and sometimes tempered (e.g. by reaffirming the reality of states)[12] the different lines of reasoning into one coherent theory of the individual's international personality. It was his theory that was most influential in subsequent legal practice, particularly in international criminal law and human rights law.[13] Therefore, in this book, ideas on the individual's international legal status put forward earlier in the context of the interwar period are considered, where appropriate, as part of the origins of the individualistic conception of international personality.[14] The conception itself is, however, presented as formulated by Hersch Lauterpacht.

The individualistic conception has its origins in two principal assumptions, the combination of which leads to its essential claim of the individual as an a priori international person having certain basic rights and duties: the first is the view that the state is a functional entity governed by individuals who are subject to the rule of law in the interest of those being governed; the second is the notion of international law as consisting of fundamental principles of law being superior to expressions of state will (constitutional principles of *ius cogens* character). It is important to note that none of these assumptions alone leads to the individualistic conception, but only their combination. For example, Alfred Verdross was one of the originators of the second assumption regarding constitutional principles in international law, but he did not advocate the individualistic conception of international personality for he did not share the functional view of the state.[15]

8 Foremost Scelle, Politis, and Alvarez. But see for natural law elements of this approach Truyol y Serra, 'Doctrines du Droit des Gens', at 38 and 203.

9 Foremost Krabbe. 10 Foremost Brierly and Bourquin. 11 Scelle, *Précis*, 42.

12 See e.g. Lauterpacht, 'Subjects', at 521.

13 On a more general level not limited to international personality, a similar argument in favour of Lauterpacht's lasting influence in contrast to other important international lawyers from the interwar period is put forward by Koskenniemi, *Gentle Civilizer*, 357.

14 For the still inspirational character of these ideas see e.g. Jouannet, Emmanuelle, 'L'Idée de Communauté Humaine à la Croisée de la Communauté des États et de la Communauté Mondiale', *Archives de Philosophie du droit*, 47 (2003), 191–232, esp. at 207–8.

15 See e.g. Verdross, *Verfassung*, 156–63, where individuals are considered only as exceptional subjects of international law where states have agreed on certain individual rights.

In part due to Lauterpacht's personal involvement, the most memorable legal manifestation of the individualistic conception of international personality are the Nuremberg judgments and the developments in international criminal law following from them. The conception has recently also been employed in litigation against private actors for violations of international human rights law. Human rights law can also more generally be understood as manifesting the individualistic conception. In today's doctrine, the conception is prominently promoted by Antônio Augusto Cançado Trindade[16] and, less resolutely, by Antonio Cassese.[17]

Basic propositions

According to the individualistic conception as formulated by Hersch Lauterpacht, the individual human being is the ultimate international person and in that function is capable of holding international rights and being subjected to international duties:

> There is no rule of international law which precludes individuals and bodies other than States from acquiring directly rights under customary or conventional international law and, to that extent, becoming subjects of the Law of Nations. . . . The conferment of such rights may cover either particular rights or the so-called fundamental rights of the individual in general. With regard to the latter, there is room for the view that having regard to the inherent purposes of international law, of which the individual is the ultimate unit, he is in that capacity a subject of international law. . . . Similar considerations apply to the question of subjects of duties imposed by international law. . . . there has been an increasing realization that the direct subjection of the individual to the rule of international law is an essential condition of the strengthening of the ethical basis of international law . . .[18]

The individualistic conception is directed against what is understood to be the positivist doctrine of international personality. By implication, this means that both the states-only conception and the recognition conception of international personality are rejected.[19] The states-only

[16] Cançado Trindade, Antônio Augusto, 'International Law for Humankind: Towards a New Jus Gentium: General Course on Public International Law', RCADI, 316–17 (2005), 9–440 (Vol. 316) and 9–312 (Vol. 317), at 252–84 (Vol. 316).

[17] Cassese, *International Law*, 165–6. For a similar, but somewhat ambiguous, statement see Mosler, 'Subjects', at 726.

[18] Lauterpacht, 'Subjects', at 526–7.

[19] Lauterpacht, Hersch, *International Law and Human Rights* (London: Stevens, 1950), 6–9. See also Lauterpacht, 'Subjects', at 488–91 (identical formulation).

conception is criticized for its primarily Hegelian idea of statehood leading it to advocate a view of international personality clearly inconsistent with international practice.[20] The recognition conception (though praised for at least accepting the possibility of non-state entities becoming international persons)[21] is disapproved of for requiring an act of recognition by states in the case of individuals becoming international persons. Such requirement is understood as being strongly linked to the ill-conceived positivist view of accepting only state will as a source of international law, a view that ignores the moral basis of international law.[22] In sum, the individualistic conception criticizes the notion of statehood and the idea of the sources of law present in the states-only and the recognition conception of international personality.

The primarily Hegelian notion of statehood employed in the positivist doctrine is rejected by the individualistic conception of international personality because it essentially misconceives the nature of the state and its relation to individuals. The state is not to be understood as a 'mystical entity',[23] an 'anthropomorphic or organic conception'[24] solely able to bring the individual human being into its full moral existence.[25] The state simply represents a corporate entity created by individuals[26] for pursuing their own interests.[27] Accordingly, there is no higher reason for the existence of the state than to safeguard the interests and the well-being of those individuals

[20] Lauterpacht, Hersch, *Private Law Sources and Analogies of International Law* (London: Longmans, Green, and Co., 1927), 44, 49, and 74–5; Lauterpacht, Hersch, 'Spinoza and International Law' in Elihu Lauterpacht (ed.), *International Law: Being the Collected Papers of Hersch Lauterpacht* (Cambridge University Press, 1975) (originally published 1927), 366–84, at 381–3; Lauterpacht, *Human Rights*, 8–12.

[21] See the acknowledgment of Cavaglieri's and Strupp's work in this respect in Lauterpacht, *Analogies*, 77–8, and Lauterpacht, Hersch, 'Westlake and Present Day International Law' in Elihu Lauterpacht (ed.), *International Law: Being the Collected Papers of Hersch Lauterpacht* (Cambridge University Press, 1975) (originally published 1925), 385–403, at 389–90.

[22] Lauterpacht, *Human Rights*, 9. Lauterpacht, 'Subjects', at 491 (identical formulation).

[23] Lauterpacht, *Analogies*, 80.

[24] Lauterpacht, Hersch, 'The Grotian Tradition in International Law' in Elihu Lauterpacht (ed.), *International Law: Being the Collected Papers of Hersch Lauterpacht* (Cambridge University Press, 1975) (originally published 1946), 307–65, at 336.

[25] Lauterpacht, *Analogies*, 44.

[26] Lauterpacht, 'Spinoza', at 370 and 373 (by clear implication).

[27] Lauterpacht, 'Subjects', at 532; Lauterpacht, 'Grotian Tradition', at 336; Lauterpacht, *Analogies*, 72–3; Lauterpacht, *Human Rights*, 123. Lauterpacht, Hersch, 'International Law – The General Part' in Elihu Lauterpacht (ed.), *International Law: Being the Collected Papers of Hersch Lauterpacht* (Cambridge University Press, 1975) (not previously published), 1–178, at 31.

composing it.[28] With this view of the process through which states come into being, there are no grounds for considering states as special or even mystical bodies pursuing higher interests than other social groups or individuals: the state simply is a corporation representing certain interests of the individuals composing it and in particular is under a duty to preserve individual freedom.[29]

Four main consequences follow from this view of the state related to international legal personality. First, there can be no fundamental distinction between the interests states pursue internationally and the interests of the individuals composing them: international norms agreed on by states will in general be intended for strengthening the well-being of individuals in some form.[30] Accordingly, there is no merit in stipulating an 'impenetrable barrier' (as the states-only and the recognition conception do) between the domestic and the international sphere.[31] Moreover, with the essential similarity between state and individual interests the distinction between public law and private law also becomes less rigid: both are concerned with the same individual interests pursued by the same human beings and therefore there is no fundamental difference between the two branches of law.[32] Second, individuals might not entrust the state with safeguarding all their interests. They will consequently take part in the international sphere in order to engage in specific international transactions. Such transactions might be regulated by international law.[33] As a third consequence, the individualistic conception stresses the fact that state actions are always exercised by individual human beings.[34] As the state is not a mystical and impersonal body, but a corporation of individuals in which some of them are entrusted by the community to act on their behalf, these competent individuals are personally responsible for their actions and cannot hide behind the abstract entity of the state.[35] In principle, international responsibility can therefore be invoked not only against states, but also against individuals acting on behalf of the state.[36] Yet it is important to emphasize that

[28] Lauterpacht, 'Spinoza', at 374; Lauterpacht, 'Subjects', at 532; Lauterpacht, 'Westlake', at 398–9; Lauterpacht, *Human Rights*, 123.

[29] Lauterpacht, *Analogies*, 73; Lauterpacht, 'General Part', at 31; Lauterpacht, *Human Rights*, 69–70 and 123–4.

[30] Lauterpacht, 'Grotian Tradition', at 336; Lauterpacht, *Analogies*, 305–6.

[31] Lauterpacht, 'Subjects', at 532.

[32] Lauterpacht, *Analogies*, 72.

[33] Lauterpacht, *International Law*, §13a (pp. 20–1); Lauterpacht, 'Subjects', at 532; Lauterpacht, 'General Part', at 31; Lauterpacht, *Human Rights*, 68.

[34] Lauterpacht, *Analogies*, 72.

[35] Lauterpacht, 'Subjects', at 520–1.

[36] Lauterpacht, 'Westlake', at 402; Lauterpacht, 'General Part', at 148.

the individualistic conception as presented here does not postulate that individuals are the only subjects of international law.[37] It is agreed that states are corporate bodies having rights and duties under international law and that states, and not individuals, can become internationally responsible for not fulfilling normal obligations of treaties and customary international law (e.g. in commerce, finance, or international administration).[38] Fourth, with the state not being 'an end onto itself but the trustee of the welfare and of the final purpose of man',[39] individuals have certain fundamental rights a state and other individuals cannot interfere with.[40] There is hence, on the level of principle, a strong link between the individual having basic rights as well as duties and being a subject of international law: the justification of the international legal order, like any legal system, rests in protecting individual freedom and well-being. Hence, this law must necessarily address the individual in direct terms.[41]

As regards the sources of international law, the individualistic conception of international personality includes natural law principles in order to supplement international treaties and custom.[42] The inclusion of these principles is logically necessary for it is thought impossible to uphold the binding nature of international law without affirming at least that the basic rule *pacta sunt servanda* is independent of state will.[43] In addition, without natural law principles, there would be the threat of a *non liquet* in international law, that is, international judicial bodies might have to end proceedings brought before them without substantively ruling on the matter when treaties and custom provide no applicable rule.[44] Such a *non liquet* must be prohibited because it amounts to a denial of justice.[45] This fundamental legal principle is thought to find support in municipal legal systems, which regularly compel judges to hand down a decision in all matters in which jurisdiction is established, notwithstanding the absence of rules applicable to the dispute.[46] In international law, the individualistic conception contends, the principle of excluding a *non liquet* finds its

[37] Cf. Scelle, *Précis*, 42; Krabbe, *Moderne Staatsidee*, 275–6 (with some qualifications); Brierly, 'Règles Générales', at 47.

[38] Lauterpacht, 'Subjects', at 521. [39] Lauterpacht, *Human Rights*, 123–4.

[40] Ibid., 70–1, 91–2, 123–4. [41] Ibid., 69 and 71.

[42] Lauterpacht, 'Grotian Tradition', at 331–3; Lauterpacht, *Analogies*, 60–71; Lauterpacht, 'Westlake', at 393–4; Lauterpacht, Hersch, *The Function of Law in the International Community* (Oxford: The Clarendon Press, 1933), 66.

[43] Lauterpacht, *Analogies*, 54–9. [44] Lauterpacht, *Function of Law*, 51–69.

[45] Lauterpacht, *Analogies*, 68; Lauterpacht, *Function of Law*, 63.

[46] Lauterpacht, *Function of Law*, 60–3. Examples include Article 1 of the Swiss Civil Code and Article 4 of the French Civil Code.

most authoritative statement in the Statute of the PCIJ, its Article 38(3) authorizing the Court to apply 'general principles of law recognized by civilized nations'.[47] This provision is understood to endorse the view, also to be found in international arbitration practice,[48] that natural law is an accepted source of international law supplementing treaties and custom.[49] Importantly, the individualistic conception of international personality thus conceives natural law principles as consisting of general principles recognized by civilized nations; it does not postulate natural law as deriving from a particular theological or philosophical system, but regards the law of nature as synonymous with general principles to be found in municipal legal systems, a 'generalization of the legal experience of mankind'.[50] Though such experience is primarily to be found in municipal private law, there can also be instances where domestic public law can become pertinent.[51] In conclusion, the individualistic conception includes natural law as a source of international law in order to ensure international law's binding nature and the completeness of the legal system.

With the acknowledgement of general principles of law as an independent source of international law, it becomes possible for the individualistic conception of international personality to confer international legal status to entities without requiring express or tacit agreement by states.[52] With regard to international personality of individuals, there is now no need for an expression of state will because it is a general principle of law in the view of this conception that 'in relation to both rights and duties, the individual is the final subject of all law'.[53] Accordingly, the individual is a subject of international law irrespective of explicit or tacit recognition of this status by states. With this general presumption of individuals as international persons, a set of fundamental rights held by the individual are also seen as emanating from general principles of law.[54]

In sum, the individualistic conception of international personality puts forward two interrelated propositions:

[47] Lauterpacht, *Analogies*, 67–71; Lauterpacht, *Function of Law*, 66–7. The Article has been incorporated into Article 38(1)(c) ICJ Statute.

[48] Lauterpacht, *Analogies*, 60–2. [49] Lauterpacht, 'Grotian Tradition', at 332.

[50] Lauterpacht, 'General Part', 74–5; Lauterpacht, *Analogies*, 71; Lauterpacht, 'Grotian Tradition', at 332–3 (by implication).

[51] Lauterpacht, *Analogies*, 71.

[52] Lauterpacht, 'Subjects', at 491 and 532–3. See also Lauterpacht, *Human Rights*, 8–9.

[53] Lauterpacht, 'Subjects', 532; Lauterpacht, *Human Rights*, 69.

[54] Lauterpacht, *Human Rights*, 32–3; Lauterpacht, 'Subjects', at 514–5 (identical formulation). See also Lauterpacht, 'Grotian Tradition', at 354–8.

(1) The state is a corporation consisting of individuals, some of them being authorized to exercise public functions. The state is not a higher organic body having a special moral status. Correspondingly, there is no difference of principle between state and individual interests. The strict distinction between international and municipal law as well as between public and private law essentially disappears, too. On a level of fundamental principle, therefore, international law, like all law, can direct rights and duties towards individuals (be they acting on behalf of the state or in private matters) and entails basic rights and duties of the individual.
(2) The sources of international law include general principles of law. In result, international personality of the individual does not depend on expressions of state will (e.g. recognition), but is established through the general principle proclaiming individuals to be the ultimate addressees of all law. Certain fundamental international rights and duties are attached to the individual's status as an international person.

As concerns the relationship between the two propositions, the first one formulates a principle whereas the second one materializes it in the existing international legal system. This is so because it does not follow automatically from the particular view of the state advocated in the first proposition that individuals are international persons; it only formulates the principle that all law, including public law, is ultimately addressed to individual human beings and that, in principle, there are basic individual rights and duties. It then requires the second proposition accepting general legal principles as sources of international law to fully introduce a formal international legal status of the individual and to attach certain fundamental international rights and duties to it.

Origins of the basic propositions

Hersch Lauterpacht's lasting influence with respect to his conception of international personality is primarily due to his ability to encapsulate new ideas on statehood and law emerging in the broader European context.[55] It is therefore this European socio-political background in

[55] Lauterpacht himself regularly acknowledged the influence of, among others, Léon Duguit, Georges Scelle, François Gény, Hugo Krabbe, Alfred Verdross and Hans Kelsen in this respect (see e.g. Lauterpacht, *Analogies*, 58, 79 and 304–5; Lauterpacht, 'Westlake', at 393; Lauterpacht, 'Subjects', at 520 and 532; Lauterpacht, *Function of Law*, 61; Lauterpacht, *Human Rights*, 91–2).

the interwar period that provides the context for the individualistic conception of international personality. This context was characterized by a widespread reaction against state-centrism and legal positivism. However, it is important to emphasize that it is not this far-reaching anti-positivist reaction itself that provides the origins for the basic propositions of the individualistic conception, but only particular combinations of elements prevalent therein. Other views of the same developments generated different conceptions of international personality, as for example the formal conception formulated by Hans Kelsen and partly shared by Alfred Verdross.

Interwar Europe

Before entering the broader European context, it is useful to briefly review Hersch Lauterpacht's biography. Lauterpacht was born in 1897 in Eastern Galicia, at the time a part of the Austro-Hungarian Empire.[56] He started university in the regional centre Lwów, but moved to the University of Vienna in 1920. In Vienna, Lauterpacht studied law and political science, under the guidance of Hans Kelsen, among others.[57] After obtaining doctorates in both law and political science, Lauterpacht moved on to London in 1923.[58] In London, Lauterpacht enrolled in graduate studies in international law and built a lasting professional and personal relationship with his teacher, Arnold Duncan McNair, who was also the supervisor of his London dissertation *Private Law Sources and Analogies of International Law.* Lauterpacht subsequently obtained a position at the London School of Economics' Department of Political Science, which was at the time dominated by Harold J. Laski, a controversial academic and public figure who shared Lauterpacht's emerging critique of the traditional notion of state sovereignty.[59] In 1937, Lauterpacht was appointed to the Whewell Chair at the University of Cambridge. During his tenure as Whewell Professor, he published widely on international law issues, his most important contribution being his 1946 article on *The Grotian Tradition in International*

[56] The following biographical information is based on Koskenniemi, Martti, 'Hersch Lauterpacht (1897–1960)' in Jack Beatson and Reinhard Zimmermann (eds.), *Jurists Uprooted: German-Speaking Émigré Lawyers in Twentieth-Century Britain* (Oxford University Press, 2004), 603–61, and on the nearly identical Koskenniemi, *Gentle Civilizer*, 353–412.

[57] See also Kelsen, Hans, 'Tribute to Sir Hersch Lauterpacht', EJIL, 8 (1997), 309–10, at 309.

[58] See also ibid., at 309.

[59] Koskenniemi, 'Lauterpacht', at 612–14.

Law.[60] In addition to research, Lauterpacht was actively involved in advising the British government, perhaps most influentially on the legal basis of the Nuremberg trials, as a member of the British War Crimes Executive.[61] After World War II, Lauterpacht was one of the first international lawyers to deal with human rights in his *International Law and Human Rights*. Appointed to the ICJ after McNair's retirement from the bench in 1955, Lauterpacht could fully participate as a Judge in only ten cases brought before the Court. He died prematurely in 1960.

Given his biography, Lauterpacht was exposed to the Austro-Hungarian socio-political context in the first two decades of the twentieth century. This context was characterized by the retreat of the formerly dominant Austrian liberalism as a political and cultural force and its replacement by nationalism, socialism and anti-Semitism.[62] Austrian liberalism has been described as 'garden-variety Victorianism ... morally ... secure, righteous and repressive; politically, it was concerned for the rule of law, under which both individual rights and social order were subsumed. It was intellectually committed to the rule of the mind over the body and to a latter-day Voltairism: to social progress through science, education, and hard work.'[63] This 'Victorian' form of liberalism had offered the Jewish population of the multi-ethnic Empire 'emancipation, opportunity, and assimilation to modernity'; its demise and the ascendance of anti-liberal forces 'left the Jew a victim'.[64] It was therefore common in the Jewish community of early twentieth-century Vienna (a community Lauterpacht was actively involved in as the president of student organizations) to regard Austrian liberalism and its values as a cherished ideal for political and cultural rule: firm moral values, scientific analysis, and individual freedom under the rule of law were treasured components of a social order of the past that had to be re-established in the future.[65] It was this aim for a liberal reconstruction in parts of society that provided the particular socio-political context for Lauterpacht during his years in Vienna, an exposure that according to Martti Koskenniemi manifested itself in Lauterpacht's 'Victorian faith'

[60] See the account of Sir Elihu Lauterpacht of conversations with his father attached to Lauterpacht, 'Grotian Tradition', at 307.
[61] Crawford, 'International Law in Twentieth-Century England', at 698.
[62] See Schorske, Carl E., *Fin-de-Siècle Vienna: Politics and Culture* (New York: Alfred A. Knopf, 1980), 3–6.
[63] Ibid., 6. [64] Ibid., 118.
[65] This was also true for, among others, Theodor Herzl at the beginning of the Zionist movement (see ibid., 146–7).

in rationalism, individualism, cosmopolitanism and human goodness.[66] With this 'Victorian faith', Lauterpacht could not be too out of place in the British socio-political context following his move to London in 1923, although his arrival there was two decades after Queen Victoria's death and the domestic scene doubtless had changed to a considerable extent.[67] In any event, Lauterpacht himself regarded his own ideals associated with Austrian liberalism as compatible with his new context, and he primarily showed this by presenting liberal ideas as firmly established in British international legal thought and political philosophy.[68]

Lauterpacht's own Austrian liberalism may help to understand his alignment with new ideas on statehood and the role of the individual emerging in the broader European context. But to understand these ideas, one has to look more closely at the broader European situation in which they arose. A particularly fertile ground proved to be the French socio-political context at the turn of the twentieth century. In this environment, a far-reaching political and intellectual debate took place on the basis and the role of the state, similar in its intensity to discussions on statehood in Germany and Italy at the time.[69] However, contrary to the German and Italian context, the major issue in France was not the very existence of the state (which had gradually developed in France since the Middle Ages and was thought to be firmly established by the time of the debate),[70] but the legitimacy of a particular form of government, that is, the Third Republic (1870–1940).[71] The French Third Republic was characterized by an apparent paradox: on the one

[66] Koskenniemi, 'Lauterpacht', at 603–4. See also Koskenniemi, *Gentle Civilizer*, 359.

[67] The latter point is emphasized by Crawford, 'International Law in Twentieth-Century England', at 682.

[68] See in particular Lauterpacht, 'Westlake', at 400–3 (on John Westlake); Lauterpacht, *Analogies*, 23–9 (on British thought in general); Lauterpacht, 'Grotian Tradition', at 334 (on John Locke's view of the human person). More concerned with legal method, Lauterpacht also denied a fundamental difference between the Anglo-American and Continental approaches (according to his understanding) in Lauterpacht, Hersch, 'The so-called Anglo-American and Continental Schools of Thought in International Law' in Elihu Lauterpacht (ed.), *International Law: Being the Collected Papers of Hersch Lauterpacht* (Cambridge University Press, 1975) (originally published 1931), 452–83, esp. at 482. On this topic, see also Jenks, Wilfried C., 'Hersch Lauterpacht – The Scholar as Prophet', BYIL, 36 (1960), 1–103, at 1.

[69] Jones, H. S., *The French State in Question: Public Law and Political Argument in the Third Republic* (Cambridge University Press, 1993), 14–15.

[70] Price, Roger, *A Concise History of France*, 2nd edition (Cambridge University Press, 2005), 13.

[71] Jones, *French State in Question*, 14 (by implication).

hand, it showed severe institutional weaknesses and was impotent to address social problems arising in an only recently industrialized French society;[72] on the other hand, it could seriously endanger personal freedom, as had been emphasized by the infamous Dreyfus Affair.[73] Taken together, these two aspects contributed to the French 'crisis of the state': it was debated what functions the state should exercise in an industrial society and to what extent the state was allowed to interfere with personal matters. The so-called *Dreyfusards* thereby insisted on firm limits on state power in the interest of individual freedom.[74] In short, the legitimacy of the state (represented by the Third Republic) was put into doubt. This was also accompanied by an increasing awareness that a strictly positivist legal method focusing on expressions of state will could not offer answers to emerging social problems. All this took place against the broader background of French–German adversity. French resentment against Germany went back to France's humiliating defeat in the war of 1871[75] (leading to Germany's unification) and was reinforced by aggressive German policy leading to World War I. Both events, particularly the latter, were perceived in France to be closely linked to the German conception of statehood and law.[76] Similarly, the same conception was

72 See Price, *Concise History*, 178 and 229–35.

73 See Caron, François, *Geschichte Frankreichs Band 5: Frankreich im Zeitalter des Imperialismus 1851–1918* (Stuttgart: Deutsche Verlags-Anstalt, 1991), 467–71. In short, the affair concerned the conviction of Alfred Dreyfus, a French army officer of Jewish origin, for selling military secrets to Germany in 1894. It later emerged that Dreyfus was innocent and that the proceedings leading to his conviction had been highly irregular. Such emerging evidence was, however, suppressed by the competent French authorities. The matter was made public by Emile Zola in 1898 in his memorable open letter *J'accuse*. The affair now had widespread public attention and two camps formed: the nationalist anti-*Dreyfusards* (believing in Dreyfus's guilt as well as a wider Jewish–German conspiracy against France and calling for Zola to be sentenced for his accusations), and the liberal *Dreyfusards* (believing in Dreyfus's innocence and calling for measures to limit state power in the interest of personal liberty). Amid public uproar, Zola was sentenced for libel and imprisoned. Due to confessions by the real traitors, a retrial was finally granted to Dreyfus in 1899. Though again convicted, he was pardoned by the President of the Republic. In 1906, in a retrial in a civilian court, Dreyfus was finally found innocent.

74 See also Laborde, Cécile, 'Pluralism, Syndicalism and Corporatism: Léon Duguit and the Crisis of the State', *History of European Ideas*, 22 (1996), 227–44, at 227.

75 See Schulze, *Staat und Nation*, 244.

76 See e.g. Duguit, Léon, *Traité de Droit Constitutionnel*, 2nd edition (Paris: E. de Boccard, 1921), IX: 'On a dit très justement que la guerre … était la lutte de l'idée de l'État puissance commandante, souveraine, contre l'idée de l'État collaboration des membres d'un même groupe national, travaillant ensemble à la réalisation de la justice et du mieux-être. L'idée de l'État puissance, affirmée par tous les publicistes et tous les juristes

associated with Germany breaking up the collective security system of the League of Nations in the 1930s (and in this case threatening France's very existence for the system of Versailles had been constructed primarily in order to protect France from another German attack). As a result, the widespread examination in France of the bases and limits of statehood were partly seen as an attempt to make clear the shortcomings and essential dangers inherent in the German conception of statehood.

On the wider European scene, the French view that German ideas on statehood had contributed to World War I and were again threatening world peace was generally shared. A passage from Erich Kaufmann's 1911 book on *Das Wesen des Völkerrechts und die Clausula Rebus Sic Stantibus* was often quoted to underline this claim: 'Nicht "die Gemeinschaft frei wollender Menschen", sondern der siegreiche Krieg ist das soziale Ideal: der siegreiche Krieg als das letzte Mittel zu jenem obersten Ziel. Im Kriege offenbart sich der Staate in seinem wahren Wesen, er ist seine höchste Leistung, in dem seine Eigenart zur höchsten Entfaltung kommt.'[77] In light of such statements by academics, there existed a dominant view in European international law in the interwar period that German positivism with its emphasis on the role of states had been an academic expression of nationalist policies and a mere apology for the use of force.[78] Under this impression, Hugo Krabbe of the Netherlands, James Leslie Brierly of Great Britain, as well as Hans Kelsen and his Vienna School were working on new conceptions of statehood and international relations directed against the German approach.[79] Closely linked to new theories of the state was the renaissance of natural law in international legal scholarship. By denying the state a higher moral standing it was also implausible to reduce the notion of law to expressions of state will as predominant German positivism had done. There was therefore an emerging anti-positivist reaction in European international law. Similarly, it also became apparent in municipal

allemands, s'est heurtée à l'idée de l'État collaboration, dont la France est l'initiatrice et qui a vaincu aux bords de la Marne et dans les ravins de Verdun.'

77 Kaufmann, Erich, *Das Wesen des Völkerrechts und die Clausula Rebus Sic Stantibus: Rechtsphilosophische Studie zum Rechts-, Staats- und Verfassungsbegriffe* (Tübingen: J. C. B. Mohr (Paul Siebeck), 1911), 146. The reference to 'die Gemeinschaft frei wollender Menschen' is directed towards the neo-Kantian legal philosopher Rudolf Stammler and the latter's formulation of the social ideal.

78 It should be noted though that Kaufmann in later years advocated an institutional theory with natural law tendencies (see also Truyol y Serra, Antonio, *Histoire du droit international public* (Paris: Economica, 1995), 147–8).

79 Koskenniemi, *Gentle Civilizer*, 172–3 (on Brierly) and 330 (on Krabbe); Koskenniemi, 'Lauterpacht', at 618 (on Kelsen).

law that a strictly positivist view of law was not able to solve legal problems arising in industrialized societies.

Moreover, there was a changing international environment. The League of Nations and other international organizations had been created. These evolutions questioned to some extent the supremacy of the state in international relations. As is well known, however, the new institutional framework could not prevent the crises of the 1930s and finally World War II. The collective security system of Versailles had shown its basic ineffectiveness in the Manchurian and Abyssinian crises and the world was again at war by 1939, once again mainly initiated by Germany. After destruction and losses of life on an unprecedented scale and the horror of the Holocaust, the international legal system had to be rebuilt in 1945 under the impression of these shocking experiences. In this post-World War II context, the individualistic conception of international personality was formulated in its final form and applied in the process of settling the war in legal terms at Nuremberg.

The state as a functional entity shaped by individuals

The origins of the individualistic conception's first proposition lie in a functional view of statehood. The state is seen as a multitude of relations between individuals. This allows the imposition of legal limits to state power. The theory was primarily formulated by Léon Duguit in the French socio-political context at the turn of the twentieth century. Duguit's teachings exercised widespread influence in Europe in the interwar period[80] (particularly through the works of Georges Scelle,[81] Nicolas Politis[82] and Alejandro Alvarez[83]) and were introduced to the English-speaking world by an enthusiastic Harold J. Laski, describing Duguit as 'without doubt the first of living political thinkers'.[84] It is

80 See also Truyol y Serra, 'Doctrines du Droit des Gens', at 33 and 39–40.

81 See e.g. Scelle, Georges, 'La doctrine de L. Duguit et les fondements du droit des gens', *Archives de Philosophie du droit et de sociologie juridique*, 2 (1932), 83–119, wherein Scelle emphasized Duguit's relevance for international law.

82 See e.g. Politis, *Nouvelles Tendances*, 9–26. See also Koskenniemi, *Gentle Civilizer*, 305.

83 See e.g. Alvarez, *Codification*, 29–57 and 122. See also Koskenniemi, *Gentle Civilizer*, 302.

84 The quote is reproduced in Laborde, 'Crisis of the State', at 228, and was originally offered by Laski in one of his letters to Oliver Wendell Holmes. On the introduction of Duguit's political ideas to an English-speaking audience by Laski see Laborde, Cécile, 'The Concept of the State in British and French Political Thought', *Political Studies*, 48 (2000), 540–57, at 545. See also the introductory notes by Laski in Duguit's *Harvard Law Review* article (Duguit, 'Law and the State', at 186–192).

possible that Hersch Lauterpacht was particularly alert to Duguit's thought because of his professional contacts with Laski at the London School of Economics. In any event, Duguit's functional view of the state, stressing the role of individuals and the importance of limiting state power, must have fit well with Lauterpacht's own association with Austrian liberalism. Duguit's theory was subsequently adopted by Hugo Krabbe, thereby modifying to a certain extent Duguit's strict sociological approach. Such modifications are reflected in the individualistic conception of international personality as advocated in its most influential form by Hersch Lauterpacht.

As noted earlier, at the turn of the twentieth century it was in the French socio-political context that the basis and the role of the state was perhaps most intensely debated in Europe. Consequently, it was primarily against the background of the French 'crisis of the state' that new ideas on statehood emerged, thereby challenging the hitherto dominant German and Italian doctrine (the two European countries where thought on the state had previously been most widespread) and providing inspiration for international legal scholarship. The most influential new theory of the state was formulated by Léon Duguit, professor of law in Bordeaux and the doyen of French constitutional law.[85] Being a committed *Dreyfusard*,[86] Duguit defined the essence of public law (comprising municipal and international law) to lie in limiting state power for the benefit of individual freedom.[87] Of course, this was a radically different task for public law compared to the German (and, for that matter, identical Italian)[88] tradition wherein public law for decades had primarily been concerned with establishing statehood. German public law, as has been noted earlier in this book, was not interested so much in limiting state power as in creating it. Having established statehood, the dominant theory in Germany did not regard state power and individual freedom as contradictory concepts; it was exactly in and through the sovereign state that the individual was able to realize its autonomy and freedom. Therefore, in the German tradition, there could be no

[85] On the generally strong influence of jurists on the debate on statehood in France see Jones, *French State in Question*, 29. On Duguit's fame see Laborde, 'Crisis of the State', at 228.

[86] See Jones, *French State in Question*, 161.

[87] Duguit, 'Law and the State', at 2–6; Duguit, *Traité*, 478; Duguit, Léon, *Études de Droit Public I: L'État: Le Droit Objectif et la Loi Positive* (Paris: Albert Fontemoing, 1901), 12. See also Jones, *French State in Question*, 163–4, and Laborde, 'Crisis of the State', at 229.

[88] The general identity of Italian public law thought and German doctrine was also observed by Duguit, *Traité*, 464.

limitation on state power other than through voluntary acts of the state (theory of auto-limitation), for the individual interest was exactly to have a fully sovereign state not being constrained by any outside will.[89] For Duguit, such equation of state power and individual freedom, having its roots in Jean-Jacques Rousseau's *volonté générale* and G. W. F. Hegel's political philosophy, was unacceptable, as was the unaccountable state following from it.[90] In effect, Duguit noted, such doctrine implied the negation of public law in favour of simple power and led to the absolute state threatening individual freedom and world peace:

> If the State is not subject to such jural principle (*une règle de droit*), there is no longer any public municipal law (*droit public interne*) nor any international law (*droit public international*). There is no longer any limit to the material power of the State, to the *Macht* as the Germans call it. The State is *Macht* and nothing more. Individuals become the property of the State and small nations become the predestined slaves of powerful states.[91]

In light of these consequences of the German approach, Duguit saw a pressing need to formulate a different public law theory better equipped to limit state power in order to protect individual freedom and peace in international relations. His own theory was therefore partly, if not primarily, intended to offer a different approach to public law than the German tradition provided.[92] This different conception had to offer limits on state power in the interest of individual freedom.

At first sight, Duguit could find such an approach in traditional French public law. Since the Declaration of the Rights of Man and of the Citizen in 1789, the French tradition, contrary to German doctrine, had regarded state power and individual rights as potentially conflicting.[93] It was therefore accepted in French legal thought that there were limits to state power in the

89 See Duguit's observations on the German doctrine in ibid., 486–91, and, more extensively, in Duguit, 'Law and the State', at 119–44.

90 Duguit, *Traité*, 461, and 483–4; Duguit, 'Law and the State', 103.

91 Duguit, 'Law and the State', at 6 (original emphasis).

92 See the revealing introductory remarks in Duguit, *Traité*, X: 'Pourquoi . . . faire si souvent appel aux juristes allemands? Voici la réponse. Il n'est douteux que, sauf de très rares exceptions, les juristes publicistes allemands en édifiant leurs théories, souvent ingénieuses, ont été avant tout déterminés par le désir de fonder sur des bases d'apparence juridique la souveraineté illimitée de l'Etat, l'absolutisme des gouvernants à l'intérieur et la politique de conquête et de rapine à l'extérieur. Il est indispensable de dénoncer cette tendance, et personnellement . . . mon effort constant a été de les combattre.'

93 See Duguit, 'Law and the State', at 11; Duguit, *Traité*, 479; Duguit, *Études de Droit Public (I)*, 13–15.

form of individual rights being anterior and superior to the state.[94] The origins of this idea lay in the natural rights theory of John Locke and had been most forcefully advocated in France by Benjamin Constant, the latter's writings mainly constituting a critique of Rousseau's *volonté générale*.[95] However, for a devoted *Dreyfusard* like Duguit, the protection of individual freedom rested on too precarious a basis by simply grounding it in natural rights and opposing them to state sovereignty. For these were two concepts that were essentially contradictory: either a state was sovereign (implying that there could be no natural rights derived from an external will limiting sovereignty), or there were natural rights (and the state necessarily ceased to be sovereign as its will was in that case limited by an external source); it was not possible to affirm both state sovereignty and natural rights.[96] The question therefore was which of the two would have priority. From Duguit's perspective, evidently shaped by the experience of the Dreyfus Affair, it was extremely likely that state sovereignty would prevail and individual freedom consequently be curtailed.[97] It was therefore not enough to simply accept natural rights as an intended limit to state sovereignty. What lay at the heart of the problem was the concept of state sovereignty itself; to really secure individual freedom, this concept had to be addressed.[98]

For Duguit, state sovereignty was a metaphysical concept without justification in the modern world:

> [La souveraineté] est purement et simplement l'expression d'un concept d'ordre métaphysique sans valeur, quel que soit le nom dont on le décore . . .. Les deux explications qu'on en donne sont aussi artificielles et chimériques l'une que l'autre. Dire que la puissance publique est de création divine, ou dire quelle est de création populaire, sont deux affirmations d'un même ordre et de même valeur, c'est-à-dire de valeur égale à zéro, parce qu'elle sont aussi indémontrées et indémontrables l'une que l'autre.[99]

This statement has to be related to Auguste Comte's philosophical (not legal) positivism, the influence of which can hardly be overstated in the French context of the nineteenth and early twentieth century.[100] Comte,

[94] Duguit, 'Law and the State', at 12; Duguit, *Traité*, 478–9.

[95] Duguit, 'Law and the State', at 105–14. Duguit's fondness of Constant becomes very clear in these paragraphs, as does his aversion to Rousseau.

[96] Ibid., at 25. [97] Ibid., at 10. [98] Duguit, *Traité*, 494–9. [99] Ibid., 494.

[100] On the general influence of Comte's positivism in France see Caron, *Geschichte Frankreichs (V)*, 363. On Comte's influence on Duguit see Jones, *French State in Question*, 162, and Diggelmann, *Völkerrechtssoziologie*, 171. See also Duguit, 'Law and the State', at 181–2 (referring to Comte's philosophical positivism).

under the influence of the ambiguous legacy of the French Revolution and the subsequent struggle between revisionist and revolutionary forces, conceived intellectual development as consisting of three stages: theological, metaphysical and positive.[101] In the theological stage (pre-Revolution period), divine will was the accepted point of reference for explaining social or moral phenomena; in the metaphysical stage (French Revolution and its immediate aftermath), abstract secular principles took over this function; in the positivist stage (present era), social and moral values had to be in accordance with empirically observable facts. Duguit's statement on state sovereignty fits well into this 'law of the three stages'. It seems that Duguit regarded state sovereignty as a concept originating from the theological and metaphysical stages of intellectual development: it had first been justified by recourse to divine will, and subsequently by reference to abstract principles (like Rousseau's *volonté générale* or Hegel's realization of the moral idea). These theological or metaphysical justifications for state sovereignty, according to Duguit's reading of history, had regularly been put forward by those people representing the government in a given state in order to legitimate their power over the rest of the population:[102] by reference to a higher principle, their acts were not understood to be individual undertakings, but to be actions of the collective will. This was no longer possible in the modern positive stage. On a realistic view, one simply had to admit that a state was a group of people (*gouvernants*) able to impose their wills on the rest of the population (*gouvernés*).[103] This coercive power of the *gouvernants* over the *gouvernés* could not be legitimized by some abstract principle, but was just the outcome of the interplay between economic and political factors in a society. With reference to the sociologist Emile Durkheim, his university colleague at Bordeaux, Duguit conceived the state as a set of social relationships between individuals, the personal status of these individuals (*gouvernants* or *gouvernés*) being determined by social differentiation.[104] Accordingly, a state existed the moment this social differentiation had enabled some individuals to impose their wills

[101] Comte, Auguste, *Cours de Philosophie Positive. Tome Quatrième et Dernier: La Philosophie Sociale et les Conclusions Générales*, 1st edition (Paris: Bachelier, 1839), 653–92.

[102] Duguit, *Traité*, 501.

[103] Duguit, *Études de Droit Public (I)*, 242; Duguit, *Traité*, 499–500 and 512–4; Duguit, 'Law and the State', at 162–3.

[104] Duguit, *Études de Droit Public (I)*, 246–55; Duguit, *Traité*, 501–12; Duguit, 'Law and the State', at 163. See also Laborde, 'Crisis of the State', at 229.

upon others, that is, when some persons were accepted as *gouvernants* and the rest were *gouvernés*.[105]

With this view of the state as consisting of social relations between those individuals governing and those being governed (without the former being an organ of some higher interest), the problem of the limits of state power in the interest of individual freedom was solved: 'L'État est une pure abstraction. La réalité, ce sont les individus qui exercent la puissance étatique; ils sont soumis à la prise du droit comme tous les autres individus, et le problème de la subordination de l'État au droit et de la limitation de la puissance étatique se trouve résolu ainsi de lui-même.'[106] With the state being a metaphor for individual relations between *gouvernants* and *gouvernés*, the individuals who exercised power were subject to law like any other individual. In consequence, the division between public and private law essentially disappeared for all law addressed individuals and there was no sovereign personality of the state requiring special legal rules.[107] As law in general, and private law in particular, tended to protect individual freedom, the individual was safeguarded from abuses of power by the *gouvernants* through subjection of the latter to ordinary legal principles.[108] But what exactly was the foundation of these principles? Duguit followed the social solidarity approach stemming from Emile Durkheim's 1893 book *De la Division du Travail Social*.[109] In accordance with Durkheim, Duguit regarded individuals as essentially dependent on one another in an industrial society which led to the fundamental principle of '*solidarité par division du travail*'.[110] This solidarity between individual members of a society was reflected in the objective law, i.e. social rules existing in a developed society in order to ensure that individual behaviour was in line with solidarity and for that purpose stipulating individual rights and duties.[111] Crucially, as also those individuals exercising a government function in society were subject to these rules, the state (understood as a metaphor for the *gouvernants*) had a legal duty to enhance social solidarity; this

105 Duguit, *Traité*, 512. 106 Ibid., 515.

107 Ibid., 522–6. It has to be noted though that Duguit in the end maintained a minor difference between private and public law with regard to sanctions (539–50). See also Jones, *French State in Question*, 165.

108 Duguit, *Traité*, 526; Duguit, *Études de Droit Public (I)*, 262–7.

109 Duguit, 'Law and the State', at 164–5.

110 Durkheim, Emile, *De la Division du Travail Social*, 8th edition (Paris: Presses Universitaires, 1967) (originally published 1893), 83–97. See the extensive treatment of the topic in Duguit, *Études de Droit Public (I)*, 23–79.

111 Duguit, *Études de Droit Public (I)*, 80–137; Duguit, 'Law and the State', at 178.

implied that the existence of the state was legitimized only by the services it provided for the well-being of individuals.[112] This was a functional and managerial view of the state stressing public services as opposed to the old conception of public commands mainly present in German thought.[113]

Duguit's functional view of the state was taken up and slightly modified by the Dutch public lawyer Hugo Krabbe in his 1919 book *Die moderne Staatsidee*.[114] Krabbe, too, started from the fact that there existed a dualism between state sovereignty and limits to state power.[115] To overcome this dilemma, he also rejected the view of the state as a commanding power and conceived it as a functional entity wherein individuals fulfilled governmental tasks and in doing so were bound by general legal principles.[116] However, modifying Duguit's approach, the basis of the *gouvernants*' status was not seen by Krabbe to lie directly in social differentiation, but in positive legal norms. By focusing on positive rules when constituting state power, Krabbe in a sense moved towards Hans Kelsen's theory of the state, the latter being the other significant theory demystifying statehood in the early twentieth century apart from Duguit's. For Kelsen, the state and law were identical: the state was the legal system and the legal system was the state.[117] By basing the functions of the *gouvernants* on legal rules, Krabbe seemed to endorse this view, for state authority then depended on the existence of a legal system. However, as Kelsen noted when critically assessing Krabbe's contribution,[118] Krabbe still regarded the state as existing independently of a legal order: it was precisely the task of the legal order to legitimize pre-existent state power as exercised by the *gouvernants*.[119] Contrary to Kelsen, then, the state and the legal order were still two separate concepts in Krabbe's opinion. Even with Krabbe modifying Duguit's theory, in that he emphasized the role of positive law as opposed to Duguit's concern with social facts, there remained this basic difference regarding the nature of the state between Krabbe and Duguit on the one hand and Kelsen on the other: for Krabbe and Duguit, the state (as a metaphor for

112 Duguit, 'Law and the State', at 184–5.

113 See also Laborde, 'Crisis of the State', at 230, and Jones, *French State in Question*, 169–71.

114 The similarity of Duguit's and Krabbe's approach is also highlighted by Truyol y Serra, *Histoire*, 146, and Diggelmann, *Völkerrechtssoziologie*, 173–4, as well as by Duguit himself in Duguit, *Traité*, 463–4, and by Krabbe in Krabbe, *Moderne Staatsidee*, 258–9.

115 Krabbe, *Moderne Staatsidee*, 1. 116 Ibid., esp. 255–63.

117 See e.g. Kelsen, *Staatsbegriff*, 86–91. Kelsen's theory is analysed in depth in the next chapter presenting the formal conception of international personality.

118 Ibid., 184–91. 119 Krabbe, *Moderne Staatsidee*, 235.

individual relationships) existed per se and had to be limited by law, whereas for Kelsen the state and law were identical.[120] It therefore seems fair to say that when Lauterpacht and other adherents to the individualistic conception of international personality made reference to Duguit, Krabbe and Kelsen jointly,[121] they merely denoted their shared goal of demystifying state sovereignty, and not a common understanding of the state.[122]

In conclusion, it is the functional theory of the state as formulated by Duguit and modified by Krabbe that the first proposition of the individualistic conception of international personality has to be related to. The basic assumption of this line of thought is that state power endangers individual freedom; correspondingly, the equation of individual liberty and statehood as in German public law thought is strongly rejected. It follows from this basic assumption that the task for municipal and international public law is to limit state power in the interest of individual freedom (a task Lauterpacht was arguably particularly attracted to as it fit well with his Austrian liberalism[123]). However, imposing limits on state power is not possible as long as one adheres to the purely metaphysical concept of state sovereignty. Hence, the latter concept has to be rejected and replaced with a functional view of statehood. On such a view, the state is simply a metaphor for relations between those governing (*gouvernants*) and those being governed (*gouvernés*), the former working in the interest of the latter. As all these individuals are subject to the same legal rules, the separation between international and municipal, as well as private and public, law disappears, making it possible, in principle, to apply international law to individuals. In effect, the functional view of the state stemming from Duguit and Krabbe leads to a legal principle according to which international law, like all law, addresses individual human beings, be they *gouvernants* or *gouvernés*. Moreover, the principle also includes that law's purpose is to protect the individual human being from state power and this leads to fundamental rights and duties of the individual.

[120] See also Eulau, Heinz, 'The Depersonalization of the Concept of Sovereignty', *Journal of Politics*, 4 (1942), 3–19, at 9–14 (by implication), and the discussion of Kelsen's theory by Duguit in the third edition of his textbook (Duguit, Léon, *Traité de Droit Constitutionnel*, 3rd edition (Paris: E. de Boccard, 1927), 63–5).

[121] See e.g. Lauterpacht, *Analogies*, 79 and 304–5; Lauterpacht, 'Westlake', at 393; Lauterpacht, 'Subjects', at 520.

[122] See also Lauterpacht, Hersch, 'Kelsen's Pure Science of Law' in Elihu Lauterpacht (ed.), *International Law: Being the Collected Papers of Hersch Lauterpacht* (Cambridge University Press, 1975) (originally published 1933), 404–30, at 414–19.

[123] See also Koskenniemi, 'Lauterpacht', at 657.

Constitutional principles as sources of law

The second proposition of the individualistic conception of international personality has its origins in the view that international law encompasses certain universal principles independent of state will; such principles also contain guidelines for international personality. Partly linked to the critique of the predominant German theory of the state, there was an anti-positivist reaction in international legal scholarship in the interwar period. By denying the state special authority, it could not be accepted that international law was created only by state will. It seemed necessary to complement state will with certain principles, some of them of such a fundamental nature that without them international law was hardly possible. The intellectual basis of this reaction lies in developments in legal philosophy at the end of the nineteenth century particularly associated with François Gény. In international law, these developments were taken up after the calamity of World War I. Particularly influential was the work of Alfred Verdross whose basic ideas on an international constitution consisting of certain fundamental legal principles were widely adopted in interwar scholarship. The theory could rely to a certain extent on Article 38(3) of the recently created PCIJ and was also shared, in its fundamental assumptions, by Lauterpacht.

Under the impression of increasingly industrialized societies and the various new legal issues they brought about, it was increasingly acknowledged in European legal philosophy at the end of the nineteenth century that a strictly positivist view on the sources of law could not offer rewarding answers.[124] Also in light of some more fundamental philosophical problems of legal positivism (like the foundation of law), a broadening of legal method seemed necessary. This 'renaissance of natural law'[125] can be illustrated by the influential work of François Gény on legal method,[126] put forward in the particular circumstances of the French state and the social issues arising therein. In France, the Napoleonic *Code Civil* of 1804 had been the sacred text for jurists in all fields of law during most of the nineteenth century.[127] It

[124] Truyol y Serra, 'Doctrines du Droit des Gens', at 199–200 ; Kolb, *Réfléxions*, 22.

[125] Truyol y Serra, 'Doctrines du Droit des Gens', at 199.

[126] As concerns Gény's influence, see e.g. Lauterpacht, 'Anglo-Amercian and Continental Schools of Thought', at 472, and Lauterpacht, *Function of Law*, 61; Truyol y Serra, 'Doctrines du Droit des Gens', at 200; Kolb, Robert, 'Principles as Sources of International Law (With Special Reference to Good Faith)', NILR, 53 (2006), 1–36, at 4 n. 11; Ago, 'Positive Law', at 699 n. 20; Koskenniemi, *Gentle Civilizer*, 281 and 372 n. 92.

[127] Koskenniemi, *Gentle Civilizer*, 274–5. On the Code Civil in general see Fikentscher, *Methoden des Rechts (I)*, 426–31.

was presumed that all legal problems could be solved by recourse to the provisions contained in the *Code Civil*, as it had been intended to cover all aspects of social life. The corresponding methodological approach of the so-called *École de l'exégèse* was solely to apply formal logic to the text of the *Code Civil* and to refrain from making reference to any historical, moral or sociological aspects.[128] The shortcomings of this strictly positivist method appeared with the emergence of new and acute social issues (e.g. employment conditions for industrial workers) that were not, or not satisfactorily, dealt with in the Code enacted in 1804.[129] The question therefore arose as to how lawyers should approach such issues not covered by positive law. Gény proposed a broadening of legal method. He first proclaimed customary rules as part of the sources of law and second accepted legal precedent and doctrinal works as subsidiary means for establishing the applicable law. Crucially, for Gény, such incorporation of other sources of law and means of interpretation did not exhaust the whole process of legal reasoning: the legal constructs (*construits*) had to be related to the social conditions (*données*) of a given case, that is, to the sociological, moral and historical context in which the legal issue at hand had to be situated. By including such aspects, Gény in effect reaffirmed that some form of natural law principles play a role in legal reasoning.[130] It was then through the interaction of the *construits* and the *données* that a lawyer arrived at a conclusion in a given case.[131] To Gény's delight, his theory of legal method was swiftly incorporated into Article 1 of the newly enacted Swiss Civil Code of 1907.[132]

Gény's approach illustrates the broadening of legal method advocated in different variations in most of Europe at the beginning of the twentieth century.[133] In international legal scholarship, these ideas were well received. One reason was that international law in particular found it difficult to assert its binding force with a purely positivist conception of

[128] Fikentscher, *Methoden des Rechts (I)*, 433. This approach is perhaps most accurately encapsulated by Charles de Montesquieu's famous line of the judge being '*la bouche de la loi*'.

[129] Ibid., 457. [130] Truyol y Serra, 'Doctrines du Droit des Gens', at 200.

[131] See also Arnaud, André-Jean, *Les juristes face à la société du XIXème siècle à nos jours* (Paris: Presses Universitaires de France, 1975), 120.

[132] Fikentscher, *Methoden des Rechts (I)*, 459. Article 1 of the Swiss Civil Code authorizes the judge to apply customary law where no applicable provision is to be found in the Codex and, in the absence of a customary rule, to apply a principle she would enact as law if she were a legislator (para. 2); in applying this principle, she has to take into account doctrine and historical experience (para. 3).

[133] For an overview of these developments in Europe see Truyol y Serra, 'Doctrines du Droit des Gens', at 199–201.

law. Another motive was that after the calamity of World War I, legal positivism, with its emphasis on state will as the only source of law, was seen merely as an apology for aggressive foreign policies.[134] In this context, diverse approaches emerged aimed at broadening the notion of international law and thereby providing a more convincing foundation for its binding force than the positivist theory had been able to do with its *Vereinbarungslehre*.[135] The common point of departure for such critical approaches was that, in order to assume international law as binding, there had to be one basic norm (*Grundnorm*) not dependent on state will; this basic norm stipulated international law's binding nature. The theory of the *Grundnorm* was prominently articulated by the so-called Vienna School of law, the idea itself originating from a 1914 article by Hans Kelsen on matters of Austrian constitutional law.[136] With particular attention to international law, the theory of the *Grundnorm* was further developed by Kelsen's Viennese colleague Alfred Verdross: '... das positive Recht als System von objektiv gültigen Normen [kann] nur begriffen werden, wenn wenigstens eine einzige nicht positive, nicht gesetzte Norm vorausgesetzt wird.... Soll demnach dem positiven Rechte objektive normative Geltung zukommen, dann muss es durch seine Grundnorm im objektiven Reiche der Werte verankert werden.'[137]

While Kelsen stopped short of going any further than assuming one (hypothetical) *Grundnorm* in his legal theory and otherwise strictly rejected any non-positive rules, Verdross saw the admission of one basic norm as only the first step for accepting other fundamental legal principles as sources of international law.[138] In Verdross's view, there was a whole set of fundamental principles without which the international legal system could not function and which could therefore not be based on possibly arbitrary state will.[139] These principles included rules on international personality ('norms determining which persons are

[134] See also Kolb, *Réfléxions*, 22 (by implication).
[135] See also Ago, 'Positive Law', at 701–7.
[136] For the original article see Kelsen, Hans, 'Reichsgesetz und Landesgesetz nach österreichischer Verfassung', AöR, 32 (1914), 202–45, at 216–17. See also Ago, 'Positive Law', at 704. For the role of the *Grundnorm* in international law see Kelsen, *Reine Rechtslehre*, 70–1.
[137] Verdross, *Verfassung*, 21 and 23.
[138] See also Truyol y Serra, 'Doctrines du Droit des Gens', at 32, and Ago, 'Positive Law', at 706.
[139] Verdross, Alfred, *Die Einheit des rechtlichen Weltbildes auf Grundlage der Völkerrechtsverfassung* (Tübingen: J. C. B. Mohr, 1923), 120–35. See also Verdross, Alfred, 'Jus Dispositivum and Jus Cogens in International Law', AJIL, 60 (1966), 55–63, at 58–60.

endowed with the capacity to act in international law'[140]), international responsibility, and basic humanitarian and moral concerns.[141] As regards the rules on international personality, Verdross did not argue that they contained any presumption in favour of individuals; his concern was just that such fundamental rules on personality had to exist for the international legal system to function. But for Verdross the fundamental principle was a presumption for states, not for individuals.[142] Such fundamental principles necessary for international law to operate represented the international constitution and, as such, had *ius cogens* character:

> [A] compulsory norm cannot be derogated either by customary or by treaty law; if it were not so, compulsory norms could never be applied in international law. In this case, the most essential and indispensable principles of law would be excluded from the realm of international law, a situation which necessarily leads to absurd results. A treaty norm, violative of a compulsory general principle of law, is, therefore, void; on the other hand, a general norm of customary international law in contradiction to a general principle of law cannot even come into existence because customary law must be formed by constant custom based on a general juridical conviction.[143]

In consequence, any deviations by states from *ius cogens* rules were void as a matter of international law. With the admission of such peremptory principles leading to a hierarchy of international norms, Verdross clearly re-approached natural law theories.[144]

Verdross was one of the earliest, but by far not the only, scholar in the European interwar context to advocate the idea of peremptory norms

[140] Verdross, Alfred, 'Forbidden Treaties in International Law', AJIL, 31 (1937), 571–77, at 572. See also Kolb, Robert, *Théorie du ius cogens international: Essai de relecture du concept* (Paris: Presses Universitaires de France, 2001), 98–100 (on a more general level not restricted to Verdross).

[141] Verdross, 'Jus Cogens', at 59–60.

[142] Verdross, *Verfassung*, 156–63; Verdross, Alfred, *Völkerrecht*, 1st edition (Berlin: Julius Springer, 1937), 66–9. This underlines the point that it is not enough to accept fundamental legal principles as independent sources of international law in order to come to an individualistic conception of international personality. This aspect on the sources of law has to be combined with a functional view of the state, something Verdross did not advocate.

[143] Verdross, 'Forbidden Treaties', at 573. See also Simma, Bruno, 'The Contribution of Alfred Verdross to the Theory of International Law', EJIL, 6 (1995), 33–54, at 49–52, and Kolb, *Ius Cogens*, 110.

[144] See also Truyol y Serra, 'Doctrines du Droit des Gens', at 32 and 224–8; Simma, 'Contribution of Verdross', at 50–2; Kolb, *Ius Cogens*, 110.

representing an international constitution. First of all, Santi Romano's theory of social institutionalism – which represents part of the origins of the recognition conception of international personality – also promoted the existence of fundamental norms constituting the international legal order. However, as noted earlier, Romano's constitution rested in the institutions of social life and not in general legal principles of a potentially moral character. Romano's constitutional approach therefore has to be distinguished from the one originating with Verdross for they start from essentially different premises.[145] But also apart from Romano's rather different approach, it became an increasingly accepted position among international lawyers in the course of the general anti-positivist reaction and the corresponding broadening of legal method that state will could be neither the foundation nor the sole source of international law. The inclusion of natural law aspects in international legal reasoning became particularly apparent in the General Courses held at The Hague in the early 1930s by prominent figures like James Leslie Brierly,[146] Maurice Bourquin,[147] Gabriele Salvioli,[148] and Louis Le Fur.[149] In addition, the same idea of a hierarchy of norms was also at the centre of the objective law theory of social solidarity stemming from Duguit's functional view of the state and being proclaimed in international law by Georges Scelle[150] and Nicolas Politis.[151] According to this view, positive law was valid only if in accordance with the objective law of social solidarity; there was thus also a hierarchy of norms.[152] Though in their own view this hierarchy did not rest on natural law principles but was the result of purely sociological observations, Duguit's, Scelle's and Politis' approach was in effect very close to the natural law theories of Verdross, Brierly and others, for they all referred to the 'nature of things' for finding fundamental legal rules.[153] There was then a movement in international legal doctrine to include basic principles of law as anterior and superior to state will as part of the sources of international law.

145 Kolb, *Bonne Foi*, 65–6, Kolb, *Ius Cogens*, 100–12, and Kolb, *Réflexions*, 23.

146 Brierly, 'Règles Générales', at 73–81.

147 Bourquin, 'Règles Générales', at 75–80 (with especially favourable reference to Verdross at pp. 78–9 n. 2).

148 Salvioli, Gabriele, 'Les Règles Générales de la Paix', RCADI, 46 (1933-IV), 1–164, at 13–15.

149 Le Fur, Louis, 'Règles Générales du Droit de la Paix', RCADI, 54 (1935-IV), 1–308, at 196–213.

150 Scelle, 'Règles Générales', at 348–52.

151 Politis, *Nouvelles Tendances*, 48–9.

152 See e.g. Scelle, 'Règles Générales', at 350.

153 This essential similarity is highlighted by Truyol y Serra, 'Doctrines du Droit des Gens', at 38.

The doctrinal claim that basic legal principles were a superior source of international law was often reinforced by reference to Article 38(3) of the PCIJ Statute which enumerated 'general principles of law recognized by civilized States' as part of the applicable law of the Court. The provision had been incorporated after difficult deliberations in the Advisory Committee of Jurists when drafting the Statute of the Court.[154] It had not been disputed in the Advisory Committee that treaties and custom were sources of international law. However, the proposition of its president, Baron Descamps, to include, according to the first draft, 'the rules of international law as recognized by the legal conscience of civilized nations'[155] had led to a fierce debate. It had seriously been questioned whether states could be subject to any rules not stemming from expressions of their will.[156] In the end, the major concern had been that the exclusion of general principles as an additional source to treaties and custom would lead the Court to declare a *non liquet* in certain cases, a threat that the majority of the Committee had preferred to avoid. Accordingly, a consensus to include general principles of law in Article 38 PCIJ Statute had been reached.[157] However, positivist writers in general did not accept this provision as indicating an independent third source of international law: they either argued that the principles mentioned in Article 38(3) were already covered by treaties and custom or contended that they concerned only the applicable law for the Court and therefore had no relevance for other authorities when applying international law.[158] On the contrary, proponents of the anti-positivist reaction regarded Article 38(3) PCIJ Statute exactly as proving their point that there were sources of international law other than expressions of state will.[159] It seems fair to say in this respect that the *Procès-verbaux* of the Advisory Committee's deliberations hinted strongly at general principles as an

[154] See Spiermann, Ole, '"Who Attempts too Much does Nothing Well": The 1920 Advisory Committee of Jurists and the Statute of the Permanent Court of International Justice', BYIL, 73 (2002), 187–260, at 187, and Spiermann, *International Legal Argument in the PCIJ*, 7. The Committee had been formed by the Council of the League of Nations and was composed of ten members.

[155] See Spiermann, 'Statute of the Permament Court', at 214.

[156] Spiermann, *International Legal Argument in the PCIJ*, 58–60; Spiermann, 'Statute of the Permament Court', 214.

[157] Kolb, 'Principles', at 30–1; Spiermann, 'Statute of the Permament Court', at 217–18. The different formulation from Descamps's first draft was put forward by Elihu Root and was strongly endorsed by Lord Phillimore.

[158] See for these different views Kolb, *Bonne Foi*, 24–34.

[159] See e.g. Verdross, *Verfassung*, 59. It has to be said that this does not hold true for Scelle who regarded general principles of law in the sense of Article 38 PCIJ Statute as being part of customary international law (see Scelle, 'Règles Générales', at 435–7).

independent source of international law (and were therefore often quoted by anti-positivists like Verdross, but not by positivists),[160] precisely because it was intended to avoid a *non liquet*. Yet, neither the wording of the provision nor the *Procès-verbaux* offered clear indications that these general principles, even when of a fundamental nature, were superior to treaties and custom in the sense of constitutional rules. In any event, in the line of reasoning of Verdross, the provision provided a positivist source (being declarative, not constitutive) for the essential truth that there also had to be non-positive rules of international law for an international legal order: these rules were the general principles of law, of which the fundamental ones constituted *ius cogens* and in this sense represented the constitution of the international legal order.

In sum, the individualistic conception's second proposition, according to which international personality of individuals is a matter of legal principle, has to be related to this view of the sources of international law including general legal principles, some of them of *ius cogens* nature. The proposition has its origins in a general reconsideration of legal positivism in Europe at the turn of the twentieth century. Such adjustment in general legal method was well received in international law where the main issue was that the international legal system could not properly function when based exclusively on state will. The position was promoted that a set of fundamental legal principles was necessary to provide the basis for international law. These principles essentially had a moral character and were hence reminiscent of natural law; it was, however, not natural law derived from a certain theological or philosophical school of thought, but from general legal principles present in legal systems in general. These were the principles referred to in Article 38(3) PCIJ Statute.[161]

[160] See e.g. Verdross, *Einheit des rechtlichen Weltbildes*, 122–4.

[161] Lauterpacht's ideas with respect to sources were very close to those of Verdross. See Lauterpacht's acknowledgement of Verdross's pioneering role in this respect in Lauterpacht, Hersch, 'Règles Générales du Droit de la Paix', RCADI, 62 (1937-IV), 95–422, at 151–2, and, more restrained, in Lauterpacht, 'General Part', at 91 n. 2. See also Lauterpacht's proposal of an Article 15 in his first report on the law of treaties in the ILC and his comment thereto, which is very reminiscent of Verdross's 1937 article on 'Forbidden Treaties' (Lauterpacht, Hersch (Special Rapporteur), *First Report on the Law of Treaties*, ILC 1953, UN Doc. A/CN.4/63, YILC (1953-II), pp. 154–5). For the similarity of Verdross's and Lauterpacht's approach with respect to the law of treaties see also Byers, Michael, 'Conceptualising the Relationship between Jus Cogens and Erga Omnes Rules', NJIL, 66 (1997), 211–39, at 224 n. 50. For their similar view on constitutional principles see also Kolb, *Ius Cogens*, 110 nn. 396 and 397, Simma,

Main manifestations in legal practice

The individualistic conception of international personality was most memorably manifested in the Nuremberg judgment. The principle regarding individual responsibility for international crimes enunciated therein lies at the heart of international criminal law in general and has been widely adopted by international and national courts ever since. Whereas the Nuremberg judgment primarily dealt with individual responsibility for actions taken on behalf of the state, more recent jurisprudence in US courts in the context of the Alien Tort Claims Act (ATCA) has affirmed that purely private actions can violate international law and in particular *ius cogens* norms. This case law is also a manifestation of the individualistic conception of international personality for it rejects the distinction between the public and the private in the field of constitutional norms of the international legal system. Finally, the individualistic conception informs much of the human rights practice in the ECHR.

These practical manifestations demonstrate that the individualistic conception, while affirming the international legal status of states, maintains a qualified presumption for the individual human being as a subject of international law. The presumption is qualified because it is restricted to the field of fundamental principles of international law. In this constitutional realm partly synonymous with *ius cogens*, individuals – as a matter of legal principle – presumably are international persons and as such have certain human rights and duties.

The Nuremberg judgment and international criminal law

In a memorable judgment dated 1 October 1946, the International Military Tribunal (IMT) at Nuremberg sentenced twelve Nazi defendants to death and seven to imprisonment for committing international crimes. Crucially, the IMT punished these individuals for crimes under international law, and not under a municipal penal law. In so doing, it applied the individualistic conception of international personality. This is not altogether surprising for Hersch Lauterpacht had 'helped to lay the foundations for the Nuremberg trials, and [had] argued powerfully

'Contribution of Verdross', at 48, and Dunoff, Jeffrey L., 'Why Constitutionalism Now? Text, Context and the Historical Contingency of Ideas', *Journal of International Law and International Relations*, 1 (2005), 191–212, at 191–2. On a more general level, the point is also made by Koskenniemi, 'Lauterpacht', at 658.

for their legal respectability'.[162] The essential legal elements of the judgment were reproduced by the International Military Tribunal for the Far East at Tokyo in 1946–8. Today, various ad hoc international criminal tribunals and the ICC, as well as numerous municipal courts, prosecute individuals for international crimes along the lines set by the Nuremberg judgment.

The idea of punishing major German war criminals was initially floated by eight governments-in-exile and the Free French National Committee in a resolution adopted in London in January 1942. The proposal was reinforced in declarations to the same effect by Franklin D. Roosevelt, Winston Churchill and Josef Stalin at their meetings in Teheran, Yalta and Potsdam (the last one with Harry Truman and Clement Attlee replacing Roosevelt and Churchill).[163] On 8 August 1945, the Allied Powers (including France) signed the London Agreement for the Prosecution and Punishment of the Major War Criminals of the European Axis establishing 'an International Military Tribunal for the trial of war criminals'.[164] Attached to the Agreement was the Charter of the International Military Tribunal[165] defining in Article 6 the international crimes for which individuals could be tried before the Tribunal, that is, crimes against peace (war of aggression), war crimes, and crimes against humanity. The Charter provided that official positions held by indicted individuals at the time of committing the crime did not free them from individual responsibility (Article 7), nor did the carrying out of superior orders (Article 8). Pursuant to Articles 14 and 15 of the Charter, the Chief Prosecutors swiftly started to prepare the indictment

[162] Crawford, 'International Law in Twentieth-Century England', at 698–9. Lauterpacht was involved in the Nuremberg trials almost from beginning to end. At the request of Arnold McNair, he had submitted a memorandum on war crimes to the Committee concerned with Crimes against International Public Order as early as July 1942. An elaborated version of the memorandum was published in Lauterpacht, Hersch, 'The Law of Nations and the Punishment of War Crimes', BYIL, 21 (1944), 58–95, and was widely appreciated. Lauterpacht was then involved, primarily through his personal relationship with United States Chief Prosecutor Robert Jackson, in drafting the London Charter (it is said that Lauterpacht came up with the idea to include 'crimes against humanity' into the Charter). Finally, Lauterpacht went to Nuremberg and wrote drafts for British Chief Prosecutor Hartley Shawcross's opening and concluding statements at the trial. See for all this information Koskenniemi, 'Lauterpacht', at 639–41.

[163] See Wright, Quincey, 'The Law of the Nuremburg Trial', AJIL, 41 (1947), 38–72, at 39.

[164] Article 1 London Agreement of 8 August 1945. The Agreement is reproduced in *AJIL Supp.*, 39 (1945), 257–58. Pursuant to Article 5 of the Agreement, nineteen other states subsequently joined it.

[165] Reproduced in ibid., 258–64.

of the accused. On 18 October 1945, at the first public meeting of the Tribunal in Berlin, twenty-four Nazi leaders were indicted. The Tribunal subsequently established itself in the Palace of Justice in Nuremberg where the trial began on 20 November 1945 with twenty-one Nazi defendants present. The judgment was announced on 1 October 1946.

According to its Charter, the Military Tribunal at Nuremberg had jurisdiction to try individuals for international crimes, that is, it was empowered to try individuals for such violations of international law considered as a crime according to the Charter. The main question was whether this jurisdiction given to the Tribunal by the Charter amounted to a violation of the *ex post facto* principle and with it of the rule *nullum crimen sine lege*: had individual responsibility for these crimes been part of international law at the time of their performance, or had they only been constituted through the Charter? The issue was particularly pertinent with regard to the crime of aggressive war, which was also the first crime the Tribunal examined:

> The Charter makes the planning or waging of a war of aggression or a war in violation of international treaties a crime; and it is therefore not strictly necessary to consider whether and to what extent aggressive war was a crime before the execution of the London Agreement. But in view of the great importance of the questions of law involved, the Tribunal has heard full argument from the Prosecution and the Defense, and will express its view on the matter.
>
> It was urged on behalf of the defendants that a fundamental principle of all law – international and domestic – is that there can be no punishment of crime without a pre-existing law. '*Nullum crimen sine lege, nulla poena sine lege.*' It was submitted that *ex post facto* punishment is abhorrent to the law of all civilized nations, that no sovereign power had made aggressive war a crime at the time that the alleged criminal acts were committed, that no statute had defined aggressive war, that no penalty had been fixed for its commission, and no court had been created to try and punish offenders.[166]

As a matter of legitimacy (and, for that matter, legality), the Tribunal found it necessary to demonstrate that international law had already included individual responsibility for aggressive war at the time of Nazi rule. To achieve this aim, two elements had to be established: first, the Tribunal had to expound that aggressive war had already been prohibited

[166] *In re Goering and Others* (International Military Tribunal at Nuremberg, Judgment), 41 AJIL 1947, 172–333, at 217). See also 13 Annual Digest and Reports of Public International Law Cases (ILR) 203, at 208.

under international law in 1939; second, it had to show that this international rule had addressed individuals acting on behalf of the state. In the view of the Tribunal, the rule itself was established through the Kellogg-Briand Pact of 1928 to which Germany was a party.[167] The legal effect of the Pact, according to the Tribunal, was not only that aggressive war was illegal under international law, but that it represented an international crime.[168] This special status did not follow from the treaty itself, but from 'general principles of justice':[169] in the reasoning of the Tribunal, resort to aggressive war had 'inevitable and terrible consequences'[170] for the international community as a whole and therefore should be treated not merely as a normal international delict, but as an international crime. Associated with this special legal character of the rule was the presumption that its violation leads to individual rather than to state responsibility.[171] However, this was not clearly spelled out in this part of the judgment, but only presumed. It was only after having demonstrated that the prohibition of aggressive war was an international norm binding upon Germany from 1928 onwards and that violations of this norm had to be regarded as an international crime that the Tribunal turned to the question of individual responsibility in more detail. When faced with the submission that international law could only put obligations upon states, and not upon individuals,[172] the Tribunal memorably replied: 'That international law imposes duties and liabilities upon individuals as well as upon States has long been recognized. . . . Crimes against international law are committed by men, not by abstract entities, and only by punishing individuals who commit such crimes can the provisions of international law be enforced.'[173] With this short statement, the Tribunal considered it as established that the crime of aggression entailed international responsibility of individuals and not of state entities. Moreover, it was denied that an official function held by individuals when committing the crime led to immunity from prosecution under international law.[174] In consequence, individual defendants were sentenced for the crime of aggressive war under international law.

[167] *In re Goering and Others*, at 216–17 (AJIL). [168] Ibid., at 218 and 220.
[169] Ibid., at 219. See also Wright, 'Nuremburg Trial', at 54.
[170] *In re Goering and Others*, at 218 (AJIL). [171] See in particular ibid., at 218.
[172] In the literature, the submission was put forward e.g. by Manner, George, 'The Legal Nature and Punishment of Criminal Acts of Violence Contrary to the Laws of War', AJIL, 37 (1943), 407–35, esp. at 407–8: 'individuals are not subjects of the law of nations. . . . Individuals, therefore, cannot be held internationally liable for their acts contrary to the law of war.'
[173] *In re Goering and Others*, at 220 and 221 (AJIL). [174] Ibid., at 221.

The reasoning of the Tribunal with regard to individual responsibility for the crime of aggression has to be understood as a manifestation of the individualistic conception of international personality. It is evident that the language of the statement on individual responsibility with its observation on states not being 'abstract entities' but shaped by men is very reminiscent of the individualistic conception's line of reasoning.[175] It appears to reflect the functional view of the state wherein the active role of individuals as *gouvernants* is emphasized. Instructively, the Tribunal did not examine whether states had expressed their will to assign international legal status to individuals in the field of international crimes; nor was it analysed whether there existed a customary rule to this effect. The Tribunal simply regarded it as a basic principle that for international law to be an effective system of law, there must be individual responsibility for international crimes.[176] The link between the special status of the norm as an international crime and seemingly automatic individual responsibility for violations of it also corresponds with the individualistic conception. It is because the prohibition of aggressive war is a fundamental norm of the international community, the violation of which leads to 'terrible consequences' for humanity, that there is a presumption of this rule being binding also upon individuals.[177] This is in accordance with the individualistic view that there are fundamental international rights and duties binding upon every individual (be they *gouvernants* or *gouvernés*) in the interest of individual freedom. Finally, the fact that the tribunal had recourse to general principles of justice in order to declare aggressive war an international crime reveals the same view on sources of international law as in the individualistic conception. In conclusion, the reasoning of the Tribunal in order to declare individual responsibility for the crime of aggressive war strongly appears to be a manifestation of the individualistic conception of international personality.

[175] See the almost identical language in Lauterpacht, 'Punishment of War Crimes', at 64: 'The rules of war are binding not upon an abstract notion of Germany, but upon members of the German government, upon German individuals exercising governmental functions in occupied territory . . .'

[176] See also Lauterpacht, *Human Rights*, 44. A similar reading of the Nuremberg judgment is suggested by Kolb, Robert, 'The Jurisprudence of the Yugoslav and Rwandan Criminal Tribunals on their Jurisdiction and on International Crimes', BYIL, 71 (2000), 259–315, at 265. Also in this direction Zoller, Elisabeth, 'International Criminal Responsibility of Individuals for International Crimes' in George Ginsburg and V. N. Kudriavtsev (eds.), *The Nuremberg Trial and International Law* (Dordrecht: Martinus Nijhoff, 1990), 99–120, at 105–6.

[177] See in this respect also Lauterpacht, 'Punishment of War Crimes', at 65.

The judgment at Nuremberg marks the beginning of modern international criminal law.[178] Its basic principle regarding individual responsibility has since been reaffirmed many times by UN organs, states, and national, as well as international, tribunals. Immediately after the announcement of the judgment, the UN General Assembly unanimously adopted Resolution 95(I) affirming the 'principles of international law recognized by ... the judgment of the Tribunal'. The ILC was subsequently asked to formulate these principles, a task it completed in 1950. In Principle I it stated: 'Any person who commits an act which constitutes a crime under international law is responsible therefor and liable to punishment.'[179] In other words, the ILC held that any violation of international law that reaches the threshold of an international crime[180] necessarily involves punishment of individuals. The ILC returned to this principle in 1996 when commenting on Article 2 of the *Draft Code of Crimes against the Peace and Security of Mankind*, succinctly stating:

> The principle of individual responsibility and punishment for crimes under international law recognized at Nürnberg is the cornerstone of international criminal law. This principle is the enduring legacy of the Charter and the Judgment of the Nürnberg Tribunal which gives meaning to the prohibition of crimes under international law by ensuring that the individuals who commit such crimes incur responsibility and are liable to punishment.[181]

The close association of international crimes and individual responsibility enunciated in Nuremberg thus became firmly established in

[178] E.g. Cassese, Antonio, *International Criminal Law*, 1st edition (Oxford University Press, 2003), 40.

[179] *Principles of International Law recognized in the Charter of the Nürnberg Tribunal and in the Judgment of the Tribunal, with commentaries*, UN Doc. A/13/16, YILC (1950-II), p. 374. The comments on the principle included what appears to be a somewhat irritated acknowledgment of the Tribunal's straightforwardness in declaring that international law was directly applicable to individuals: 'The general rule underlying Principle I is that international law may impose duties on individuals directly without any interposition of internal law. The findings of the Tribunal were very definite on the question whether rules of international law may apply to individuals.' (YILC 1950-II, para. 99 (p. 374)). See also the more radical proposal by Georges Scelle in YILC 1949-I, at 206–7 (Scelle, Georges, *Formulation of the Principles recognized in the Charter of the Nürnberg Tribunal and in the Judgment of the Tribunal – Proposal by Professor Georges Scelle*, incorporated into UN Doc. A/CN.4/SR.28).

[180] This line is an adaptation from Cassese, *International Criminal Law*, 3.

[181] *Draft Code of Crimes against the Peace and Security of Mankind*, UN Doc. A/51/10, YILC 1996-II(2), p. 19. Essential elements of the Draft Code were later introduced into the Draft Statute of the International Criminal Court.

international law in the aftermath of the judgment. To a considerable extent, this Nuremberg principle was also relied upon in the jurisprudence of the International Criminal Tribunal for the Former Yugoslavia (ICTY),[182] the first international criminal tribunal after the Nuremberg and Tokyo trials.[183] However, in these ICTY judgments there was some ambiguity as to whether individual responsibility followed automatically from dealing with international crimes (as the Nuremberg principle would suggest) or whether it had to be separately established in certain cases through examination of international custom to this effect.[184] The issue was especially pertinent with respect to war crimes not listed but generally referred to in Article 3 of the ICTY Statute. Through this construction, it was left to the Tribunal to determine whether a serious violation of the laws of war not listed in the Statute entailed individual responsibility. This somewhat unfortunate situation was dealt with by the Tribunal primarily by relying on the Nuremberg principle of automatic individual responsibility for international crimes and at the same time declaring this principle part of international customary law (without serious investigation of state practice).[185] In result, then, the ICTY jurisprudence strongly reaffirmed that individual responsibility is implicit in the category of international crimes and therefore followed the Nuremberg principle in general, notwithstanding some efforts to ground this principle in international custom (which would make it to some extent dependent on expressions of state will). An overall similar approach can be found in the practice of the International Criminal Tribunal for Rwanda (ICTR)[186] which – though indirectly, it appears – also followed the Nuremberg principle regarding

[182] See *Prosecutor* v. *Tadic* (Jurisdiction), ICTY Trial Chamber Case IT-94-1, 10 August 1995, para. 70; *Prosecutor* v. *Tadic* (Jurisdiction), ICTY Appeals Chamber, 2 October 1995, paras 128–9 (applying the Nuremberg principle also to internal armed conflicts); *Prosecutor* v. *Tadic* (Judgment), ICTY Trial Chamber, 7 May 1997, para. 621 (p. 223) and para. 665 (p. 245); *Prosecutor v. Furundzija* (Judgment), ICTY Trial Chamber Case IT-95-17/1-T, 10 December 1998, para. 140 (p. 54) and para. 169 (p. 67).

[183] The ICTY was established under Chapter VII of the UN Charter by Security Council Resolution 808 (1993), adopted on 22 February 1993.

[184] See also Kolb, 'Jurisprudence of the Yugoslav and Rwandan Criminal Tribunals', at 265–6, and Shraga, Daphna and Ralph Zacklin, 'The International Criminal Tribunal for the Former Yugoslavia', EJIL, 5 (1994), 360–80, esp. at 366.

[185] This becomes especially clear in *Prosecutor v. Furundzija*, para. 140 (p. 54). See also Kolb, 'Jurisprudence of the Yugoslav and Rwandan Criminal Tribunals', at 266.

[186] The ICTR was also established under Chapter VII UN Charter by Security Council Resolution 955 (1994), adopted on 8 November 1994.

individual responsibility.[187] In the same vein, the newly created International Criminal Court (ICC) in The Hague has jurisdiction over natural persons according to Article 1 and Article 25 of the Rome Statute. Influenced by these developments concerning international tribunals,[188] national courts, too, by relying on the related principle of universal jurisdiction, have dealt with individual responsibility for international crimes and have thereby followed the basic ideas enunciated at Nuremberg.[189]

In conclusion, international criminal law as developed after Nuremberg follows the Nuremberg principle. Accordingly, the individualistic conception of international personality has been continuously manifested. In this sense, the individual is regarded as responsible for international crimes for an international crime is defined as a violation of a fundamental value of the international community.[190] Such fundamental norms – in contrast to 'normal' international rules, e.g. stemming from bilateral trade agreements – impose duties upon individuals and not only (or even primarily) on collective state entities, for only with individual responsibility can these fundamental values be effectively preserved. In consequence, according to this principle, there is no need to specifically establish individual responsibility for an international crime: there is a strong presumption of individual responsibility with international crimes. This presumption recently became apparent in the *Bosnian Genocide Case*, with the ICJ forced to contend at length that an international crime (in this case genocide) could be

187 See *Prosecutor* v. *Akayesu* (Judgment), ICTR Trial Chamber Case 96-4-T, 2 September 1998, paras 671–5.

188 Cassese, *International Criminal Law*, 8.

189 Most famous is perhaps *Regina* v. *Bow Street Metropolitan Stipendiary Magistrate, ex parte Pinochet Ugarte No. 3* (UK House of Lords, 1999), 119 ILR 136. In this case, as in most others dealt with by national courts, the question of state immunity necessarily arose (the matter is less pertinent in the ICTY or ICC because Article 7(2) ICTY Statute and Article 27 ICC Statute exclude claims of immunity). It must be noted that the issue of state immunity has to be distinguished from individual responsibility for international crimes as such: immunity is only an exception to the principle of universal jurisdiction which in turn depends on there being an international crime; accordingly, immunity does not directly deny individual responsibility, but only jurisdiction. The distinction has been made admirably clear by the Joint Separate Opinion of Judges Higgins, Kooijmans and Buergenthal in the *Yerodia* Case (*Case concerning the Arrest Warrant of 11 April 2000* (Democratic Republic of the Congo v. Belgium), Judgment, ICJ 14 February 2002, esp. at p. 84 (para. 71 of the Joint Separate Opinion).

190 See also the association of *ius cogens* and individual responsibility in *Prosecutor* v. *Furundzija*, para. 155 (p. 60).

committed not only by individuals but also by states.[191] Though the Nuremberg principle was quoted in the judgment, it was held that in accordance with this principle there existed a dual criminal responsibility in international law (individual and state).[192] In several separate opinions, this view was questioned and it was argued by reference to the same Nuremberg principle that an international crime could only be committed by individuals.[193] The case illustrates that in international criminal law, there is a presumption of the individual being an international person; in fact, international criminal law only exists because the individual is considered as the addressee of fundamental international rules in the sense of the individualistic conception of international personality. Nevertheless, it is perfectly in line with the individualistic conception as understood in this book that there is a dual responsibility, that is, that there is also state responsibility for international crimes. On balance, this seems to be the position today, notwithstanding a presumption of individuals.[194]

Civil responsibility of private parties for ius cogens *violations*

In the context of applying the United States Alien Tort Claims Act (ATCA), US courts have repeatedly had to deal with alleged violations of international law by private parties, including corporations. The private and partly

[191] *Case concerning the Application of the Convention on the Prevention and Punishment of the Crime of Genocide* (Bosnia and Herzegovina v. Serbia and Montenegro), Judgment, ICJ 26 February 2007, paras 155–79.

[192] Ibid., paras 172–3.

[193] Separate Opinion of Judge Owada, paras 49–50 and Separate Opinion of Judge Tomka, esp. para. 45.

[194] See also Cassese, *International Criminal Law*, 19, and Article 25(4) of the Rome Statute. The topic of criminal responsibility of states was intensely debated in the course of the ILC's work on state responsibility. It was Special Rapporteur Roberto Ago who introduced a distinction between criminal and delictual responsibility of states into what became provisional Article 19 of the state responsibility project in the ILC (see Ago, Roberto (Special Rapporteur), *Fifth Report on State Responsibility*, UN Doc. A/CN.4/291 and Addendum 1 and 2, YILC (1976-II(1)), pp. 24–54). Accordingly, Ago advocated that states could become criminally responsible and certain special consequences were attached to this. However, the topic being controversial and the distinction not substantively reflected in international practice, it was later dropped on the recommendation of James Crawford (see Crawford, James (Special Rapporteur), *First Report on State Responsibility*, UN Doc. A/CN.4/490/Add.3, para. 101; see also *Draft Articles on Responsibility of States for Internationally Wrongful Acts with Commentaries*, YILC (2001-II(2)), pp. 110–12). For a view emphasizing the importance of criminal responsibility of states see Pellet, Alain, 'Can a State Commit a Crime? Definitely, Yes!' EJIL, 10 (1999), 425–34, esp. at 426–30.

corporate nature of these entities were new features compared to the Nuremburg judgment and its subsequent application in international criminal law. The latter had primarily dealt with actions taken by individuals on behalf of the state and not with purely private matters. Starting with the seminal decision in *Kadic* v. *Karadzic II*,[195] US courts have repeatedly affirmed that private entities can violate international law of *ius cogens* character; in so doing these non-state actors commit a tort in the meaning of the ATCA and are ordered to pay compensation. This jurisprudence is a manifestation of the individualistic conception of international personality.

The ATCA is a civil procedure law enacted in 1789 declaring US courts competent to hear tort petitions for violations of 'the law of nations' that have taken place outside the United States.[196] In essence, the ATCA is a municipal statute of jurisdictional character embodying a *renvoi* to violations of international law. The statute was brought back to the courts' attention in 1980 in *Filartiga* v. *Peña-Irala*[197] in which a Paraguayan official was sued for committing torture. The case concerning state action exercised by an individual, the court could draw from the Nuremberg principle for establishing whether agents of a state could violate international law. The matter was different in 1984 in *Tel-Oren* v. *Libyan Arab Republic.*[198] In this case, the Palestine Liberation Organization (PLO) was sued for committing torture when seizing a civilian bus in Israel. The PLO was clearly not a state for the purposes of the tort proceedings. This led Judge Edwards to draw a distinction between the case at hand and *Filartiga* as well as the Nuremburg principle with regard to the possibility of non-state actors violating international law:

> The Palestine Liberation Organization is not a recognized state, and it does not act under color of any recognized state's law. In contrast, the Paraguayan official in *Filartiga* acted under color of state law, although in violation of it. The Second Circuit surveyed the law of nations and concluded that *official torture* constituted a violation of it. Plaintiffs in the case before us do not allege facts to show that official or state-initiated

[195] *Kadic* v. *Karadzic II* (US Court of Appeals, Second Circuit, 1995) (Chief Judge Newman), 104 ILR 135, at 149–65.

[196] 28 USC §1350. The ATCA reads in its entirety: 'The district courts shall have original jurisdiction of any civil action by an alien for a tort only, committed in violation of the law of nations or a treaty of the United States'. For the history of the ATCA see Burley, Anne-Marie, 'The Alien Tort Statute and the Judiciary Act of 1789: A Badge of Honor', AJIL, 83 (1989), 461–93, esp. at 464–88.

[197] *Filartiga* v. *Peña-Irala* (US Court of Appeals, Second Circuit, 1980), 77 ILR 169.

[198] *Tel-Oren* v. *Libyan Arab Republic* (US Court of Appeals, District of Columbia Circuit, 1984) (Judge Edwards, concurring), 77 ILR 193.

> torture is implicated in this action. Nor do I think they could, so long as the PLO is not a recognized member of the community of nations.[199]

In view of the fact that there was no action on behalf of a state involved, the question also arose as to whether private action would constitute a violation of international law:

> The extension would require us to venture out of the comfortable realm of established international law – within which *Filartiga* firmly sat – in which states are the actors. It would require an assessment of the extent to which international law imposes not only rights but also obligations on individuals. It would require a determination of where to draw the line between persons or groups who are or are not bound by dictates of international law, and what the groups look like.[200]

Judge Edwards was not prepared to 'venture out of the comfortable realm of established international law' without guidance from the Supreme Court. While hinting at the possibility that international law also puts obligations on private parties not acting on behalf of a state – 'a number of jurists and commentators either have assumed or urged that the individual is a subject of international law'[201] – Judge Edwards concluded that the Nuremberg principle was not applicable to the present case where there was no state action involved.[202] A similar reasoning was put forward by Judge Scalia one year later in *Sanchez-Espinoza* v. *Reagan*,[203] a case concerning conduct on behalf of the Nicaraguan Contra Forces ('Contras'). The Contras neither representing a state entity nor their actions being attributable to a state, their conduct was declared private and as such per se not in a position to interfere with rules of international law. In a sense, this early jurisprudence on the ATCA represents a mixture of the states-only and the individualistic conception of international personality: individual responsibility is only accepted when conduct leading to it is exercised on behalf of the state, i.e. in the function of a *gouvernant*. A strict application of the individualistic conception would entail that actions of *gouvernés* are relevant for international law as well, in particular when fundamental norms of the international legal order are concerned.

[199] Ibid., at 220 (original emphasis). [200] Ibid., at 221.

[201] Ibid., at 221. Judge Edwards also made reference in this respect towards Lauterpacht's view on the subjects of international law.

[202] Ibid., at 223.

[203] *Sanchez-Espinoza* v. *Reagan*, (US Court of Appeals, District of Columbia Circuit, 1985) (Judge Scalia), 80 ILR 586, at 590–1.

The latter view was, however, clearly manifested in 1995 in *Kadic* v. *Karadzic II*.[204] The case arose out of the Yugoslav crisis and its complex and violent process of secession in the early 1990s. The specific context was the case of Bosnia and Herzegovina. Being one of the republics constituting the Yugoslav federation, Bosnia and Herzegovina had proclaimed its will to secede from Yugoslavia on 15 October 1991 and, after a referendum boycotted by its Serbian population, officially declared independence on 3 March 1992.[205] After the declaration of Bosnia and Herzegovina's will to secede, the area's Serbian population declared the independent state Republika Srpska of which Radovan Karadzic was the president.[206] On 6 April 1992, Bosnia and Herzegovina was recognized as a state by the members of the European Community while no recognition was granted to the Republika Srpska. The latter was considered part of Bosnia and Herzegovina without a right to external self-determination and in consequence lacking statehood. Subsequently, hostilities between the Bosnian Serbs and the government of Bosnia and Herzegovina escalated into civil war. Radovan Karadzic was later sued under the ATCA by a group of Bosnian Muslims for acts of genocide, war crimes, and other human rights violations. The District Court of the Southern District of New York decided on 7 September 1994 that it lacked jurisdiction under the ATCA because the Republika Srpska was not a state and the acts allegedly committed by Karadzic were therefore not attributable to a state. In the absence of state action, and in line with the principles stated in *Tel-Oren* v. *Libyan Arab Republic* and *Sanchez-Espinoza* v. *Reagan*, there was no violation of international law.[207] The District Court thus accepted Karadzic's contention that 'acts committed by non-state actors do not violate the law of nations'. On appeal, the Second Circuit replied to this reasoning: 'We do not agree that the law of nations, as understood in the modern era, confines its reach to state action. Instead, we hold that certain forms of conduct violate the law of nations whether undertaken by those acting under the auspices of states or only as private individuals.'[208] The Second Circuit readily specified which international law norms could be violated by private individuals: 'offenses of *universal concern* include those capable of being committed

[204] *Kadic* v. *Karadzic II* (US Court of Appeals, Second Circuit, 1995) (Chief Judge Newman), 104 ILR 135, at 149–65.

[205] See Crawford, *Creation of States*, 398. [206] Ibid., 406–7.

[207] *Kadic* v. *Karadzic I* (US District Court for the Southern District of New York, 1994), 104 ILR 135, at 146.

[208] *Kadic* v. *Karadzic II*, at 152.

by non-state actors.'[209] Accordingly, there was a 'limited category of violations of universal concern' which could also be committed by private individuals, not only by individuals acting on behalf of the state. As subsequent practice confirmed, such international law rules of 'universal concern' were synonymous with international *ius cogens*.[210]

In sum, the *Kadic* v. *Karadzic II* judgment proclaims that when it comes to international *ius cogens*, there is no private–public distinction: such fundamental norms apply irrespective of whether an individual is acting on behalf of the state or of a non-state entity. This view reflects the individualistic conception of international personality, in particular with respect to three elements. First, it contains the proposition that the public and private spheres should not be distinguished too strictly. In this line of thought, it is not possible to treat violations of fundamental values of humanity committed by the leader of a non-state entity in a different way from those committed by state agents; they all affect fundamental rights of human beings and therefore cannot be judged by different standards. Second, the view on *ius cogens* as representing international norms of universal concern is also in line with the individualistic conception of international personality. In this tradition, international law is not simply regarded as a set of horizontal obligations but as a system of law containing constitutional principles pertinent to all members of the international community. Third, it is not attempted to ground the universal application of *ius cogens* norms in international customary law; it is merely treated as a matter of legal principle. This, too, corresponds with the individualistic conception of international personality.

The principle originating with *Kadic* v. *Karadzic II* and manifesting the individualistic conception of international personality has since been applied several times in the context of corporations having allegedly violated international *ius cogens*.[211] From the point of view of the individualistic conception, this is not surprising for acts by corporations can also possibly endanger basic individual rights and freedoms and there

209 Ibid., at 153 (emphasis added).

210 See e.g. the statement in *Presbyterian Church of Sudan* v. *Talisman Energy, Inc.* (US District Court for the Southern District of New York, 2003), 244 F.Supp.2d 289, at 313.

211 *Iwanowa* v. *Ford Motor Company* (US District Court for the District of New Jersey, 1999), 67 F.Supp.2d 424, at 443–5; *Doe I* v. *Unocal Corporation* (US Court of Appeals, Ninth Circuit, 2002), 395 F.3d 932, at 945–7; *Ken Wiwa v. Royal Dutch Petroleum Company* (US District Court for the Southern District of New York, 2002), WL 319887, at *12; *Presbyterian Church of Sudan* v. *Talisman Energy Inc.*, at 311–9. See for an overview of the case law Seibert-Fohr and Wolfrum, 'Einzelstaatliche Durchsetzung', at 155–64.

seems to be no reason why corporations, being legal persons, should be treated differently from natural persons.[212] Correspondingly, courts have often not taken much effort to show that corporate liability for violations of international law originated from treaty or customary international law. It has primarily been dealt with as a matter of principle and legal logic: 'Given that private individuals are liable for violations of international law in certain circumstances, there is no logical reason why corporations should not be held liable, at least in cases of *jus cogens* violations.'[213] In result, courts have treated corporations according to the principle formulated in *Kadic* v. *Karadzic II* and thereby manifested the individualistic conception of international personality. However, it is not entirely clear to what extent the US Supreme Court is prepared to confirm this jurisprudence of lower courts. Although the opinion offers much room for interpretation, the Supreme Court at least hinted in *Sosa* v. *Alvarez-Machain et al.* that *Kadic* v. *Karadzic II* might have gone too far in stipulating liability of private actors for violations of international law. If confirmed, this view would have repercussions for whether corporations can be sued under the ATCA for violations of international law.[214] It might well be, therefore, that the Supreme Court eventually will not apply the individualistic conception of international personality when dealing with the ATCA.

International human rights law in the ECHR

At least in the context of the European Court of Human Rights (ECHR), it is submitted that international human rights law has to be considered a manifestation of the individualistic conception of international personality.[215] In this respect, it has to be readily admitted that aspects of international personality are normally not specifically addressed in the jurisprudence of the ECHR. It is thus difficult to trace information on the international legal status of individuals directly from the case law. Accordingly, in the present section the argument is developed by relating

[212] See e.g. also Ratner, 'Corporations and Human Rights', esp. at 492–6, and Vazquez, 'Obligations of Corporations', at 944.

[213] *Presbyterian Church of Sudan* v. *Talisman Energy Inc.*, at 319.

[214] *Sosa* v. *Alvarez-Machain et al.* (US Supreme Court, 2004), 127 ILR 691, at 794 (with specific reference to *Kadic* v. *Karadzic*, note 20).

[215] The present analysis is confined to the ECHR. Its basic conclusions, however, *mutatis mutandi* hold true in the context of the IACHR (see also Caflisch and Cançado Trindade, 'Conventions Américaine et Européenne', *passim* (by implication).

the general reasoning in *Loizidou* v. *Turkey*[216] and its subsequent employment in the case law to the basic propositions and origins of the individualistic conception. By analysing these incidents, it can also be illustrated that there are tendencies in international human rights jurisprudence to indirectly re-approach the states-only conception of international personality in the same paradoxical sense as in European Community law. This is done by insisting so much on the idiosyncratic nature of international human rights law and its concern for individuals as to separate it from the overall international legal system.[217] It is then only when firmly situating international human rights law in the context of general international law that the individualistic conception of international personality is truly manifested. On balance, this is the case in international human rights law as pursued in the ECHR.

The case of *Loizidou* v. *Turkey* concerned Ms Titina Loizidou, a Cypriot national who lived in Southern Cyprus but held property in the northern part of the island. After Turkish occupation of Northern Cyprus in 1974, Ms Loizidou was prevented by Turkish forces from returning to her property. On 19 March 1989, the applicant participated in a demonstration in the course of which she crossed the border to Northern Cyprus and was arrested. After being released, the government of Cyprus and Ms Loizidou brought suit against Turkey claiming that the latter had violated Article 1 of Protocol No. 1 and several other provisions of the European Convention on Human Rights[218] by preventing Ms Loizidou from returning to her property and peacefully enjoying it as well as by arresting her. Turkey, for its part, denied that the ECHR had jurisdiction over the matter. It referred to a reservation filed on 28 January 1987 with the intended effect of precluding Northern Cyprus from jurisdiction of the Court. The reservation had been renewed several times afterwards and there was no question that it was still in force. What was at issue was whether the reservations of Turkey were permissible

[216] *Loizidou* v. *Turkey I* (Grand Chamber, Preliminary Objections, 1995), ECHR Series A No 310; *Loizidou* v. *Turkey II* (Grand Chamber, Merits), ECHR Reports 1996-VI.

[217] On whether international human rights law in the ECHR is a so-called 'self-contained regime' see Report of the Study Group (Finalized by Martti Koskenniemi), *Fragmentation of International Law: Difficulties Arising from the Diversification and Expansion of International Law*, ILC 2006, UN Doc. A/CN.4/L.682, paras 161–4 (denying it). See also Caflisch and Cançado Trindade, 'Conventions Américaine et Européenne', esp. at 60–1 (also denying it).

[218] Convention for the Protection of Human Rights and Fundamental Freedoms, 4 November 1950, 213 UNTS 222.

under Articles 25[219] and 46[220] of the European Convention on Human Rights.

Turning to the interpretation of Articles 25 and 46 of the European Convention on Human Rights, the Court first elaborated how it had to approach the two provisions. The Court observed:

> Articles 25 and 46 of the Convention are provisions which are essential to the effectiveness of the Convention system since they delineate the responsibility of the Commission and Court 'to ensure the observance of the engagements undertaken by the High Contracting Parties' ... *In interpreting these key provisions it must have regard to the special character of the Convention as a treaty for the collective enforcement of human rights and fundamental freedoms.*[221]

To strengthen its argument, the Court referred back to a statement on the nature of the European human rights system it had already made in the context of *Ireland* v. *United Kingdom* in 1976: 'Unlike international treaties of the classic kind, the Convention comprises more than mere reciprocal engagements between Contracting States. It creates, over and above a network of mutual, bilateral undertakings, objective obligations which, in the words of the Preamble, benefit from a "collective enforcement".'[222]

In effect, the Court stressed the special character of human rights in these statements. The European Convention on Human Rights did not represent mere bilateral undertakings, but amounted to an objective legal order. It followed:

[219] In relevant part, Article 25 stated at the time: '1. The Commission may receive petitions addressed to the Secretary General of the Council of Europe from any person, non-governmental organization or group of individuals claiming to be the victim of a violation by one of the High Contracting Parties of the rights set forth in [the] Convention, provided that the High Contracting Party against which the complaint has been lodged has declared that it recognizes the competence of the Commission to receive such petitions. Those of the High Contracting Parties who have made such a declaration undertake not to hinder in any way the effective exercise of this right.'

[220] '1. Any of the High Contracting Parties may at any time declare that it recognizes as compulsory ipso facto and without special agreement the jurisdiction of the Court in all matters concerning the interpretation and application of the ... Convention. 2. The declarations referred to above may be made unconditionally or on condition of reciprocity on the part of several or certain other High Contracting Parties or for a specified period. 3. These declarations shall be deposited with the Secretary General of the Council of Europe who shall transmit copies thereof to the High Contracting Parties.'

[221] *Loizidou* v. *Turkey I*, para. 70 (references omitted, emphasis added).

[222] *Ireland* v. *United Kingdom* (Judgment, 1976), ECHR Series A No 25, para. 239.

> . . . that these provisions cannot be interpreted solely in accordance with the intentions of their authors as expressed more than forty years ago . . . the object and purpose of the Convention as an *instrument for the protection of individual human beings* requires that its provisions be interpreted and applied so as to make its safeguards practical and effective . . . a system, which would enable States to qualify their consent under the optional clauses, would not only seriously weaken the role of the Commission and Court in the discharge of their functions but would also diminish the effectiveness of the Convention as a *constitutional instrument of European public order* (ordre public).[223]

By implication, the Court held that the restrictions on its jurisdiction as declared by Turkey, though perhaps acceptable under general international law, were not permissible in the special circumstances of the European Convention on Human Rights:[224] its Articles 25 and 46 had to be interpreted in light of the fundamental values incorporated into the Convention and in these circumstances it was not possible to allow Turkey effectively to exclude Northern Cyprus from the protection of the Convention. It was stressed that the European human rights system was not only a treaty system, but a constitutional legal order intended for the protection of the individual human being. Such status of human rights law, in the opinion of the Court, strongly suggested that special considerations with respect to treaty interpretation applied which made Turkey's reservation with regard to Northern Cyprus impermissible. These rather strong statements in favour of special considerations when international human rights law was at issue were put into perspective in the merits phase of the proceedings: 'In the Court's view, the principles underlying the Convention cannot be interpreted and applied in a vacuum. Mindful of the Convention's special character as a human rights treaty, it must also take into account any relevant rules of international law . . .'[225] In result, the ECHR made it clear that despite human rights representing constitutional norms which, to a certain extent, had to be distinguished from 'normal' treaty norms, this did not imply that international human rights law was a self-contained legal system. Unlike the conclusions drawn by the ECJ in the *van Gend en Loos* case[226] and subsequent jurisprudence, the concern with individuals was no reason for the ECHR to separate human rights law from general international

[223] *Loizidou* v. *Turkey I*, paras 71–2 and 75 (references omitted, emphasis added).
[224] Ibid., para. 89. [225] *Loizidiou v. Turkey II*, para. 43.
[226] Case 26/62, *Van Gend en Loos* v. *Netherlands Inland Revenue Administration*, 1963 ECR 1, at 12.

law. At the same time, however, it insisted on some special considerations to be taken into account when objective and constitutional norms intended for the protection of individual human beings were at issue. Thus, the Court, while maintaining the constitutional character of international human rights law, also firmly situated the latter in the overall international legal system.

This balanced approach formulated in the merits phase of *Loizidou* v. *Turkey* was confirmed in subsequent judgments of note. In *Al-Adsani* v. *United Kingdom*, the ECHR stated in this respect: 'The Court must be mindful of the Convention's special character as a human rights treaty, and it must also take the relevant rules of international law into account (see, *mutatis mutandis*, *Loizidou v. Turkey* (merits), . . . § 43). The Convention should so far as possible be interpreted in harmony with other rules of international law of which it forms part . . .'[227] And in *Bankovic* v. *Belgium et al.*, the Court, summarizing its previous jurisprudence, held in similar vein:

> . . . the Court recalls that the principles underlying the Convention cannot be interpreted and applied in a vacuum. The Court must also take into account any relevant rules of international law when examining questions concerning its jurisdiction and, consequently, determine State responsibility in conformity with the governing principles of international law, although it must remain mindful of the Convention's special character as a human rights treaty (the above-cited *Loizidou* judgment (*merits*), at §§ 43 and 52). The Convention should be interpreted as far as possible in harmony with other principles of international law of which it forms part (*Al-Adsani v. the United Kingdom*, . . .).[228]

Consequently, it can be said that the ECHR upheld its approach of considering international human rights law as special while nevertheless situating it in the overall international legal system. There was no new legal order, there were only constitutional norms protecting individual human beings in the framework of existing general international law.

On balance, the jurisprudence of the ECHR has to be understood as a manifestation of the individualistic conception of international personality. Though not directly addressing the topic, the style of reasoning and the use of certain expressions like 'constitutional norms', 'fundamental

[227] *Al-Adsani* v. *United Kingdom* (Grand Chamber, Judgment), ECHR Reports 2001-XI, para. 55.

[228] *Bankovic and Others* v. *Belgium and Others* (Grand Chamber, Decision on Admissibility), ECHR Reports 2001-XII, para. 57.

freedoms', or 'objective obligations', as well as their link to the 'protection of individual human beings', strongly indicate this conclusion. In particular, the use of these categories underlines that international human rights law in the ECHR is not considered a matter of normal treaty interpretation as the formal conception of international personality would suggest; there is an a priori idea that human rights conventions serve a higher purpose – namely, protecting the individual – calling for special considerations alien to formal treaty interpretation. At the same time, as the *Al-Adsani* and *Bankovic* judgments in particular made clear, the ECHR regards the international legal system capable of providing the overall legal framework in which these constitutional norms for the protection of individual freedoms can be situated. There is no need to establish a self-contained legal system separated from general international law in order to protect individual human beings. This is also in accordance with the individualistic conception which precisely considers it the basic purpose of international law to protect individuals.[229] By implication, it follows that the individual must be considered an international person in the European human rights system: it is an international person because of the very nature of human rights representing constitutional norms of the international legal system.[230]

[229] Admittedly, there are also some tendencies in ECHR jurisprudence to separate international human rights law from the overall international legal system and by doing so to manifest the states-only conception in the same paradoxical sense as in European Community law. This tendency shines through in the preliminary objection phase of *Loizidou* v. *Turkey*, but was restrained in the merits phase of the same case and in subsequent judgments under review.

[230] See also Caflisch and Cançado Trindade, 'Conventions Américaine et Européenne', at 33, and Wildhaber, 'Human Rights and International Law', at 227. *Contra*: Orakhelashvili, 'Position of the Individual', at 254–5.

8

The formal conception

The formal conception articulates no presumption for a particular entity to be an international person. The international legal system is declared completely open: anyone being the addressee of an international norm (right, duty or capacity) is an international person. Consequently, international personality is an *a posteriori* concept. In principle, there are also no direct legal consequences attached to being an international person. In particular, the capacity to create international law does not follow from personality. Hans Kelsen formulated the formal conception as part of his pure theory of law. It has been advocated, among others, by Paul Guggenheim,[1] D. P. O'Connell[2] and, perhaps most prominently, Julio A. Barberis.[3] The main legal manifestations of the conception are the *LaGrand* and *Avena* decisions of the ICJ as well as mixed claims under BITs and human rights treaties in general.

Basic propositions

The formal conception declares personality in international law an essentially open concept. There are no limits as to which entities can be international persons:

> Examinant le domaine de validité personnel du droit international, il convient de se demander pour quels sujets vaut cet ordre, à qui il s'adresse, c'est-à-dire quels sont les sujets dont il règle la conduite, les droits et les devoirs. Nous aurons à montrer qu'à cet égard la validité du droit international ne connaît pas de limites.[4]

1 Guggenheim, Paul, *Lehrbuch des Völkerrechts: Unter Berücksichtigung der internationalen und schweizerischen Praxis* (Basel: Verlag für Recht und Gesellschaft, 1948), 161.
2 O'Connell, D. P., 'La Personnalité en Droit International', RGDIP, 34 (1963), 5–43, at 8.
3 Barberis, 'Personnalité Juridique', at 168–70 (with some minor addenda).
4 Kelsen, Hans, 'Théorie Générale du Droit International Public', RCADI, 42 (1932-IV), 121–351, at 141. An almost identical formulation can be found in Kelsen's second General

There is thus no a priori presumption for a specific entity possessing international personality. The system is considered completely open. The mechanism by which international personality is acquired is by interpreting international norms: any entity on which the international legal system confers rights, duties or capacities is an international person.[5] Personality in international law is then not a precondition for holding international obligations or authorizations, but is the consequence of possessing them. In other words, personality is not an a priori concept, but an a posteriori legal construction. In fact, personality is not regarded as a concept belonging to positive law, but is considered a merely descriptive device belonging to the realm of legal doctrine and as such being without concrete legal implications: being an international person thus simply reflects the sum of legal norms addressing a certain entity.[6] Accordingly, it is a matter for every international norm to determine its addressees and as such its legal persons: whenever the interpretation of an international norm leads to it addressing the conduct of a particular entity, this entity is an international person.

On a fundamental level, international norms, like all legal rules, are thought to regulate the conduct of individual human beings. Therefore, according to the formal conception, every international norm in the first place addresses individuals:

> All law is a regulation of human behaviour. The only social reality to which legal norms can refer are the relations between human beings. Hence, a legal obligation as well as a legal right cannot have for its contents anything but the behaviour of human individuals. If, then, international law should not obligate and authorize individuals, the obligations and rights stipulated by international law would have no contents at all and international law would not oblige or authorize anybody to do anything.[7]

However, the fact that, on a fundamental level, international law regulates conduct of individual human beings does not imply that in the

Course (Kelsen, Hans, 'Théorie du Droit International Public', RCADI, 84 (1953-III), 1-203, at 66).

5 Kelsen, Hans, *General Theory of Law and State* (Cambridge (Mass.): Harvard University Press, 1945), 99 and 342, and Kelsen, *Reine Rechtslehre*, 52. By implication: Kelsen, 'Théorie (II)', at 67–8; Kelsen, 'Théorie (I)', at 143–4. See also the enlightening statements by Barberis, 'Personnalité Juridique', at 169–70.

6 Kelsen, 'Théorie (II)', at 67; Kelsen, 'Théorie (I)', at 143; Kelsen, *Law and State*, 96. See also Barberis, 'Personnalité Juridique', at 169.

7 Kelsen, *Law and State*, 342. See also Kelsen, 'Théorie (I)', at 142, and Kelsen, 'Théorie (II)', at 66.

formal conception only individuals are international persons. For individuals are often not addressed by international law in their private matters, but in their function as an organ of a corporate body. In this case, the legal actions of the individual are attributed (*Zurechnung*) to a corporate body such as the state or some other form of collective organization. It is then this corporate body which is in effect the addressee of the particular international norm and as such an international person:

> Quand on dit d'une personne juridique, d'une société par exemple, qu'elle a des obligations ou des droits subjectifs, cela signifie qu'il existe des obligations ou des droits subjectifs se rapportant à la conduite d'un individu, mais que cet individu a les obligations et les droit subjectifs en question en sa qualité de membre ou d'organe de la société. Nous disons que ses obligations et droits sont ceux de la société. Nous les lui rapportons, nous les lui imputons, parce que l'individu qui est le vrai sujet de ces obligations et droits subjectifs les a en qualité de membre ou d'organe de la société.[8]

Accordingly, states and other corporate bodies do become international persons when an international norm is directed towards an individual whose conduct is attributed to the corporate body as a matter of the pertinent legal system.[9] Importantly, thus, these corporate entities, including states, are never international persons by their very existence. In fact, states are not regarded to have an existence at all apart from norms of imputation: states are not thought to exist as a social fact; they only exist as far as the national legal order creates state organs, that is, attributes individual action to the state.[10] States then acquire international legal status only when an international norm is directed towards an individual whose conduct is imputable to the state according to the national legal system.

Apart from being indirectly addressed by international norms as organs of corporate bodies, individuals can also be direct addressees of international norms in the formal conception. This is the case when their conduct is regulated by international norms in matters not attributable to a corporate entity according to the national legal system.[11] In this event, individuals are direct international persons. Analysing the totality of international norms in 1932, it follows for Kelsen that at that time

[8] Kelsen, 'Théorie (II)', at 67. [9] Kelsen, *Law and State*, 343; Kelsen, 'Théorie (I)', at 148.

[10] Kelsen, *Law and State*, 191–2; Kelsen, 'Théorie (II)', at 77–9.

[11] Kelsen, 'Théorie (II)', at 93–7; Kelsen, 'Théorie (I)', at 148–58; Kelsen, *Law and State*, 342–8.

various forms of collective organizations, most prominently states, and individuals are international persons: 'Le droit international a, en règle générale, pour sujets les Etats, c'est-à-dire des individus d'une façon médiate – exceptionnellement aussi des individus d'une façon immédiate. Il n'est pas contraire à la nature du droit international que ce qui est aujourd'hui une exception devienne un jour la règle.'[12] Thus, there is nothing in the international legal system that prevents individuals from becoming regular international persons; it all depends on what addressees international norms stipulate at a given moment in time. It is also possible that, as a matter of empirical observation, individuals become regular international persons whereas the international legal status of states might become the exception.

As concerns the consequences of being an international person, there are no additional legal implications related to possessing personality in international law other than those determined by the totality of the applicable international norms. Hence, there are no fundamental rights and duties or certain capacities attached to being an international person according to the formal conception. All these powers and competences are determined by particular international norms to their effect, not by the concept of international personality itself:[13] '[An entity] is an international personality because it is a subject of international rights and duties. The concept of international personality is a thoroughly formal concept. Hence it is impossible to deduce from the fact that [an entity] is an international personality any definite rights and duties ...'[14] It is therefore senseless in the view of the formal conception to recognize certain entities as international persons: such status in itself does not entail any international legal rights, duties or capacities whatsoever.[15] It is a matter for international norms to confer such legal obligations or authorizations upon social entities. By implication, it is also not a consequence of being an international person to possess the competence to create international law. It is only through customary international norms authorizing individuals as organs of states to create international law that such competence is acquired. The difference between law-creation and law-application is hence essentially non-existent in the formal conception: law-creation is simply the application of a hierarchically higher norm authorizing a particular entity to create law.[16] In the case of international law, general customary law contains rules declaring

[12] Kelsen, 'Théorie (I)', at 170. [13] Kelsen, *Law and State*, 248–52. [14] Ibid., 250.
[15] Barberis, 'Personnalité Juridique', at 169–70. [16] Kelsen, 'Théorie (II)', at 119–20.

that states are competent to create law by concluding international treaties. Customary law is thereby thought to apply irrespective of whether a specific entity participated in its creation. Indeed, in the formal conception, international custom is not considered a tacit treaty, but law emerging from general use among competent organs and as such generally pertinent in international relations.[17]

In sum, the formal conception can be encapsulated in the following two basic propositions:

(1) International personality is an open concept. It is used to describe which entities are addressees of international rights, duties and capacities. International personality is not a precondition for, but a consequence of being addressed by a norm of international law. There can thus be no a priori presumption for a certain entity to be an international person as personality is only acquired a posteriori.
(2) There are no further consequences attached to being an international person. In particular, international persons do not automatically possess so-called fundamental rights and duties nor are they automatically authorized to formally contribute to the creation of international law.

The origins of these two basic propositions will now be considered in order to understand their pertinence and to evaluate whether they should still be considered legally sound.

Origins of the basic propositions

Unlike other conceptions of international personality, which mostly encapsulated intellectual assumptions developed over a long period of time by different authors, the formal conception is almost uniquely the contribution of Hans Kelsen himself. Though there are certain key assumptions adopted from other contexts – like the fundamental distinction between 'is' and 'ought' – the origins of the conception's basic propositions are primarily found in Kelsen's highly original general theory of law and the state. These origins are the normative view of the state declaring law and statehood identical, and the purely positive theory of the sources of law rejecting any natural law principles. It is important to note that these two elements do not exclusively inform one

[17] Kelsen, *Law and State*, 351–4; Kelsen, 'Théorie (II)', at 122–9.

of the two propositions. Although certainly more relevant for the first proposition, the normative view of statehood also determines to a certain extent the second one. In turn, the purely positivist theory of sources also has some influence on the first proposition's definition of international norms. However, it is still possible to consider the origins of the two propositions separately.

Devolution of empire and scientific method

In order to locate the relevant context of the formal conception of international personality, it is useful to start with some biographical information on Hans Kelsen. Kelsen is regularly described as the 'jurist of the twentieth century'.[18] He was born in Prague in 1881, which was at the time a part of the Austro-Hungarian Empire.[19] Shortly after his birth, Kelsen's family moved to Vienna where he earned a doctorate in law in 1906. While doing military service in World War I, Kelsen was appointed extraordinary professor of public law at the University of Vienna, an appointment obtained not without opposition from within the faculty because of Kelsen's Jewish origins. In 1919, he was finally promoted to an ordinary professorship. In the same year, with the Austro-Hungarian Empire breaking up, Kelsen was called on to draft a constitution for the Austrian Republic. He succeeded in incorporating a section on the establishment of a true constitutional court and was subsequently appointed a judge serving in that court from 1921 to 1929. At the time, Kelsen was an active participant in Viennese intellectual life and assembled his own School of Vienna (including Adolf Merkl, Josef L. Kunz and Alfred Verdross) from which the pure theory of law emerged. He also took a vivid interest in German public law debates, actively taking part in some of the more memorable sessions of the German public law association in the 1920s.[20] Partly due to a political controversy originating with cases on the suspension of marriage in which he played a decisive role as a judge, Kelsen left Vienna in 1930 and took up a professorship at the University of Cologne. With the establishment of

[18] See e.g. Métall, Rudolf Aladár, *Hans Kelsen: Leben und Werk* (Vienna: Franz Deuticke, 1969), III, or Jabloner, Clemens, 'Kelsen and his Circle: The Viennese Years', EJIL, 9 (1998), 368–85, at 371.

[19] The following biographical sketch is primarily based on Métall, *Kelsen*, 1–101, the most comprehensive work on Kelsen's life.

[20] See on these sessions and Kelsen's prominent involvement therein the overview provided by Stolleis, *Geschichte des öffentlichen Rechts (III)*, 189–94.

Nazi rule, Kelsen lost his position at Cologne and left Germany, finding refuge in Geneva at the Graduate Institute of International Studies. At the Institute, he published his *Reine Rechtslehre* in 1934, a book encapsulating his thought on legal theory so far. With the outbreak of World War II, Kelsen, like so many other European scholars of Jewish origin, was forced to escape from Europe. After an adventurous journey, he arrived in the United States in 1940 and temporarily found a position at Harvard University. In 1943, Kelsen was appointed lecturer in political science at the University of California at Berkeley. Kelsen died in Berkeley in 1973.

In light of this biographical information, the formal conception of international personality has to be situated in the decaying years of the Austro-Hungarian Empire, in particular in *fin-de-siècle* Vienna,[21] and in German public law scholarship at the turn of the twentieth century. In the American period, Kelsen did not substantially alter his conception of personality in international law, but primarily reiterated his main points in English. The wider European context, which is identical to the one in which the recognition conception and the individualistic conception were formulated, is not of primary interest because the formal conception in general did not have recourse to these general developments, but very much emerged out of its specific Viennese and German public law context.[22] In order to elucidate the origins of the formal conception's main propositions, it is therefore sufficient to review the socio-political and intellectual context of the faltering Danube monarchy in *fin-de-siècle* Vienna and to look for the specific situation in German public law in which Kelsen put forward his original conception of personality.

As regards the Austro-Hungarian context at the turn of the twentieth century, the multi-ethnic state created by treaty in 1867 (consisting of eleven constituent nations) had come under constant strain from within. Mass movements – including Czech nationalism, pan-Germanism, and Slavic patriotism – threatened the very existence of the Empire.[23] The heterogeneous nature of the Austrian-Hungarian state was constantly

[21] The term '*fin-de-siècle* Vienna' has been coined by Schorske, *Fin-de-Siècle Vienna*, esp. 3–10. See also Fischer, Kurt Rudolf, 'Zur Theorie des Wiener Fin de Siècle' in Jürgen Nautz and Richard Vahrenkamp (eds.), *Die Wiener Jahrhundertwende* (Vienna: Böhlau, 1993), 110–27, at 111.

[22] By implication, this also follows in more general terms from Koskenniemi, *Gentle Civilizer*, 238–49.

[23] Schorske, *Fin-de-Siècle Vienna*, 118; Janik, Allan and Stephen Toulmin, *Wittgenstein's Vienna* (London: Weidenfeld and Nicolson, 1973), 55–8.

displayed in daily struggles for political influence among the different national movements. This experience proved formative for the pure theory of law and its understanding of statehood; as Kelsen himself put it in his unpublished autobiography:

> Angesichts des österreichischen Staates, der sich aus so vielen nach Rasse, Sprache, Religion und Geschichte verschiedenen Gruppen zusammensetzte, erwiesen sich Theorien, die die Einheit des Staates auf irgendeinen sozial-psychologischen oder sozial-biologischen Zusammenhang der juristisch zum Staat gehörigen Menschen zu gründen versuchten, ganz offenbar als Fiktionen. Insofern diese Staatstheorie ein wesentlicher Bestandteil der Reinen Rechtslehre ist, kann die Reine Rechtslehre als eine spezifisch österreichische Theorie gelten.[24]

In the years leading to World War I, it became increasingly probable that the multi-ethnic state would break up and that its constituent nations would seek autonomy. The devolution of the Austro-Hungarian state finally ensued in the aftermath of World War I, with the Empire breaking up into several separate states and Austria becoming a republic abolishing the Habsburg monarchy. Kelsen was actively involved in this process of devolution and, as the drafter of the constitution, in the creation of the new Austrian republic. The new Austrian state, however, was immediately exposed to huge economic and social problems with public unrest and political rivalries. There was a constant danger that the democratic and parliamentary institutions would not prevail.[25]

In these unstable socio-political circumstances of the final years of the Austro-Hungarian Empire and the creation of the Austrian republic, Vienna provided an exceptionally stimulating intellectual and cultural environment.[26] *Fin-de-siècle* Vienna was characterized by a variety of intellectual subcultures – so-called circles – ranging from Sigmund Freud's group on psychoanalysis to the one surrounding the composer Arnold Schönberg dealing with twelve-tone music.[27] What was

[24] Quoted in Métall, *Kelsen*, 42 and in Jabloner, 'The Viennese Years', at 373 (translated into English).

[25] Janik and Toulmin, *Wittgenstein's Vienna*, 239–41.

[26] For the link between the general perception of a political crisis and the extremely productive intellectual environment see e.g. Mantl, Wolfgang, 'Modernisierung und Dekadenz' in Jürgen Nautz and Richard Vahrenkamp (eds.), *Die Wiener Jahrhundertwende* (Vienna: Böhlau, 1993), 80–100, at 92–7.

[27] For an overview of the different intellectual circles see Timms, Edward, 'Die Wiener Kreise: Schöpferische Interaktionen in der Wiener Moderne' in Jürgen Nautz and Richard Vahrenkamp (eds.), *Die Wiener Jahrhundertwende* (Vienna: Böhlau, 1993), 128–43, at 129–34.

particular to this intellectual culture (apart from its productiveness), and which distinguished it from other intellectual settings in Europe at the time, was the dynamic interaction taking place between the different circles: there was constant exchange between them and many protagonists were members of several groups at the same time.[28] Perhaps the most famous of these groups was the Vienna Circle properly so called, from which philosophical neo-positivism (also called logical positivism or logical empiricism) emerged.[29] The Vienna Circle was composed of philosophers, mathematicians and physicists and was concerned with the possibility of scientific knowledge, that is, the philosophy of science. Deeply influenced by the works of two non-members, Bertrand Russell's *Principia Mathematica*[30] and Ludwig Wittgenstein's *Tractatus Logico-Philosophicus*,[31] the Vienna Circle's neo-positivism insisted on a unified science (i.e. a scientific method applicable to every field of study) based on the combination of logic and empirical observation; by implication, it forcefully excluded any a priori statements from scientific undertakings.[32] Importantly, Kelsen was not a member of the Vienna Circle properly so called.[33] But his own intellectual circle dealing with legal theory had interactions with the Vienna Circle[34] and Kelsen was undoubtedly influenced by its concern with scientific method and by its rejection of metaphysical (i.e. a priori) reasoning.[35] On the other hand, it

[28] Ibid., at 132.

[29] For a useful overview of the Vienna Circle see Haller, Rudolf, *Neopositivismus: Eine historische Einführung in die Philosophie des Wiener Kreises* (Darmstadt: Wissenschaftliche Buchgesellschaft, 1993), 13. See also Jabloner, 'The Viennese Years', at 378–9.

[30] The book was actually co-authored by Alfred North Whitehead who, however, did not exercise such an influence on the Vienna Circle as did Russell.

[31] Haller, *Neopositivismus*, 13–14 and 82–100. However, Wittgenstein was associated to some extent with the Vienna Circle during the late 1920s at the request of the original members.

[32] Ibid., 11–17. The originality of neo-positivism compared to classical philosophical positivism as formulated by Auguste Comte or David Hume primarily lies in the pivotal role of logic and the corresponding importance of language.

[33] Jabloner, 'The Viennese Years', at 378–82.

[34] Timms, 'Wiener Kreise', at 140; Jabloner, 'The Viennese Years', at 378–9. According to Timms's examination, Kelsen's circle also overlapped with the one headed by Ludwig von Mises on economic theory, including Friedrich August von Hayek and Joseph Schumpeter.

[35] Rub, Alfred, *Hans Kelsens Völkerrechtslehre: Versuch einer Würdigung* (Zürich: Schulthess, 1995), 147–9, and Dreier, Horst, *Rechtslehre, Staatssoziologie und Demokratietheorie bei Hans Kelsen* (Baden-Baden: Nomos, 1986), 29, 35 (n. 52) (by implication). See also Janik and Toulmin, *Wittgenstein's Vienna*, 133.

is important to note that Kelsen disagreed on there being a unified scientific approach to all fields of study and insisted on distinguishing between causal and normative sciences.[36]

Apart from this specific Austro-Hungarian and Viennese context, the formal conception has to be situated in German public law debates in the first decades of the twentieth century. Austrian public law, particularly in the years between 1914 and 1945, was generally understood and pursued as part of overall German public law.[37] It was therefore the latter context in which Austrian public lawyers like Kelsen mainly operated. The general situation was thereby characterized, as has been demonstrated in the course of presenting the origins of the states-only and recognition conceptions of international personality, by the predominance of the so-called *Gerber–Laband Gesetzespositivismus* and by the two-sided theory of the state as advocated by Georg Jellinek. However, by the turn of the twentieth century, at least in legal theory if not yet in public law, new approaches to legal study were put forward in the German context. One of the main driving forces behind these new approaches was the philosophy of Neo-Kantianism. Neo-Kantianism was the dominant philosophical school in Germany from 1870 onwards demanding, as the name suggests, a return to the philosophy of Immanuel Kant.[38] In particular, neo-Kantianism called for reconsidering Kant's theory of knowledge in order to ensure philosophy's independent status as science in response to increasingly speculative idealism and the success of natural sciences.[39] This dominant neo-Kantian view in philosophy was taken over into German legal theory, most famously by Rudolf Stammler.[40] It was argued that Kant himself had failed to live up to his critical method in the field of law and had essentially remained a natural lawyer.[41] It was hence thought necessary to apply Kant's theory of knowledge to legal

[36] This already becomes clear in Kelsen, Hans, *Hauptprobleme der Staatsrechtslehre – entwickelt aus der Lehre vom Rechtssatze* (Tübingen: J. C. B. Mohr, 1911), V and 6–17. See also Jabloner, 'The Viennese Years', at 379.

[37] Stolleis, *Geschichte des öffentlichen Rechts (III)*, 145–7.

[38] Köhnke, Klaus Christian, *Entstehung und Aufstieg des Neukantianismus: Die deutsche Universitätsphilosophie zwischen Idealismus und Positivismus* (Frankfurt a.M.: Suhrkamp, 1986), 302–19.

[39] See ibid., 23–105.

[40] Stolleis, *Geschichte des öffentlichen Rechts (III)*, 165; Truyol y Serra, 'Doctrines du Droit des Gens', at 200.

[41] See e.g. Stammler, Rudolf, *Theorie der Rechtswissenschaft* (Halle a.d. Saale: Buchhandlung des Waisenhauses, 1911), 35–6. See also Kelsen, *Law and State*, 444–5. On the whole topic see Dreier, *Rechtslehre*, 70.

study in order to formulate a more scientific juristic method (in the 'true' Kantian sense) than traditionally pursued in German public law. It was in this context of neo-Kantian legal theory criticizing the still predominant juristic method for its unscientific reasoning that Kelsen operated.[42] However, it has to be said that neo-Kantianism as pursued by Stammler did not completely delete aspects of natural law theories from their legal reasoning. The strict anti-metaphysical outlook is the contribution of Kelsen himself under the possible influence of Viennese neo-positivism.[43]

The normative view of the state

The state, in the view of Kelsen, was '[die] wahre crux unserer Wissenschaft' from which most problems of national and international public law theory developed.[44] This certainly held true for the concept of legal personality. The state being the primary example in which a corporation had been thought to exist on its own as a 'juristic person' apart from individuals constituting it,[45] any reconsideration of legal personality had to start with the nature of statehood.[46] Accordingly, it is Kelsen's own theory of the state and its accompanying assumptions that provide the origins of the first proposition of the formal conception according to which international personality is only a consequence of, but not a precondition for, having international rights, duties and capacities. In the particular Viennese context at the turn of the twentieth century, and in the broader realities of the Austrian state at the time, the traditional German public law notion of statehood (with its insistence on the state being a historical fact absorbing individuals) thereby appeared unconvincing. From an intellectual point of view, in accordance with

42 See also Rub, *Kelsens Völkerrechtslehre*, 143–7; Koskenniemi, *Gentle Civilizer*, 241; Kolb, *Les Cours Généraux*, 77; Paulson, Stanley L., 'The Neo-Kantian Dimension of Kelsen's Pure Theory of Law', *Oxford Journal of Legal Studies*, 12 (1992), 311–32, at 312–13; Lauterpacht, 'Pure Science of Law', at 405–6.

43 Dreier, *Rechtslehre*, 73–4 and 83.

44 Kelsen, *Problem der Souveränität*, 13 (n. 1). See also Kelsen, Hans, 'Was ist die reine Rechtslehre?' in *Demokratie und Rechtsstaat: Festgabe zum 60. Geburtstag von Zaccaria Giacometti* (Zürich: Polygrapischer Verlag, 1953), 143–62, at 155.

45 As noted earlier, a most influential formulation of this view in international law was put forward by Vattel, *Le Droit des Gens*, §2 (p. 1). For German public law, see e.g. Gerber, *Deutsches Staatsrecht*, §7 (pp. 19–21).

46 On a more general level, the same point is made e.g. by Truyol y Serra, 'Doctrines du Droit des Gens', at 24–5.

emerging scientific postulates, traditional theory intolerably mixed different methods of enquiry. From a socio-political perspective, in light of the realities of the decaying Austro-Hungarian Empire and the subsequent creation of new states, it seemed necessary to replace a theory stressing the organic evolution of states and their anteriority and superiority to law with a more realistic one. In this environment, Kelsen regarded the state as a purely legal construction – a legal fiction – effectively being identical with the national legal system. Consequently, there was no separate existence of the state as a historical fact preceding the law. Anyone pretending that the state really existed made unacceptable use of a legal fiction for the purpose of legitimizing an illiberal political theory. From this view of statehood followed a general theory of legal personality: in analogy to the state, any legal person was simply a reflection of the sum of legal norms addressing and constituting it. There was no real existence of legal persons, and there was no legal existence previous to being addressed by international norms. Thus, it is this normative view of statehood and its implications for collective legal organizations more generally to which the first proposition of the formal conception of international personality must be related.

The starting point of the normative view of statehood is the fundamental distinction between 'is' and 'ought'. David Hume is generally credited with having formulated the 'is-ought problem' in his *Treatise of Human Nature* published in 1739–40:

> In every system of morality, which I have hitherto met with, I have always remarked, that the author proceeds for some time in the ordinary way of reasoning, and establishes the being of a God, or makes observations concerning human affairs; when of a sudden I am surprised to find, that instead of the usual copulations of propositions, *is*, and *is not*, I meet with no proposition that is not connected with an *ought*, or an *ought not*. This change is imperceptible; but is, however, of the last consequence. For as this *ought*, or *ought not*, expresses some new relation or affirmation, it is necessary that it should be observed and explained; and at the same time that a reason should be given, for what seems altogether inconceivable, how this new relation can be a deduction from others, which are entirely different from it.[47]

[47] Hume, David, *A Treatise of Human Nature* (Oxford: Clarendon Press, 2007) (originally published 1739–40), Book 3, Part 1, Section 1, para. 27 (p. 302; SB 469–70 [SB denoting the classical Oxford University Press edition edited by Selby-Bigge]) (original emphasis, spelling modernized). For Hume's influence on Kelsen see Dreier, *Rechtslehre*, 32 (n. 31).

It follows from Hume's classic statement that one has to draw a distinction between the actual and the normative: it does not follow from a fact ('is') that it is normatively desirable ('ought') or not ('ought not') and, conversely, a normative injunction does not necessarily conform with the actual outcome. The point was elaborated on by Immanuel Kant some forty years later in his epoch-making *Kritik der reinen Vernunft*:

> Denn in Betracht der Natur gibt uns die Erfahrung die Regel an die Hand und ist der Quell der Wahrheit; in Ansehung der sittlichen Gesetze aber ist Erfahrung (leider!) die Mutter des Scheins, und es ist höchst verwerflich, die Gesetze über das, was ich tun soll, von demjenigen herzunehmen, oder dadurch einschränken zu wollen, was getan wird.[48]

By implication, for Kant, the distinction between 'is' and 'ought' was also linked to different modes of acquiring knowledge: whereas knowledge about nature ('is') was acquired through a process in which experience and a priori categories of the mind interacted,[49] the former part – experience or empirical observation – was not present when moral questions ('ought') were the object of study.[50] It was only reason without any recourse to empirical observation that could guide statements about normative judgments.[51] As a result, normative and descriptive sciences also had to be distinguished with regard to scientific method.

The 'is-ought distinction' and its implied differences in scientific analysis were taken up by neo-Kantian philosophy at the end of the nineteenth century.[52] In accordance with Kant, it was postulated that there were two kinds of scientific undertakings: those describing the actual and those prescribing the normative. Crucially, law was declared to form part of the latter realm:[53] law stipulated how things ought to be, and not how things actually were. Two main consequences followed from this somewhat reductionist interpretation of Kant (the reductionist

[48] Kant, Immanuel, *Kritik der reinen Vernunft*, 3rd edition (Hamburg: Felix Meiner, 1990) (originally published 1781), A 319, B 375 (p. 353) [following general custom, A denotes the 1781 version, B the reworked 1787 version].

[49] Ibid., A 124–8 (pp. 181a–8a). This is what is called 'Kant's Copernican Turn': knowledge about nature is not acquired by observing pre-existing laws of nature, but by applying transcendental mental categories to natural phenomena.

[50] Kant, Immanuel, *Kritik der praktischen Vernunft*, 10th edition (Hamburg: Felix Meiner, 1990) (originally published 1788), 55–6 (pp. 36–7).

[51] Ibid., 30–1 (pp. 16–7).

[52] See e.g. Simmel, Georg, *Einleitung in die Moralwissenschaft: Eine Kritik der ethischen Grundbegriffe*, 2nd edition (Berlin and Stuttgart: Cotta, 1904) (originally published 1892–3), esp. 8, 12 and 27.

[53] See e.g. Stammler, *Theorie*, 68–74 (though with different terminology).

aspect being the corresponding rejection of natural law tendencies undoubtedly present in Kant's legal theory):[54] first, there was no room for applying natural science methods – including causal social sciences like sociology, psychology or history – as part of legal analysis, for this would imply deriving an 'ought' from an 'is'; second, any tendencies to hold legal concepts as truly existing in the realm of natural or social facts were declared to be fundamentally mistaken for such construction would amount to deriving an is from an ought.[55] As an effect of neo-Kantian legal philosophy, legal science was declared to be strictly limited to the domain of normative statements without taking into account factual observations or concluding that legal concepts truly existed.

This development in neo-Kantian legal philosophy had important repercussions for German public law theory with regard to the view of the state. The introduction of neo-Kantian legal thought into German public law was accomplished primarily by Kelsen himself.[56] Applying neo-Kantian postulates, Kelsen attacked the hitherto predominant two-sided theory of the state according to which statehood was considered a historical fact to be examined from a sociological as well as a legal perspective, with both approaches considered public law methods. His first criticism was of a general methodological nature: in line with neo-Kantian thought, Kelsen attacked the '*Methodensynkretismus*'[57] of the two-sided theory of the state. According to Kelsen, this violated the first order scientific postulate that legal analysis was not to be concerned with historical, sociological or psychological aspects, but with stating the law: a certain factual state of affairs was only legally relevant if there was a legal norm attaching certain legal consequences to it, and not by its mere existence.[58] By implication, the focus of a legal analysis of the state, like

[54] E.g. Paulson, 'Neo-Kantian Dimension', at 312. See also the subsequent section dealing with the sources of law.

[55] See also Dreier, *Rechtslehre*, 70–82, and Stolleis, *Geschichte des öffentlichen Rechts (III)*, 164–5 (in more general terms).

[56] Stolleis, *Geschichte des öffentlichen Rechts (III)*, 164; Jabloner, 'The Viennese Years', at 374.

[57] Kelsen, *Reine Rechtslehre*, 2; Kelsen, 'Was ist die Reine Rechtslehre', 147. See also Kelsen, *Problem der Souveränität*, 1–2, wherein the term '*Methodenanarchismus*' is used to highlight the same issue.

[58] Kelsen, Hans, 'La Naissance de l'État et la Formation de sa Nationalité: Les Principes et leur Application au Cas de la Tchécoslovaquie', RDI, 4 (1929), 613–41, at 615 (and 617): 'Si l'on envisage la question du passage d'un simple état de fait à un état de droit . . ., il est évidemment impossible de trouver cette justification dans le fait même à justifier.' See also Kelsen, *Problem der Souveränität*, 10–12, and Dreier, *Rechtslehre*, 209.

all legal analysis, had to be on legal norms, and not on perceived social facts. In consequence, there was no room for social science methods in a legal analysis of the state.

In addition to this general methodological criticism, the use of social science methods was thought particularly erroneous in the case of the state: there simply was no social reality of statehood to be examined. According to Kelsen, every sociological, historical or psychological analysis of the state had to have recourse to a legal definition of statehood:

> Gegeben ist aber auch die von den Soziologen vorausgesetzte Staatseinheit durch die Rechtswissenschaft und die Zugehörigkeit zum Staate wird, durchaus juristisch, nach der einheitlichen Geltung einer als gültig vorausgesetzten Rechtsordnung bestimmt. Diese Rechts- und Staatsordnung aber stellt einen vom kausalgesetzlichen System der Natur gänzlich verschiedenen, spezifisch eigengesetzlichen Zusammenhang der Elemente dar.[59]

The legal aspect of statehood to which a social science undertaking had to have recourse was thus public power. Of course, population and territory were two additional and more tangible elements of statehood according to traditional public law doctrine (*Drei-Elementen Lehre*). Yet, according to Kelsen, these two elements depended on the establishment of a public order, making the latter the decisive characteristic of statehood for it defined population and territory of the state in the first place.[60] Being hence obliged to refer to the legal concept of public power[61] when defining statehood, it followed that traditional public law doctrine started from a legal definition of the state when examining it with historical, sociological or psychological means. By implication, public lawyers had recourse to the realm of 'ought' (the legal definition of public power and thus statehood) in order to define their object of study belonging to the realm of 'is' (the state as a social phenomenon).

It followed for Kelsen that traditional public law theory of statehood operated with an untenable fiction (*eine gänzlich unzulässige Fiktion*).[62] It is necessary to explain what exactly Kelsen meant by the term 'fiction'

[59] Kelsen, *Staatsbegriff*, 8–9 (emphasis omitted).

[60] Kelsen, 'Naissance de L'État', at 614; Kelsen, *Staatsbegriff*, 84–6. A very useful summary of this argument is provided by Lauterpacht, 'Pure Science of Law', at 414–15.

[61] For public power being synonymous with a legal order see also Kelsen, 'Naissance de L'État', at 614.

[62] Kelsen, *Staatsbegriff*, 9 (emphasis omitted). See also Kelsen, *Hauptprobleme*, VIII: 'Die Verquickung einander ausschliessender Betrachtungsweisen führt notwendig zur Fiktion, der Behauptung einer Realität im bewussten Widerspruche zur Wirklichkeit.'

in addition to its being related to deriving an 'is' from an 'ought'. By making use of the term, Kelsen referred to the 'philosophy of as-if' (*Philosophie des Als-ob*) as formulated by the neo-Kantian philosopher Hans Vaihinger in 1911.[63] According to Vaihinger, human knowledge was often acquired through a process in which, at some point, ideas were taken to exist even though it was obvious that in reality they did not.[64] In other words, there was a conscious contradiction with reality for the exact purpose of comprehending reality. The main danger when operating with such fictions, Vaihinger pointed out, was when these were not taken as a provisional means in an intellectual process, but held to truly exist.[65] In this case, fictions led to self-constructed problems and contradictions that were difficult to get rid of.[66] In Kelsen's view, this is exactly what happened when public lawyers held the state to truly exist:[67]

> Diese Verdoppelung [= Fiktion der Person des Staates] bleibt insolange ein nützlicher Denkbehelf, als man sich ihres Charakters bewusst bleibt. Sie wird aber zu einer gefährlichen Fehlerquelle, zu einem steten Anlass der törichtesten Scheinprobleme, wenn man die Personifikation real setzt, hypostasiert und mit der Person des Staates als mit einer von dem Personifikationssubstrat, der Rechtsordnung, verschiedenen selbständigen Wesenheit operiert, den Staat das Recht 'erzeugen', 'tragen' lässt, als ob der Staat noch etwas anderes wäre als einen Menschen verpflichtende Ordnung, und sich so plötzlich vor die Frage gestellt sieht, wie es denn möglich sei, dass der Staat, der das Recht 'erzeugt', durch eben dieses Recht selbst 'gebunden' werden könne.[68]

Thus, there was no problem in using the fiction of statehood as long as the state was not taken to truly exist, but only to represent a mental device reflecting the total of the legal order. Difficulties arose when public lawyers thought that the state, in the sense of a 'hypostasis',[69] truly existed in the realm of facts. In this case, seemingly unsolvable problems,

[63] See Kelsen, *Staatsbegriff*, 205–8; Kelsen, *Problem der Souveränität*, 18 (n. 1); Kelsen, Hans, 'Zur Theorie der juristischen Fiktionen: Mit besonderer Berücksichtigung von Vaihingers Philosophie des Als-ob' in Hans Klecatsky, René Marcic and Herbert Schambeck (eds.), *Die Wiener Rechtstheoretische Schule* (Vienna: Europa Verlag, 1968) (originally published 1919), 1215–41, *passim*. See also, though in the different context of diplomatic protection, Vermeer-Künzli, Annemarieke, 'As If: The Legal Fiction in Diplomatic Protection', EJIL, 18 (2007), 37–68, at 45–8.

[64] Vaihinger, Hans, *Die Philosophie des Als Ob: System der theoretischen, praktischen und religiösen Fiktionen der Menschheit auf Grund eines idealistischen Positivismus*, 6th edition (Leipzig: Felix Meiner, 1920), 175.

[65] Ibid., 173. [66] Ibid., 230. [67] See also Kelsen, *Staatsbegriff*, 205–6.

[68] Kelsen, *Problem der Souveränität*, 18. [69] E.g. Kelsen, 'Fiktionen', at 1219.

like the relationship between law and the state, arose even though in reality the issue did not exist, for the legal order, as demonstrated above, exactly defined statehood and was hence identical with, not opposed to it.[70] The two-sided theory, by using fictions in the sense declared problematic by Vaihinger, consequently construed problems that did not exist. The whole point of traditional public law doctrine concerning the state was therefore based on an untenable use of a fiction. In a sense, traditional German doctrine – that is, self-proclaimed legal positivists rejecting natural law – thus made the same unacceptable use of a fiction as natural lawyers did when conceiving the state as a social contract entered into by its citizens, even though it was clear that such a contract in reality did not exist.[71]

According to Kelsen, the reason why public lawyers had held the fiction of statehood to truly exist was political.[72] The fiction of the state was rooted in the ideology of illiberal democracy in the sense of Jean-Jacques Rousseau's *volonté générale*:[73] by conceiving the state as a person on its own, the loss of individual freedom resulting from becoming subject to state power was offset by the freedom of the collective body in which the individual was totally absorbed. In the words of Kelsen:

> Der Wandel des Freiheitsbegriffes, der von der Vorstellung eines Freiseins des Individuums von staatlicher Herrschaft zur Vorstellung einer Beteiligung des Individuums an der staatlichen Herrschaft führt, bedeutet zugleich die Loslösung des Demokratismus vom Liberalismus . . . Die . . . *Freiheit des Individuums* tritt allmählich in den Hintergrund und die *Freiheit des sozialen Kollektivums* in den Vordergrund. Der Protest gegen die Herrschaft von meinesgleichen führt im politischen Bewusstsein zu einer Verschiebung des Subjekts der – auch in der Demokratie unvermeidbaren – Herrschaft: zur Konstruktion der anonymen *Person des Staates*. Von ihr und nicht von äusserlich sichtbaren Menschen lässt man das Imperium ausgehen. . . . Hier verdeckt der Schleier der Staatspersonifikation das dem demokratischen Empfinden unerträgliche Faktum einer Herrschaft von Mensch über Mensch . . . Die . . . Konsequenz erfordert, dass, weil die Staatsbürger nur in ihrem Inbegriffe, dem Staate frei sind, eben nicht der einzelnen Staatsbürger, sondern die Person des *Staates* frei sei . . . An die Stelle des freien Individuums tritt die Souveränität des Volkes . . .[74]

[70] Kelsen, *Problem der Souveränität*, 18. [71] Kelsen, *Hauptprobleme*, VIII.

[72] Kelsen, *Staatsbegriff*, 127: 'Hier verrät sich die Theorie, ihr politischer Charakter guckt hervor.' See also Kelsen, 'Was ist die Reine Rechtslehre', at 155–6.

[73] Kelsen, Hans, *Vom Wesen und Wert der Demokratie* (Tübingen: J. C. B. Mohr, 1929), 6–12; Kelsen, *Law and State*, 285–6.

[74] Kelsen, *Demokratie*, 10–13 (original emphasis).

Considering the state a collective person of social life was thus the result of an illiberal ideology of democracy putting the collective good above the individual one. It was an ideology that saw no need for basic individual rights (*Grund- und Freiheits- oder Menschen- und Bürgerrechte*) because individuals and minority groups did not need protection in a state that was in itself the vehicle for their highest freedom and fulfilment.[75] It was the idea of the absolute state as expounded by Rousseau and Hegel that lay behind the fiction of the state being a truly existing social body.[76] Kelsen rejected these views for they profoundly misunderstood the nature of individual freedom: according to Kelsen, and contrary to Rousseau and Hegel, individual liberty precisely lay outside, not inside the state.[77]

It follows that for Kelsen – having demonstrated that theories contending the existence of states as a social fact were mistakenly entertaining a fiction in order to foster an illiberal political ideology – the state was identical with the domestic legal system. The national legal order is the only and decisive characteristic of statehood: 'Die Person des Staates ist nur in vergrössertem Massstabe was jede andere juristische Person ... ist: die Personifikation von Rechtsnormen.'[78] By implication, the state was not anterior to law, but corresponded with the existence of a legal system. Only because there was a legal system could one speak of a state and not, as traditional doctrine had claimed, vice versa. Put succinctly, statehood was not a precondition for the existence of legal norms, but the consequence thereof. With statehood only being the personification of the national legal order and therefore posterior to law, it was also demonstrated what other legal persons were:[79] they just represented those legal norms constituting and addressing them, that is, attributing individual behaviour to them.[80] In analogy to statehood, legal persons did not exist previously to legal norms constituting and addressing them; and also corresponding to statehood, a legal person did not exist at all in the realm of things, but only in the realm of law.[81] In consequence,

75 Ibid., 53.
76 Ibid., 106–13 (nn. 16–19) (by implication, with reference to Heinrich Triepel).
77 Kelsen, *Law and State*, 284–7.
78 Kelsen, *Problem der Souveränität*, 20. See also Kelsen, 'Was ist die Reine Rechtslehre', at 155.
79 Truyol y Serra, 'Doctrines du Droit des Gens', at 25 (by implication).
80 Kelsen, *Law and State*, 96–7 and 191–2. In what follows, when speaking of norms addressing a certain legal entity, it is always implied that the mechanism in which these norms are directed at such an entity is through imputation of individual behaviour towards it.
81 Kelsen, 'Fiktionen', at 1221.

personality could never be a precondition for, but only the consequence of legal norms addressing a certain entity. There simply was no legal person, just as there was no state, before legal norms were directed at it.

It is these principles on statehood and legal personality formulated in domestic public law that the first proposition of the formal conception of international personality has to be related to. With the state only representing the total of a domestic legal order, the international legal system, too, could not be based on state power as a social phenomenon. Statehood could only be understood to reflect a national legal order, that is, a legal person of domestic law lacking any factual existence. Accordingly, the status of states in international law depended on international norms constituting and addressing them.[82] By implication, a state's personality in international law was determined by those international norms directed at it.[83] This held true for any other type of international personality. As a result, international personality was only an a posteriori legal concept not to be confused with reality. It is this view that informs the formal conception's claim that international personality is only the consequence of, but not a precondition for, having international rights, duties and capacities and the corresponding proposition that international personality is an entirely open concept not stating any presumption regarding the entities enjoying such legal status in international law.

Law as a formally complete system of positive norms

The formal conception stipulates in its second proposition that there are no legal consequences attached to being an international person. Admittedly, the origins of this proposition are anticipated in the normative view of statehood. For it seems inherent in this view that the legal status of an international person cannot lead to more legal rights, duties and capacities than are included in the very international norms constituting international personality. In a sense, the origins of the first proposition thus partly inform the second one as well. However, notwithstanding a normative view of statehood and its implications for legal personality, there is room for arguing that once an entity is addressed by international law and consequently considered an international person,

[82] Kelsen, 'Naissance de L'État', at 617–18 (and at 635 in application to the case of Czechoslovakia). See also Crawford, *Creation of States*, 5.

[83] Kelsen, 'Naissance de L'État', at 617.

certain fundamental international authorizations and obligations follow from this status (for example the capacity to bring international claims or the obligation to prevent genocide). The decisive reason for nevertheless not attaching such consequences to international personality according to the formal conception's second proposition lies in considering international law as a system of positive norms emanating neither from state will nor from principles of natural law. International norms are thought to result only from hierarchically higher international norms. At the top of this hierarchical system is a basic norm (*Grundnorm*), which constitutes the legal character of the international legal order. Again, unlike other conceptions, these assumptions were primarily formulated by Kelsen himself and did not so much represent the end of a wider intellectual development.[84] The origins of the second proposition then primarily lie in Kelsen's own theory of the sources of (international) law.

To a certain extent, Kelsen's view on the sources of law can be associated with the philosophy of the Vienna Circle.[85] As noted earlier, Viennese neo-positivism insisted that there could be no a priori statements in science and that all scientific undertakings consequently had to be a combination of empirical observation and logic.[86] Kelsen had defected from neo-positivist theory in that he maintained the fundamental distinction between 'is' and 'ought'. In the view of the Vienna Circle, such categories already represented an unacceptable use of a priori reasoning.[87] Yet, Kelsen proved to be more faithful to philosophical positivism when drawing a sharp distinction inside the realm of 'ought' between the disciplines of law and those of morals or theology. For Kelsen, law's status as an independent science depended not only on distinguishing it from natural and causal social sciences belonging to the realm of 'is', but also on separating it, inside the realm of 'ought', from ethical and theological perspectives:

> Dadurch, dass die Aussageform der das System 'Staat' oder 'Recht' darstellenden Urteile das 'Sollen' ist, wird wohl die Abscheidung gegenüber dem System 'Natur' vollzogen, aber eine Vermengung mit anderen Systemen zur Gefahr, die ebenso bedenklich ist wie die eben vermiedene. Das Sollen ist ebenso die Sphäre der Moral ... Die

[84] By implication, this also follows from Lauterpacht, 'Pure Science of Law', at 404–5.

[85] See e.g. Rub, *Kelsens Völkerrechtslehre*, 148; Dreier, *Rechtslehre*, 35 (n. 52); Jabloner, 'The Viennese Years', at 378 (referring to a letter in which Kelsen declared that the 'antimetaphysical thrust' had connected him to the Vienna Circle).

[86] Haller, *Neopositivismus*, 11–17.

[87] See also the reference in Jabloner, 'The Viennese Years', at 379.

> Vermengung des Systems 'Recht' oder 'Staat' mit dem System der Moral ist das Wesen der Naturrechtstheorie und ebenso abzulehnen wie die Vermengung mit dem System der Natur . . .[88]

Incorporating moral or divine truths – that is: a priori statements in the sense resisted by neo-positivism – into legal analysis was the central feature of natural law theory.[89] By separating law from other normative sciences like morals or theology, Kelsen thus banned natural law from legal reasoning. In accordance with postulates of neo-positivism, Kelsen declared any a priori statements invoking the 'nature of things' to be alien to law. In historical perspective, this invocation had only served political purposes, but no scientific advancement:

> Naturrecht ist juristische Metaphysik. Und der Schrei nach Naturrecht tönt jetzt – nach einer Periode des Positivismus und des Empirismus – wieder allenthalben und auf allen Erkenntnisgebieten . . . Die Frage, auf die das Naturrecht zielt, ist die ewige Frage, was hinter dem positiven Recht steckt. Und wer die Antwort sucht, der findet, fürchte ich, nicht die absolute Wahrheit einer Metaphysik . . . Wer den Schleier hebt und sein Auge nicht schliesst, dem starrt das Gorgonenhaupt der Macht entgegen.[90]

Hence, for Kelsen natural law was an unacceptable part of traditional legal reasoning for it historically served a political-ideological function. Positive law, on the contrary, was empirically observable and therefore less prone to be abused by political interests. Although belonging to the realm of 'ought', positive law was, in a normative sense, also a reality, for it was defined as law artificially created and laid down by human beings: 'Das Problem des positiven Rechts besteht gerade darin: dass dieses zugleich als Sollen und Sein erscheint, obgleich sich diese beiden Kategorien logisch ausschliessen.'[91] Whereas positive law was empirically and logically observable in line with neo-positivist postulates, natural law was speculative and dependent on a priori statements

[88] Kelsen, *Staatsbegriff*, 77–8.

[89] Kelsen, Hans, *Die philosophischen Grundlagen der Naturrechtslehre und des Rechtspositivismus*, 'Philosophische Vorträge veröffentlicht von der Kant-Gesellschaft' (Paul Menzer and Arthur Liebert, eds.) (Berlin: Pan-Verlag, 1928), 8–9.

[90] Comment by Kelsen in Kaufmann, 'Gleichheit vor dem Gesetz', at 53 (Votum Kelsen-Wien). See also Kelsen, *Grundlagen der Naturrechtslehre*, 37–41, and Kelsen, 'Was ist die Reine Rechtslehre', at 154–5.

[91] Kelsen, *Grundlagen der Naturrechtslehre*, 10. Identical formulation in Kelsen, *Law and State*, 394. See also Kelsen, 'Was ist die Reine Rechtslehre', at 146; Kelsen, *Grundlagen der Naturrechtslehre*, 8–10.

referring to the 'nature of things'. It was therefore only positive law, that is, law artificially created by human beings, that was really law; moral and theological principles, to the contrary, were not to be regarded as law.[92]

By restricting the notion of law to positive law, the question naturally arose as to the basis on which such humanly created and empirically observable statements of the law had normative force and were therefore to be obeyed. For example,[93] why was a decision issued by an administrative department addressed to a particular individual to be complied with? Obviously, moral or theological justifications did not suffice to establish the directive's normative force because such reasoning did not form part of the legal realm. Neither could there be a causal social science explanation, presumably referring to the sociological or psychological fact of obedience towards public authorities. The reason for the validity of the administrative directive could only be found in positive law itself. By implication, a specific legal norm was valid because there was a higher positive norm declaring it so.[94] In the event of an administrative decision, its validity had to be based on a statute authorizing the administration to take the decision in question and obligating those addressed by it to comply with the decision. Yet the problem was not entirely solved but rather shifted to the next level, for one could subsequently ask why the statute enacted by parliament had normative force. The answer was that there was a positive constitutional rule to the effect that acts by parliament had to be obeyed. Again, it was a hierarchically higher positive norm declaring an inferior norm valid. Finally, the question arose why the constitution itself had normative force. And at this point, Kelsen referred to the basic norm (*Grundnorm*): '. . . positive norms are valid only on one assumption: that there is a basic norm which establishes the supreme, law-creating authority. The validity of this basic norm is unproved and must remain so within the sphere of positive law itself.'[95] The validity of positive law, the only law properly so called, was therefore dependent on assuming the basic norm to exist. Being outside the realm of positive law, the lawyer was not competent to

[92] Kelsen, *Law and State*, 249: 'Legal principles can never be presupposed by a legal order; they can only be created by this order.'

[93] The example is taken from Kelsen, *Grundlagen der Naturrechtslehre*, 12–13. It is also used by Lauterpacht, 'Pure Science of Law', at 407.

[94] Kelsen, *Grundlagen der Naturrechtslehre*, 12.

[95] Kelsen, *Law and State*, 395.

examine whether such a rule existed. Lawyers just had to assume that it did in order to found their system.

This general theory on the sources of law and their foundation was applied by Kelsen to international law.[96] Consequently, all aspects of natural law or sociology had to be erased from international legal argument. In analogy to domestic law, international law was considered to represent a hierarchy of positive norms (that is, norms artificially created and not merely supposed to exist) in which the normative force of a legal norm depended on a superior positive norm to this effect.[97] A convenient starting point to survey this hierarchy was a decision issued by an international institution, in this case an international court.[98] The normative force of such a decision depended on a treaty norm instituting the court and declaring its decisions valid. Treaties, in turn, had normative force because of a customary international rule, *pacta sunt servanda*, according to which treaties entered into by states were binding sources of international law.[99] This left the validity of international custom to be determined:

> Quelle est alors la raison de validité du droit international coutumier? . . . Une théorie positiviste, c'est-à-dire une théorie qui ne recourt pas à une autorité transcendante, n'a pas de réponse à cette question. Elle se borne à constater qu'en affirmant qu'un État est juridiquement obligé de se comporter de la manière dont les autres États se comportent habituellement, on suppose que la coutume internationale est un fait créateur de droit. Une telle affirmation est une hypothèse pour l'interprétation des relations internationales. Elle n'a pas le caractère d'une norme de droit positif; car elle n'a pas été créée par un acte de volonté. Elle est une norme supposée ou hypothétique. En tant que fondement du droit coutumier elle a le caractère d'une norme fondamentale.[100]

The normative force of international custom thus depended on a basic norm – situated, as in national law, outside the realm of positive law – according to which 'States ought to behave as they have customarily behaved'.[101] Customary international law developed in application of this basic norm was then superior to treaty law and in turn provided the basis for the latter's normative force. There were no other primary sources of international law apart from custom and treaty. In particular, general principles of law were not considered sources of international

[96] See ibid., 369. [97] Kelsen, 'Théorie (II)', at 119.
[98] The example is taken from Kelsen, *Law and State*, 369.
[99] Ibid., 366 and 369; Kelsen, 'Théorie (II)', at 129. [100] Kelsen, 'Théorie (II)', at 129.
[101] Kelsen, *Law and State*, 369.

law.[102] For Kelsen, positive international law was formally complete and any attempt to use general principles of law in order to make it complete in material terms amounted to a return to natural law for it involved moral and political judgments.[103] Article 38 of the PCIJ and ICJ Statutes and their references to general principles of law could therefore only be understood as delegating the power to create international law to the court for the purposes of a particular case.[104] In consequence, only custom and treaties provided positive sources of international law.

In conclusion, it is this view, which conceives international law as a hierarchical system of positive norms, that the formal conception's second proposition on international personality has to be related to. By obliterating natural law (understood to include general principles of law) from the sources of international law, there could be no such thing as fundamental rights and duties of international persons.[105] For in order to associate the status of a legal person with certain fundamental rules of conduct in international affairs, a role had to be given to general legal principles enabling such association as a matter of law; without such principles, there was no legal basis on which to establish fundamental authorizations and obligations corresponding with being an international person. By implication, all rights and duties possessed by international persons had to emanate from positive international norms directed at them. Similarly, international personality could not imply the competence to create international law: international law-creation was entirely determined by superior positive norms.[106] Accordingly, it could not be part of international personality itself to have the competence to create law; law-creating authority was only the result of a positive international norm to this effect. In sum, international personality could have no further consequences than those included in customary and treaty norms which addressed a specific legal person because there were no additional legal sources capable of assigning such consequences.

[102] Kelsen, 'Théorie (II)', at 121–2.

[103] Ibid., at 122. For the essential difference between formal and material completeness see also Koskenniemi, *Apology to Utopia*, 53.

[104] Kelsen, 'Théorie (II)', at 121.

[105] This becomes especially clear in Kelsen, *Law and State*, 248–50.

[106] Of course, the hypothetical basic norm, which represents the starting point of this hierarchical system, included non-positivist elements. See the convincing critique by Truyol y Serra, 'Doctrines du Droit des Gens', at 30–2.

Main manifestations in legal practice

The formal conception of international personality is mainly manifested in legal practice when the direct effect of treaties on individuals (including corporations) is at issue. It has been applied in the *LaGrand* case and beyond in the context of individual treaty rights. In *Amco* v. *Indonesia* (resubmitted case, 1990), the formal conception was manifested with respect to the application of international law to state contracts.

The ICJ's decision in LaGrand *and individual treaty rights*

The *LaGrand* case is certainly the leading modern case concerning the direct effect of treaties on individuals. Unlike the PCIJ in *Jurisdiction of the Courts of Danzig*, the ICJ unambiguously held in *LaGrand* that an international treaty provision – in the event Article 36(1)(b) of the Vienna Convention on Consular Relations (VCCR)[107] – 'creates individual rights'.[108] Importantly, the judgment focused exclusively on the interpretation of the treaty norm in question and did not state any presumption with regard to its personal scope. The decision has been widely interpreted to affirm the position of the individual as a subject of international law.[109] It clearly represents, it is submitted, a manifestation of the formal conception of international personality.

The case was brought before the ICJ under somewhat unusual circumstances at the end of several sets of judicial proceedings in the United

[107] 569 UNTS 262.

[108] *LaGrand Case* (Germany v. United States), Judgment, 2001 ICJ Reports 466, para. 77. Compare with *Jurisdiction of the Courts of Danzig* (Advisory Opinion), 1928 PCIJ Series B No. 15, at 17–18. The essential difference between *LaGrand* and *Jurisdiction of the Courts of Danzig* is disputed by Crawford, 'The ILC's Articles on Responsibility of States', at 887, and Spiermann, 'LaGrand Case', at 209. However, their insistence on the similarity between the two cases rests on a somewhat different reading of *Jurisdiction of the Courts of Danzig* than the one suggested in this study, and not on a different understanding of *LaGrand*.

[109] See e.g. Gaja, Giorgio (Special Rapporteur), *First Report on responsibility of international organizations*, ILC 2003, UN Doc. A/CN.4/532, para. 17 ('The Court stated in the *LaGrand* case that individuals are also subjects of international law'); Spiermann, 'LaGrand Case', at 208–11 (by implication); Oellers-Frahm, Karin, 'Die Entscheidung des IGH im Fall LaGrand – Eine Stärkung der internationalen Gerichtsbarkeit und der Rolle des Individuums im Völkerrecht', *Europäische Grundrechte-Zeitschrift*, 28 (2001), 265–72, at 267; Greszick, Bernd, 'Rechte des Einzelnen im Völkerrecht: Chancen und Gefahren völkerrechtlicher Entwicklungstrends am Beispiel der Individualrechte im allgemeinen Völkerrecht', ARV, 43 (2005), 312–44, at 320–6.

States of America.[110] In 1982, Walter and Karl LaGrand, two brothers of German nationality, had been arrested in the United States for supposed involvement in an attempted armed robbery in the course of which one person had been murdered and another seriously injured. On 17 February 1984, the LaGrand brothers were convicted of murder in the first degree, attempted murder in the first degree, attempted armed robbery and two counts of kidnapping. On 14 December 1984, they were sentenced to death. During all these proceedings, the competent United States authorities had by their own admission failed to provide Walter and Karl LaGrand with information on consular assistance pursuant to Article 36(1)(b) VCCR;[111] neither had the US authorities informed the relevant German consular post of the arrest, conviction or sentencing of the LaGrand brothers.[112] It was not until 1992 that the LaGrands, having heard from other sources that they could get consular assistance, contacted the German Consulate post and subsequently obtained counsel through the German authorities. In 1995, the LaGrands filed applications for writs of habeas corpus with the competent United States District Court based on the Arizona authorities' failure to provide them with information on consular assistance pursuant to Article 36(1)(b) VCCR. The application was rejected on the grounds of 'procedural default', a legal principle of United States law stating that federal courts could only take into account legal arguments already presented in state courts (in the present case, the LaGrand brothers

[110] For the facts of the case, see *LaGrand Case*, paras 10–34.

[111] Article 36(1)(b) VCCR reads:

> 1. With a view to facilitating the exercise of consular functions relating to nationals of the sending State:
>
> (b) if he so requests, the competent authorities of the receiving State shall, without delay, inform the consular post of the sending State if, within its consular district, a national of that State is arrested or committed to prison or to custody pending trial or is detained in any other manner. Any communication addressed to the consular post by the person arrested, in prison, custody or detention shall be forwarded by the said authorities without delay. The said authorities shall inform the person concerned without delay of his rights under this subparagraph;

[112] There was some dispute as to why the US authorities had failed to provide the information pursuant to Article 36(1)(b) VCCR. The United States claimed that their authorities had not been aware at the time that the LaGrands were German citizens because, having spent most of their lives in the United States, their demeanour and speech had appeared as those of a native American. Germany, however, disputed this claim. See *LaGrand Case*, para. 16.

had obviously not presented a claim based on the VCCR in the state court for they had only later learned of this provision).[113] On 15 January 1999, the Supreme Court of Arizona ordered that Karl LaGrand be executed on 24 February 1999 and Walter LaGrand on 3 March 1999. Though the German government tried to intervene, Karl LaGrand's execution took place on 24 February 1999. At this point, the issue was brought before the ICJ. On 2 March 1999, Germany filed an application with the ICJ instigating proceedings against the United States for violations of the VCCR and requesting provisional measures. On 3 March 1999, the ICJ granted the request for provisional measures and ordered the United States to prevent the execution of Walter LaGrand pending the final decision in these proceedings. Four hours after the Court had delivered its order, Walter LaGrand was executed.

The proceedings before the ICJ nevertheless continued. In relevant part, the German government submitted that the United States, by failing to provide information on consular assistance to the LaGrand brothers, had not only violated Germany's rights under Article 36(1)(b) VCCR (something the United States readily admitted), but also Walter and Karl LaGrand's individual rights under the same treaty provision.[114] The issue of individual rights was significant in order to determine whether the United States had also violated obligations towards Germany under Article 36(2) VCCR,[115] which required that domestic law had to give full effect to the 'rights referred to in paragraph 1'. If one considered the term 'rights referred to in paragraph 1' to include individual rights, it could be argued that the United States had to provide domestic law remedies in criminal proceedings to give effect to these individual rights. Such remedies had obviously been lacking when the LaGrands' appeal for reconsideration of their sentence had been denied in federal court on grounds of domestic law. The United States, for its part, contended that the rights enumerated in Article 36(1)(b) VCCR 'are rights of States, and not of individuals, even though these rights may benefit individuals'.[116] In consequence, according to the United States government, there was no obligation stemming from Article 36(2) VCCR to provide domestic

[113] On 'procedural default', see ibid., para. 23.
[114] See the submissions by Germany: ibid., para. 11 (written) and 12 (oral).
[115] Article 36(2) VCCR reads: '2. The rights referred to in paragraph 1 of this article shall be exercised in conformity with the laws and regulations of the receiving State, subject to the proviso, however, that the said laws and regulations must enable full effect to be given to the purposes for which the rights accorded under this article are intended.'
[116] *LaGrand Case*, para. 76.

remedies for situations in which public authorities had failed to provide information on consular assistance. The right to this information was not held by individuals, but only by states; states, however, were not party to criminal proceedings in the United States and therefore there was no need for such a remedy.

In result, the ICJ was faced with the issue whether an international treaty provision, in addition to constituting rights and duties of state parties to the treaty, conferred international rights on individuals. The ICJ's response was instructive as much for the aspects it preferred to neglect as for the ones it chose to address. The Court stated:

> The Court notes that Article 36, paragraph 1(b), spells out the obligations the receiving State has towards the detained person and the sending State. It provides that, at the request of the detained person, the receiving State must inform the consular post of the sending State of the individual's detention 'without delay'. It provides further that any communication by the detained person addressed to the consular post of the sending State must be forwarded to it by authorities of the receiving State 'without delay'. Significantly, this subparagraph ends with the following language: 'The said authorities shall inform the person concerned without delay of *his rights* under this subparagraph' (emphasis added [by the Court]). . . . The clarity of these provisions, viewed in their context, admits of no doubt. It follows, as has been held on a number of occasions, that the Court must apply these as they stand . . .[117]

The Court thus focused on the text of Article 36(1)(b) VCCR when determining its application to individuals. In its own view, the text of the provision was sufficiently clear and, referring to a set of somewhat elderly precedents, the Court consequently felt obliged to apply the provisions 'as they stand'.[118] However, it is important to note that the precedents cited had nothing to do with direct effect of treaties, but with treaty interpretation more generally. The Court hence considered the direct effect of treaties as a matter of general principles of treaty interpretation.[119] There was no (rebuttable) presumption against or for direct effect of treaties on individuals; it all depended on the treaty provision in question. From this approach followed the Court's often-cited

[117] Ibid., para. 77 (list of references omitted).

[118] The Court obviously paraphrased the principle formulated in *Questions Concerning Acquisition of Polish Nationality* (Advisory Opinion), 1923 PCIJ Series B No. 7, at 20 (the opinion it also put first in its list of references): 'Having before it a clause which leaves little to be desired in the nature of clearness, it is bound to apply this clause as it stands . . .'.

[119] See also Spiermann, 'LaGrand Case', at 209, and Jennings, 'LaGrand', at 29.

conclusion: 'Based on the text of these provisions, the Court concludes that Article 36, paragraph 1, creates individual rights, which, by virtue of Article 1 of the Optional Protocol, may be invoked in this Court by the national State of the detained person. These rights were violated in the present case.'[120]

Accordingly, the Court, by interpreting the wording of the provision, concluded that Article 36(1)(b) VCCR conferred a direct right to information regarding consular assistance on individuals. It followed from this interpretation of the said provision that the United States was obliged pursuant to Article 36(2) VCCR to introduce domestic law remedies enabling full effect to be given to this individual right:

> The Court cannot accept the argument of the United States which proceeds, in part, on the assumption that paragraph 2 of Article 36 applies only to the rights of the sending State and not also to those of the detained individual. The Court has already determined that Article 36, paragraph 1, creates individual rights for the detained person in addition to the rights accorded the sending State, and that consequently the reference to 'rights' in paragraph 2 must be read as applying not only to the rights of the sending State, but also to the rights of the detained individual.[121]

In consequence, the Court ordered the United States to implement remedies which 'by means of its own choosing shall allow the review and reconsideration of the conviction and sentence by taking account of the violation of the rights set forth in that Convention'.[122]

The German government argued that, in addition to representing an individual right, the right to information on consular assistance was also to be considered a human right.[123] Indeed, the parties engaged in lengthy discussions on this point in oral argument.[124] Germany attempted to foster its position by extensive reference to Advisory Opinion OC-16/99 on the *Right to Information on Consular Assistance in the Framework of*

[120] *LaGrand Case*, para. 77. [121] Ibid., para. 89 (reference omitted).

[122] Ibid., para. 128. For the lack of such implementation so far see Hoppe, Carsten, 'Implementation of LaGrand and Avena in Germany and the United States: Exploring a Transatlantic Divide in Search of a Uniform Interpretation of Consular Rights', EJIL, 18 (2007), 317–36, at 322–3.

[123] *LaGrand Case*, para. 78. See also *Memorial of the Federal Republic of Germany*, 16 September 1999, paras 4.108–4.111.

[124] Compare the statements by Professor Bruno Simma, appearing on behalf of the Federal Republic of Germany, in Verbatim Record 2000/26, paras 7–14, as well as in Verbatim Record 2000/27, at paras 15–25, with Professor Stefan Trechsel, appearing on behalf of the United States of America, in Verbatim Record 2000/31, paras 6.6–6.8.

the Guarantees of the Due Process of Law which had been announced a year earlier by the Inter-American Court of Human Rights (IACHR).[125] In its opinion, the IACHR had declared the right to information on consular assistance a human right and concluded that the relevant provisions of the VCCR had to be interpreted in 'evolutive' terms in the tradition of interpreting human rights treaties.[126] It also followed, in the view of the IACHR and the German government, that it was even more important to give full effect to the right to information on consular assistance in domestic law for it was not only a 'normal' treaty right, but a human right. The Court, however, refrained from entering such reasoning:

> At the hearings, Germany further contended that the right of the individual to be informed without delay under Article 36, paragraph 1, of the Vienna Convention was not only an individual right but has today assumed the character of a human right. In consequence, Germany added, 'the character of the right under Article 36 as a human right renders the effectiveness of this provision even more imperative'. The Court having found that the United States violated the rights accorded by Article 36, paragraph 1, to the LaGrand brothers, it does not appear necessary to it to consider the additional argument developed by Germany in this regard.[127]

For the ICJ, then, it was not instructive whether the right contained in Article 36(1)(b) VCCR had a special status in international law or not; it sufficed to look at the treaty provision in question and to interpret it according to normal rules of treaty interpretation.[128]

By implication, it is submitted that the reasoning of the ICJ in *LaGrand* is a manifestation of the formal conception of international personality. As the conception asserts, the Court did only focus on the treaty norm in question in order to determine whether it conferred a direct international right to individuals. Unlike the *Jurisdiction of the Courts of Danzig* opinion,[129] there was no (rebuttable) presumption articulated against direct application of treaty provisions to individuals. Neither did the Court express any presumption in favour of direct effect,

[125] *Right to Information on Consular Assistance in the Framework of the Guarantees of the Due Process of Law* (Advisory Opinion OC-16/99), 1999 IACHR Series A No. 16, paras 85–7.

[126] Ibid., paras 114–15. [127] *LaGrand Case*, para. 78.

[128] Jennings, 'LaGrand', at 27, comments on this aspect with his usual vigour: 'The Court wisely decided that it had already disposed of this aspect of the case . . . For this wise forbearance all international lawyers should give heartfelt thanks.'

[129] *Jurisdiction of the Courts of Danzig*, at 17.

for example by referring to the status of the norm (as a human right) in international law. Such reasoning would have hinted at the individualistic conception of international personality, of which the above mentioned IACHR Advisory Opinion OC-16/99, with its focus on the status of the norm as a human right, tends to be a manifestation. The Court's decision in *LaGrand*, conversely, sees no reason to deviate from general principles of treaty interpretation. It considers the direct effect of treaties on individuals only as an issue concerning the interpretation of a treaty norm. Without even mentioning the concept of international personality, the Court stated that Article 36(1)(b) VCCR directly applies to individuals. International personality is then only a device of legal doctrine to conceptualize the fact that the individual holds a direct international right, but no legal concept stating any material presumptions or consequences. This clearly is in conformity with the formal conception of international personality.

After *LaGrand*, the ICJ was concerned with the same issue of the individual right to information on consular assistance in *Avena*. Mexico had brought a claim against the United States after around fifty of its nationals had been sentenced to death in the United States without having been informed of their right to consular assistance. In this context, the Court explicitly reaffirmed its interpretation of Article 36(1)(b) VCCR as articulated in *LaGrand*.[130] In consequence, *Avena*, too, has to be considered as a manifestation of the formal conception of international personality. In the United States, the same issue was brought before the Supreme Court in *Sanchez-Llamas* v. *Oregon*, but the Court only assumed, without deciding on the matter, that Article 36(1)(b) VCCR conferred rights upon the individual.[131] It is therefore not entirely clear which conception of international personality the Supreme Court's decision has to be related to, even more so because the Court also stated that there was 'a long established presumption that treaties and other international agreements do not create judicially enforceable individual rights'. It is also interesting to note in this respect that before *LaGrand*, a Canadian Court of Appeal had denied that Article 36(1)(b) VCCR entailed individual rights.[132] In the event, this Court appears

[130] *Case Concerning Avena and Other Mexican Nationals* (Mexico v. United States), 2004 ICJ Reports 12, para. 40.

[131] *Sanchez-Llamas* v. *Oregon* (US Supreme Court), 548 U.S. (2006).

[132] *The Queen* v. *Van Bergen* (Alberta Court of Appeal), 261 A.R. 387, para. 15 ('The Vienna Convention creates an obligation between states and is not one owed to the national').

to have applied the states-only or recognition conception of international personality by not interpreting the text of the particular treaty but limiting itself to state the general principle that a treaty creates rights and duties of states, not of individuals. In the tradition of the *LaGrand* case and the formal conception of international personality, such principled considerations are mistaken. All that is needed in order to determine whether a treaty norm has direct effect is to interpret the norm according to general rules of treaty interpretation.

The impact of *LaGrand* has not been restricted to the law of consular relations. In particular, the ICJ's approach towards individual treaty rights has found resonance in international investment arbitration law. There have been signs that arbitrators do not consider individuals (understood to encompass corporations) as mere beneficiaries of rights contained in bilateral or multilateral investment treaties that are actually held by their state of nationality, but as direct holders of these international rights. For example, after the *LaGrand* judgment and apparently influenced by it,[133] a tribunal under ICSID declared that 'both the substantive and procedural rights of the individual in international law have undergone considerable development' and thereby indicated that certain rights under NAFTA were directly held by individuals.[134] And with express reference to the ICJ's judgment in *LaGrand*, it was declared in *SGS* v. *Philippines* that 'under modern international law, treaties may confer rights, substantive and procedural, on individuals'.[135] By referring to *LaGrand*, these tribunals appear to have affirmed direct rights of corporations under international investment treaties and thereby to have transcended the *Mavrommatis*-formula. In doing so, they have manifested the formal conception of international personality.[136]

*The effect of Article 42 ICSID Convention (*Amco v. Indonesia*)*

As noted earlier, there is often uncertainty about whether and to what extent international law is applicable to so-called state contracts. In particular, it is unclear what effect the choice of international law

[133] Spiermann, 'Individual Rights', at 185, also assumes a link between the *LaGrand* judgment and this statement.

[134] *Mondev International Ltd.* v. *United States* (Award, 2002), 42 ILM 85, para. 116.

[135] *Société Générale de Surveillance (SGS)* v. *Republic of the Philippines* (Decision on Objections to Jurisdiction, 2004), 8 ICSID Reports 518, para. 154.

[136] A similar, albeit not identical, point is put forward by Leben, 'La Théorie du Contrat d'État', at 308–10.

(either by directly selecting it as the law governing the contract or by referring disputes to a tribunal authorized by statutory provisions to apply it) exercises on the proper law of contract. In this context, it is submitted that legal reasoning as found in *Amco* v. *Indonesia* (resubmitted case, 1990)[137] is a manifestation of the formal conception of international personality.[138] In line with the conception, there is no presumption against international law being applicable and there are no a priori restrictions attached to the role of international law. International law is fully applied because Article 42(1) ICSID Convention so stipulates.

The *Amco* v. *Indonesia* case concerned contracts entered into by Amco Asia Corporation, a company incorporated in the United States, and a state-owned Indonesian company as well as the Indonesian government. There had been no choice of law clauses in these contracts. By 1980, several disagreements between Amco and its Indonesian partners had arisen, in the course of which the competent Indonesian authorities, including Indonesian courts, had cancelled Amco's licence to invest in Indonesia and permitted Indonesian business partners of Amco to take control of its property. Amco subsequently brought suit against Indonesia under ICSID seeking compensation for damages arising from seizure of property and cancellation of its investment licence. The tribunal, after being challenged by Indonesia, declared itself competent to hear the case. With respect to the law applicable to the contractual relationships, the tribunal referred to Article 42(1) ICSID Convention.[139] The provision states: 'The Tribunal shall decide a dispute in accordance with such rules of law as may be agreed by the parties. In the absence of such agreement, the Tribunal shall apply the law of the Contracting State party to the dispute (including its rules on the conflict of laws) and such rules of international law as may be applicable'. The tribunal then proceeded by relying primarily on general principles of law and public international law in order to award Amco considerable compensation for damage.[140] Indonesia subsequently applied for annulment proceedings pursuant to Article 52 ICSID Convention. The ad hoc committee

137 *Amco Asia Corporation and Others* v. *The Republic of Indonesia* (Resubmitted Case: Award on the Merits, 1990), 1 ICSID Reports 569, paras 37–40.

138 See also Leben, Charles, 'Hans Kelsen and the Advancement of International Law', EJIL, 9 (1998), 287–305, at 303.

139 *Amco Asia Corporation and Others* v. *The Republic of Indonesia* (Award on the Merits, 1984), 1 ICSID Reports 413, paras 147–8.

140 Ibid., para. 291.

annulled the findings of the tribunal inter alia on the grounds that, by mostly focusing on general principles of law and public international law, it had failed to apply Indonesian law to the state contract and thus came short of stating appropriate reasons for its decision in the meaning of Article 52(1)(e) ICSID Convention.[141] The committee made reference to the annulment proceedings in *Klöckner* v. *Cameroon* in which it had also been held that domestic law had mistakenly been ignored in favour of applying public international law.[142] With reference to this decision, and recounting reasons inherent in the system of international investment arbitration, the ad hoc committee in *Amco* v. *Indonesia* declared:

> It seems to the *ad hoc* committee worth noting that Article 42(1) of the Convention authorizes an ICSID tribunal to apply rules of international law only to fill up lacunae in the applicable domestic law . . . The above view on the supplemental and corrective role of international law in relation to the law of the host State as substantive applicable law, is shared in ICSID case law [reference to annulment decision in *Klöckner* v. *Cameroon*].[143]

After the annulment, however, the newly established committee took issue with this restrictive view on the effect of Article 42(1) ICSID Convention:

> This Tribunal notes that Article 42(1) refers to the application of host-state law and international law. If there are no relevant host-state laws on a particular matter, a search must be made for the relevant international laws. And, where there are applicable host-state laws, they must be checked against international laws, which will prevail in the case of conflict. Thus international law is fully applicable and to classify its role as 'only' 'supplemental and corrective' seems a distinction without a difference.[144]

In the view of the newly established committee dealing with the resubmitted case, international law was fully applicable to the state contract under review. There were no restrictions inherent in international investment arbitration that called for restraint when applying principles of public international law to matters concerning a state contract. On the

[141] *Amco Asia Corporation and Others* v. *The Republic of Indonesia* (Decision on Annulment, 1986), 1 ICSID Reports 509, paras 38–44.

[142] *Klöckner Industrie-Anlagen GmbH and Others* v. *Republic of Cameroon* (Decision on Annulment, 1985), 2 ICSID Reports 95, paras 122–5, and 156.

[143] *Amco* v. *Indonesia* (Decision on Annulment), paras 20 and 22.

[144] *Amco* v. *Indonesia* (Resubmitted Case: Award on the Merits), para. 40.

contrary, international law, because of Article 42(1) of the Convention and the general principle that international law prevailed over national law, was the proper law of state contract under ICSID whenever the parties decided to submit their dispute to this forum without specifically choosing another legal system to govern the contract.

The reasoning in the final phase of *Amco* v. *Indonesia* has to be considered a manifestation of the formal conception of international personality. Conversely, as has been noted in the context of examining the *Serbian Loans* statement, the annulment declaration in the course of the same proceedings manifests the states-only conception (as does *Klöckner* v. *Cameroon* to which it refers). The difference between the two approaches is that the award on the resubmitted case follows strictly the text of Article 42(1) ICSID Convention (and opts for the superiority of international law in case of conflict between the two *applicable* legal systems)[145] whereas the annulment decision restricts the effect of the treaty provision for systemic reasons. As regards the reasoning in the resubmitted case, there is no presumption against international law being applicable to a state contract and hence there are no reservations about the plain meaning of Article 42(1) ICSID Convention. At the same time, the only reason for the application of international law is that the statutory provision so provides. There are no other considerations – such as, for example, the status of the legal norms in question or effective actor-quality of the parties – attached to the affirmation that international law directly and fully applies to the contract. Similarly, there are no further implications drawn from this conclusion: there is no indication articulated in the award that the private party has certain international rights or capacities associated with being an international person. By implication, the company may a posteriori be considered an international person; but this status does not imply any legal consequences.[146] This approach followed in *Amco* v. *Indonesia* is in accordance with the formal conception of international personality.

[145] The point here is not so much that applicable rules of international law prevail over the domestic ones in case of conflict; the point is that international law is applicable at all without restrictions.

[146] See also Leben, 'Kelsen', at 303–4, and Leben, 'La Théorie du Contrat d'État', at 302–14. A similar argument is made by Lauterpacht, Elihu, 'International Law and Private Foreign Investment', *Indiana Journal of Global Legal Studies*, 4 (1997), 259–76, at 272–4.

9

The actor conception

The actor conception of international personality considers all entities exercising 'effective power' in the international 'decision-making process' international persons. To be precise, the notion of international personality is avoided and the term 'participant' or indeed 'actor' preferred. It is not exactly argued that all participants are international persons because in principle the concept of international personality does not exist in this conception. However, there is often reference to the status of certain participants as 'subjects of international law' or 'international persons'. And, functionally, the notion of participant is used to the same end as is the concept of international personality, namely, to describe which social entities are relevant in international law.

The actor conception is often associated with the work of Rosalyn Higgins, the President of the International Court of Justice. But while her work on the topic was certainly influential, she was not, and has never claimed to be,[1] original in her statements on international personality. She mostly followed the path designated by Myers S. McDougal and Harold D. Lasswell (both from Yale Law School[2]), who had formulated the actor conception after the end of World War II as part of their policy-oriented approach to international law. Later on, W. Michael Reisman joined McDougal and Lasswell in finalizing the conception and forcefully promoting it in theory and practice.[3] Rosalyn Higgins's

[1] See e.g. Higgins, Rosalyn, 'Conceptual Thinking about the Individual in International Law' in Richard Falk, Friedrich Kratochwil and Saul H. Mendlovitz (eds.), *International Law: A Contemporary Perspective* (London: Westview Press, 1985) (originally published in *British Journal of International Studies*, 4 1978), 476–94, at 478–9 (explicit acknowledgment of McDougal's theory); Higgins, 'General Course', at 81 (by implication).

[2] In this context it might be interesting to note that McDougal was the supervisor of Higgins's doctorate at Yale Law School (see the account in Higgins, Rosalyn, 'McDougal as Teacher, Mentor, and Friend', YLJ, 108 (1999), 957–60, esp. at 958–9).

[3] On a more general level, a similar point is made by Voos, Sandra, *Die Schule von New Haven: Darstellung und Kritik einer amerikanischen Völkerrechtslehre* (Berlin: Duncker und Humblot, 2000), 15.

main contribution, it might be said, lay in familiarizing European international lawyers with the actor conception – particularly through her General Course in 1991 – by using terms and lines of arguments perhaps better comprehensible for a European international law audience than the original works of McDougal, Lasswell and Reisman had been. In this book, Higgins's work is consequently used in order to present the basic propositions of the conception; the origins of the conception, however, have to be inferred from the context in which McDougal and Lasswell (and to a lesser extent Reisman) had originally formulated the actor conception.

To a certain extent, some aspects of the actor approach had already been anticipated by Philip C. Jessup[4] and Wolfgang M. Friedmann.[5] From a somewhat different angle, mainly focused on the role of international organizations but with very similar results, Scandinavian authors led by Finn Seyersted also postulated one form of the actor conception.[6] More recently, the conception has also been put forward by John Dugard in the context of the ILC's work on diplomatic protection[7] and can also be found in works by Anne-Marie Slaughter[8] and Robert

[4] Jessup, Philip C., 'The Subjects of a Modern Law of Nations', *Michigan Law Review*, 45 (1947), 383–408, esp. at 384:

> There is . . . no occasion here to continue the debate as to whether under existing international law individuals are subjects of the law or only its 'destinataires'. Those who will may consider some of the observations here as *lex lata*, while others will deal with them as made *de lege ferenda*. It remains true . . . that it is 'obvious that international relations are not limited to relations between states'. The function of international law is to provide a legal basis for the orderly management of international relations. The traditional international law was keyed to the actualities of the past centuries in which international relations were inter-state relations. The actualities have changed; the law is changing.

[5] Friedmann, *Changing Structure*, e.g. 173–6 and 223–4 (with regard to private corporations). But see the apparently more traditional discussion on the status of individuals at 232–49. On the latter point, compare the critical remarks by McDougal, Myers S. and W. Michael Reisman, '"The Changing Structure of International Law": Unchanging Theory for Inquiry', *Columbia Law Review*, 65 (1965), 810–35, at 816.

[6] Seyersted, *Objective International Personality*, 44–5. Compare with the almost identical statements in Higgins, 'General Course', at 78.

[7] Dugard, John R. (Special Rapporteur), First Report on Diplomatic Protection, ILC 2000, UN Doc. A/CN.4/506, para. 24 (with references to Rosalyn Higgins, Myers McDougal and Harold Lasswell): 'The debate over the question whether the individual is a mere "object" of international law (the traditional view) or a "subject" of international law is unhelpful. It is better to view the individual as a participant in the international legal order.'

[8] Slaughter, Anne-Marie, 'International Law in a World of Liberal States', EJIL, 6 (1995), 503–38, at 504.

McCorquodale.[9] Its main manifestations in legal practice are *Reineccius et al.* v. *Bank for International Settlements* (on the Bank's powers to expropriate its private shareholders), the *International Tin Council* cases (on the liability of member states of an international organization vis-à-vis third parties) and the award in *Sandline* v. *Papua New Guinea* (concerning the law applicable to state contracts).

Basic propositions

The actor conception contends, with some qualifications to be readily enunciated, that all participants in the international legal system are international persons.[10] The qualifications concern the fact that the actor conception – in principle, but not entirely – avoids using the notion of 'international personality' or 'subject of international law'. It is one of the main characteristics of this conception that it considers the dichotomy between subjects (or persons) and mere objects of international law as essentially misleading:

> [I]t is not particularly helpful either intellectually or operationally to rely on the subject–object dichotomy that runs through so much of the writings. It is more helpful, and closer to perceived reality, to return to the view of international law as a particular decision-making process. Within that process (which is a dynamic and not a static one) there are a variety of participants, making claims across State lines, with the object of maximizing various values. Determinations will be made on those claims by various authoritative decision-makers – Foreign Office Legal Advisers, arbitral tribunals, courts. Now, in this model, there are no 'subjects' or 'objects', but only *participants*. Individuals *are* participants along with States, international organizations (such as the United Nations, or the IMF, or the ILO), multinational corporations, and indeed private non-governmental groups.[11]

In the actor conception, thus, the more flexible notion of 'participants' is employed instead of 'persons' or 'subjects'. Participants in the international

[9] McCorquodale, 'Individual', at 310–11 (with reference to Higgins).

[10] McDougal, Myers S., 'International Law, Power, and Policy: A Contemporary Conception', RCADI, 82 (1953-I), 133–259, at 160–2; McDougal, Myers S., Harold D. Lasswell and W. Michael Reisman, 'The World Constitutive Process of Authoritative Decision' in Richard A. Falk and Cyril E. Black (eds.), *The Future of the International Legal Order: Volume I: Trends and Patterns* (Princeton University Press, 1969), 73–154, at 81; Higgins, 'General Course', at 68 and 77–82. See also Voos, *Schule von New Haven*, 80–2 (not distinguishing at all between participants and persons).

[11] Higgins, 'General Course', at 81 (original emphasis). See also McDougal and Reisman, 'Unchanging Theory', at 815–16.

legal system are states, international and non-governmental organizations, multinational corporations and private individuals.[12] However, the traditional notion of personality or subjectivity is nevertheless used at times, if only to phrase arguments in language familiar to international lawyers.[13] On balance, it seems fair to say that, in a broad sense, the actor conception considers being a participant in the international legal order as functionally similar to being an international person. The actor approach can thus be considered a qualified conception of international personality.

In the actor conception, the international legal order is not considered a system of rules, but a process of authoritative decision-making:

> [Traditional] views – and the reasoning on which they are based – carry with them so many assumptions that, in disagreeing with them, it is hard to know where to begin. The most basic assumption, of course, is that international law – indeed, any legal system – is a set of rules. Yet . . . law can be seen rather as a process: a particularized form of decision-making process, distinguished from mere political decision-making by the significance of reference to the accumulated trends of past decisions, the emphasis on the authority of the persons making the decision . . .[14]
>
> Operating within th[e] global process of effective power is . . . a comprehensive process of authoritative decision, in the sense of a continuous flow of decisions made by the persons who are expected to make them, in accordance with criteria expected by community members, in established structures of authority, with enough bases in power to secure consequential control, and by authorized procedures.[15]

This authoritative decision-making process has to be distinguished from the political process of 'naked' power.[16] The process of authoritative decision-making is more predetermined than a mere political process, but at the same time it is not confined to legal adjudication. It includes other organized arenas like formal diplomatic negotiations as well as unorganized settings more focused on public persuasion.[17] These

[12] See also McDougal, Lasswell and Reisman, 'World Constitutive Process', at 81–94; McDougal, 'Contemporary Conception', at 161; Reisman, W. Michael, 'The View from the New Haven School of International Law', ASIL Proc., 86 (1992), 118–25, at 122.

[13] E.g. McDougal, 'Contemporary Conception', at 161; McDougal, Lasswell and Reisman, 'World Constitutive Process', at 81 and 93; Higgins, 'General Course', at 68 and 76–8.

[14] Higgins, 'Conceptual Thinking', at 478–9.

[15] McDougal, Myers S., Harold D. Lasswell and Lung-chu Chen, *Human Rights and World Public Order: The Basic Policies of an International Law of Human Dignity* (New Haven and London: Yale University Press, 1980), 162.

[16] See also McDougal, Lasswell and Reisman, 'World Constitutive Process', at 76.

[17] Higgins, 'Conceptual Thinking', at 480; McDougal, Lasswell and Reisman, 'World Constitutive Process', at 100–2.

interactions cumulate in decisions which themselves enjoy authority not because international rules exist to this effect, but because the relevant participants effectively accept, to varying degrees in different contexts, the decision as compulsory in the self-interest of stability in international relations.[18]

Yet participation in this international decision-making process depends merely on *factual* power. There is no legal rule conferring legal capacity onto an entity allowing it to participate in this process. All actors actually taking part in authoritative decision-making processes of an international kind are participants of the international legal order irrespective of the cause for participation. It might well be that an actor has access to unorganized arenas of the international decision-making process simply as a result of exercising enough power to be accepted by other more established participants. International lawyers therefore have to observe which entities actually participate in order to determine the relevant persons of the international legal order. They do not have to look for particular rules or formal acts of recognition when determining the legal status of a particular actor.[19] For example, according to the actor conception, individuals are participants in the international legal order because they actually take part in various – mostly unorganized – international arenas concerned with authoritative decision-making; neither the lack of legal rules to this effect nor of recognition by states has any significance when determining the legal status of individuals in international law:

> The adamant stance of some observers in refusing to recognize the individual as a subject of international law is currently based on a pseudo-empirical survey of the practice of organized arenas. Since individuals do not have *locus standi* before the organized arenas which are examined, individuals are not, it is concluded, subjects of international law. The concealed assumption is that the organized arenas surveyed exhaust authoritative patterns of constitutive interaction. A more comprehensive survey of the range of constitutive arenas indicates that individuals with effective bases of power have always had access to a wide variety of arenas.[20]

To identify the participants, one has to observe the variety of international arenas in which decisions on international matters are made and to analyse which actors take part in these decisions.

[18] McDougal, Lasswell and Reisman, 'World Constitutive Process', at 76.

[19] Higgins, 'General Course', at 80; Higgins, 'Conceptual Thinking', at 478.

[20] McDougal, Lasswell and Reisman, 'World Constitutive Process', at 93. See also Higgins, 'Conceptual Thinking', at 480–2.

In conclusion, the actor conception can be encapsulated in two basic propositions:

(1) International law is not a set of rules, but an authoritative decision-making process. In this process, goals and values of the international community and outcomes in particular circumstances are determined. The process takes place in different arenas, which range from organized to unorganized. It is authoritative and therefore to be distinguished from 'naked' power.
(2) In this authoritative decision-making process, participation is not based on legal rules or specific acts of recognition, but on effective power to participate. According to the conception, all international lawyers have to do in order to establish the personal scope of the international legal order is to analyse organized and unorganized international decision-making processes and to determine which entities *effectively* partake in them. The consequences of being a participant are, in principle, governed by factual observations as well.

In the following, the origins of these two propositions will be examined in order to establish their meaning and significance as well as their underlying assumptions.

Origins of the basic propositions

The origins of the actor conception's basic propositions lie in the American context of the mid twentieth century. This context is characterized by a twofold realism: legal realism and international realism. The former, primarily informed by pragmatist philosophy, provides insights as to the origins of the first proposition of the actor conception with its focus on law as a decision-making process. The latter lies at the centre of the second proposition and the conception's concern with effective power. It is important to note the basic difference between the two forms of realism: whereas the first form is concerned with the legal process in settings with strong judicial institutions, the latter builds on the weakness of legal institutions in the international realm.[21] In result, legal realism affirms a distinct role for law, whereas international realism precisely denies such a role. In combination, these two forms of realism

[21] See also Slaughter Burley, Anne-Marie, 'International Law and International Relations Theory: A Dual Agenda', AJIL, 87 (1993), 205–39, at 209 n. 11.

provide the origin of the basic propositions of the actor conception of international personality.

American realism

As noted earlier, the actor conception, albeit influentially promoted by Rosalyn Higgins and W. Michael Reisman, was originally coined by Myers S. McDougal and Harold D. Lasswell. To determine the relevant context of the conception, it is useful to start with some biographical information on the latter two scholars. Myers S. McDougal was born in 1906 in Mississippi where he also earned his first university degree. Winning the prestigious Rhodes Scholarship in 1927, he spent three years as a graduate student at Oxford University, attending lectures in international law by James Leslie Brierly. Upon returning to the United States, McDougal earned his J.S.D. from Yale Law School in 1931. At Yale, the predominant legal theory at the time was American legal realism. McDougal enthusiastically committed himself to this school of thought after overcoming serious doubts rooted in his rather different Oxford training.[22] McDougal subsequently worked as a law professor on property law and legal philosophy at the University of Illinois and at Yale before serving as a legal advisor to the US State Department during World War II. After the war, McDougal returned full-time to Yale Law School and began to engage with international law.[23] At about the same time, his intense partnership with Harold D. Lasswell started.[24] Lasswell (born 1902) was not a lawyer, but a social scientist. Yet his influence in both political science and law might be best illustrated by the fact that he became President of the American Political Science Association as well as of the American Society of International Law.[25] Lasswell had introduced behaviouralism into political science in the 1930s under the acknowledged influence of John Dewey, his colleague at the University of

[22] See McDougal, Myers S., 'Fuller v. the American Legal Realists: An Intervention', YLJ, 50 (1941), 827–40, at 834–8 (with some ambiguity). See also Willard, Andrew R., 'Myers Smith McDougal: A Life of and about Human Dignity', YLJ, 108 (1999), 927–33, at 929, Voos, *Schule von New Haven*, 20–1, and Rosenthal, Bent, *Étude de l'œuvre de Myers Smith McDougal en Matière de Droit International Public* (Paris: Librarie Générale de Droit et de Jurisprudence, 1970), 31–2 and 70.

[23] Voos, *Schule von New Haven*, 21.

[24] On the extraordinary close collaboration between McDougal and Lasswell see Falk, Richard A., 'Casting the Spell: The New Haven School of International Law', YLJ, 104 (1995), 1991–2008, at 1994–6.

[25] Voos, *Schule von New Haven*, 27.

Chicago, and had subsequently become one of the leading political scientists in the United States.[26] After World War II, Lasswell moved to Yale where his cooperation with McDougal started: Lasswell provided the general framework of inquiry for international legal studies whereas McDougal filled this framework with his legal knowledge.[27] As part of their collaborative endeavour, McDougal and Lasswell were calling for reforms in law studies at graduate level. According to them, law had to be understood as a decision-making process to be approached from different disciplinary angles, including political science and sociology.[28] This view of law and legal education became known as the policy-oriented school or, because of its close relation to Yale Law School, the New Haven School.

Thus, the relevant context of the actor conception is international (legal) scholarship in the United States in the mid twentieth century and its socio-political environment. The latter was – and still is – characterized by the extraordinarily important position of the judiciary in the American polity. As Alexis de Tocqueville observed in 1835: 'Il n'est presque pas de question politique, aux États-Unis, qui ne se résolve tôt ou tard en question judiciaire.'[29] Two factors contributed to this peculiar role of law in the American political process: the first is, of course, the self-proclaimed power of the Supreme Court to review and declare unconstitutional enactments of Congress;[30] the second is the doctrine known as 'substantive due process' which enables the Supreme Court to strike down state laws that pass formal procedural criteria but fail material standards of reasonableness and desirability.[31] The latter doctrine developed in relation to the Fourteenth Amendment to the American Constitution, which had been passed by Congress in 1866

[26] Marvick, Dwane, 'The Work of Harold D. Lasswell: His Approach, Concerns, and Influence', *Political Behaviour*, 2 (1980), 219–229, esp. at 220–4. Merelman, Richard M., 'Harold D. Lasswell's Political World: Weak Tea for Hard Times', *British Journal of Political Science*, 11 (1981), 471–97, at 485–6.

[27] Voos, *Schule von New Haven*, 27–9; Falk, 'New Haven School', at 1995.

[28] McDougal, Myers S. and Harold D. Lasswell, 'Legal Education and Public Policy: Professional Training in the Public Interest', YLJ, 52 (1943), 203–95, *passim* (the article was written during the war in Washington before Lasswell moved to Yale).

[29] Tocqueville, Alexis de, *De la démocratie en Amérique* (Paris: Gallimard, 1986) (originally published 1835), Deuxième Partie, Ch. VIII, ii (p. 401).

[30] *Marbury* v. *Madison* (US Supreme Court, 1803), 5 U.S. 137.

[31] See Hart, H. L. A., 'American Jurisprudence through English Eyes: The Nightmare and the Noble Dream' in H. L. A Hart (ed.), *Essays in Jurisprudence and Philosophy* (Oxford: Clarendon Press, 1983) (originally published 1977), 123–44, at 124–5.

and ratified in 1868.[32] The Amendment was an effect of the American Civil War: whereas a similar proposal by James Madison had not found approval by Congress in 1789, the battle over slavery demonstrated that citizens had to be protected not only from the federal government (which was provided for in the Fifth Amendment as part of the Bill of Rights), but also from their local governments.[33] However, the main obstacle to using the Fourteenth Amendment as a device to protect the basic rights of individuals from infringements by their local governments was the 'due process of law' clause. If interpreted in formal terms, the clause meant that states could act in ways that resulted in depriving their citizens of 'life, liberty, or property' whenever basic requirements of fair procedure were upheld.[34] Yet, the Supreme Court, from the 1890s onwards, understood 'due process of law' in substantive terms, allowing it to materially consider the constitutionality of state-made law.[35] By implication, the Fourteenth Amendment became a central factor for the Supreme Court's power in the American political process, for it allowed the Court to ultimately rule on the constitutionality of a variety of laws enacted by state parliaments in the normal democratic process.

Arguably, there is a link between the importance of the judicial process in the American polity and the desire of American diplomats after World War I to create a new international order based on the rule of law.[36] In this respect, United States foreign policy had encountered a dramatic change under the presidency of Woodrow Wilson when it – temporarily, as it turned out – abandoned its century-old Monroe Doctrine (which affirmed American influence in the Western hemisphere and pledged not to take part in European great power politics) to intervene in World War I

[32] It reads in relevant part: 'No State shall . . . deprive any person of life, liberty, or property, without due process of law; nor deny to any person within its jurisdiction the equal protection of the laws.'

[33] Tribe, Laurence H., *American Constitutional Law: Volume One*, 3rd edition (New York: Foundation Press, 2000), 9–10.

[34] See also ibid., 1332–3 (although contesting this formal view). [35] Ibid., 1343–5.

[36] Such a link is suggested by Kennan, George F., *American Diplomacy 1900–1950* (University of Chicago Press, 1951), 95–6. On a more general level, Kennedy, David, 'The Disciplines of International Law and Policy', *Leiden Journal of International Law*, 12 (1999), 9–133, at 18, and Cot, Jean-Pierre, 'Tableau de la Pensée Juridique Américaine', RGDIP, 110 (2006), 537–96, at 537–8, put forward similar arguments. On American international law tradition before 1919 and idealistic aspects in it, see Raymond, John M. and Barbara J. Frischholz, 'Lawyers who Established International Law in the United States, 1776–1914', AJIL, 76 (1982), 802–29, esp. at 825–6.

and to build a new international order.[37] Accordingly, Wilson was one of the main architects of the League of Nations system created at the Peace Conference in Paris.[38] Albeit the United States subsequently did not join the League and returned to a period of isolationism for domestic political reasons, most American international lawyers – who were mostly associated with the State Department – remained committed to Wilsonian legalism in the interwar period.[39] Yet, by the end of World War II, this commitment was seriously discredited: after the crises over Manchuria, Abyssinia and German rearmament in the 1930s and the apparent inability of the League system to decisively deal with them, legalist approaches in the tradition of Wilson seemed to many to be completely out of touch with the realities of international relations.[40] In addition to these past experiences, after World War II the United States was faced with an entirely different international power structure. By 1945, the British Empire was in clear retreat whereas the influence of the United States and the Soviet Union had increased tremendously. In this new situation, the United States renounced pre-war isolationism and pledged, in what is known as the Truman doctrine, to actively engage in world politics. There was thus a practical need for alternative visions of international politics than the one offered by discredited Wilsonian idealism. This vision was provided by the emerging theory of international realism.[41]

The rule-sceptic view of law

In the American polity with its extraordinary high standing of the judiciary, there emerged a realist approach to law at the turn of the

[37] See Kissinger, Henry, *Die Vernunft der Nationen: Über das Wesen der Aussenpolitik* (Berlin: Goldmann, 1996), 40–52 (from a strictly realist perspective).

[38] Ibid., 250–8.

[39] Koskenniemi, *Gentle Civilizer*, 465–6. A more heterogeneous picture is provided by Kennedy, David, 'The Twentieth-Century Discipline of International Law in the United States' in Austin Sarat, Bryant Garth and Robert A. Kagan (eds.), *Looking Back at Law's Century* (Ithaca: Cornell University Press, 2002), 386–433, at 402. See also Carr, E. H., *The Twenty Years' Crisis*, reissue of the 2nd edition (New York: Palgrave, 2001) (originally published 1939), 15.

[40] Kennedy, 'International Law in the United States', at 402; Koskenniemi, *Gentle Civilizer*, 466.

[41] Hoffmann, Stanley, 'An American Social Science: International Relations' in *Janus and Minerva: Essays in the Theory and Practice of International Politics* (London: Westview Press, 1987), 3–24, at 10–1; Koskenniemi, *Gentle Civilizer*, 469–70.

twentieth century stressing the law-making capacity of judges. In the view of this so-called 'American Legal Realism', judges did not merely apply pre-existing legal rules to a particular situation, but first of all created the law to be applied. Indeed, in this tradition, judges were precisely called upon to take into account the practical consequences of their reasoning instead of merely applying formal legal principles according to legal logic.[42] The task of lawyers was therefore not, as in the traditional sense, to infer rules from the acknowledged sources of law, but to determine legal outcomes by taking into account a variety of aspects, including economic and philosophical ones. By implication, in the lack of formal rules, legal outcomes depended considerably on the political and philosophical predispositions of judges. This led to what H. L. A. Hart famously called 'a concentration, almost to the point of obsession, on the judicial process' in American jurisprudence.[43] It is this view of law as essentially created – instead of merely applied – in the judicial decision-making process that the first proposition of the actor conception of international personality has to be associated with.

As already noted, the power of the judiciary in the American polity partly depends on the doctrine of 'substantive due process', which was developed after the Civil War in the context of the Fourteenth Amendment. In this respect, a milestone decision was handed down in 1905 in *Lochner* v. *New York*.[44] The matter was the constitutionality of a New York state law that limited the maximum amount a baker was allowed to work. In its controversial decision, the Supreme Court, by a 5–4 margin, declared the law unconstitutional on the grounds that it interfered with the guarantee of contractual freedom implicit in the Fourteenth Amendment. Writing for the majority, Judge Peckham called the law an 'unreasonable, unnecessary and arbitrary interference with the right and liberty of the individual to contract in relation to labor, and, as such, it is in conflict with, and void under, the Federal Constitution'. In other words, the 'due process of law' clause of the Fourteenth Amendment was interpreted in substantial terms: to be constitutional, it was not enough for the New York state law to fulfil procedural requirements; it also had to pass tests of fairness, reasonableness and appropriateness. In the view of the majority, the New York bakery law

[42] This normative tendency of legal realism is persuasively highlighted by Verdirame, Guglielmo, 'The Divided West: International Lawyers in Europe and America', EJIL, 18 (2007), 553–80, at 562. Only as an aside, it appears, it is also mentioned by Hart, 'American Jurisprudence', at 128.

[43] Hart, 'American Jurisprudence', at 123.

[44] *Lochner* v. *New York* (US Supreme Court), 198 U.S. 45 (1905).

failed this test. Judge Oliver Wendell Holmes took issue with this reasoning and filed a memorable dissent:

> This case is decided upon an economic theory which a large part of the country does not entertain. If it were a question whether I agreed with that theory, I should desire to study it further and long before making up my mind. But I do not conceive that to be my duty, because I strongly believe that my agreement or disagreement has nothing to do with the right of a majority to embody their opinions in law . . . The 14th Amendment does not enact Mr. Herbert Spencer's Social Statics . . . a Constitution is not intended to embody a particular economic theory, whether of paternalism and the organic relation of the citizen to the state or of laissez faire. It is made for people of fundamentally differing views, and the accident of our finding certain opinions natural and familiar, or novel, and even shocking, ought not to conclude our judgment upon the question whether statutes embodying them conflict with the Constitution of the United States.[45]

Holmes's main criticism was that the majority opinion simply followed a general economic theory it thought enacted in the Fourteenth Amendment, namely the nearly absolute principle of freedom of contract. Starting from this dogma, any social welfare policy restricting contractual freedom was in some sense precluded. For Holmes, such reliance on a general theory was essentially mistaken because '[g]eneral propositions do not decide concrete cases. The decision will depend on a judgment or intuition more subtle than any articulate major premise.'[46] Accordingly, what the majority opinion had failed to do was to consider the specifics of the case at hand. In Holmes's view, a legal matter was not dealt with by relying on some general dogma; it was rather by considering the subtleties of the specific circumstances and the practical consequences of a decision that a legal issue was to be approached. In *Lochner* v. *New York*, the majority had failed to seriously acknowledge the consequences of its decision, that is, the imposition of a certain economic theory on the New York legislature.[47] Such abstract reasoning with its reliance on a general theory was unacceptable for Holmes.

Holmes's *Lochner* dissent was remarkably influential in American jurisprudence and, indeed, philosophy.[48] Part of this impact is explained

[45] *Lochner* v. *New York*, (Holmes, J., dissenting) (references omitted). [46] Ibid.

[47] The matter is at least addressed in the majority opinion when Justice Peckham states that 'this is not a question of substituting the judgment of the court for that of the legislature'.

[48] See e.g. Pound, Roscoe, 'Mechanical Jurisprudence', *Columbia Law Review*, 8 (1908), 605–23, at 615–16, and Dewey, John, 'Logical Method and Law', *Philosophical Review*, 33 (1924), 560–72, at 563–6.

by the fact that it was no isolated critique of legal formalism, but formed an authoritative part of a wider jurisprudential and philosophical endeavour generally associated with the philosophy of pragmatism.[49] In the 1870s, Holmes had been a member of an informal group at Harvard University ('The Metaphysical Club') which included William James and Charles Sanders Peirce, two of the principal architects of pragmatist philosophy.[50] In fact, it might be said, with some degree of simplification, that the philosophy of pragmatism arose out of the gatherings of this informal group.[51] In order to understand Holmes's criticism in the *Lochner* dissent, it is thus fitting to situate it into the larger philosophy of pragmatism as perhaps most influentially coined by William James.[52] James's main claim was that the value of a theoretical concept was not to be judged by its logical consistency or perceived abstract-philosophical soundness, but by its practical consequences: 'truth is what works best'.[53] Put more meticulously:

> ... *ideas* (which themselves are but parts of our experience) *become true just in so far as they help us to get into satisfactory relation with other parts of our experience*, to summarise them and get about among them by

[49] For a balanced account of Holmes's legal approach and its relation to pragmatism, see Grey, Thomas C., 'Holmes and Legal Pragmatism', *Stanford Law Review*, 41 (1989), 787–870, esp. at 787–93. See also Hart, 'American Jurisprudence', at 130 (with some reservations). White, Morton, *Social Thought in America: The Revolt against Formalism* (Oxford University Press, 1976) (originally published 1947), 15–18, puts Holmes's critique in the wider context of American social thought and its general rejection of formalism.

[50] One has to be mindful not to forget the considerable differences that exist inside pragmatist philosophy and in particular between James and Peirce. For present purposes, however, these differences have not be elaborated on, for it is only the basic (and similar) premises that are of relevance. And see the acknowledgement of Peirce's influence in James, William, 'Philosophical Conceptions and Practical Results' in *William James: Writings 1878–1899* (New York: The Library of America, 1992) (originally delivered 1898), 1077–97, at 1079.

[51] See e.g. Fisch, M. H., 'Justice Holmes, the Prediction Theory of Law, and Pragmatism', *Philosophical Review*, 39 (1942), 85–97, esp. at 88–90. Of course, this is not to forget John Dewey, who, slightly later, formulated his own influential version of pragmatism. See also White, *Social Thought in America*, 59.

[52] It has to be admitted that Holmes showed considerable ambiguity as regards his association with the philosophical pragmatism of James. However, as far as the presently relevant general propositions of pragmatism are concerned, it is possible to trace some of Holmes's basic premises back to pragmatist philosophy as articulated by James (see also Grey, 'Legal Pragmatism', esp. at 788).

[53] James, William, 'Pragmatism: A New Name for Some Old Ways of Thinking' in *William James: Writings 1902–1910* (New York: The Library of America, 1987) (originally delivered 1907), 479–624, at 522.

> conceptual short-cuts instead of following the interminable succession of particular phenomena. Any idea upon which we can ride, so to speak; any idea that will carry us prosperously from any one part of our experience to any other part, linking things satisfactorily, working securely, simplifying, saving labor; is true for just so much, true in so far forth, true *instrumentally* . . . truth in our ideas means their power to 'work' . . .[54]

Ideas or concepts were thus only meaningful when they made an intended contribution in concrete situations of social life. In the view of pragmatist philosophy, contemporary philosophy had often taken the discussion too far away from concrete situations.[55] Thus, pragmatism as articulated by James argued for setting aside overly abstract theoretical discussions and instead focusing on what effects different ideas had in practice.

Manifestly, a very similar preference for practical consequences over abstract principle was advocated by Holmes in *Lochner* v. *New York*. Already before his dissent, and in line with James's main pragmatist claims, Holmes had argued that the fallacy in legal studies was 'the notion that the only force at work in the development of the law is logic'.[56] In his view, instead of merely applying abstract legal principles without any further practical considerations, it was precisely the task of lawyers to examine the effects of a particular legal rule in practice:

> For the rational study of the law the black-letter man may be the man of the present, but the man of the future is the man of statistics and the master of economics. It is revolting to have no better reason for a rule of law than that so it was laid down in the time of Henry IV. It is still more revolting if the grounds upon which it was laid down have vanished long since, and the rule simply persists from blind imitation of the past.[57]

According to Holmes, the incorporation of practical considerations into legal decision-making implied a much more complex judicial process in which economic and social aspects played an important part. Adjudication was no more a matter of finding the relevant legal rules,

[54] Ibid., at 512 (original emphasis). See also the formulation in James, 'Philosophical Conceptions', at 1080: 'the effective meaning of any philosophic proposition can always be brought down to some particular consequence . . .'.

[55] James, 'Philosophical Conceptions', at 1095–6 (especially critical of Kant). See also James, 'Pragmatism', at 508: 'It is astonishing to see how many philosophical disputes collapse into insignificance the moment you subject them to this simple test of tracing a concrete consequence.'

[56] Holmes, Oliver Wendell, 'The Path of the Law', HLR, 10 (1897), 457–78, at 465. See also Dewey, 'Logical Method', at 564.

[57] Holmes, 'Path of the Law', at 469.

but an exercise in making a sound decision in terms of economic or other social considerations. Therefore, lawyers had to be educated in economics and other social sciences in order to fulfil their task as decision-makers in the political process.[58] It is in this context that one has to situate Holmes's perhaps most famous line: 'The prophecies of what the courts will do in fact, and nothing more pretentious, are what I mean by the law.'[59] This pragmatist view of law – correctly understood not as a mere description of how the legal process worked, but as a call upon lawyers as to how it should work[60] – was widely shared in American jurisprudence in the first decades of the twentieth century.[61] Influential protagonists of American legal realism were the Harvard scholar Roscoe Pound and Karl N. Llewellyn of Columbia University.[62] It was Roscoe Pound who familiarized international lawyers in 1939, in a presentation to the American Society of International Law, with the by then dominant realist view of law, which had not yet found resonance in international law quarters.[63] For present purposes, it might be added, as noted earlier, that Myers S. McDougal defended the realist school of thought in a paper in 1941 against attacks put forward by the natural lawyer Lon Fuller.[64]

It is to this rule-sceptic view of law as advocated by American legal realism that the first proposition of the actor conception of international personality has to be related.[65] Primarily articulated in the context of pragmatist philosophy and the Supreme Court's reliance on an absolute principle of contractual freedom in matters of social welfare (a key political issue at the turn of the twentieth century), legal realism in the tradition of Oliver Wendell Holmes calls upon lawyers to prefer practical considerations over the blind application of abstract legal principles. It follows that law is not a system of rules which are merely applied by the judiciary according to legal logic, but a decision-making process in which

58 Ibid., at 474. 59 Ibid., at 461. 60 See also Verdirame, 'Divided West', at 562.

61 Hart, 'American Jurisprudence', at 131; Cot, 'Pensée Juridique Américaine', at 545–8.

62 Pound, Roscoe, 'The Call for a Realist Jurisprudence', HLR, 44 (1931), 697–711, esp. at 709–11; Llewellyn, Karl N., 'A Realistic Jurisprudence – The Next Step', *Columbia Law Review*, 30 (1930), 431–65, *passim*. However, the versions of legal realism advocated by Pound and Llewellyn differed to a considerable extent. See Llewellyn, Karl N., 'Some Realism about Realism: Responding to Dean Pound', HLR, 44 (1931), 1222–64, esp. at 1223–6.

63 Quoted in Cot, 'Pensée Juridique Américaine', at 547.

64 McDougal, 'American Legal Realists', *passim*. See also Cot, 'Pensée Juridique Américaine', at 546 and 564.

65 In more general terms, see also Kennedy, 'International Law in the United States', at 403, and Kolb, *Réfléxions*, 131–2.

economic, philosophical or social considerations are employed in order to solve legal issues. In this way, the fallacy of blindly applying formal rules is thought to be avoided and more practical aspects of specific problems are paid attention to in legal adjudication. Law then becomes synonymous with the process in which persons authorized to do so make decisions by taking into account a multitude of factors; there are no pre-existing formal rules that determine the outcome of a legal matter. The actor conception's insistence on international law being a decision-making process has its origin in this pragmatist view of law.

The reconciliation of the normative and the actual

Any legal theory informed by philosophical pragmatism is oriented towards the empirically observable.[66] However, the more immediate origin of the actor conception's concern with effectiveness in its second proposition is the turn to international realism in American international studies after World War II and the response by international lawyers to the challenge this posed. As an effect of this development, which had been initiated by Hans J. Morgenthau, the normative and the actual were brought closer together in the study of international affairs. In fact, in this tradition, international law could only claim validity when it reflected effective action or interests. It is this view which informs the second proposition's concern with organized as well as unorganized authoritative decision-making processes and its attentiveness to those entities actually taking part in them.

With Wilsonian legalism essentially in disrepute in the American context after World War II, international realism offered an alternative approach to international politics. This new approach coincided with and was partly shaped by America's new role in international affairs as a world power and as the major antagonist of the Soviet Union in the emerging Cold War.[67] Curiously, though, the main advocates of international realism, with the exception of George F. Kennan, were not established American figures, but German émigré international lawyers led by Hans J. Morgenthau.[68] Morgenthau, born in 1904, had arrived in the United States only in 1937 and his thought was deeply influenced by

[66] Verdirame, 'Divided West', at 558, highlights the role of pragmatism as the main reason for the concern with effectiveness in American international law scholarship.
[67] Hoffmann, 'American Social Science', at 10–11.
[68] Koskenniemi, *Gentle Civilizer*, 465–7.

his previous German and European experience.[69] Having spent his formative years in the Weimar Republic, Morgenthau had endured first hand how formal legal rules had failed to control political and societal life.[70] Similarly, in the international realm, the apparent success of Gustav Stresemann's diplomatic initiatives in the 1920s – aimed at revising territorial aspects of the Versailles settlement and integrating Germany into the League of Nations[71] – illustrated the dependence of international norms on political realities.[72] For Morgenthau, accordingly, the main issue confronting legal studies, and in particular international legal studies, were not technical and logical niceties, but the question whether legal norms could indeed influence actual behaviour.[73] Consequently, in his 1934 Geneva *Habilitation* entitled *La réalité des normes*, Morgenthau took issue with Kelsen's strict separation between *Sein* and *Sollen*.[74] According to Morgenthau, and contrary to Kelsen, the normative only had value in so far as it had effect in reality, that is, was really observed.[75] Thus, any *Sollen* had to represent a physical or psychological *Sein* in order to be relevant.[76] By implication, the strictly formal validity of norms in Kelsen's hierarchical system (with the basic norm at the top of it) was put into question and replaced by a focus on actual compliance:[77] the normative and the actual were brought closer together again, for there was no sense in a norm that had no effect in the reality of things according to Morgenthau's own painful experience.[78]

[69] Frei, Christoph, *Hans J. Morgenthau: Eine intellektuelle Biographie* (Berne/Stuttgart/Vienna: Paul Haupt, 1993), *passim*, has mainly contributed to an understanding of Morgenthau's European and particularly German heritage. See also Cot, 'Pensée Juridique Américaine', at 551.

[70] Koskenniemi, *Gentle Civilizer*, 449–50; Frei, *Morgenthau*, 120–9.

[71] See Kissinger, *Vernunft der Nationen*, 294–300.

[72] Koskenniemi, *Gentle Civilizer*, 445.

[73] See the introductory remarks in Morgenthau, Hans J., *Die internationale Rechtspflege, ihr Wesen und ihre Grenzen* (Leipzig: Universitätsverlag von Robert Noske, 1929), esp. 3. See also Frei, *Morgenthau*, 141.

[74] Morgenthau, Hans J., *La Réalité des Normes, en Particulier des Normes du Droit International: Fondements d'une Théorie des Normes* (Paris: Librarie Felix Alcan, 1934), 7–9. Interestingly, Kelsen was one of the driving forces behind accepting Morgenthau's study as a *Habilitation* at Geneva in 1934 (see Koskenniemi, *Gentle Civilizer*, 457, and Frei, *Morgenthau*, 51–6).

[75] Morgenthau, *Réalité des Normes*, 34–5.

[76] Ibid., 10 (by implication).

[77] Ibid., 7, 17 and esp. 76–84.

[78] Frei, *Morgenthau*, 142–4. Frei goes on arguing that Morgenthau's focus on the actual was influenced by the philosophy of Friedrich Nietzsche, a link that was seldom mentioned by American commentators.

With this approach aimed at reconciling the actual and the normative, the question arose as to what instrument ensured effect of legal norms in the reality of things. Morgenthau's answer was:

> A rule of international law does not, as positivism was prone to believe, receive its validity from its enactment into a legal instrument, as, for instance, an international treaty. There are rules of international law which are valid, although not enacted in such legal instruments, and there are rules of international law which are not valid, although enacted in such instruments . . . A rule . . . is valid when its violation is likely to be followed by an unfavourable reaction, that is, a sanction against its violator. An alleged rule, the violation of which is not followed by such a sanction, is a mere idea, a wish, a suggestion, but not a valid rule.[79]

Accordingly, international rules the violation of which was not actually followed by sanctions (or would in all likelihood be followed by them) were no rules at all in Morgenthau's view.[80] For example, the fact that no sanctions had been imposed upon Germany for violating the Treaty of Locarno by remilitarizing the Rhineland in 1936 implied that the particular rules of this treaty were invalid and Germany's action therefore not illegal in the proper meaning of the term.[81] Crucially, sanctions were thereby not understood in the sense of a legal norm providing for them (as is Kelsen's definition of sanctions), but as unfavourable reactions actually taking place.[82] It followed that one had to look at the interests and actions of relevant actors (and thus on the likelihood or past experience of effective sanctions) in order to determine the validity of a rule. In result, an international rule only existed as an effect of actual deeds or interests: 'The science of international law, completely absorbed by practical problems as to what the rules of international law should be, is paying almost no attention to the psychological and sociological laws governing the actions of men in the international sphere, nor to *the possible legal rules growing out of such action*.'[83] By implication, according to Morgenthau's functional perspective on international law, one had to analyse the actual in order to find the normative content of the

[79] Morgenthau, Hans J., 'Positivism, Functionalism, and International Law', AJIL, 34 (1940), 260–84, at 276. See also the almost identical reasoning in Morgenthau, *Réalité des Normes*, 45–7.

[80] Morgenthau, 'Functionalism', at 277–8.

[81] Ibid., at 277. A very similar point is made by Carr, *Twenty Years' Crisis*, 100–2.

[82] See Koskenniemi, *Apology to Utopia*, 198–9.

[83] Morgenthau, 'Functionalism', at 283 (emphasis added).

international legal order.[84] Kelsen's strict separation between *Sein* and *Sollen*, if not entirely eliminated,[85] was at least severely tempered.

In a sense, Morgenthau never delivered on his call for a functionalist approach to international law.[86] In his subsequent work, he did not examine whether legal rules corresponded with actual behaviour or interests, but focused almost entirely on psychological and sociological elements shaping effective action of men in the international realm.[87] Though Morgenthau never went so far as to completely deny international law any influence in international affairs, he nevertheless gave up studying it and turned to the analysis of effective action. This resulted in 'international realism' as a conscious effort to approach the international sphere from an anti-formalist and non-legalistic perspective. In consequence, a new academic discipline called 'international relations', at the beginning synonymous with international realism, emerged in American academia.[88] Partly due to 'a remarkable chronological convergence' between the emergence of international realism and the needs of the United States government for policy advice in the post-World War II international environment, the discipline of international relations quickly succeeded in establishing itself and in recruiting talent.[89] Following Morgenthau's lead, and of course influenced by E. H. Carr's seminal study on the *Twenty Years' Crisis*,[90] a variety of European émigré – such as John H. Herz, Henry Kissinger, and, although already with constructivist tendencies, Karl W. Deutsch – subsequently worked on realist approaches to international affairs. On the more practical side, diplomats like George F. Kennan put forward influential realist analyses of international relations which provided the basis for American foreign policy in the early stages of the Cold War.[91] Hence, as far as the study of

84 On this general tendency in Morgenthau's work see also Hoffmann, 'American Social Science', at 6–7.

85 Morgenthau, *Réalité des Normes*, 8. See also Frei, *Morgenthau*, 142.

86 Koskenniemi, *Gentle Civilizer*, 460.

87 See e.g. Morgenthau, Hans J., *Politics among Nations: The Struggle for Power and Peace*, 5th edition (New York: Alfred Knopf, 1978) (originally published 1948), esp. 14.

88 Frei, *Morgenthau*, 125 (by implication); Koskenniemi, *Gentle Civilizer*, 467; Hoffmann, 'American Social Science', at 6.

89 Hoffmann, 'American Social Science', at 10.

90 On the particular influence of Carr in the United States see the introductory remarks by Michael Cox in Carr, *Twenty Years' Crisis*, xxxv–xli.

91 See e.g. Kennan, *American Diplomacy*, *passim*. As is well known, Kennan also provided the blueprint for America's containment policy in his 'Long Telegram' from Moscow in 1946 and in a subsequent article in *Foreign Affairs* signed under the pseudonym 'Mister X'.

international affairs was concerned, the dominant approach in the United States in the years following World War II was international realism as articulated in the growing academic discipline of 'international relations' and as put into practice by the main foreign-policy makers in the United States government.

In this practical and academic environment of predominant international realism, any approach insisting on the role of law in international affairs had to re-conceptualize the relation between law and politics, or, in the sense of the early Morgenthau, between *Sein* and *Sollen*.[92] In order not to be considered utopian in the discredited tradition of interwar international scholarship, American international lawyers in the post-World War II period had to pay closer attention to the realities of international life as postulated by international realism. In consequence, as a response to international realism, American international law after World War II was focused more on actual political power and empirical facts than on formal law.[93] Though not agreeing with strict realist postulates that the international realm was entirely dominated by naked power (a claim that only few realists actually made, and in particular not Morgenthau), international lawyers were inclined to agree that law had to find resonance in actual behaviour in order to be valid. In a sense, it might be said that by focusing on the actual when making a legal analysis, American international lawyers fulfilled the task Morgenthau had formulated in 1940 to come up with a functionalist approach to international law.[94]

It is this concern for the actual in American international law scholarship that provides the origin of the actor conception's second proposition. The latter's focus on effective power has to be understood as reflecting the general tendency to prefer the actual over the normative: the determination of the participants in the international decision-making process could therefore not depend on a formal principle or concept, but had to focus on those entities actually having the power to make themselves heard in all those arenas of authoritative decision-making that effectively existed. In

92 Slaughter Burley, 'Dual Agenda', at 209; Kennedy, 'International Law in the United States', at 403; Koskenniemi, *Gentle Civilizer*, 474; Kolb, *Réflexions*, 132.

93 Slaughter Burley, 'Dual Agenda', at 209. Of course, American international law was no monolithic block at the time. But it was a generally shared tendency under the influence of international realism to prefer the actual over formal normative concepts. See on this also Koskenniemi, *Gentle Civilizer*, 478–9.

94 A similar point is made by Simpson, Gerry, 'Duelling Agendas: International Relations and International Law (Again)', *Journal of International Law and International Relations*, 1 (2005), 61–74, at 65.

result, there was no discrepancy between a normative postulate as to the relevant entities for the international legal system and those entities effectively taking part in this system. The normative and the actual were brought together and the latter took prominence. In this sense, the actual determined the normative with respect to the personal scope of international law. It was effective power, not formal criteria, that established the quality of an entity to take part in the international legal system. This was in line with the point of departure of international realism and how international law scholarship had adapted to it in the American context.

Main manifestations in legal practice

The actor conception has been manifested mainly in the context of dealing with entities that are somehow attached to a domestic legal system but nevertheless possess essentially international characteristics. In these manifestations, a tendency of the actor conception becomes apparent that is not readily detectable in its scholarly articulation, namely to attach certain legal consequences to the status of a participant in international law. This pattern has its origins in this reconciliation of the normative and the actual.

The Bank for International Settlements *arbitration*

Combining aspects of an international institution and a municipal legal person, the legal status of the Bank for International Settlements (BIS) has long been a matter of scholarly debate.[95] In 2002, the issue became pertinent in *Reineccius et al.* v. *Bank for International Settlements*, a case concerning the recall of BIS shares held by private persons.[96] In its partial award, the tribunal, by clear implication, declared the BIS an international person. The reasoning of the tribunal, it is suggested, manifests the actor conception of international personality.

[95] See Williams, 'Bank for International Settlements', at 672, and Schwarzenberger, *Internationale Banken*, 51–8. See also Bederman, David J., 'The Unique Legal Status of the Bank for International Settlements Comes into Focus', *Leiden Journal of International Law*, 16 (2003), 787–94, at 788–9.

[96] *Dr. Horst Reineccius, First Eagle SoGen Funds, Inc., Mr. Pierre Mathier and La Société de Concours Hippique de la Châtre*, v. *Bank for International Settlements* (Partial Award on the Lawfulness of the Recall of the Privately Held Shares on 8 January 2001 and the Applicable Standards for Valuation of those Shares, Permanent Court of Arbitration, 2002), 15 World Trade and Arbitration Materials 73.

The BIS was created in 1930 in the context of the Young plan which reorganized the German reparation payments imposed in the Versailles Peace Treaties.[97] As part of the scheme, the BIS was to be created as an international financial institution with the purpose of collecting and administering German annuities and distributing them among the creditor countries. Two international agreements were concluded to this effect: one between Germany on the one hand and the creditor countries on the other,[98] and one between the creditor countries plus Germany on the one hand and Switzerland on the other.[99] Whereas the first agreement concerned the essentials of the Young plan and its execution through the establishment of the BIS, the second treaty put an obligation upon Switzerland to grant the annexed Constituent Charter of the Bank. As a result, the BIS existed not only on the basis of two international treaties, but also as an effect of incorporation in Switzerland in the form of a 'Company limited by shares'.[100] To complicate matters further, some of the contracting governments (in the event, the American, Belgian and French) were not willing or not able to hold shares in the BIS and, pursuant to Article 16 of the Statutes of the Bank, sold their shares to private parties.[101] Although these shares did not imply any rights to participate in the governance of the Bank, the Board of Directors nevertheless proposed at the end of the year 2000 to amend the Statutes of the Bank to the effect that private shareholders would not be tolerated anymore. On 8 January 2001 the Statutes were amended with Article 18A allowing the forcibe recall of all privately held shares against payment of compensation of 16,000 Swiss Francs per share. Several of the affected private shareholders, pursuant to Article 54(1) BIS Statutes, referred the matter to arbitration and requested a ruling on the lawfulness of the recall and on the level of compensation. A tribunal under the chairmanship of W. Michael Reisman was formed to consider the case through the good offices of the Permanent Court of Arbitration.

97 The following historical background of the case is based on Williams, 'Bank for International Settlements', at 667–72. For the facts of the actual case see *Reineccius et al.* v. *Bank for International Settlements*, paras 1–6.

98 Agreement regarding the Complete and Final Settlement of the Question of Reparations, 20 January 1930, 104 LNTS 244.

99 Convention respecting the Bank for International Settlements, with Annex, 20 January 1930, 104 LNTS 443.

100 Statutes of the Bank for International Settlements, 20 January 1930, 104 LNTS 449, Article 1.

101 By the year 2000, around 14 per cent of BIS shares were in private hands.

In order to determine the lawfulness of the share recall, the tribunal had to decide on the applicable law. The main issue was whether the recall was to be judged on the basis of international law or municipal law (or a combination of both of them). In order to decide this issue, the tribunal first found it necessary to consider the legal character of the Bank. In relevant part, the tribunal stated over several paragraphs:

> The Bank is chartered as a company limited by shares under Swiss law . . . While the internal structure of the Bank was, according to Article 1 of the Statutes, 'a Company limited by shares' . . . the essential international character of the Bank is apparent from its treaty origin. Moreover, the functions of the Bank were essentially public international in their character . . . From its inception, the Bank was charged with the performance of a particularly urgent international task [the management of the Young Plan].[102]

Noting that the BIS had also been recognized as an international organization in three host country agreements,[103] the tribunal drew its conclusion: '. . . the Tribunal finds that the Bank for International Settlements is a *sui generis* creation which is an international organization.'[104] It is worth recording that the tribunal did not declare the BIS an international person; it only pronounced it an international organization. However, the arbitrators understood an international organization to be subject to international law and thus, functionally, equivalent to an international person.[105] In consequence, the tribunal proceeded by stating that only public international law, and not municipal shareholder law, was to be applied to the matter at hand.[106]

The tribunal next considered the conformity of the recall with the Constitutive Instruments, that is, with the Bank's internal law based on the 1930 treaties on the establishment of the Bank. There was no violation of these instruments in the view of the tribunal.[107] Yet, the conformity to the Statutes was not the only standard by which the tribunal examined the recall of the shares as a matter of international law. It deemed it necessary to further analyse whether the BIS also complied with general international law on expropriation when it had recalled the shares and had offered a certain amount of compensation.[108] According

[102] *Reineccius et al.* v. *Bank for International Settlements*, paras 108–14.
[103] Ibid., para. 115. [104] Ibid., para. 118. [105] Ibid., para. 172.
[106] Ibid., paras 123 and 142. See also Bederman, 'Unique Legal Status of the BIS', at 793.
[107] *Reineccius et al.* v. *Bank for International Settlements*, paras 147–8.
[108] Ibid., paras 142 and 148.

to the tribunal, this meant that the recall also had to meet the public interest and non-discrimination requirements inherent in international expropriation law. With regard to the former requirement, the tribunal found itself compelled to make some general statements about the applicability of the expropriation regime to an international organization like the BIS:

> Now, obviously, the Bank is not a state. If public interest were understood as meaning the public interest of a state, the Bank's actions could not meet the public interest test and would be *eo ipso* unlawful. The reason for this conclusion would not derive from the nature and the purpose of the action, but from the fact that the Bank is not a state. That argument ... would be circular and quite sterile ... When applied to an actor which is an international entity, but is not a state, public interest must be understood, *mutatis mutandis*, as an action rationally, proportionately and necessarily related to the performance of one of the legitimate international public purposes of the actor undertaking it.[109]

In the event, the latter precondition was judged to be fulfilled, as was the non-discriminatory requirement. The tribunal thus declared the share recall 'prima facie' lawful also under general international law.[110] However, the treatment of the matter was rather short and indecisive.[111] Having judged the recall lawful as a matter of general international expropriation law, it remained to be determined whether the level of compensation offered by the Bank was in accordance with international legal standards. The tribunal restated in this respect that 'the Bank is an international organization' and 'thus subject to international law'.[112] Accordingly, it again looked at the Constituent Instruments of the BIS and general international law – including extensive research into international case law on compensation for expropriation and particularly relying on jurisprudence in the context of the Iran–US Claims Tribunal – and found that on account of both, particular Statutes and general international law, full compensation was to be paid to the private shareholders.[113] The remainder of the award was concerned with the valuation method for full compensation, with the tribunal concluding that the accurate value of the shares at the time of the recall was 33,820 Swiss Francs per share, and not merely 16,000 as offered by the Bank.[114] The

[109] Ibid., para. 150. [110] Ibid., para. 158.
[111] Ibid., para. 155. See also Bederman, 'Unique Legal Status of the BIS', at 791.
[112] *Reineccius et al.* v. *Bank for International Settlements*, para. 172.
[113] Ibid., paras 161–71. [114] Ibid., para. 203.

exact amount owed by the Bank to its former shareholders, including possible interest, was determined in the final award and is of no immediate relevance for present purposes.

It is submitted that, on balance, the reasoning and wording of the partial award in *Reineccius et al.* v. *Bank for International Settlements* manifest the actor conception of international personality. The arguments put forward by the tribunal for considering the BIS an international organization were primarily based on the effective role of the Bank in international affairs. Although the treaty origins of the BIS played a role, as did recognition in three headquarter agreements, the decisive reason for the Bank's accepted international status were the effective international functions that it fulfilled in international financial affairs. Only because of this actual international role did the Bank's international character prevail over its formal municipal status. In addition, as in the actor conception, there was also no differentiation between being an international organization, an international actor or an international person: all terms (or functional equivalents of them) were used to describe the same public international character of the Bank.[115] With regard to the applicable law, it is further evocative of the actor conception that the tribunal not only referred to the Bank's Constituent Instruments when determining the lawfulness of the share recall and the level of compensation, but also took into account general international law on expropriation. Especially significant is that the latter was seemingly automatically applied, without articulating any general justification or interpreting specific rules with respect to their applicability to international organizations.[116] It was just presumed that it was to some extent relevant. This approach is certainly in line with the actor conception and with its insistence on law being a decision-making process rather than the application of formal legal rules: international standards of expropriation were just one element in the process of deciding the matter. Clear indications as to what their exact legal relevance and indeed content was were deemed unnecessary. In essence, the award shows the tendency of the actor conception, not readily detectable in its scholarly formulation, to attach certain legal consequences to being an international actor without any principled justification. In a sense, this reflects the rapprochement of the actual and the normative as one of the main aspects of the actor conception.

[115] See esp. ibid., para. 172.

[116] See also the criticism by Bederman, 'Unique Legal Status of the BIS', at 791 and 793.

The International Tin Council *cases and beyond*

In several cases dealing with the financial collapse of the International Tin Council (ITC), it was held that member states were not liable for outstanding debts of the organization. Where this conclusion was arrived at by relying on international law, the main rationale was that the ITC's international personality was an 'objective reality' which precluded secondary or concurrent member-state liability. Subsequently, the same approach was followed in the Institut de Droit International and in the project on responsibility of international organizations in the ILC. On balance, this line of reasoning is a manifestation of the actor conception of international personality.

By the time of its collapse, the ITC was the executive arm of the Sixth International Tin Agreement (ITA6) concluded on 26 June 1981 in Geneva.[117] The parties to the agreement comprised twenty-one producer and consumer countries of tin plus the European Economic Community (EEC). The purpose of the ITA6 was to 'provide for adjustment between world production and consumption of tin' and to 'prevent excessive fluctuations in the price of tin'.[118] To this end, the ITC managed a buffer stock, which was financed by contributions of member states and bank loans. After the supported price of tin collapsed in 1985, the ITC was no longer able to meet its outstanding financial commitments. Having sold all remaining buffer stock, there remained debts to private creditors estimated at 150 million Pounds Sterling. Albeit some private creditors had arbitration clauses in their contracts and initiated proceedings, there were no assets left with which awards in their favour could have been satisfied. As for the ITA6 member countries, they did not voluntarily step in. In this situation, creditors started to bring claims against member states in domestic courts and before the European Court of Justice (ECJ). In relevant part, the submission was that member states of the ITA6, qua members, were concurrently liable for the outstanding debts of the ITC. This raised the difficult question whether the ITC had separate legal personality and, if so, whether this personality precluded secondary or concurrent liability of its members.

[117] 1282 UNTS 294. For background information on the ITC see McFadden, Eric J., 'The Collapse of Tin: Restructuring a Failed Commodity Agreement', AJIL, 80 (1986), 811–30, at 812–29, and Sadurska, Romana and C. M. Chinkin, 'The Collapse of the International Tin Council: A Case of State Responsibility?' *Virginia Journal of International Law*, 30 (1990), 845–90, at 849–51.

[118] Sixth International Tin Agreement, Article 1(a) and (b).

The issue was addressed most extensively in litigation in English courts. However, the matter was thereby partly dealt with on the basis of domestic law. The ITC had been headquartered in London by virtue of a headquarters agreement[119] and a statutory instrument giving effect to this agreement stated that the ITC should 'have the legal capacities of a body corporate' in English law. This formula was understood to the effect that the ITC had separate domestic legal personality.[120] In consequence, concurrent liability of member states could arguably be analysed on the grounds of English law. This was the route generally pursued in the High Court[121] and, with somewhat more extensive references to international law, in the House of Lords.[122] By contrast, the Court of Appeal discussed the issue predominantly on the basis of international law, although its reasoning was still strongly influenced by English law and its relationship to the international legal system (especially with respect to the establishment, but not the consequences, of legal personality).[123] The European Court of Justice has also been concerned with the collapse of the ITC. While the ECJ did not have to hand down a decision in the end, the opinion of Advocate-General Darmon is still significant as to how personality was understood under international law independently of pecularities of a domestic legal system. In the present section, thus, the ITC cases will be analysed primarily based on the English Court of Appeal judgment and the Advocate-General's opinion in the ECJ proceedings, with exclusive focus on their interpretation of the matter according to international law.

In the English Court of Appeal, Kerr LJ, determined that the first issue to be addressed was whether the ITC possessed separate legal personality. He started his examination by stating in a rather unequivocal manner that '... the ITC in the same way as virtually every other international organisation is

[119] Headquarters Agreement between the United Kingdom of Great Britain and Northern Ireland and the International Tin Council, 9 February 1972, 834 UNTS 288.

[120] E.g, *Maclaine Watson & Co Ltd* v. *Department of Trade and Industry* (England, High Court, 1987), 80 ILR 39, at 43–4 (Millett, J).

[121] *Maclaine Watson & Co Ltd* v. *Department of Trade and Industry*, at 41–4 (Millett, J).

[122] *Australia & New Zealand Banking Group Ltd and Others* v. *Commonwealth of Australia and 23 Others; Amalgamated Metal Trading Ltd and Others* v. *Department of Trade and Industry and Others; Maclaine Watson & Co Ltd* v. *Department of Trade and Industry; Maclaine Watson & Co Ltd* v. *International Tin Council* (England, House of Lords, 1989), 29 ILM 670, e.g. at 672–5 (Lord Templeman).

[123] *Maclaine Watson & Co Ltd* v. *Department of Trade and Industry; J. H. Rayner (Mincing Lane)* v. *Department of Trade and Industry and Others*, (England, Court of Appeal, 1988), 80 ILR 49, esp. at 86–8 and 90 (Kerr LJ).

a legal entity on the plane of international law.'[124] Yet, in what followed, it did not become entirely clear what kind of legal personality Kerr LJ exactly established. It seems, presumably because the matter was still approached to some extent from the perspective of English law, that no distinction was drawn between legal personality in international law and municipal legal personality conferred upon an entity by way of international law. Arguably, Kerr LJ understood the two concepts to be very similar, if not identical, and it is therefore difficult to trace clear statements on the ITC's international personality properly so called from his reasoning.[125] The statements by Advocate-General Darmon are much clearer in this respect. First of all, Darmon declared that it was not sufficient to rely on Article 16(1) of the ITA6 according to which the 'Council shall have legal personality . . . in particular the capacity to contract' when international personality was concerned: personality in the sense of Article 16(1) was merely 'civil', that is, restricted to municipal law.[126] The question whether the ITC had separate legal personality in international law hence had to be decided according to other criteria. It is convenient to quote the Advocate-General's opinion at length in this respect:

> The question arising here is whether the ITC may be regarded as an 'independent legal entity' in relation to its members, that is an entity separate from the latter. It was precisely that question of international personality that the International Court of Justice was called upon to examine in respect of the United Nations in its Opinion on 'Reparations for injuries suffered in the service of the United Nations' in which the International Court of Justice stated: 'The Charter has not been content to make the Organization created by it merely a centre for harmonizing the actions of nations in the attainment of these common ends . . . It has equipped that centre with organs, and has given it special tasks. It has defined the position of the Members in relation to the organization by requiring them to give it every assistance in any action undertaken by it, and to accept and carry out the decisions of the Security Council.' Those criteria, laid down in order to circumscribe the personality of the United Nations in its relations with its Member States, would seem to be amply fulfilled in the case of the ITC.
>
> First, the International Tin Council, when implementing the Sixth Agreement, is charged with pursuing the attainment of the latter's objectives:

[124] Ibid., at 92.

[125] See also ibid., at 94, and the references to Jenks, Wilfried C., 'The Legal Personality of International Organizations', BYIL, 22 (1945), 267–75, at 267, which predominantly concerns municipal personality of international organizations.

[126] *Maclaine Watson & Company Limited* v. *Council and Commission of the European Communities* (Advocate-General's Opinion), 1990 ECR I-01797, para. 133.

> namely, essentially to ensure world-wide equilibrium in the market in tin. It is not limited to 'harmonizing' the members' efforts in this respect, but in any event carries out the task itself, using means that are its own. In so doing, the Council exercises its own decision-making power distinct from that of the members who make up the organization . . .
>
> Consequently, it does appear that the ITC is an entity distinct from its members vested with its 'own decision-making power'.[127]

Advocate-General Darmon apparently understood the *Reparation for Injuries* Advisory Opinion as having enunciated certain objective criteria the fulfilment of which by an international organization leads to personality in international law.[128] Following this interpretation, the ITC was considered an international person because it was an independent organ having its own decision-making power. There was no doubt in the Advocate-General's view that the ITC, in view of its effective and independent powers, possessed personality in international law.

Having established international personality of the ITC (or, in the case of the English Court of Appeal, legal personality as considered relevant for English courts), the question remained whether this legal status precluded liability of member states as a matter of international law. In this respect, the reasoning in the English Court of Appeal was not decisively influenced by particularities of English law, but focused more exclusively on general international law. It is therefore more pertinent for present purposes. Kerr LJ noted:

> The preponderant view of the relatively few international jurists to whose writings we were referred, since we were told that there are no others, appears to be in favour of international organizations being treated in international law as 'mixed' entities, rather than bodies corporate. But their views, however learned, are based on their personal opinions; and in many cases they are expressed with a degree of understandable uncertainty. As yet there is clearly no settled jurisprudence about these aspects of international organizations. There is no other source from which the position in international law can be deduced with any confidence.[129]

Apparently, Kerr LJ was aware of views in international legal scholarship according to which the legal status of international organizations

[127] Ibid., paras 134–6.

[128] The present study disputes this interpretation of the *Reparation of Injuries* opinion, as has been argued in the context of the recognition conception of international personality. Advocate-General Darmon's interpretation is, however, in accordance with e.g. Seyersted, *Objective International Personality*, esp. 9.

[129] *J. H. Rayner (Mincing Lane)* v. *Department of Trade and Industry and Others*, at 108 (Kerr LJ).

resembled a mixed entity, that is, an entity in which members remain liable towards third parties that have not recognized the organization. However, these views did not seem convincing. For Kerr LJ, the presumption was that legal personality precluded member-state liability unless there was an international rule rebutting this presumption. Such a rule, however, could not be found in international legal material:

> In sum, I cannot find any basis for concluding that it has been shown that there is any rule of international law, binding upon the member States of the ITC, whereby they can be held liable – let alone jointly and severally – in any national court to the creditors of the ITC for the debts of the ITC resulting from contracts concluded by the ITC in its own name.[130]

It followed that the submission of the private creditors, according to which the member states of the ITC were to be declared liable for the debts of the organization qua members, was dismissed on the ground that there was no international rule declaring such secondary liability.[131] In other words, the presumption against liability stemming from legal personality of the ITC in international law had not been rebutted by international rules to this effect to the satisfaction of the Court. In the ECJ, Advocate-General Durmon proposed a similar conclusion, though more focused on the lack of actual influence on the part of the EEC.[132]

Taken together, the ITC cases, as far as international law was concerned, put forward two propositions: first, international legal personality of international organizations is a matter of objective criteria; second, the consequence of international personality of international organizations is a presumption that liability of member states towards third parties is precluded. These two propositions were mostly adopted in the Institut de Droit International and, more recently, in the ILC. In the former, deliberations were decisively influenced by Rapporteur Rosalyn Higgins.[133] She proposed to consider personality of international organizations primarily as a matter of 'objective reality', that is, of

[130] Ibid., at 109 (Kerr LJ).

[131] Lord Gibson concurred in this finding, while Lord Nourse dissented: ibid., at 174–5 (Gibson LJ), and at 147 (Nourse LJ).

[132] *Maclaine Watson & Company Limited* v. *Council and Commission of the European Communities*, paras 137–42.

[133] Higgins, Rosalyn, *Provisional Report: The legal consequences for member states of the non-fulfilment by international organizations of their obligations toward third parties*, 66-I Ann. IDI 1995, 373–420. See also Stumer, Andrew, 'Liability of Member States for Acts of International Organizations: Reconsidering the Policy Objections', HILJ, 48 (2007), 553–80, at 565.

effective 'structure, powers, purposes and functions' that are 'opposable to third parties ... not dependent upon any recognition by them'.[134] Such a definition was, however, considered to exceed the task of the Commission and was dropped in the Final Resolution.[135] Simply presuming that an international organization possessed international personality (according to criteria left undefined), the Final Resolution of the Institut adopted the propositions enunciated in the ITC cases and declared liability of member states, in principle, excluded as a matter of international law.[136] The ILC subsequently adopted a very similar approach in its project on responsibility of international organizations. Though it was also not defined in the articles themselves how an international organization acquired international personality, the commentary made clear that personality was considered a matter of 'objective fact' and not necessarily of recognition or formal treaty provisions.[137] With respect to liability of member states, the ILC again followed the lead of the Institut: in Draft Article 29(1), it adopted the principle that member states were excluded from secondary or concurrent liability for obligations of the organization.[138] Interestingly, one basis for adopting this solution in the ILC, in addition to existing jurisprudence, was 'policy reasons': Special Rapporteur Gaja argued, with reference to Higgins's Provisional Report in the Institut, that liability of member states for obligations of international organizations would lead to constant interference by governments in the decision-making processes of international organizations.[139] This was the explicitly enunciated policy

[134] *The legal consequences for member states of the non-fulfilment by international organizations of their obligations toward third parties: Draft Resolution of October 1994*, 66-I Ann. IDI 1995, 465–69, at 465 (Article 2); Higgins, *Provisional Report*, at 385–6.

[135] See e.g the comments by James Crawford, 66-I Ann. IDI 1995, at 450.

[136] *The legal consequences for member states of the non-fulfilment by international organizations of their obligations toward third parties: Resolution adopted 1 September 1995*, 66-II Ann. IDI 1995, 445–53, at 449 (Article 1 and Article 6).

[137] *Report of the International Law Commission: Fifty-fifth Session*, ILC 2003, UN Doc. A/58/10, at 41–2. See also Gaja, Giorgio (Special Rapporteur), *First report on responsibility of international organizations*, ILC 2003, UN Doc. A/CN.4/532, esp. para. 19.

[138] *Report of the International Law Commission: Fifty-eighth Session*, ILC 2006, UN Doc. A/61/10, at 286–91. The wording of Article 29(1) at first sight seems to indicate that member states are in principle liable and there are exceptions when they are not. However, the commentary makes clear that there is no (or not much) difference to the article proposed by Gaja which stated the principle more unequivocally (see Gaja, Giorgio (Special Rapporteur), *Fourth report on responsibility of international organizations: Addendum*, ILC 2006, UN Doc. A/CN.4/564/Add.2, esp. paras 78–96).

[139] Gaja, *Fourth report*, para. 94; Higgins, *Provisional Report*, at 419.

factor determining that, in principle, there could be no liability of member states.[140]

On balance, the approach chosen in the ITC cases, and subsequently adopted in the Institut de Droit International and the ILC, has to be considered a manifestation of the actor conception of international personality. Personality of the ITC and international organizations in general is considered a matter of objective fact rather than of recognition or formal treaty provisions. It is hence effective 'decision-making power' as well as actual structure and purpose of an organization that is pertinent when deciding on its legal status. This insistence on effectiveness and objective reality is certainly reminiscent of the origins of the actor conception. Related to the 'objective reality'[141] of international organizations and their personality in international law, there is a presumption that member states are not liable for obligations of the organization. Accordingly, a third party cannot rely on not having recognized the organization for the latter is considered an objective entity opposable to third parties. This view can be understood as drawing a legal consequence from a factual observation: the non-liability of member states is drawn from the objective reality of international organizations as international persons. Again, the actual and the normative are brought closer together. Finally, the actor conception is also reflected in the straightforward way in which policy considerations (admittedly, in the context of law codification) are taken as legal arguments at least supplementing, if not overcoming, formal legal rules or acts of recognition. It follows that, on balance, the ITC cases and the adoption of principles enunciated in the course of them strongly implicate a manifestation of the actor conception of international personality.

The award in Sandline *v.* Papua New Guinea

In *Sandline* v. *Papua New Guinea*, an arbitration tribunal declared international law fully applicable to a state contract notwithstanding the acknowledged fact that the parties had expressly chosen English law to govern the contract. In result, Papua New Guinea (PNG) could not rely on its own constitutional law as a defence for non-compliance with its contractual obligations to Sandline International Inc. The

[140] But see the convincing critique of this policy reason by Stumer, 'Liability of Member States', at 570–9.

[141] Higgins, *Provisional Report*, at 386. See also Higgins, 'General Course', at 78.

award undoubtedly manifests the actor conception of international personality.

The facts of the case are as follows.[142] On 31 January 1997 the Deputy Prime Minister of Papua New Guinea signed an agreement with Sandline International Inc., a company incorporated in the Bahamas and 'specialising in rendering military and security services ... particularly in situations of internal conflict'. In signing the contract, the Deputy Prime Minister had acted with the knowledge and the approval of the Prime Minister and the Minister of Defence as well as further government officials. According to the terms of the agreement, Sandline would support PNG Forces in regaining control over Bougainville, an island which at the time was dominated by separatist forces. In return, PNG would pay Sandline a fee of 18 million US Dollars immediately after signing the contract and another 18 million within 30 days of deployment of a Sandline command squad. PNG complied with the first obligation and Sandline subsequently deployed its team. The second payment, however, had not been made by 16 March 1997, when a mutiny occurred in the PNG defence forces in the course of which Sandline employees were put under arrest. On 21 March 1997 the Sandline personnel were safely evacuated. In light of these events, the PNG government refused to pay the second fee on the grounds that it had become impossible to perform the contract. Sandline reacted by initiating proceedings pursuant to an arbitration clause in the contract. It claimed payment of the outstanding sum plus interest. PNG, after first relying on impossibility of performance, finally amended its defence to the effect that the whole contract was unlawful under section 200 of its Constitution, partly because those who had negotiated and signed it had lacked capacity to do so. In the view of PNG, the contract was void and it counterclaimed reimbursement of the initial payment.

The arbitration tribunal – incidentally including Sir Michael Kerr, the Court of Appeal judge who provided some of the memorable statements in the *Tin Council* cases – declared it unnecessary to decide whether the contract was indeed illegal under the law of PNG; it just assumed that it was.[143] It proceeded by examining what effect this assumed illegality had on the validity of the contract. It first recounted that according to clause 6.3 of the agreement between PNG and Sandline, the contract was 'to be construed and governed in accordance with English law'.[144]

[142] The facts are taken as presented in *Sandline International Inc.* v. *Papua New Guinea* (Interim Award, 1998), 117 ILR 552, at 554–8.

[143] Ibid., para. 8.2. [144] Ibid., para. 9.1.

Consequently, there was an express choice of English law as the proper law of contract. The arbitrators acknowledged that under English law the contract would be void according to the *Ralli Brothers* principle.[145] However, this general principle did not apply in the present case in the view of the tribunal:

> The proposition upon which PNG relies [the *Ralli Brothers* principle] clearly applies where the contract in question is between private parties. In such cases the principle is based upon public policy which is based in turn upon the comity of nations. But where a contract is concluded by a State, one enters the realm of public international law and public policy wears a different aspect.[146]

Accordingly, the tribunal considered it mistaken to rely on the *Ralli Brothers* principle in the present circumstances: there were different policy reasons relevant in the context of a state contract as opposed to an agreement between private parties:

> An agreement between a private party and a state is an international, not a domestic, contract. This Tribunal is an international, not a domestic, arbitral tribunal and is bound to apply the rules of international law. Those rules are not excluded from, but form part of, English law, which is the law chosen by the parties to govern their contract.[147]

Accordingly, in view of the parties to the agreement and the nature of the arbitration, the tribunal declared that international law had to be applied to the contract instead of English domestic law. This was not necessarily seen as a contradiction of the choice of law by the parties as, according to the arbitrators, international law formed part of English law and the choice of law clause was therefore respected when international law was declared to govern the agreement.

In consequence, the tribunal looked at international law in order to examine what effect the assumed illegality of the agreement under the law of PNG had on its overall validity. In this respect, the tribunal referred to the fundamental international legal principle that a state cannot rely on its internal law for justifying the non-performance of an international obligation:[148] 'In international law . . . a State cannot rely upon its own internal laws as the basis for a plea that a contract

[145] The *Ralli Brothers* principle states that a contract will not be enforced under English law when 'it is illegal in the place of performance if that place is a friendly country and the courts of that country would not enforce the contract'. Ibid., para. 9.1.

[146] Ibid., para. 9.2 (references omitted).

[147] Ibid., para. 10.1.

[148] Codified in Article 27 VCLT and Article 32 ARSIWA.

concluded by it is illegal. It is a clearly established principle of international law that acts of a State will be regarded as such even if they are *ultra vires* or unlawful under the internal law of the state.'[149] It followed for the tribunal that the assumed fact that the contract was illegal under the law of PNG had no effect on the validity of the contract whatsoever; the contractual obligations still existed pursuant to international law, which was the law governing the contract according to the reasoning of the arbitrators. In result, PNG was considered liable for its failure to perform the contract and ordered to pay the outstanding 18 million US Dollars plus interest to Sandline.[150]

The reasoning of the arbitrators is clearly reminiscent of the actor conception of international personality. In order to apply international law to the state contract, the tribunal referred to public policy reasons related to the nature of a state contract and the international character of the arbitration. Neither did the tribunal explain why the specific international principle it invoked (that PNG could not rely on its internal law for justifying non-performance of an international obligation) should apply to a state contract, nor did it refer to implied recognition of the private party as an international person to foster the relevance of international law. Indeed, the concept of international personality was not mentioned at all in the award. It appears that there was again a reconciliation of the actual and the normative: the effective international character of the contract led to the normative conclusion that international law should govern the agreement. In order not to openly disregard the choice of law by the parties, international and English law were then simply considered to form a whole, notwithstanding the rather complex relationship between the two systems of law.[151] In sum, the award has to be understood to have automatically 'internationalized' the legal personality of Sandline by stressing effective characteristics and policy factors, an approach which corresponds with the origins of the actor conception of international personality.

[149] *Sandline* v. *Papua New Guinea*, para. 10.2.

[150] Ibid., para. 13.1. The award was subsequently challenged by PNG in the Supreme Court of Queensland, Australia (the seat of the arbitration had been Cairns), on the grounds that it contained a 'manifest error of law'. However, the appeal was denied because of lack of subject matter jurisdiction. See *In the Matter of the Commercial Arbitration Act 1990 and In the Matter of an Application pursuant to Section 38 thereof by the Independent State of Papua New Guinea against Sandline International Inc.* (Australia, Supreme Court of Queensland, 1999), 117 ILR 565, at 575–87 (Ambrose, J).

[151] Compare only Brownlie, *Principles*, 41–4.

PART III

A framework for personality in international law

In the preceding part, it has been demonstrated what original assumptions the conceptions of international personality are based on and how they were manifested as well as substantiated in legal practice. It is now possible, in line with the basic purpose of this book, to determine in Part III which assumptions are still to be considered legally sound today and which ones have been discarded in international law over time. It is argued that while the assumptions of the individualistic and formal conceptions are supported in international law today, those of the states-only, recognition and actor conceptions generally are not. It follows that personality in international law has to be allocated and understood according to a legal framework primarily informed by the individualistic and formal conceptions. In order to substantiate this contention, this Part starts with a short recapitulation of the main points enunciated in Part II and evaluates the original assumptions and substantiations articulated therein in light of the present international legal system (1). Subsequently, a legal frame of reference combining the formal and individualistic conception is outlined and briefly illustrated by applying it to the four legal issues enumerated at the outset of this book (2).

10

Appraisal of the conceptions and their assumptions

This section starts with a short summary. Afterwards, the assumptions informing the different conceptions of international personality are related to the respective positions in present international law.

Recapitulation

It has been argued in the preceding analysis that assumptions about the nature of statehood and the role of individuals therein as well as about the sources of international law primarily inform the conceptions of international personality. In practice, these different assumptions have been substantiated by stating (expressly or by implication) different presumptions concerning which social entities are international persons and, in some instances, by attaching certain legal consequences to this status. It is convenient to encapsulate these insights in the following table presenting the conceptions with respect to their founders, original assumptions, main practical manifestations and the presumptions as well as consequences substantiated in the latter.

For now, the relevant column is the one enunciating the original assumptions that underlie the conceptions of international personality. As the table indicates, these assumptions differ in several respects. The four most pertinent differences concern

(1) the nature and the powers of the state,
(2) the relationship between statehood and individual freedom,
(3) the role of legal sources not derived from state will, and
(4) the relationship between the actual and the normative as a matter of international law.

It is submitted that in light of the foregoing analysis, serious debate about personality in international law requires to engage with these four topics and to determine which views on them correspond with the position in

Overview of the conceptions of personality in international law

Conception	Founders	Original assumptions	Main manifestations	Presumption	Consequences
States-only	Heinrich Triepel, Dionisio Anzilotti, Lassa Oppenheim	– State is a historical fact enabling true freedom of individuals. – Law is created by state will.	– *Mavrommatis*, – *Jurisdiction of the Courts of Danzig*, – *Serbian Loans*, – *van Gend en Loos*	Only states (non-rebuttable)	Same as statehood
Recognition	Karl Strupp, Georg Schwarzenberger, Arrigo Cavaglieri	– Same as states-only. – Supplementation with a sociological perspective.	– *Reparation for Injuries*, – ICRC, – Holy See and Order of Malta, – *Texaco* v. *Libya*	For states (rebuttable)	Analogous to those of statehood
Individualistic	Hersch Lauterpacht (Léon Duguit, Georges Scelle)	– State is a functional entity representing relations between individuals. – International law includes constitutional principles.	– Nuremberg and inter-national criminal law, – *Kadic* v. *Karadciz II* and beyond, – Human rights law in the ECHR	For individuals when international norms of a fundamental nature are concerned (rebuttable)	International responsibility

Formal	Hans Kelsen	– State is a juridical construction. – Law is a formally complete system of positive norms.	– *LaGrand* and *Avena*, – Effect of Article 42 ICSID Convention (*Amco* v. *Indonesia*)	None	None
Actor	Myers S. McDougal, Harold D. Lasswell (W. Michael Reisman, Rosalyn Higgins)	– Law is a decision-making process, not a set of rules. – The actual and the normative coincide in international law.	– *Bank for International Settlements* Arbitration, – *International Tin Council* cases, – *Sandline* v. *PNG*	For effective actors (non-rebuttable)	Determined by policy considerations or effective action

international law today. Of course, it has to be readily admitted that these are vast and controversial areas. However, it is possible to make general statements regarding the direction international law has taken on these issues and thereby to denote those assumptions that are out of touch with the present international legal system as opposed to those that are supported therein.

Evaluation

It is submitted that the assumptions underlying the states-only, recognition and actor conceptions of international personality are discarded in contemporary international law. By contrast, the predispositions of the individualistic and formal conceptions find considerable support in current international legal doctrine and practice.

The state: fact vs. legal status

The question of the nature and the powers of the state, in terms of international law, essentially breaks down to whether statehood is considered a fact existing outside the realm of law or whether it is a legal status determined by law. The former view lies at the heart of the states-only and recognition conceptions whereas the latter particularly informs the formal one. When considering the state as fact, international law is understood simply to take account of the social reality of statehood and its powers: the state precedes the law and becomes a 'natural', 'original' or 'absolute' international person existing a priori.[1] By contrast, when conceiving statehood as a legal status, its formation as well as its rights, duties and capacities are determined by the international legal system itself: the law precedes the state and the latter's international status is acquired a posteriori.[2] The question to be answered now is what the position in international law is with regard to the concept of statehood.

Before exploring this question, it is necessary to address the related issue of recognition and the 'great debate' over its constitutive or

[1] This assumption is especially well summarized by Cavaglieri, 'Règles Générales', at 321: 'Pour nous, l'État est un phénomène social, avant d'être un phénomène juridique; il est une formation historique, à laquelle le droit se rattache, mais qu'il est incapable de créer par ses règles. Ce n'est pas l'État qui est le produit de droit, mais le contraire.'

[2] See e.g. Kelsen, 'Naissance de L'État', at 617–18.

declaratory nature in the formation of statehood.[3] In the present context, the question is not whether recognition is constitutive for, or declaratory of, the creation of states in international law, but whether legal rules determine this creation. In principle, both a constitutive and a declaratory theory of recognition can thereby accustom a role for legal principles: in the former case, recognition of states can be understood as a legal act subject to legal criteria from which a legal duty of recognition or non-recognition arises;[4] in the latter, the formation of statehood can be deemed as governed by legal criteria in addition to effectiveness. Similarly, in both cases, the formation of states can be dealt with as a matter of fact in that recognition, according to a constitutive theory, is understood as a purely discretionary political act dealing with a factual situation, or, pursuant to a declaratory theory, in that the existence of the state is considered as synonymous with effectiveness. Accordingly, the question for present purposes is not so much whether recognition is constitutive or declaratory – on balance, the position today is that it is declaratory[5] – but whether the formation of a state and its powers are governed by international law. For although the states-only and recognition conceptions generally assume a constitutive role for recognition in matters of statehood, the important point is that they do so on the basis of conceiving the state as a fact and recognition as a discretionary political act instead of an act determined by law;[6] and albeit the formal conception adheres to the declaratory as well as to the constitutive theory,[7] they do so in both cases on the basis that there exist legal criteria determining statehood. The important division, therefore, is not whether recognition is constitutive or declaratory, but whether statehood is considered a fact lying outside the international legal system or a legal status determined by that system.

[3] A convenient summary of the debate is provided by Lauterpacht, Hersch, *Recognition in International Law* (Cambridge University Press, 1947), 38–42, Crawford, *Creation of States*, 19–28, or by Talmon, Stefan, *Kollektive Nichtanerkennung illegaler Staaten* (Tübingen: Mohr Siebeck, 2006), 214–59.

[4] The classic example is Lauterpacht, *Recognition*, 26–37, postulating a legal duty to recognize when legal criteria of statehood are fulfilled.

[5] See e.g. Talmon, *Kollektive Nichtanerkennung*, 218, and Brownlie, *Principles*, 86–8.

[6] See e.g. Cavaglieri, 'Règles Générales', at 340–6.

[7] Compare Kelsen, 'Naissance de L'État', at 617–18 (declaratory theory according to the legal principle of effectiveness) with Kelsen, Hans, 'Recognition in International Law: Theoretical Observations', AJIL, 35 (1941), 605–17, at 609–10 (constitutive theory which deems recognition unlawful when granted to an entity not fulfilling the legal criteria of statehood).

The view of the state as a fact is codified in the Montevideo Convention of 1933.[8] According to its Article 1, a state exists when it possesses '(*a*) a permanent population, (*b*) a defined territory, (*c*) government, and (*d*) capacity to enter into relations with other States'. This clearly reflects the assumptions concerning statehood that are inherent in the states-only and the recognition conceptions of international personality. The relevant question now is whether the Montevideo Convention can still be considered to represent the position in international law today, that is, whether states fulfilling the four criteria of effectiveness enumerated in Article 1 of the Convention are states in terms of international law. In light of various practical incidents since World War II, the answer to this question must be no. In the words of John Dugard: 'Although Rhodesia, Transkei, Bophuthatswana, Venda, Ciskei and, possibly, the Turkish Republic of Northern Cyprus met or meet the traditional requirements of statehood expounded in the Montevideo Convention of 1933, it is absurd to contend that any of these entities . . . acquired the status of "State".'[9] Significantly, in all instances enumerated by Dugard the duty of collective non-recognition was invoked in relation to claims to statehood by these effective entities.[10] In order to grasp the precise connotation of this instrument for the nature of statehood in international law and the role of legal criteria in this process, one has to look at the *Namibia* opinion[11] wherein the ICJ, although not exactly in the context of state creation, dealt with the principle of non-recognition.[12]

[8] Convention on Rights and Duties of States adopted by the Seventh International Conference of American States, 26 December 1933, 165 LNTS 19. The Convention had only a limited number of signatories (the United States and mostly Latin American countries), but is nevertheless considered as articulating a general consensus at the time. See also Crawford, *Creation of States*, 45–6.

[9] Dugard, John, *Recognition and the United Nations* (Cambridge: Grotius, 1987), 123. See also Crawford, *Creation of States*, esp. 97–107, and Grant, Thomas D., *The Recognition of States: Law and Practice in Debate and Evolution* (Westport: Praeger, 1999), esp. 83–4 and 213–14. *Contra*: Talmon, *Kollektive Nichtanerkennung*, 238.

[10] SC Resolution 216 of 12 November 1965, SC Resolution 217 of 20 November 1965, and SC Resolution 277 of 18 March 1970 (Rhodesia); GA Resolution 31/6A of 26 October 1976 and SC Resolution 402 of 22 December 1976 (South African homelands); SC Resolution 541 of 18 November 1983 and SC Resolution 550 of 11 May 1984 (Northern Cyprus). See also Crawford, *Creation of States*, 159.

[11] *Legal Consequences for States of the Continued Presence of South Africa in Namibia (South West Africa) notwithstanding Security Council Resolution 276 (1970)* (Advisory Opinion), 1971 ICJ Reports 16.

[12] See also Dugard, *Recognition*, 117, and Crawford, *Creation of States*, 162–8. For early practice on the principle of non-recognition, including the resolutions of the League of Nations in the Manchurian crisis, see Lauterpacht, *Recognition*, 417–20.

In the event, the Court was concerned with the continuing presence of South Africa in Namibia after its Mandate to administer the territory had been revoked, partly on the grounds that South Africa had violated the Mandate's provisions by extending its apartheid policy to Namibia.[13] As South Africa was unwilling to relinquish control over the territory, the Security Council expressly called upon states not to recognize South Africa's unlawful administration in Namibia.[14] Subsequently, it referred the matter to the ICJ, asking for the legal consequences of South Africa occupying Namibia without valid title. The Court upheld that the revocation of the Mandate was valid on the ground that South Africa had violated its provisions. To reach this conclusion, the Court considered the Mandate in the broader context of evolving international legal principles in the area of self-determination:

> . . . an international instrument [the Mandate] has to be interpreted and applied within the framework of the entire legal system prevailing at the time of the interpretation. In the domain to which the present proceedings relate, the last fifty years, as indicated above, have brought important developments. These developments leave little doubt that the ultimate objective of the sacred trust was the self-determination and independence of the peoples concerned. In this domain, as elsewhere, the *corpus iuris gentium* has been considerably enriched, and this the Court, if it is faithfully to discharge its functions, may not ignore.[15]

In addition to developments concerning self-determination, the Court also took into account developments in the field of human rights when determining that South Africa had violated its position as the Mandatory by extending its apartheid policy to Namibia.[16] From this reasoning it followed that the continuing presence of South Africa was illegal and that there was a duty binding upon on all states – members and non-members of the UN – not to recognize the South African administration in Namibia.[17] The duty of non-recognition was thereby defined to include obligations

> to abstain from entering into treaty relations with South Africa in all cases in which the Government of South Africa purports to act on behalf of or concerning Namibia . . . to abstain from sending diplomatic or special

[13] GA Resolution 2145 (XXI) of 27 October 1966; SC Resolution 276 of 30 January 1970.
[14] SC Resolution 283 of 29 July 1970.
[15] *Legal Consequences for States of the Continued Presence of South Africa in Namibia*, para. 53.
[16] Ibid., para. 131. [17] Ibid., para. 115.

> missions to South Africa including in their jurisdiction the Territory of Namibia, to abstain from sending consular agents to Namibia, [and] to abstain from entering into economic and other forms of relationship or dealings with South Africa on behalf of or concerning Namibia which may entrench its authority over the Territory.[18]

The Court hence attributed considerable legal content to the duty of non-recognition as an obligation of states under customary international law.[19] This obligation was derived from the fact that South Africa's presence in Namibia was unlawful according to international standards informed by the principles of self-determination and respect for human rights.[20]

By analogy, when the principle of non-recognition is invoked in true cases of state creation like Rhodesia, the South African homelands or Northern Turkey, it has to be understood along the lines derived and substantiated in the *Namibia* opinion. In this sense, a duty not to recognize an effective entity has to be interpreted as a legal consequence of the entity in question not meeting fundamental international legal principles (like the right to self-determination and the respect for human rights).[21] In other words, there is a customary legal obligation binding upon all states not to accommodate an effective entity into the international legal system if that entity fails to respect peremptory international norms and other fundamental legal norms. Yet there is some degree of controversy as to exactly what the existence of such an obligation means for the concept of statehood, that is, whether such an entity is non-existent as a state for not meeting the criteria of statehood,[22] whether it is initially existent in legal terms but void for violating peremptory norms,[23] or whether its statehood, though sociologically existent, is illegal and without effect in international law.[24] For present purposes, it is not necessary to enter into this discussion.[25] The important point

[18] Ibid., paras 122 and 124. [19] See also Crawford, *Creation of States*, 165.

[20] Dugard, *Recognition*, 122. In more general terms: Crawford, *Creation of States*, 160.

[21] See also Dugard, *Recognition*, 127.

[22] Crawford, *Creation of States*, 105 and 107 (by clear implication).

[23] Dugard, *Recognition*, 131.

[24] Talmon, *Kollektive Nichtanerkennung*, 258–9. To considerable extent, Talmon adheres to the two-sided theory of the state as coined by Jellinek (see esp. 238–9). As a result, he envisages the creation of a state as a 'politisch-soziologischer Vorgang' (238) and at the same time considers legal criteria as relevant for the legal status of statehood (259–61). It seems that the better view would be that, in terms of international law, the entity in question is simply no state, leaving aside considerations of sociology or political science.

[25] By implication, see also Dugard, *Recognition*, 130.

here is that statehood, along all these lines, is considered a legal status which is denied in some way or another when specific international norms are not respected. By implication, statehood is clearly not a matter transcending international law, but is precisely governed by that law: an effective entity qualifying as a state according to the effectiveness criteria lacks statehood in international law when its formation fails to meet legal standards related to peremptory international rules and the principle of self-determination. Accordingly, an entity like Rhodesia, although undoubtedly satisfying the criteria of effectiveness as enunciated in the Montevideo Convention, could not be considered a state in terms of international law under its white minority government from 1965–79, for it violated the principle of self-determination and human rights through its apartheid regime.[26] The same holds true for the South African homelands (the Bantustans)[27] as well as, perhaps, and for different reasons,[28] for Northern Cyprus. In all these cases, international law denied (or still denies) the status of statehood although they represent(ed) effective entities.

In result, in present international law statehood is not simply a matter of effectiveness, but is to a considerable degree regulated by international law. A state does not simply exist as a matter of fact: the existence of a state is determined by meeting international legal standards and failure to do so implies denial of statehood in international law. The state is then not a given fact from which international law simply starts, but a legal entity deriving its status and its powers from the international legal system itself. Correspondingly, the notion of state sovereignty cannot be understood to represent natural powers, but only 'the totality of international rights and duties recognized by international law'.[29] James Crawford has summarized these aspects succinctly: 'A State is not a fact in the sense that a chair is a fact; it is a fact in the sense in which it may be said a treaty is a fact: that is, a legal status attaching to a certain state of affairs by virtue of certain rules or practices.'[30] It follows that the assumption underlying the states-only and recognition conceptions of international personality, according to which states are facts

[26] Ibid., 90–8, and Crawford, *Creation of States*, 97 and 129–30.

[27] Dugard, *Recognition*, 98–108, and Crawford, *Creation of States*, 344–5.

[28] Dugard, *Recognition*, 108–111, and Crawford, *Creation of States*, 133–4.

[29] *Reparation for Injuries suffered in the service of the United Nations* (Advisory Opinion), 1949 ICJ Reports 174, at 180.

[30] Crawford, *Creation of States*, 5 (with reference to Kelsen). *Contra*: Ipsen, *Völkerrecht*, 268 (with reference to Anzilotti).

transcending the realm of international law and possessing natural absolute powers, is not supported in the present international legal system. The present position rather endorses to a considerable degree the assumption informing the formal conception, namely that statehood is a legal status derived from or denied by international norms.

Individual freedom: inside vs. outside the state

Related to the nature of the state is the relationship between statehood and individual freedom. In this respect, the states-only and recognition conceptions of international personality build on the original assumption that the fulfilment of individual liberty is enabled by being a national of a state; by implication, there is no need to limit state power in the interest of individual freedom, but rather a necessity to establish and preserve statehood. By contrast, the individualistic and, to a somewhat lesser extent, the formal conception are informed by the idea that individual liberty has to be protected from state power, for the latter (exercised by individuals authorized to do so) endangers the well-being and freedom of individuals if it remains unchecked. The position in international law today strongly supports the second idea by imposing obligations on states to treat their nationals in accordance with international standards that are a concern for the international community as a whole.

In a sense, the mere existence of various international human rights treaties[31] indicates the support in contemporary international law for the assumption that individuals have to be protected from their own state of nationality. However, such instruments can also be interpreted as simply reflecting auto-limitation of state power on the inter-state level. More pertinent is whether there are customary international norms stipulating minimal standards concerning the treatment of a state's own nationals irrespective of the state being a party to particular treaty instruments. The answer to this question must be in the affirmative: in present international law, all states are under an obligation to treat their nationals in accordance with certain basic rights of the human being, and this obligation is not only owed towards specific other states, but *erga*

[31] E.g. the European Convention for the Protection of Human Rights and Fundamental Freedoms, 4 November 1950, 213 UNTS 222, the International Covenant on Civil and Political Rights, 19 December 1966, 999 UNTS 172, or the American Convention on Human Rights, 22 November 1969, 1144 UNTS 144.

omnes.[32] The position is best illustrated by reference to the ICJ's (in)famous *South West Africa*[33] judgment of 1966 and the contrasting treatment of the matter in the subsequent *Barcelona Traction*[34] case as well as in the *Namibia* opinion[35] referred to previously.

In *South West Africa*, the Court essentially had to consider Ethiopia's and Liberia's submission that South Africa's policy of apartheid as extended to South West Africa (Namibia) was contrary to international law.[36] In the preliminary objections phase, the Court had declared itself competent to adjudicate on the matter.[37] Yet when dealing with the merits of the submission, the Court, by the casting vote of President Spender, declared that Ethiopia and Liberia lacked a proper legal interest and consequently rejected their claim.[38] In an often cited passage, the Court thereby addressed the concern for individuals living under the apartheid regime in South West Africa in the following terms:

> Throughout this case it has been suggested, directly or indirectly, that humanitarian considerations are sufficient in themselves to generate legal rights and obligations, and that the Court can and should proceed accordingly. The Court does not think so . . . Humanitarian considerations may constitute the inspirational basis for rules of law, just as, for instance, the preambular parts of the United Nations Charter constitute the moral and political basis for the specific legal provisions thereafter set out. Such considerations do not, however, in themselves amount to rules of law. All States are interested – have an interest – in such matters. But the existence of an 'interest' does not of itself entail that this interest is specifically juridical in character.[39]

In other words, the Court denied that South Africa was under any international obligation towards Ethiopia and Liberia to treat the population of South West Africa (over which it exercised public power) according to basic international standards. In the view of the majority, there simply were no such binding standards as a matter of international

[32] See e.g. Brownlie, *Principles*, 537, Ipsen, *Völkerrecht*, 814; Cassese, *International Law*, 370; Daillier, Patrick and Alain Pellet, *Droit International Public*, 6th edition (Paris: L. G. D. J., 1999, 643; Jennings and Watts, *Oppenheim's International Law*, 992–3.

[33] *South West Africa* (Ethiopia v. South Africa; Liberia v. South Africa), Second Phase (Judgment), 1966 ICJ Reports 6.

[34] *Case Concerning the Barcelona Traction, Light and Power Company, Limited* (Belgium v. Spain), Second Phase (Merits), 1970 ICJ Reports 3.

[35] *Legal Consequences for States of the Continued Presence of South Africa in Namibia*.

[36] *South West Africa* (Second Phase), at 10–14 (submissions by Ethiopia and Liberia).

[37] *South West Africa* (First Phase), at 347.

[38] *South West Africa* (Second Phase), at 51 (para. 99). [39] Ibid., at 34 (paras 49–50).

law.[40] By implication, the statement supports the assumption inherent in the states-only and recognition conceptions that individuals are of no concern for international law as they are absorbed in their state of nationality (although in the present case it was a mandated territory, not a state), which alone enabled them to enjoy their true freedom and well-being.[41] Lacking specific treaty relations, there was no legal interest on the part of members of the international community in the welfare of individuals who were subject to another state power.

Without doubt, the *South West Africa* statement does not represent the position in international law today. Indeed, the decision was immediately criticized and led to a serious crisis in the international judiciary triggering adjustments in the internal practice of the ICJ.[42] In this context of strong criticism, the statements in the *Barcelona Traction* case of 1970 can be interpreted as 'a concealed apology for the fiasco of the *Second South West Africa* decision'.[43] In its judgment, principally dealing with diplomatic protection, the ICJ introduced the concept of obligations *erga omnes*. These were international obligations in which 'all States can be held to have a legal interest in their protection ... Such obligations derive, for example, in contemporary international law, from the outlawing of acts of aggression, and of genocide, as also from *the principles and rules concerning the basic rights of the human person*, including protection from slavery and racial discrimination.'[44] In clear contrast to the *South West Africa* judgment, the Court accepted that there were international norms of legal concern to all states. Crucially, such norms included the basic rights of individual human beings. As a result, a state was not free to treat its individuals according to its own choosing, but was under an obligation owed to the international community to guarantee certain fundamental freedoms and rights. In this view, the individual was a concern for the international community as a whole, and not only for the state of nationality (nor, possibly, only for specific other states pursuant to treaty provisions). It is

40 But see the dissenting opinions by Judge Jessup (*South West Africa* (Second Phase), at 325) and by Judge Tanaka (*South West Africa* (Second Phase), esp. at 285–7).

41 A similar point is put forward by Spiermann, *International Legal Argument in the PCIJ*, 79 (n. 1).

42 See e.g. Rosenne, Shabtai, *The World Court: What it is and how it Works*, 5th completely revised edition (Dordrecht: Martinus Nijhoff, 1995), 172–3.

43 Crawford, *Creation of States*, 103. See also Tams, Christian J., *Enforcing Obligations Erga Omnes in International Law* (Cambridge University Press, 2005), 15 (with further references).

44 *Case Concerning the Barcelona Traction, Light and Power Company, Limited*, paras 33–4 (emphasis added).

in this sense that the subsequent *Namibia* opinion – already referred to when examining the position on the nature of statehood – has to be interpreted. The Court partly based the obligation *erga omnes* not to recognize the South African administration in Namibia on the violation of 'fundamental human rights' through South Africa's apartheid regime.[45] In a sense, this represents the functional view of the state as informing the individualistic conception of international personality, for non-recognition was linked to the administration not managing to protect the well-being of its population.[46]

In sum, with regard to the relationship between statehood and individual liberty, international law has moved from the discredited *South West Africa* decision to the statements in *Barcelona Traction* and *Namibia*, thereby declaring welfare and freedom of individuals a concern of the international community as a whole.[47] Hence, the position today is that individual dignity is not secured by unlimited (nor only auto-limited) state power, but by restraining the latter through general international norms for the benefit of individuals. Of course, the argument put forward here is not that international law directly confers these customary rights upon individuals (although this will be the result achieved when all assumptions are evaluated). For the moment, the point is only that the existence of these norms implies that, in terms of international law, individual freedom and well-being are considered potentially endangered, rather than enabled, by the state. This position clearly supports the assumption underlying the individualistic and formal conceptions, namely that individual liberty and welfare are best preserved by restricting state power. By the same token, the contemporary position discards the view that only inside the unchecked state will individuals find their true freedom and fulfilment.

Particular vs. general international law

With regard to sources of international law, the main division is between those conceptions conceiving international law as a set of explicit and tacit contracts among states (states-only, recognition) and those

45 *Legal Consequences for States of the Continued Presence of South Africa in Namibia*, paras 126 and 131.

46 Ibid., para. 127.

47 See also Article 48(1)(b) ARSIWA and commentary to it in YILC 2001-II(2), pp. 126–7 (esp. n. 725).

accepting general international rules pertinent for all states even though not all may have consented to them (individualistic, formal).[48] In the latter case, there is a further subdivision between the idea that general rules include fundamental legal principles and peremptory norms (individualistic) and the rejection of the legal validity of such principles and norms (formal). Of course, it has to be readily admitted that both of these divisions still represent controversial topics in international law today. However, it is possible to trace two positions in contemporary practice and doctrine indicating the overall direction international law has taken in this respect: the first is that customary international law is not a tacit treaty; the second is that the category of peremptory norms is now well established. The tendency today supports the view underlying the individualistic and the formal conceptions, namely that there are general rules of international law transcending acquiescence by particular states and, though solely informing the individualistic conception, these norms include peremptory ones. This conclusion also allows an appraisal of the actor conception's assumption that international law is not a set of rules but a decision-making process.

The first division can be encapsulated in the opposition between particular and general international law. Assuming that international law is only particular, state consent is seen as the exclusive source of law and a state is only bound by those international norms which it has explicitly or tacitly agreed on. In this view, customary international law is conceived as a tacit treaty and there follows a strict identity between creators and subjects of international law: an entity is only bound by those obligations in the creation of which it has participated. By contrast, if one accepts the existence of truly general international law, state consent is not necessarily required for a customary international rule to arise: international custom is then not understood as a tacit agreement, but as rules originating in a general – but, crucially, not universal[49] – practice to which specific states neither have to contribute nor subsequently to consent in order to be bound. In this view,

[48] There is a further division of course between all these conceptions and the actor conception, for while the former all agree that international law is a set of rules, the latter considers it a decision-making process in which policy considerations play an overwhelming role. This fundamental difference will be examined in the last paragraph of this section.

[49] This is the difference from Strupp, Cavaglieri, or Schwarzenberger who accepted general international law whenever there was *universal* practice. See e.g. Strupp, *Grundzüge*, 11; Cavaglieri, 'Règles Générales', at 323–7; Schwarzenberger, 'Fundamental Principles', at 201–2.

there is no necessary identity between creators and subjects of international law. The question now is whether the contemporary position supports conceiving customary international law as a tacit agreement or whether the position is that general rules are pertinent for a specific entity without consent. By clear implication, it is the latter view that is supported in present international legal argument.[50]

A useful starting point to underline this claim is the ICJ's line of reasoning in the *North Sea Continental Shelf Cases*.[51] The legal issue was whether Germany was under a customary international obligation to determine the boundary of the continental shelf by applying the equidistance principle as laid down in Article 6(2) of the Geneva Convention on the Continental Shelf,[52] a treaty Germany had signed but not ratified. Dealing with the submissions on behalf of Denmark and the Netherlands, the Court first examined whether Germany had in some form – 'by conduct, by public statements and proclamations, and in other ways' – tacitly consented to the rule expressed in Article 6(2).[53] In the result, the Court denied that such consent could be inferred from German conduct or statements.[54] In the tradition of the tacit agreement conception of customary international law, this would have been the end of the matter: without consent in some form by Germany to the equidistance principle, there could be no obligation for Germany to apply it.

[50] For recent statements of this position see Kolb, Robert, 'Selected Problems in the Theory of Customary International Law', NILR, 50 (2003), 119–50, at 141–5, Mendelson, Maurice, 'The Subjective Element in Customary International Law', BYIL, 66 (1995), 177–208, at 184–94 and Byers, Michael, *Custom, Power and the Power of Rules: International Relations and Customary International Law* (Cambridge University Press, 1999), 142–6; Daillier and Pellet, *Droit International* (6th edition), 319–20. For a different view see Danilenko, Gennady M., 'The Theory of International Customary Law', *German Yearbook of International Law*, 31 (1988), 9–51, at 11–14, and, though somewhat ambiguously, Villiger, Mark E., *Customary International Law and Treaties: A Manual on the Theory and Practice of the Interrelation of Sources*, 2nd edition (The Hague: Kluwer Law International, 1997), 41–2. For a very early comprehensive critique of the tacit treaty conception of international custom see Bourquin, 'Règles Générales', at 62–7. From a critical perspective, see Koskenniemi, *Apology to Utopia*, 416–7. See also Kunz, Josef L., 'The Nature of Customary International Law', AJIL, 47 (1953), 662–69, at 663–4, and Verdross, Alfred, 'Entstehungsweisen und Geltungsgrund des universellen völkerrechtlichen Gewohnheitsrechts', ZaöRV, 29 (1969), 635–53, at 636–7 (only descriptive).

[51] *North Sea Continental Shelf Cases* (Federal Republic of Germany v. Denmark; Federal Republic of Germany v. Netherlands), Judgment, 1969 ICJ Reports 3.

[52] Convention on the Continental Shelf, 29 April 1958, 499 UNTS 312.

[53] *North Sea Continental Shelf Cases*, para. 27. [54] Ibid., para. 32.

However, the Court went on to consider the second submission, namely that Germany was

> in any event bound to accept delimitation on an equidistance-special circumstances basis, because the use of this method is not in the nature of a merely conventional obligation, but is, or must now be regarded as involving, a rule that is part of the *corpus* of general international law; and, like other rules of general or customary international law, is binding on the Federal Republic automatically and independently of any specific assent, direct or indirect, given by the latter.[55]

The Court considered this a sound submission[56] in the abstract and went on to examine whether the equidistance principle truly represented part of customary international law. In this part of the judgment, there was no more reference to German conduct; it was only analysed whether there was a general – but not universal – state practice indicating the existence of a customary rule.[57] In the event, the Court denied that sufficient practice and *opinio iuris* existed to affirm the customary character of the equidistance principle.[58] However, it seems clear from the reasoning of the Court that had it affirmed such a norm, it would have been binding upon Germany even without the latter's consent (unless it was a persistent objector).[59]

As far as the logical structure of the judgment in the *North Sea Continental Shelf Cases* is concerned, it strengthens the claim dominating in contemporary doctrine according to which customary law is not a tacit agreement but general law also opposable to those entities which have not acquiesced in it.[60] In this sense, it seems to be settled that customary international law can be universally binding[61] even though

[55] Ibid., para. 37. [56] Ibid., para. 71. [57] Ibid., paras 47–82. [58] Ibid., paras 81–2.

[59] The concept of 'persistent objector' does not contradict but rather strengthens the position that customary law is not consensual. For the concept precisely exists because a state can be bound by customary law even without consent (see e.g. Kolb, 'Customary International Law', at 144). The only way a state can free itself from such an obligation, to which it has not consented, is then by persistently objecting to its creation. For the acceptance of the concept in practice see the *Fisheries Case* (United Kingdom v. Norway), Judgment, 1951 ICJ Reports 116, at 130–1 (by clear implication).

[60] This line of reasoning was also followed in *Case Concerning the Continental Shelf* (Libya v. Malta), Judgment, 1985 ICJ Reports 13, 229, esp. para. 25, although with somewhat different results.

[61] In addition to custom with general reach, there can also be regional or even bilateral customary law. For a pronouncement of the former, see *Asylum Case* (Colombia v. Peru), Judgment, 1950 ICJ Reports 266, at 276–8. For the latter, see *Case Concerning Rights of Nationals of the United States of America in Morocco* (France v. United States), Judgment, 1952 ICJ Reports 176, at 199–200.

it requires only general practice[62] supported by *opinio iuris* for its establishment.[63] Accordingly, the strict consensual nature, and with it the identity between creators and subjects of international law, is not supported in contemporary doctrine and practice. As a result, the assumption underlying the states-only and recognition conceptions stipulating that there is only particular international law is no longer tenable in international law.

Acknowledging the existence of general international law, the second division to be addressed is whether part of these norms can transcend the realm of ordinary custom and acquire a peremptory character.[64] In principle, it is agreed that international customary law is *ius dispositivum*, meaning that it is possible for states to derogate from it in treaties on an *inter partes* basis,[65] or to free themselves unilaterally from an emerging customary rule by persistently objecting to it. Yet, the question is whether this principle holds true in all events or whether there are general international norms, as claimed by the individualistic conception but doubted by the formal one,[66] that represent *ius cogens* and as such are not to be derogated from in treaties and in other legal acts.[67] As is well known, such norms have been authoritatively endorsed in Article 53 of the Vienna Convention on the Law of Treaties:[68]

> A treaty is void if, at the time of its conclusion, it conflicts with a peremptory norm of general international law. For the purposes of the present Convention, a peremptory norm of general international law is a

[62] See also Villiger, *Customary International Law and Treaties*, 29, and Brownlie, *Principles*, 7–8. On a more general level see Ipsen, *Völkerrecht*, 216, and Kolb, 'Customary International Law', at 142.

[63] The position of customary law's general nature finds further support in the widely accepted view that new states are bound by international custom without having to consent to the rules included in it: e.g. Byers, *Custom*, 145 (with further references); Kolb, 'Customary International Law', at 142. By implication, this view can also be inferred from *Report of the International Law Commission: Twenty-fifth Session*, ILC 1973, UN Doc. A/9010/Rev.1, at 177 (commentary on then Article 2 of the Draft Articles on State Responsibility). *Contra*: Ipsen, *Völkerrecht*, 223–4 (though somewhat ambiguously).

[64] In the terminology of Kolb, 'Customary International Law', at 136–7, these norms form 'universal' as opposed to 'general' custom.

[65] See e.g. Ipsen, *Völkerrecht*, 252.

[66] For the at times ambiguous position in the formal conception on this point see Kelsen, 'Théorie (II)', at 150–1.

[67] See for the latter effect the separate opinion by Judge *ad hoc* Lauterpacht on the request of provisional measures in the *Case Concerning the Application of the Convention on the Prevention and Punishment of the Crime of Genocide* (Bosnia and Herzegovina v. Yugoslavia), Provisional Measures, 1993 ICJ Reports 325, 407, para. 100 (at 440).

[68] 23 May 1969, 1155 UNTS 331.

> norm accepted and recognized by the international community of States as a whole as a norm from which no derogation is permitted and which can be modified only by a subsequent norm of general international law having the same character.

Beyond doubt, the category of peremptory norms is now well established in contemporary international practice[69] and doctrine,[70] thereby having been applied in other contexts than the law of treaties. However, in contrast to the well-settled acceptance of the category, its source and content are less clear,[71] and the definition in Article 53 VCLT is of little help in this respect because of its circularity.[72] What seems to be accepted is that although states play an important role in the process of creation of peremptory norms, their practice and individual wills cannot have the same weight as is the case with ordinary customary law.[73] It therefore appears that the element of *opinio iuris* must be of more importance and conceived of in more collective terms when determining a rule of *ius cogens* than when establishing ordinary custom. In effect, this brings the concept of peremptory norms closer to being a matter of legal principle.[74] However, one does not have to entirely subscribe to the

69 *Prosecutor* v. *Furundzija* (Judgment), ICTY Trial Chamber Case IT-95-17/1-T, 10 December 1998, paras 153–7; *Al-Adsani* v. *United Kingdom* (Grand Chamber, Judgment), ECHR Reports 2001-XI, paras 60–1; *Legality of the Threat or Use of Nuclear Weapons* (Advisory Opinion), 1996 ICJ Reports 226, para. 79 (by clear implication). The category has also been accepted in the ILC's State Responsibility project (see commentary to Article 40 ARSIWA in YILC 2001-II(2), p. 112).

70 See e.g. Brownlie, *Principles*, 488–9; Ipsen, *Völkerrecht*, 193; Crawford, *Creation of States*, 101; Byers, *Custom*, 183–6; Daillier and Pellet, *Droit International* (6th edition), 200–2.

71 For a comprehensive overview on the different theories of *ius cogens* see Kolb, *Ius Cogens*, 33–168. See also Byers, *Custom*, 187–95.

72 See also Crawford, *Creation of States*, 101; Daillier and Pellet, *Droit International* (6th edition), 202.

73 By implication, this also follows from commentary to Article 12 ARSIWA in YILC 2001-II(2), p. 56. See also Kolb, 'Customary International Law', at 124–5, and Byers, *Custom*, 187.

74 To a very limited extent, this argument finds some support in the reasoning of the ICJ in *Case Concerning Military and Paramilitary Activities in and Against Nicaragua* (Nicaragua v. United States), Judgment, 1986 ICJ Reports 14, para. 190. In the event, the Court related the *ius cogens* character of the prohibition of use of force to it being a 'fundamental or cardinal' principle of international law, the latter to some extent being based on an unusually strong focus on general *opinio iuris* in the international community (para. 191). Similarly, the *Corfu Channel Case* (United Kingdom v. Albania), Judgment, 1949 ICJ Reports 4, at 22, and its invocation of 'general and well-recognized principles', namely 'elementary considerations of humanity', is sometimes considered to be related to the concept of *ius cogens* (see e.g. Ipsen, *Völkerrecht*, 193). However, it has to be admitted that the latter concept was not addressed in the judgment.

individualistic conception's equation of peremptory norms and fundamental legal principles; it suffices to state that *ius cogens*, in order to discharge its function, must have a somewhat distinct source from ordinary customary law. With Ian Brownlie, it may therefore simply be stated that 'certain overriding principles of international law exist, forming a body of *jus cogens*'.[75] It is agreed that this body includes the prohibition of use of force, the prohibitions of genocide and of trade in slaves, the protection of fundamental human rights and certain rules of humanitarian international law as well as, arguably, the principle of self-determination.[76]

In effect, the acceptance of overriding principles forming a body of *ius cogens* reinforces the argument that international law today is not merely a set of bilateral relationships, but a system of law including norms of a general, or indeed universal, character. In this sense, it is further proof that the position today discards the assumption that international law is only particular. By implication, the identity between creators and subjects of international law is additionally questioned: the law-creation process for the category of peremptory norms is allocated on a level superior to the practice and will of individual states, namely on something resembling a community of states and its *opinio iuris* in the form of fundamental legal principles.[77] Therefore, individual states cannot be presumed to have truly created the *ius cogens* obligations which are binding upon them, and they certainly cannot opt out of this category of norms. In addition, and more specifically, the general acceptance of a class of peremptory norms underlines that international law today knows a body of fundamental principles which transcend ordinary customary rules and at the same time still form part of international law. This position contradicts the assumption informing the formal conception that such principles are only of a moral or meta-legal nature, or at best represent a hypothetical basic norm. To the contrary, the present position supports the individualistic conception and its underlying idea that there are certain principles related to the notion of *ius cogens* forming part of international law although they are not derived from international custom or treaty. It follows that with regard to

[75] Brownlie, *Principles*, 488.

[76] Ibid., 489; Crawford, *Creation of States*, 101; Ipsen, *Völkerrecht*, 193. See also commentary to Article 40 ARSIWA in YILC 2001-II(2), pp. 112–13.

[77] By implication, a similar understanding can be inferred from commentaries to Article 12 and 40 ARSIWA in YILC 2001-II(2), p. 56 and p. 112. See also Daillier and Pellet, *Droit International* (6th edition), 202–3.

assumptions concerning the sources of international law, the contemporary position mainly confirms the postulates informing the individualistic conception of international personality, while it partly contradicts those of the formal one and almost entirely discards the presuppositions of the states-only and recognition conceptions.

From these conclusions, it is also possible to draw certain insights with regard to the first assumption underlying the actor conception, namely that international law is not a set of legal rules but a decision-making process. In this view, the above peremptory norms cannot exist on the basis of an abstract *opinio iuris* related to fundamental legal principle. They rather have to rest on policy considerations and therefore are subject to change whenever social needs and interests so require.[78] Of course, to a certain extent, public policy considerations are present in the concept of international *ius cogens* and the *opinio iuris* necessary for its creation.[79] Similarly, it is also the case that peremptory norms are not entirely static, but can be adjusted in the same complex way as they are created.[80] But in light of the above reasoning, it seems difficult to argue that international law does not know a set of rules which on a given point in time are pertinent independently of policy considerations standing against them. It is not the case that abstract legal principles can simply be abandoned in international law in favour of what is deemed to work best in a specific situation. There are peremptory rules and principles from which no deviation is possible. Therefore, the assumption that international law is a process of authoritative decision-making in which policy reasons are instantly favoured over legal rules is difficult to reconcile with the acceptance in international practice and doctrine of general and indeed peremptory norms. These norms are non-negotiable in specific circumstances. In its generality, the first assumption of the actor conception hence does not seem to find support in contemporary international law, for the latter at least in part resembles a system of legal rules.

Effective action vs. principled justification

With regard to the normative force of effective action in international law, a crucial difference exists between, on the one hand, the actor and recognition conceptions and, on the other hand, the three other conceptions of

[78] See also Kolb, *Ius Cogens*, 82–3.
[79] Ibid., 68–83 (presenting this emphasis) and 171–81 (criticizing it).
[80] See Article 53 VCLT and commentary to Article 12 ARSIWA in YILC 2001-II(2), p. 56.

international personality. Whereas the assumption underlying the former two conceptions is that actual behaviour and power have corresponding legal value,[81] the latter three all rest on the distinction of 'is' and 'ought' and, most pertinent in the formal conception, stipulate a need for principled justification in order to transform sociological descriptions into legal prescriptions. True, the relationship between the actual and the normative represents one of the fundamental predicaments of the international legal order, if not of legal philosophy in general.[82] It therefore may be more important to stress the fundamental difference and the need for a choice between the different assumptions than to attempt to offer a definite statement on the matter. Nevertheless, with all due caution, it seems possible to make an argument on the position in international law by examining the role of *opinio iuris* in the formation of international custom. Such analysis strongly suggests that effective action does not imply a presumption of legal value in international law. On the contrary, there is significant practice in the jurisprudence of the International Court of distinguishing actual behaviour from legal intent. By analogy, the reconciliation of the actual and the normative as informing the actor and the recognition conceptions of international personality is put into question; in turn, the need for some form of principled justification finds support in international legal argument as practised by the International Court.

In a sense, the bipartite character of international customary law alone indicates that the actual and the normative are kept separate in international legal argument:[83] by requiring an element of *opinio iuris* in addition to state practice, facts have to be transformed into a normative prescription in order to acquire the status of law. In the words of Robert Kolb: '. . . the *opinio iuris* criterion has the function of transforming facts of practice devoid of intrinsic legal value into law by incorporating into them a legal element. *Opinio iuris* thus transforms facts into law. It is a sort of philosopher's stone.'[84] Yet, it is possible to interpret this process of transformation in such a way as to consider *opinio iuris* as a

[81] This tendency is certainly less apparent in the recognition conception. However, its origin in grounding the legal framework of the states-only conception in social reality includes a tendency to reconcile the normative with the actual in a similar vein as is the case in the assumptions underlying the actor approach.

[82] For a classic treatment of the matter in philosophical terms, see Searl, John R., 'How to Derive "Ought" from "Is"', *Philosophical Review*, 73 (1964), 43–58, *passim*.

[83] See Article 38(1)(b) ICJ Statute: 'international custom, as evidence of a *general practice accepted as law*' (emphasis added).

[84] Kolb, 'Customary International Law', at 127. See also Kolb, *Réflexions*, 52, and Koskenniemi, *Apology to Utopia*, 411–12. Curiously, Kelsen, the main proponent of a

more or less automatic consequence of there being a general practice.[85] On this view, the presumption is that whatever is effectively practised by sufficient numbers is automatically transformed into customary law, a position that would still fit well with the reconciliation of the actual and the normative informing the actor and, to a lesser extent, the recognition conception of international personality.[86] The question then, is whether international practice supports this interpretation of the bipartite character of international custom, that is, whether it assumes *opinio iuris* to follow automatically whenever a general practice is established, or whether it requires additional justification.

The precise role of *opinio iuris* in the formation of international customary law is a controversial topic in contemporary doctrine and practice.[87] For present purposes, the relationship between effective conduct and *opinio iuris* is of relevance.[88] In this respect, there is remarkable continuity in the jurisprudence of the International Court.[89] In the *Lotus* case, the PCIJ had to address the French contention that, as a matter of general practice, criminal proceedings dealing with incidents taking place on the high seas were generally instituted in the state whose flag was flown on the vessel concerned. From this observation of fact, the French government concluded that a customary international rule existed to the effect that other states were under an obligation to abstain from initiating criminal proceedings whenever their flag was not flown on the relevant vessel. The Court replied:

> Even if the rarity of the judicial decisions to be found among the reported cases were sufficient to prove in point of fact the circumstance alleged by

distinction between the normative and the actual, only came around to accepting a role for *opinio iuris* in the formation of international custom in 1953 (Kelsen, 'Théorie (II)', at 122). However, his earlier criticism of the notion was related to it representing a fiction in the form of state will.

85 See e.g. Brownlie, *Principles*, 8, who mentions this position without sharing it. In the same sense, see also Haggenmacher, Peter, 'La Doctrine des Deux Éléments du Droit Coutumier dans la Pratique de la Cour Internationale', RGDIP, LXXXX (1986), 5–125, at 8 (relating such a position to the New Haven School).

86 See also Koskenniemi, *Apology to Utopia*, 412.

87 On doctrinal positions, see Kolb, 'Customary International Law', at 137–41; on ambiguities in international practice see e.g. Mendelson, 'Subjective Element', at 181–4.

88 In the preceding section, as another aspect of the controversy surrounding *opinio iuris*, the question whether *opinio iuris* is a will or a belief has already been touched upon. The argument was that, especially where fundamental customary norms are concerned, the emphasis must rest on *opinio iuris* being a general belief rather than an individual will.

89 See also Daillier and Pellet, *Droit International* (6th edition), 327; Brownlie, *Principles*, 8–10; Haggenmacher, 'Doctrine des Deux Éléments', at 6–7.

> the Agent of the French Government, it would merely show that States had often, in practice, abstained from instituting criminal proceedings, and not that they had recognized themselves to be obliged to do so; for only if such abstention were based on their being conscious of having a duty to abstain would it be possible to speak of an international custom. The alleged fact does not allow one to infer that States have been conscious of having such a duty . . .[90]

Accordingly, even assuming that there was a general practice in the sense that France contended, the Court made clear that there was no accompanying *opinio iuris*. The latter had to be established independently of there being actual behaviour. It follows that there was not necessarily a corresponding legal intention when a general practice was established. There was thus a distinction made between effective state action and legal intent. The above passage from the *Lotus* was quoted by the ICJ in the *North Sea Continental Shelf Cases* and thereby endorsed in all relevant aspects:

> Not only must the acts concerned amount to a settled practice, but they must also be such, or be carried out in such a way, as to be evidence of a belief that this practice is rendered obligatory by the existence of a rule of law requiring it. The need for such a belief, i.e., the existence of a subjective element, is implicit in the very notion of the *opinio juris sive necessitatis*. The States concerned must therefore feel that they are conforming to what amounts to a legal obligation. The frequency, or even habitual character of the acts is not in itself enough.[91]

The ICJ made clear in somewhat different terms that state practice does not necessarily imply a presumption of *opinio iuris*. A relationship between the two elements of custom certainly exists, but at the same time it is also made clear that actual behaviour does not alone amount to a normative statement. The Court again reinforced this argument in *Military and Paramilitary Activities in and Against Nicaragua*.[92]

These statements in significant cases and the remarkable continuity with which they were invoked underline the carefully drawn distinction in international law between what specific entities actually do, and what legal effect such action may have: action in itself clearly is not sufficient to draw a normative conclusion. There are then strong indications that the position in

[90] *Case of the SS Lotus* (Judgment), 1927 PCIJ Series A No. 10, at 28.

[91] *North Sea Continental Shelf* cases (Federal Republic of Germany v. Denmark; Federal Republic of Germany v. Netherlands), Judgment, 1969 ICJ Reports 3, para. 77.

[92] *Case Concerning Military and Paramilitary Activities in and Against Nicaragua* (Nicaragua v. United States), Judgment, 1986 ICJ Reports 14, para. 207.

international law today assumes no necessary presumption that effective action implies legal effects. The normative value of the actual is not automatic, but requires some sort of principled transformation.

The relatively independent role of *opinio iuris* in the formation of international custom illustrates that the contemporary position in international law does not endorse the reconciliation of effective action with legal norms, which assumption informs the actor and, to a certain extent, the recognition conceptions of international personality. Certainly, it would be an overstatement to claim that this reconciliation has been discarded: the relationship between the actual and the normative is a prevailing issue in the international legal system and one that will not be settled by abstract reasoning, but has to be lived through in daily practice. Yet, the relevant statements by the ICJ and its predecessor on the complex relationship between effective behaviour and *opinio iuris* in the formation of customary law underlines that some sort of principled justification is required to transform facts into international legal norms. This does not imply that effectiveness is not or cannot be an important principle in international law; but it still has to be a *legal* principle, that is, it has to be justified on the basis of normative values. It therefore seems difficult to argue that in the field of personality or in any other field of international law there can be direct normative implications of effective behaviour or actual power: such conclusions require a principled justification in analogy to the role of *opinio iuris* in the formation of customary international law. It may therefore be concluded that the present position supports the distinction between effective action and legal implications, a distinction that is especially present in the formal conception but also informs the states-only and individualistic one. In the same manner, it is difficult to subscribe to the assumption that the actual and the normative are as closely linked in international law as the actor and recognition conceptions assume.

Conclusion

In the four main areas in which the conceptions of international personality differ with regard to their underlying assumptions, the position in contemporary international law may be encapsulated as follows:

(1) The state is a legal status determined by international law.
(2) Freedom and welfare of individuals is a concern of the international community as a whole, and not only of the state of nationality.

(3) International law consists of general rules, a portion of which are peremptory. In this sense, international law is a system of legal rules and principles.
(4) International law draws a distinction between effective action and legal implications. A principled justification – that is, an *opinio iuris* not automatically presumed with evidence of practice – is required in order to transform facts into law.

The main argument of this book is that conceptions resting on assumptions clearly at odds with these contemporary positions cannot claim legal value in present international legal argument. For international law to be a true and therefore coherent system of law, the concept of personality must conform with how statehood, the relationship between state power and individual freedom, the sources of international law, and the role of the actual in determining the normative are conceived in present international law.[93]

In this sense, one must conclude that the assumptions on which the states-only and the recognition conceptions rest – in particular their understanding of statehood as a historical fact enabling individuals to find their true fulfilment, and their view of international law as being only particular – have been discarded in international law. To a lesser extent, the same holds true for the tendency of the recognition conception to attach legal value to sociological developments. Similarly, there is very little support in international law for the basic premises of the actor conception: neither the international legal system is generally conceived a decision-making process in which policy considerations take precedence over legal rules and principles, nor is effective action directly relevant in normative terms. It is therefore submitted that the states-only, recognition and actor conceptions cannot provide a basis for allocating personality in the present international legal system. It follows that states can neither be conceived as the exclusive international persons nor are they the direct administrators of international personality through the process of recognition; similarly, there is no sound basis for effective actor quality directly leading to international legal status.

By contrast, the assumptions informing the individualistic and the formal conceptions are to a considerable degree in line with the premises of contemporary international law: the state is a legal status, the

[93] For international law being a system of law and the corresponding requirement of consistency, see also Crawford, *Creation of States*, 5–6.

individual has to be protected from state power rather than being entirely subjected to it, and there are general norms of international law transcending state consent, including overriding legal principles of peremptory character which cannot be derogated from as a result of policy considerations. In all these aspects, the two conceptions and their assumptions conform to the position in international law today. Therefore, it is submitted that international legal argument on personality must take place in a frame of reference combining the formal and the individualistic conceptions of international personality. Such a framework and its consequences in practice will be presented in the remaining chapter of this book.

11

An individualistic and formal frame of reference

A frame of reference for personality in international law must combine principles of the individualistic and the formal conceptions. The two are historically and intellectually closely related and converge in their criticism of traditional views of statehood, the role of individuals, and the sources of law. However, their concrete focus varies. The individualistic conception is almost exclusively concerned with the role of individuals and of fundamental legal principles in international law, thereby neglecting to provide an overall framework for international personality. The formal conception, on the other hand, offers a complete analysis of personality in the international legal order based on a meta-legal basic norm, but fails to take true account of the now accepted category of peremptory principles. A combination of the two conceptions can temper their respective shortcomings. Accordingly, the general approach of the formal conception has to be grounded in fundamental legal principles. These call for special considerations with regard to their personal scope.

Such a framework does not state which entities actually are international persons. This is a matter to be established in the concrete circumstances of a legal issue. What the frame of reference offers are basic principles according to which this task can consistently be fulfilled in a variety of legal situations. Hence, depending on the context, very different entities have international legal status. In order to make the implications of this framework clearer, it will be applied to the four legal issues that were outlined at the beginning of this book and have been examined throughout as practical manifestations of particular conceptions.

Basic principles

The combination of the individualistic and formal conceptions leads to international law representing an open system.[1] The starting point of this

[1] The notion has been coined by Crawford, *Open System*, 27–8.

framework is the formal conception's declaration, substantiated in legal practice, that any entity that is addressed by an international norm is an international person.[2] Unlike the states-only and actor conception, there is no restriction of the personal scope of international law. Unlike the recognition conception, states are not considered primary or normal international persons administrating personality through explicit or implied recognition. In this framework, there are no a priori international persons (except for individuals in specific circumstances), and there are no entities which are a priori precluded from becoming international persons. In principle, personality in international law hence is a strict a posteriori concept: an international person simply represents those international rights, duties and capacities directed at it. It is then a matter of norm interpretation whether a specific entity enjoys international personality in a particular legal context. In case of a treaty norm, the process of interpretation has to follow the regular principles codified in Articles 31–33 VCLT,[3] without any presumption to be rebutted. As argued above, there simply is no sound legal basis in contemporary international law for a presumption for or against certain entities with regard to the personal scope of an international norm. In case of a customary rule, the process of determining its personal scope may be more complex than with treaties, and involve a strong teleological perspective. But again, there is no presumption to be overcome: the system is completely open.

It is important to clarify the role of recognition in this process. Obviously, in the present framework, it is neither necessary nor sufficient to be recognized by states in order to acquire international legal status.[4] However, recognition can have considerable evidential value, especially when the personal scope of an international customary norm has to be determined. For recognition as an international person may provide an indication that norms of general custom apply to the entity in question.[5]

[2] The best modern formulation of this view is Barberis, 'Personnalité Juridique', at 169.

[3] See also *LaGrand Case* (Germany v. United States), Judgment, 2001 ICJ Reports 466, para. 77 (without referring to Articles 31–33 VCLT, but to a settled practice of treaty interpretation consistent with Article 31) and the comments by Spiermann, 'LaGrand Case', at 209.

[4] It is not sufficient in the sense that recognition as an international person alone does not imply any direct legal consequences as a matter of international law.

[5] To a certain extent, the reasoning in *Prosecutor* v. *Simic et al.* (Decision on the Prosecution Motion under Rule 73 for a Ruling concerning the Testimony of a Witness), ICTY Trial Chamber 27 July 1999, esp. para. 46, can be understood along these lines when the Trial Chamber declared a customary rule of confidentiality applicable to the ICRC.

In this sense, it is a legal instrument contributing to the interpretation *ratione personae* of a customary international rule. Therefore, recognition certainly plays an important role when establishing international personality, but it cannot be a necessary or a sufficient requirement. Similar considerations apply with regard to an entity's status as an effective actor. Although such status in itself cannot lead to international personality, it may have evidential value (although to a lesser extent than recognition) when determining the personal scope of particular norms.

There is one exception to the general rule that personality in international law is acquired a posteriori. The exception concerns international legal status of individuals in the context of international crimes and fundamental human rights, two areas of international law generally considered to be related to the broader category of peremptory norms.[6] In line with the individualistic conception and its substantiation in legal practice, there is a rebuttable presumption that individuals possess personality in international law when international crimes and basic human rights are concerned. By implication, as a matter of fundamental legal principle, individuals are a priori international persons in this limited context. It follows that there is no need to separately establish whether international crimes bind individual human beings: they automatically do so on the basis of legal principle without a statutory provision or customary practice necessarily indicating so.[7] This holds true irrespective of whether individuals act on behalf of a state or in a private capacity; it is just a matter of them being individual human beings and as such under an obligation to respect fundamental international norms.[8] Similarly, where fundamental human rights are concerned, it is presumed that they directly confer rights upon individuals without having to establish their direct application in a single instance.[9] The same

[6] For the link between peremptory norms and international crimes see e.g. *Prosecutor* v. *Furundzija* (Judgment), ICTY Trial Chamber Case IT-95-17/1-T, 10 December 1998, para. 155, and commentary to Chapter III ARSIWA in YILC 2001-II(2), pp. 110–11. For the link between *ius cogens* and human rights see e.g *Al-Adsani* v. *United Kingdom* (Grand Chamber, Judgment), ECHR Reports 2001-XI, paras 59–61.

[7] See the Nuremberg principle (*Principles of International Law recognized in the Charter of the Nürnberg Tribunal and in the Judgment of the Tribunal, with commentaries*, UN Doc. A/13/16, YILC 1950-II, p. 374) and its invocation in e.g. *Prosecutor* v. *Tadic* (Jurisdiction), ICTY Trial Chamber Case IT-94-1, 10 August 1995, para. 70, and *Prosecutor* v. *Furundzija*, para. 140 and para. 169.

[8] See e.g. *Kadic* v. *Karadzic II* (US Court of Appeals, Second Circuit, 1995), 104 ILR 135, at 153.

[9] See also Caflisch and Cançado Trindade, 'Conventions Américaine et Européenne', at 33.

presumption may hold true, as practical manifestations of the individualistic conception indicate, for other legal persons of municipal law insofar as there are no logical reasons precluding analogy with individual human beings.[10] Of course, the presumption for individuals in these contexts does not imply that other entities like states or international organizations are excluded from the scope of international criminal law and human rights law: the latter collective entities are international persons in this area whenever the application of these norms towards them is established a posteriori.[11] But on a level of legal principle, the a priori holders of rights and duties in this limited area are individual human beings. Therefore, whenever such a universal norm is concerned, its application towards individuals (and, arguably, municipal legal persons where analogy is not precluded on logical grounds) automatically follows without further examination of the principle's personal scope. The relevant task for the international lawyer is then to determine the status of the norm in question, and not whether it applies to individuals.

An effect of considering states natural international persons has been a tendency in the states-only and recognition conception to identify the consequences of international personality with those of statehood. It has been asserted that one of the implications of being an international person is the capacity to take part in the creation of international law. However, as submitted above, the assumptions on which these conceptions rest have been discarded in contemporary international law. Accordingly, there is no sound reason for declaring the state a natural international person and for identifying the consequences of personality in international law with those of being a state. In the present framework, international personality of states is thus not considered to be natural, but to exist a posteriori reflecting international norms addressed to them. By implication, there is no rationale for identifying the consequences attached to international personality with the rights, duties and capacities of states. In particular, enjoying international personality cannot imply the capacity to create international law: such capacity is conferred

[10] See e.g. *Presbyterian Church of Sudan* v. *Talisman Energy, Inc.* (US District Court for the Southern District of New York, 2003), 244 F.Supp.2d 289, at 319.

[11] See also *Case concerning the Application of the Convention on the Prevention and Punishment of the Crime of Genocide* (Bosnia and Herzegovina v. Serbia and Montenegro), Judgment, ICJ 26 February 2007, paras 170–9. With respect to human rights, states, apart from having obligations under these norms, also hold contractual and customary rights against other states in this respect. But such rights have to be established and are not presumed.

upon states and specific entities through a principle of international law to this effect, and is not a consequence of being an international person.[12] Of course, the question arises in this framework where this legal principle authorizing an entity to create international law would come from. Combining the individualistic and formal conceptions, the answer must be that at least some fundamental legal principles precede the existence of states as international persons. With the acceptance of legal principles as sources of international law existing independently of expressions of state will, the circularity in international law between norms and legal persons is interjected. The starting-point is then not anymore an original international person enjoying absolute powers, but rather a set of legal principles endowing states and other entities with specific capacities in international law, including that of creating the law.

The only consequence directly stemming from international personality is the capacity to invoke international responsibility and to be held internationally responsible. It is particularly clear from the origins and manifestations of the individualistic conception, especially in the context of international crimes, that the notion of international personality is closely related to the concept of international responsibility.[13] Today, it is generally agreed that international responsibility is 'in essence a ... question inseparable from that of legal personality in all its forms'.[14] This close link finds a basis in the distinction between primary and secondary rules, which informs the law of international responsibility:[15] whereas primary rules define the specific international rights and duties of relevant entities, secondary rules concern the consequences of non-fulfilment of the former. By implication, in order to apply secondary norms, there must be non-fulfilment of a primary norm; and such non-fulfilment in turn depends on whether a specific entity possesses international personality with regard to this primary norm. In a sense, thus, the notion of international personality represents the link between primary and secondary international rules: the application of the latter depends on whether an entity is an international person in the context of the former. Without personality, there can neither be a breach of a primary norm nor can an entity become the legal victim of such a breach;

[12] See also Brownlie, *Principles*, 3. [13] E.g. *Prosecutor* v. *Furundzija*, para. 140.

[14] Brownlie, *Principles*, 419. See also Crawford and Olleson, 'International Responsibility', at 452, and commentary to Article 1 ARSIWA in YILC 2001-II(2), p. 34.

[15] For the distinction between primary and secondary obligations see Ago, Roberto (Special Rapporteur), *Second Report on State Responsibility*, ILC 1970, UN Doc. A/CN.4/233, YILC 1970-II, p. 179. See also commentary to ARSIWA in YILC 2001-II(2), p. 31.

international responsibility hence presupposes international personality. However, the consequence of personality is only that the general system of secondary norms applies in the case of an internationally wrongful act; by contrast, which concrete secondary rules are pertinent in a specific context has to be determined on the basis of norm interpretation.[16] Obviously, most of these secondary norms have developed historically with regard to states and it is questionable to what extent there exists a general international law of responsibility. Equally, it may be difficult to rely on analogy in this area.[17] However, the principle put forward here is that to the extent such general secondary rules exist or that analogy is possible, the application of such norms is a consequence of international personality of the entities concerned.

It is convenient to summarize the basic principles for personality in international law, which follow from a combination of the formal and individualistic conception:

(1) International law is an open system. No entities are a priori excluded from it.
(2) International personality follows from an international norm addressing an entity. It is thus acquired a posteriori through interpretation of specific norms. In case of treaty norms, normal rules of treaty interpretation apply. In principle, there is no a priori international person.
(3) Special considerations apply when international crimes and fundamental human rights are concerned. In this context related to the category of peremptory norms, there is a presumption that these basic principles directly apply to individual human beings, irrespective of them acting in official or private capacity. In this limited sense, individuals are a priori international persons. Where analogy between individuals and legal persons of municipal law is not

[16] This is the crucial distinction between the present principle and *Reparation for Injuries*. In the latter, the consequence attached to international personality (which was established on the basis of recognition) was the capacity to bring international claims as understood in customary international law, without examining this particular customary norm and to what extent it was applicable to non-state entities (see *Reparation for Injuries suffered in the service of the United Nations* (Advisory Opinion), 1949 ICJ Reports 174, at 177). By contrast, the principle outlined here only suggests that the system of secondary norms applies, without indicating which customary rules or principles are precisely pertinent. The latter is to be determined on the basis of interpreting the secondary norms and is not a direct consequence of personality.

[17] Crawford and Olleson, 'International Responsibility', at 453.

precluded on grounds of logic, the presumption arguably holds true for the latter. The legal status of states and other public entities in this context is established according to regular principles.

(4) Recognition is neither a necessary nor a sufficient condition for acquiring international personality. However, it has considerable evidential value when interpreting the personal scope of specific norms, especially those of a customary nature. A similar function is exerted by effective actor status.

(5) The only direct consequence of possessing personality in international law is the capacity to invoke responsibility and to be held responsible for internationally wrongful acts (as far as applicable secondary rules exist). There is no further consequence of personality; in particular, there is no inherent capacity to create law.

Application of these principles leads to the conclusion that, in most instances, states and international organizations are addressed by international norms and as such are international persons. But the important point is that they are not natural legal persons in this framework, and therefore there is no reason to state a presumption for them or against other entities being international persons. Personality is never normal or exceptional in the present framework, it is just a matter of norm interpretation according to general rules. Except for the case of individuals in the context of international crimes and fundamental human rights, there is no sound legal basis for invoking presumptions as to the personal scope of international law. The system is open: this is the most basic principle of this framework.

Implications for particular legal issues

It is now possible to briefly indicate the practical implications of the basic principles enunciated above. This is done by applying them to the four legal issues enumerated at the outset of this book, namely (a) the direct application of treaties to individuals, (b) the capacities of international organizations, (c) the rights and duties of non-state actors under customary international law, and (d) the law applicable to state contracts.

(a) The direct effect of treaties upon individuals (or other municipal legal persons) is affirmed in the present framework whenever this follows from interpreting the relevant provision according to general rules of treaty interpretation.[18] In this process, there is neither a presumption

[18] The latter are codified in Articles 31–33 VCLT.

against direct application to be rebutted, nor is there a presumption for direct effect to be maintained: there is no presumed personal scope of an international treaty norm. It follows that the relevant authoritative statements in this area are *LaGrand* and *Avena*.[19] By contrast, it is mistaken to treat the matter in the sense of *Jurisdiction of the Courts of Danzig*, where, arguably, a (finally rebutted) presumption against the direct effect of treaties was articulated before entering the actual examination.[20] Similarly, it is not necessary to separate a treaty from general international law in order to make it directly applicable, an approach defining European Community law in the tradition of *Van Gend en Loos*[21] and sometimes present in international human rights law. As a matter of general international law, international treaties have direct effect upon individuals whenever the provision in question so indicates, and there is no reason to treat direct effect as an exceptional case calling for special considerations. Applying this principle, it seems that there are a considerable number of treaties, e.g. in the area of investment protection, which confer direct rights and duties upon individuals. In this sense, it also seems no longer possible to adhere to the *Mavrommatis*-formula: by exerting diplomatic protection, a state may also assert treaty rights directly held by individuals.[22]

(b) According to the principles enunciated above, international organizations are international persons to the extent that they are addressed by international norms. Such norms include the constitutive charter, other international treaties and general international law as applicable. It follows that international organizations are not international persons on the basis of objective criteria, although fulfilment of the latter may influence the interpretation of the above legal instruments.[23] Similarly, explicit or implied recognition of international personality may have considerable evidential value, but it does not in itself have direct legal

[19] *LaGrand Case* (Germany v. United States), Judgment, 2001 ICJ Reports 466, para. 77; *Case Concerning Avena and Other Mexican Nationals* (Mexico v. United States), 2004 ICJ Reports 12, para. 40. See also commentary to Article 33(2) ARSIWA in YILC-2001 (2), p. 95.

[20] *Jurisdiction of the Courts of Danzig* (Advisory Opinion), 1928 PCIJ Series B No. 15, at 17–18.

[21] *Van Gend en Loos* v. *Netherlands Inland Revenue Administration*, Case 26/62, 1963 ECR 1, at 12.

[22] See also *Draft Articles on Diplomatic Protection with commentaries*, ILC 2006, UN Doc. A/61/10, pp. 25–6.

[23] *Contra*: *Maclaine Watson & Company Limited* v. *Council and Commission of the European Communities* (Advocate-General's Opinion), 1990 ECR I-01797, paras 134–6.

implications. Accordingly, in the present framework, international personality only reflects those explicit and implied powers conferred upon an international organization by international norms. In this area, the organization holds rights, duties and capacities separate from its members and opposable to non-membes as well as to other entities. Consequently, the organization is internationally responsible and can invoke responsibility in this limited context. However, there are no additional consequences to be inferred from personality with respect to responsibility. The capacity to invoke a particular form of an international claim, e.g., a diplomatic protest, is not an effect of personality. This can only be the result of an applicable secondary norm. By implication, there seems to be no merit in the reasoning of the ICJ in the *Reparation for Injuries* opinion wherein such specific capacities were arguably determined on the basis of personality and the latter established by relying on recognition.[24] Personality only indicates that the system of secondary norms is applicable, but it has to be separately established which norms of this system are pertinent in a specific legal situation. Likewise, according to the principles outlined above and unlike the reasoning in the *Tin Council* cases,[25] when an international organization is held responsible, there is no (rebuttable) presumption stemming from personality that members of the organization are not liable. Again, such a presumption would have to be inferred from statutory or customary rules to this effect, and not from personality itself. Certainly, such a customary principle is presently emerging,[26] but it seems mistaken to directly derive it from personality. Finally, in the present framework, there can be no automatic application of general international law to an international organization simply because it is an international actor.[27] Although the latter status may have evidential value when determining

[24] *Reparation for Injuries suffered in the service of the United Nations* (Advisory Opinion), 1949 ICJ Reports 174, esp. at 177.

[25] *Maclaine Watson & Co Ltd* v. *Department of Trade and Industry; J. H. Rayner (Mincing Lane)* v. *Department of Trade and Industry and Others* (England, Court of Appeal, 1988), 80 ILR 49, at 109 (Kerr, LJ).

[26] See Draft Article 29(1) on Responsibility of International Organizations with commentary (*Report of the International Law Commission: Fifty-eight Session*, ILC 2006, UN Doc. A/61/10, at 286–91).

[27] *Contra*: *Dr. Horst Reineccius, First Eagle SoGen Funds, Inc., Mr. Pierre Mathier and La Société de Concours Hippique de la Châtre*, v. *Bank for International Settlements* (Partial Award on the Lawfulness of the Recall of the Privately Held Shares on 8 January 2001 and the Applicable Standards for Valuation of those Shares, Permanent Court of Arbitration, 2002), 15 World Trade and Arbitration Materials 73, para. 150.

the application of such norms, it nevertheless has to be established by thoroughly interpreting the personal scope of the norm or regime in question.

(c) Rights and duties of so-called non-state actors under general international law are not a priori excluded in the present framework. With one exception, such rights and duties are, however, not presumed to exist. It is important to distinguish two categories in this respect: ordinary customary norms and fundamental principles of the international legal order related to *ius cogens*. In the former case, while there is no presumption against non-state actors, there is also no presumption for them having international rights and duties. In this context, it all depends on interpreting the personal scope of the norm in question. As the example of the ICRC illustrates, recognition as an international person (or, for that matter, effective power in international relations) can play a significant role in this process, although without having direct legal effect.[28] In general, it may often be difficult to find convincing arguments for the application of such ordinary custom to non-state actors, for they have historically developed in relation to states and analogy may be delicate. With respect to international crimes and fundamental human rights, however, the matter must be approached differently. In this context, there is a presumption for their direct application towards individuals. In so far as analogy with individual human beings is not precluded on logical grounds, this also holds true for other non-state actors, for example private corporations.[29] Accordingly, when international crimes are concerned, there is a presumption that they impose direct international duties upon individuals and analogous non-state actors, irrespective of whether they act in a private or public capacity.[30] Likewise, in the context of fundamental human rights, it is presumed that they confer direct rights upon individuals and, possibly, other entities where analogy is not precluded. In the limited context of fundamental international principles that form part of *ius cogens*, private parties presumably have international rights and duties. In all other areas of

[28] *Prosecutor* v. *Simic et al.* (Decision on the Prosecution Motion under Rule 73 for a Ruling concerning the Testimony of a Witness), ICTY Trial Chamber 27 July 1999, esp. para. 46. However, in terms of the present framework, the trial chamber seems to have overstated the effect of recognition.

[29] See also *Presbyterian Church of Sudan* v. *Talisman Energy, Inc.* (US District Court for the Southern District of New York, 2003), 244 F.Supp.2d 289, at 319.

[30] See also *Kadic* v. *Karadzic II* (US Court of Appeals, Second Circuit, 1995) (Chief Judge Newman), 104 ILR 135, at 153.

customary law, however, the system is open without there being any presumption.

(d) Contrary to the *Serbian Loans* statement,[31] there are no principled reservations against applying international law to state contracts. At the same time, international law cannot automatically be imposed on such contracts.[32] Neither does recognition of the private party as an international person have a specific effect on the proper law.[33] The only way for international law to govern the contract – apart from the parties so choosing – is on the basis of an international norm so stipulating. Such a norm is represented, for example, by Article 42(1) ICSID Convention. In a sense, whenever such a provision is applicable to a legal situation, it indirectly confers international rights and duties – and therefore a posteriori personality – upon the parties to the contract, and there is no sound legal reason why these international norms should be only restrictively applied.[34] It follows that international law can govern state contracts whenever an overriding treaty or statutory provision so indicates. In that case, international law fully applies. On the other hand, according to the basic principles enunciated above, there is no reason to apply international law if no treaty or statutory norm, or the will of the parties, so requires.

[31] *Case Concerning the Payments of Various Serbian Loans Issued in France* (Judgment), 1929 PCIJ Series A No. 20, at 41–2.

[32] *Contra*: *Sandline International Inc.* v. *Papua New Guinea* (Interim Award, 1998), 117 ILR 552, para. 10.1.

[33] *Contra*: *Texaco Overseas Petroleum Company and California Asiatic Oil Company* v. *The Government of the Libyan Arab Republic* (Award on the Merits, Sole Arbitrator Dupuy, 1977), 53 ILR 422, paras 47–8.

[34] See *Amco Asia Corporation and Others v. The Republic of Indonesia* (Resubmitted Case: Award on the Merits, 1990), 1 ICSID Reports 569, para. 40.

Conclusion

This book argues that there are five conceptions of personality in modern international legal argument. These conceptions consider different entities to be international persons, state different criteria as to how to become one, and attach different consequences to being one. Deliberately, it has not been attempted to examine in depth which of these conceptions find direct support in international doctrine and practice – all of them do to some extent. The present book has rather ventured to engage with the five conceptions by spelling out the original assumptions on which they rest and by examining how they were manifested as well as substantiated in legal practice. The assumptions so derived mainly concern particular views on the nature of statehood, the link between individual freedom and state power, the sources of international law and the relationship between social facts and legal norms. The specific assumptions on these matters could then be related to the respective positions in contemporary international law.

The main insight of this analysis is that conceptions which put overwhelming emphasis on the role of states or effective actors in the international legal system rely on assumptions that have been discarded in present international law: the state is not considered a historical fact, but a legal status; individual freedom is not regarded best preserved inside the state, but by making it a concern for the international community as a whole; international law is not only particular or a mere decision-making process, but includes rules and principles of a general nature; and factual developments do not have direct legal value, but have to be transformed into law through a principled justification. For international law to be a consistent system of law, it is not possible to apply such conceptions whose underlying assumptions are at odds with basic premises of the contemporary international legal order. By contrast, conceptions stressing the role of individuals and of fundamental legal principles in the international legal system and insisting on a strictly legal construction of personality find support in international law with regard to their original assumptions. It is therefore according to them that a frame of reference for international personality was outlined.

The main point of this framework is that international law is an open system from which no entity is a priori excluded. Equally, there can be no natural or primary as opposed to derived or secondary international persons. International personality is an a posteriori concept simply reflecting those international norms directed at a specific entity. Thus, the personal scope of an international rule, with the exception of certain fundamental principles in which there is a presumed personality of individuals, is determined according to general rules of interpretation without starting from a particular presumption. In this process, recognition of international legal status may have considerable evidential value, but is not in itself necessary or sufficient for constituting personality in international law; similar considerations apply with respect to effective actor status. It ensues that the sole consequence of being an international person is to be able to invoke international responsibility and to be held internationally responsible as far as applicable secondary rules exist. Crucially, it is not a consequence of personality to have the capacity to create international law.

True, such a framework for personality offers very little normative content. But this minimal approach seems to be best prepared for reconciling the concept of personality with the international legal system as a whole. The main point of this framework is to make clear that there are at present no sound legal reasons to restrict the personal scope of international law a priori. At the same time, the inclusion into the legal system cannot depend solely on actual power, but must be a matter of legal norms and principles. With certain exceptions, there is no more to declare in a framework for personality in international law than that the system is open and that inclusion depends on legal norms to this effect. This may not amount to much, but perhaps this is one of those instances in which less is more. For the less the concept of personality is employed to a priori exclude social entities from the international legal system or to declare automatic legal consequences, the more the international law of persons conforms with the basic premises of the contemporary international legal order.

BIBLIOGRAPHY

Ago, Roberto, 'Positive Law and International Law', *AJIL*, 51 (1957), 691–733 ['Positive Law']

Akande, Dapo, 'International Organizations' in Malcolm D. Evans (ed.), *International Law*, 2nd edition (Oxford University Press, 2006) 277–305 ['International Organizations']

Alvarez, Alejandro, *La Codification du Droit International: Ses Tendances – Ses Bases* (Paris: A. Pedone, 1912) [*Codification*]

Anzilotti, Dionisio, 'La condizione giuridica internazionale della Santa Sede in seguito agli accordi del Laterano', *Rdi*, 9 (1929), 165–76 ['Santa Sede']

Lehrbuch des Völkerrechts, translation of the 3rd edition (Berlin and Leipzig: Walter de Gruyter, 1929) [*Völkerrecht*]

'Teoria Generale della Responsibilità dello Stato nel Diritto Internazionale' in Società Italiana per l'Organizzazione Internazionale (ed.), *Opere di Dionisio Anzilotti: Scritti di diritto internazionale pubblico* (Padova: Cedam, 1955) (originally published 1902), 1–147. [*Responsibilità*]

'Il diritto internazionale nei giudizi interni' in Società Italiana per l'Organizzazione Internazionale (ed.), *Opere di Dionisio Anzilotti: Scritti di diritto internazionale pubblico* (Padova: Cedam, 1955) (originally published 1905), 281–539 [*Giudizi interni*]

'Corso di Diritto Internazionale' in Società Italiana per l'Organizzazione Internazionale (ed.), *Opere di Dionisio Anzilotti* (Padova: Cedam, 1955) (originally published 1928) ['Corso']

'Notion et Fondement de la Responsabilité Internationale des États à Raison des Dommages Soufferts par des Étrangers' in Società Italiana per l'Organizzazione Internazionale (ed.), *Opere di Dionisio Anzilotti: Scritti di diritto internazionale pubblico* (Padua: Cedam, 1956) (originally published 1906), 149–207 ['Responsabilité des États à Raison des Dommages Soufferts par des Étrangers']

Arangio-Ruiz, Gaetano, *Diritto Internazionale e Personalità Giuridica* (Bologna: Cooperativa Libraria Universitaria, 1972) [*Personalità Giuridica*]

Arnaud, André-Jean, *Les juristes face à la société du XIXème siècle à nos jours* (Paris: Presses Universitaires de France, 1975) [*Les juristes*]

Austin, John, *The Province of Jurisprudence Determined*. 'Cambridge Texts in the History of Political Thought' (Wilfrid D. Rumble, ed.) (Cambridge University Press, 1995) (originally published 1832) [*Province of Jurisprudence*]

Balladore Pallieri, Giorgio, *Diritto Internazionale Pubblico*, 5th edition (Milano: Giuffré, 1948) [*Diritto Internazionale*]

Barberis, Julio A., 'Nouvelles Questions Conçernant la Personnalité Juridique Internationale', *RCADI*, 179 (1983-I), 145–304 ['Personnalité Juridique']

Beaulac, Stéphane, *The Power of Language in the Making of International Law: The Word Sovereignty in Bodin and Vattel and the Myth of Westphalia* (Leiden/Boston: Martinus Nijhoff, 2004) [*Making of International Law*]

Beckett, W. E., 'Decisions of the Permanent Court of International Justice on Points of Law and Procedure of General Application', *BYIL*, 11 (1930) 1–54 ['Decisions of the PCIJ']

Bederman, David J., 'The Unique Legal Status of the Bank for International Settlements Comes into Focus', *Leiden Journal of International Law*, 16 (2003) 787–94 ['Unique Legal Status of the BIS']

Bentham, Jeremy, *An Introduction to the Principles of Morals and Legislation* (Kitchener: Batoche Books, 2000) (originally published 1781) [*Principles of Morals and Legislation*]

Bergbohm, Carl, *Staatsverträge und Gesetze als Quellen des Völkerrechts* (Dorpat: C. Mattiesen, 1877) [*Staatsverträge*]

Berlin, Isaiah, 'Does Political Theory Still Exist?' in Henry Hardy and Roger Hausherr (eds.), *The Proper Study of Mankind: An Anthology of Essays* (New York: Farrar, Strauss and Giroux, 2000), 59–90 ['Political Theory']

Bernstorff, Jochen von, 'Georg Jellinek – Völkerrecht als modernes öffentliches Recht im fin de siècle' in Stanley L. Paulson and Martin Schulte (eds.), *Georg Jellinek: Beiträge zu Leben und Werk* (Tübingen: Mohr Siebeck, 2000), 183–206 ['Völkerrecht als modernes öffentliches Recht']

Binding, Karl, 'Die Gründung des Norddeutschen Bundes' in Leipziger Juristenfakultät (ed.), *Festgabe für Dr. Bernhard Windscheid* (Leipzig: Duncker und Humblot, 1888), 3–72 ['Gründung des Norddeutschen Bundes']

Bindschedler, Rudolf L., 'Die Anerkennung im Völkerrecht', *AVR*, 9 (1961–62), 377–97 ['Anerkennung']

Bindschedler-Robert, Denise, 'Red Cross', *EPIL*, 4 (2003) 56–63 ['Red Cross']

Bluntschli, Johan Caspar, *Das moderne Völkerrecht der civilisierten Staaten: als Rechtsbuch dargestellt*, 3rd revised edition (Nördlingen: C.H. Beck, 1878) [*Das moderne Völkerrecht*]

Bobbio, Norberto, 'Trends in Italian Legal Theory', *American Journal of Comparative Law*, 8 (1959), 329–40 ['Italian Legal Theory']

Boucher, David and Paul Kelly, 'The Social Contract and its Critics: An Overview' in David Boucher and Paul Kelly (eds.), *The Social Contract from Hobbes to Rawls* (London/New York: Routledge, 1994), 1–34 ['Social Contract']

Bourquin, Maurice, 'Règles Générales du Droit de la Paix', *RCADI*, 35 (1931-I), 5–232 ['Règles Générales']

Bowett, Derek William, *The Law of International Institutions*, 4th edition (London: Stevens, 1982) [*International Institutions*]

'State Contracts with Aliens: Contemporary Developments on Compensation for Termination or Breach', *BYIL*, 59 (1988), 49–74 ['State Contracts']

Breycha-Vauthier, Arthur C. and Michael Potulicki, 'The Order of St. John in International Law: A Forerunner of the Red Cross', *AJIL*, 48 (1954), 554–63 ['Order of St. John']

Brierly, James Leslie, 'Règles Générales du Droit de la Paix', *RCADI*, 58 (1936-IV), 1–242 ['Règles Générales']

'The Covenant and the Charter', *BYIL*, 23 (1946), 83–94 ['Covenant']

Brownlie, Ian, 'The Place of the Individual in International Law', *Virginia Law Review*, 50 (1964), 435–62 ['Individual']

'Legal Status of Natural Resources in International Law (Some Aspects)', *RCADI*, 162 (1979-I), 245–318 ['Natural Resources']

Treaties and Indigenous Peoples: The Robb Lectures 1991 (Oxford: The Clarendon Press, 1992) [*Treaties and Indigenous Peoples*]

Principles of Public International Law, 6th edition (Oxford University Press 2003) [*Principles*]

Bugnion, François, *Le Comité international de la Croix-Rouge et la protection des victimes de la guerre*, 2nd edition (Geneva: Comité international de la Croix-Rouge, 2000) [*Le Comité international de la Croix-Rouge*]

Burley, Anne-Marie, 'The Alien Tort Statute and the Judiciary Act of 1789: A Badge of Honor', *AJIL*, 83 (1989), 461–93 ['Alien Tort Statute']

Byers, Michael, 'Conceptualising the Relationship between Jus Cogens and Erga Omnes Rules', *NJIL*, 66 (1997), 211–39 ['Jus Cogens and Erga Omnes Rules']

Custom, Power and the Power of Rules: International Relations and Customary International Law (Cambridge University Press, 1999) [*Custom*]

Caflisch, Lucius and Antonio Augusto Cançado Trindade, 'Les Conventions Américaine et Européenne des Droits de l'Homme et le Droit International Général', *RGDIP*, CVIII (2004), 5–62 ['Conventions Américaine et Européenne']

Cançado Trindade, Antônio Augusto, 'International Law for Humankind: Towards a New Jus Gentium: General Course on Public International Law', *RCADI*, 316–17 (2005) 9–440 (Vol. 316) and 9–312 (Vol. 317) ['General Course']

Caron, François, *Geschichte Frankreichs Band 5: Frankreich im Zeitalter des Imperialismus 1851–1918* (Stuttgart: Deutsche Verlags-Anstalt, 1991) [*Geschichte Frankreichs (V)*]

Carr, E. H., *The Twenty Years' Crisis*, reissue of the 2nd edition (New York: Palgrave, 2001) (originally published 1939) [*Twenty Years' Crisis*]

Carty, Anthony, 'Why Theory? – The Implications for International Law Teaching' in Philip Allott, Anthony Carty, Martti Koskenniemi and Colin Warbrick (eds.), *Theory and International Law: An Introduction* (London: British Institute of International and Comparative Law, 1991), 75–104 ['Why Theory?']

Cassese, Antonio, *International Law* (Oxford University Press, 2001) [*International Law*]

International Criminal Law, 1st edition (Oxford University Press, 2003) [*International Criminal Law*]

Cavaglieri, Arrigo, 'La Conception Positive de la Société Internationale', *RGDIP*, XVIII (1911) 259–92 ['Conception Positive']

'I soggetti del diritto internazionale', *Rdi*, 20 (1925), 18–32, 169–87 ['Soggetti']

'Règles Générales du Droit de la Paix', *RCADI*, 26 (1929-I), 315–585 ['Règles Générales']

Clapham, Andrew, *Human Rights Obligations of Non-State Actors* (Oxford University Press, 2006) [*Non-State Actors*]

Collingwood, R. G., *An Autobiography* (Oxford University Press, 1939) [*Autobiography*]

Comte, Auguste, *Cours de Philosophie Positive. Tome Quatrième et Dernier: La Philosophie Sociale et les Conclusions Générales*, 1st edition (Paris: Bachelier, 1839) [*Philosophie Positive*]

Cosnard, Michel, 'Rapport Introductif' in Société Française pour le Droit International (ed.), *Colloque du Mans: Le Sujet en Droit International* (Paris: Editions A. Pedone, 2005), 13–53 ['Rapport']

Cot, Jean-Pierre, 'Tableau de la Pensée Juridique Américaine', *RGDIP*, 110 (2006), 537–96 ['Pensée Juridique Américaine']

Crawford, James R., *International Law as an Open System: Selected Essays* (London: Cameron May, 2002) [*Open System*]

'The ILC's Articles on Responsibility of States for Internationally Wrongful Acts: A Retrospect', *AJIL*, 96 (2002), 874–90 ['The ILC's Articles on Responsibility of States']

'Public International Law in Twentieth-Century England' in Jack Beatson and Reinhard Zimmermann (eds.), *Jurists Uprooted: German-Speaking Emigré Lawyers in Twentieth Century Britain* (Oxford University Press, 2004), 681–707 ['International Law in Twentieth-century England']

The Creation of States in International Law, 2nd edition (Oxford University Press, 2006) [*Creation of States*]

Crawford, James R. and Simon Olleson, 'The Nature and Forms of International Responsibility' in Malcolm D. Evans (ed.), *International Law*, 2nd edition (Oxford University Press, 2006), 451–77 ['International Responsibility']

Currie, John, *Public International Law* (Toronto: Irwin Law, 2001) [*International Law*]

Daillier, Patrick and Alain Pellet, *Droit International Public*, 5th edition (Paris: L.G.D.J., 1994) [*Droit International* (5th edn.)]

Droit International Public, 6th edition (Paris: L.G.D.J., 1999) [*Droit International* (6th edn.)]

Danilenko, Gennady M., 'The Theory of International Customary Law', *German Yearbook of International Law*, 31 (1988), 9–51 ['International Customary Law']

Dewey, John, 'Logical Method and Law', *Philosophical Review*, 33 (1924), 560–72 ['Logical Method']

Dickinson, Edwin D., 'Changing Concepts and the Doctrine of Incorporation', *AJIL*, 26 (1932), 239–60 ['Changing Concepts']

Diena, Giulio, 'La Sante Sede e il diritto internazionale dopo gli accordi Lateranensi dell'11 febbraio 1929', *Rdi*, 9 (1929), 177–87 ['Santa Sede']

Diggelmann, Oliver, *Anfänge der Völkerrechtssoziologie: Die Völkerrechtskonzeptionen von Max Huber und Georges Scelle im Vergleich* (Zürich: Schulthess, 2000) [*Völkerrechtssoziologie*]

Doehring, Karl, *Völkerrecht*, 2nd edition (Heidelberg: C.F. Müller, 2004) [*Völkerrecht*]

Dominicé, Christian, 'La personnalité juridique internationale du CICR' in Christophe Swinarski (ed.), *Études et essais sur le droit international humanitaire et sur les principes de la Croix-Rouge en l'honneur de Jean Pictet* (Geneva and The Hague: Martinus Nijhoff, 1984), 663–73 ['CICR']

Dreier, Horst, *Rechtslehre, Staatssoziologie und Demokratietheorie bei Hans Kelsen* (Baden-Baden: Nomos, 1986) [*Rechtslehre*]

Dugard, John, *Recognition and the United Nations* (Cambridge: Grotius, 1987) [*Recognition*]

Duguit, Léon, *Études de Droit Public I: L'État: Le Droit Objectif et la Loi Positive* (Paris: Albert Fontemoing, 1901) [*Études de Droit Public (I)*]

'The Law and the State', *HLR*, 31 (1917), 1–185 ['Law and the State']

Traité de Droit Constitutionnel, 2nd edition (Paris: E. de Boccard, 1921) [*Traité*]

Traité de Droit Constitutionnel, 3rd edition (Paris: E. de Boccard, 1927) [*Traité* (3rd edn.)]

Dumberry, Patrick, 'L'Entreprise, Sujet de Droit International? Retour sur la Question à la Lumière des Développements Récents du Droit International des Investissements', *RGDIP*, CVIII (2004), 103–21 ['L'Entreprise, Sujet du Droit International?']

Dunoff, Jeffrey L., 'Why Constitutionalism Now? Text, Context and the Historical Contingency of Ideas', *Journal of International Law and International Relations*, 1 (2005), 191–212 ['Constitutionalism']

Durkheim, Emile, *De la Division du Travail Social*, 8th edition (Paris: Presses Universitaires, 1967) (originally published 1893) [*Division du Travail*]

Dworkin, Ronald, *Taking Rights Seriously* (London: Duckworth, 1977) [*Taking Rights Seriously*]

Eulau, Heinz, 'The Depersonalization of the Concept of Sovereignty', *Journal of Politics*, 4 (1942) 3–19 ['Depersonalization']

Falk, Richard A., 'Casting the Spell: The New Haven School of International Law', *YLJ*, 104 (1995), 1991–2008 ['New Haven School']

Fatouros, A. A., 'International Law and the Internationalized Contract', *AJIL*, 74 (1980), 134–41 ['Internationalized Contract']

Fikentscher, Wolfgang, *Methoden des Rechts in vergleichender Darstellung Band I: Frühe und Religiöse Rechte, Romanischer Rechtskreis* (Tübingen: J.C.B. Mohr (Paul Siebeck), 1975) [*Methoden des Rechts (I)*]

Fiore, Pasquale, *Trattato di Diritto Internazionale Pubblico*, 3rd edition (Turin: Unione Tipografico-Editrice, 1887) [*Diritto Internazionale*]

Fisch, M. H., 'Justice Holmes, the Prediction Theory of Law, and Pragmatism', *Philosophical Review*, 39 (1942), 85–97 ['Justice Holmes']

Fischer, Kurt Rudolf, 'Zur Theorie des Wiener Fin de Siècle' in Jürgen Nautz and Richard Vahrenkamp (eds.), *Die Wiener Jahrhundertwende* (Vienna: Böhlau, 1993), 110–27 ['Wiener Fin de siècle']

Fitzmaurice, Gerald, 'The Law and Procedure of the International Court of Justice: International Organizations and Tribunals', *BYIL*, 29 (1952), 1–62 ['Law and Procedure']

Frei, Christoph, *Hans J. Morgenthau: Eine intellektuelle Biographie* (Berne/ Stuttgart/Vienna: Paul Haupt, 1993) [*Morgenthau*]

Friedmann, Wolfgang, *The Changing Structure of International Law* (London: Stevens & Sons, 1964) [*Changing Structure*]

Friedrich, Manfred, 'Der Methoden- und Richtungsstreit: Zur Grundlagendiskussion der Weimarer Staatsrechtslehre', *AöR*, 102 (1977), 161–209 ['Methoden- und Richtungsstreit']

Fusinato, Guido, 'La Personalità Giuridica dell'Istituto Internazionale d'Agricoltura', *Rdi*, 8 (1914), 149–55 ['Istituto Internazionale d'Agricoltura']

Gaja, Giorgio, 'Positivism and Dualism in Dionisio Anzilotti', *EJIL*, 3 (1992), 123–38 ['Positivism and Dualism']

Gallie, W. B., 'Essentially Contested Concepts', *Proceedings of the Aristotelian Society*, 56 (1956), 167–98 ['Essentially Contested Concepts']

Gassner, Ulrich M., *Heinrich Triepel: Leben und Werk* (Berlin: Duncker und Humblot, 1999) [*Triepel*]

Gentili, Alberico, *De Iure Belli Libri Tres*. 'The Classics of International Law' (James Brown Scott, ed.) (Oxford: The Clarendon Press, 1933) (1598) [*De Iure Belli*]

Gerber, Carl Friedrich von, *Grundzüge des deutschen Staatsrechts*, 3rd edition (Leipzig: Bernhard Tauchnitz, 1880) [*Deutsches Staatsrecht*]

Giacometti, Zaccharia, 'Zur Lösung der Römischen Frage', *Zeitschrift für die gesamte Staatswissenschaft*, 90 (1931), 8–50 ['Römische Frage']

Grant, Thomas D., *The Recognition of States: Law and Practice in Debate and Evolution* (Westport: Praeger, 1999) [*Recognition of States*]

Greenwood, Christopher, 'State Contracts in International Law – The Libyan Oil Arbitrations', *BYIL*, 53 (1982), 27–81 ['Libyan Oil Arbitrations']

Greszick, Bernd, 'Rechte des Einzelnen im Völkerrecht: Chancen und Gefahren völkerrechtlicher Entwicklungstrends am Beispiel der Individualrechte im allgemeinen Völkerrecht', *AVR*, 43 (2005), 312–44 ['Rechte des Einzelnen']

Grewe, Wilhelm G., *Epochen der Völkerrechtsgeschichte*, 2nd edition (Baden-Baden: Nomos, 1988) [*Völkerrechtsgeschichte*]

Grey, Thomas C., 'Holmes and Legal Pragmatism', *Stanford Law Review*, 41 (1989), 787–870 ['Legal Pragmatism']

Grotius, Hugo, *De Jure Bellis ac Pacis. Libri Tre.* 'The Classics of International Law' (James Brown Scott, ed.) (Oxford: The Clarendon Press, 1925) (originally published 1625) [*De Jure Belli*]

Guggenheim, Paul, *Lehrbuch des Völkerrechts: Unter Berücksichtigung der internationalen und schweizerischen Praxis* (Basel: Verlag für Recht und Gesellschaft, 1948) [*Lehrbuch*]

Haddock, Bruce, 'Hegel's critique of the theory of social contract' in David Boucher and Paul Kelly (eds.), *The Social Contract from Hobbes to Rawls* (London/New York: Routledge, 1994), 147–63 ['Hegel's critique']

Haggenmacher, Peter, *Grotius et la Doctrine de la Guerre Juste* (Paris: Presses Universitaires de France, 1983) [*Grotius*]

'La Doctrine des Deux Éléments du Droit Coutumier dans la Pratique de la Cour Internationale', *RGDIP*, LXXXX (1986), 5–125 ['Doctrine des Deux Eléments']

Hall, Stephen, 'The Persistent Spectre: Natural Law, International Order and the Limits of Legal Positivism', *EJIL*, 12 (2001), 269–307 ['Persistent Spectre']

Haller, Rudolf, *Neopositivismus: Eine historische Einführung in die Philosophie des Wiener Kreises* (Darmstadt: Wissenschaftliche Buchgesellschaft, 1993) [*Neopositivismus*]

Hart, H. L. A., *The Concept of Law* (Oxford: Clarendon Press, 1961) [*Concept of Law*]

'American Jurisprudence through English Eyes: The Nightmare and the Noble Dream' in H. L. A. Hart (ed.), *Essays in Jurisprudence and Philosophy* (Oxford: Clarendon Press, 1983) (originally published 1977), 123–44. [*American Jurisprudence*]

Hegel, Georg Friedrich Wilhelm, *Grundlinien der Philosophie des Rechts.* 'Georg Friedrich Wilhelm Hegel: Sämtliche Werke' (Georg Lasson, ed.) (Leipzig: Felex Meiner, 1930) (originally published 1821) [*Philosophie des Rechts*]

Vorlesungen über die Philosophie der Weltgeschichte. 'Georg Friedrich Wilhelm Hegel: Sämtliche Werke' (Georg Lasson, ed.) (Leipzig: Felix Meiner, 1930) (originally published 1830) [*Philosophie der Weltgeschichte*]

Die Verfassung des deutschen Reiches: Eine politische Flugschrift (Georg Mollat, ed.) (Stuttgart: Frommanns, 1935) (originally published 1801) [*Verfassung des deutschen Reiches*]

Heilborn, Paul, *Das System des Völkerrechts entwickelt aus den völkerrechtlichen Begriffen* (Berlin: Verlag von Julius Springer, 1896) [*System des Völkerrechts*]
'Les Sources du Droit International', *RCADI*, 11 (1926-I), 1–63 ['Sources']
Herdegen, Matthias, *Völkerrecht*, 3rd edition (Munich: C.H. Beck, 2004) [*Völkerrecht*]
Higgins, Rosalyn, 'Conceptual Thinking about the Individual in International Law' in Richard Falk, Friedrich Kratochwil and Saul H. Mendlovitz (eds.), *International Law: A Contemporary Perspective* (London: Westview Press, 1985) (originally published in *British Journal of International Studies*, 4 (1978)), 476–94 ['Conceptual Thinking']
'International Law and the Avoidance, Containment and Resolution of Disputes: General Course on Public International Law', *RCADI*, 230 (1991-V), 9–342 ['General Course']
Problems and Process: International Law and How we Use it (Oxford: Clarendon Press, 1994) [*Problems and Process*]
'McDougal as Teacher, Mentor, and Friend', *YLJ*, 108 (1999) 957–60 ['McDougal']
Hobbes, Thomas, *Leviathan*. 'Cambridge Texts in the History of Political Thought' (Richard Tuck, ed.) (Cambridge University Press, 1996) (originally published 1651) [*Leviathan*]
Hoffmann, Stanley, 'An American Social Science: International Relations' in *Janus and Minerva: Essays in the Theory and Practice of International Politics* (London: Westview Press, 1987), 3–24 ['American Social Science']
Holmes, Oliver Wendell, 'The Path of the Law', *HLR*, 10 (1897), 457–78 ['Path of the Law']
Hoppe, Carsten, 'Implementation of LaGrand and Avena in Germany and the United States: Exploring a Transatlantic Divide in Search of a Uniform Interpretation of Consular Rights', *EJIL*, 18 (2007), 317–36. ['Implementation of LaGrand']
Huber, Max, *Die soziologischen Grundlagen des Völkerrechts*. 'Internationalrechtliche Abhandlungen' (Peter Klein and Herbert Kraus, eds.) (Berlin: Walther Rothschild, 1928) (originally published 1910) [*Soziologische Grundlagen*]
Hume, David, *A Treatise of Human Nature* (Oxford: Clarendon Press, 2007) (originally published 1739–40) [*Treatise*]
Ipsen, Knut, *Völkerrecht*, 5th edition (Munich: C.H. Beck, 2004) [*Völkerrecht*]
Jabloner, Clemens, 'Kelsen and his Circle: The Viennese Years', *EJIL*, 9 (1998), 368–85 ['The Viennese Years']
James, William, 'Pragmatism: A New Name for Some Old Ways of Thinking' in *William James: Writings 1902–1910* (New York: The Library of America, 1987) (originally delivered 1907), 479–624 ['Pragmatism']
'Philosophical Conceptions and Practical Results' in *William James: Writings 1878–1899* (New York: The Library of America, 1992) (originally delivered 1898), 1077–97 ['Philosophical Conceptions']

Janik, Allan and Stephen Toulmin, *Wittgenstein's Vienna* (London: Weidenfeld and Nicolson, 1973) [*Wittgenstein's Vienna*]

Jeannet, Stéphane, 'Recognition of the ICRC's Long-standing Rule of Confidentiality – An Important Decision by the International Criminal Tribunal for the Former Yugoslavia', *International Review of the Red Cross* (2000) 403–25 ['ICRC's Long-standing Rule of Confidentiality']

Jellinek, Georg, *Die rechtliche Natur der Staatenverträge: Ein Beitrag zur juristischen Construction des Völkerrechts* (Vienna: Alfred Hölder, 1880) [*Staatenverträge*]

Allgemeine Staatslehre, 3rd edition (Berlin: Julius Springer, 1921) (originally published 1900) [*Allgemeine Staatslehre*]

Jenks, Wilfried C., 'The Legal Personality of International Organizations', *BYIL*, 22 (1945), 267–75 ['Personality of International Organizations']

'Hersch Lauterpacht – The Scholar as Prophet', *BYIL*, 36 (1960), 1–103 ['Scholar as Prophet']

Jennings, Robert Y., 'State Contracts in International Law', *BYIL*, 37 (1961), 156–82 ['State Contracts']

'The LaGrand Case', *The Law and Practice of International Courts and Tribunals*, 1 (2002) 13–54 ['LaGrand']

Jennings, Robert Y. and Arthur Watts, *Oppenheim's International Law Volume I: Peace*, 9th edition (London: Longman, 1992) [*Oppenheim's International Law*]

Jessup, Philip C., 'The Subjects of a Modern Law of Nations', *Michigan Law Review*, 45 (1947), 383–408 ['Subjects']

Jones, H. S., *The French State in Question: Public Law and Political Argument in the Third Republic* (Cambridge University Press, 1993) [*French State in Question*]

Jouannet, Emmanuelle, *Emer de Vattel et l'Émergence Doctrinale du Droit International Classique* (Paris: A. Pedone, 1998) [*Vattel*]

'L'Idée de Communauté Humaine à la Croisée de la Communauté des États et de la Communauté Mondiale', *Archives de Philosophie du droit*, 47 (2003), 191–232 ['Communauté Humaine']

Kant, Immanuel, *Kritik der reinen Vernunft*, 3rd edition (Hamburg: Felix Meiner, 1990) (originally published 1781) [*KrV*]

Kritik der praktischen Vernunft, 10th edition (Hamburg: Felix Meiner, 1990) (originally published 1788) [*KpV*]

Kaufmann, Erich, *Das Wesen des Völkerrechts und die Clausula Rebus Sic Stantibus: Rechtsphilosophische Studie zum Rechts-, Staats- und Verfassungsbegriffe* (Tübingen: J.C.B Mohr (Paul Siebeck), 1911) [*Wesen*]

'Die Gleichheit vor dem Gesetz im Sinne des Art. 109 der Reichsverfassung' in Vereinigung der Deutschen Staatsrechtslehrer (ed.), *Veröffentlichungen der Vereinigung der Deutschen Staatsrechtslehrer* (Berlin and Leipzig: Walter de Gruyter & Co., 1927), 2–62 ['Gleichheit vor dem Gesetz']

Kelsen, Hans, *Hauptprobleme der Staatsrechtslehre – entwickelt aus der Lehre vom Rechtssatze* (Tübingen: J.C.B. Mohr, 1911) [*Hauptprobleme*]

'Reichsgesetz und Landesgesetz nach österreichischer Verfassung', *AöR*, 32 (1914), 202–45 ['Reichsgesetz und Landesgesetz']

Der soziologische und der juristische Staatsbegriff: Kritische Untersuchung des Verhältnisses von Staat und Recht (Tübingen: J.C.B. Mohr (Paul Siebeck), 1922) [*Staatsbegriff*]

Die philosophischen Grundlagen der Naturrechtslehre und des Rechtspositivismus. 'Philosophische Vorträge veröffentlicht von der Kant-Gesellschaft' (Paul Menzer and Arthur Liebert, eds.) (Berlin: Pan-Verlag, 1928) [*Grundlagen der Naturrechtslehre*]

Das Problem der Souveränität und die Theorie des Völkerrechts: Beitrag zu einer Reinen Rechtslehre, 2nd edition (Tübingen: J.C.B. Mohr (Paul Siebeck), 1928) (originally published 1920) [*Problem der Souveränität*]

Vom Wesen und Wert der Demokratie (Tübingen: J.C.B. Mohr, 1929) [*Demokratie*]

'La Naissance de l'État et la Formation de sa Nationalité: Les Principes et leur Application au Cas de la Tchécoslovaquie', *RDI*, 4 (1929), 613–41 ['Naissance de L'État']

'Théorie Générale du Droit International Public', *RCADI*, 42 (1932-IV), 121–351 ['Théorie (I)']

Reine Rechtslehre: Einleitung in die rechtswissenschaftliche Problematik (Leipzig and Vienna: Franz Deuticke, 1934) [*Reine Rechtslehre*]

'Recognition in International Law: Theoretical Observations', *AJIL*, 35 (1941), 605–17 ['Recognition']

General Theory of Law and State (Cambridge (Mass.): Harvard University Press, 1945) [*Law and State*]

The Law of the United Nations: A Critical Analysis of Its Fundamental Problems (London: Stevens, 1950) [*Law of the United Nations*]

'Was ist die reine Rechtslehre?' in *Demokratie und Rechtsstaat: Festgabe zum 60. Geburtstag von Zaccaria Giacometti* (Zürich: Polygraphischer Verlag, 1953), 143–62 ['Was ist die Reine Rechtslehre']

'Théorie du Droit International Public', *RCADI*, 84 (1953-III), 1–203 ['Théorie (II)']

'Zur Theorie der juristischen Fiktionen: Mit besonderer Berücksichtigung von Vaihingers Philosophie des Als-ob' in Hans Klecatsky, René Marcic and Herbert Schambeck (eds.), *Die Wiener Rechtstheoretische Schule* (Vienna: Europa Verlag, 1968) (originally published 1919), 1215–41 ['Fiktionen']

'Tribute to Sir Hersch Lauterpacht', *EJIL*, 8 (1997), 309–10 ['Lauterpacht']

Kennan, George F., *American Diplomacy 1900–1950* (Chicago: University of Chicago Press, 1951) [*American Diplomacy*]

Kennedy, David, 'Theses about International Law Discourse', *German Yearbook of International Law*, 23 (1980), 353–91 ['Theses']

'Primitive Legal Scholarship', *HILJ*, 27 (1986), 1–98 ['Primitive Legal Scholarship']

'International Law and the Nineteenth Century: History of an Illusion', *NJIL*, 65 (1996) 385–420 ['History of an Illusion']

'The Disciplines of International Law and Policy', *Leiden Journal of International Law*, 12 (1999), 9–133 ['Disciplines of International Law']

'The Twentieth-Century Discipline of International Law in the United States' in Austin Sarat, Bryant Garth and Robert A. Kagan (eds.), *Looking Back at Law's Century* (Ithaca: Cornell University Press, 2002), 386–433 ['International Law in the United States']

Kersten, Jens, *Georg Jellinek und die klassische Staatslehre* (Tübingen: Mohr Siebeck, 2000) [*Georg Jellinek*]

Khan, Daniel-Erasmus, 'Max Huber as Arbitrator: The Palmas (Miangas) Case and Other Arbitrations', *EJIL*, 18 (2007), 145–70 ['The Palmas Case']

Kingsbury, Benedict, 'Legal Positivism as Normative Politics: International Society, Balance of Power and Lassa Oppenheim's Positive International Law', *EJIL*, 13 (2002) 401–36 ['Lassa Oppenheim's Positive International Law']

Kissinger, Henry, *Die Vernunft der Nationen: Über das Wesen der Aussenpolitik* (Berlin: Goldmann, 1996) [*Vernunft der Nationen*]

Klabbers, Jan, 'The Life and Times of the Law of International Organizations', *NJIL*, 70 (2001), 287–317 ['Law of International Organizations']

'(I Can't Get No) Recognition: Subjects Doctrine and the Emergence of Non-State Actors' in Jarna Petman and Jan Klabbers (eds.), *Nordic Cosmopolitanism: Essays in International Law for Martti Koskenniemi* (Leiden: Brill, 2003), 351–69 ['Subjects Doctrine']

'The Concept of Legal Personality', *Ius Gentium*, 11 (2005), 35–66 ['Legal Personality']

Klueber, Johann Ludwig, *Droit des Gens Moderne de l'Europe.* (M. A. Ott, ed.) (Paris: Librairie de Guillaumin, 1861) (originally published 1818) [*Droit des gens*]

Köhnke, Klaus Christian, *Entstehung und Aufstieg des Neukantianismus: Die deutsche Universitätsphilosophie zwischen Idealismus und Positivismus* (Frankfurt a.M.: Suhrkamp, 1986) [*Neukantianismus*]

Kolb, Robert, 'Une observation sur la détermination de la subjectivité internationale', *ZöR*, 52 (1997), 115–25 ['Observation']

La Bonne Foi en Droit International Public: Contribution à l'Étude des Principes Généraux de Droit (Paris: Presses Universitaires de France, 2000) [*Bonne Foi*]

'The Jurisprudence of the Yugoslav and Rwandan Criminal Tribunals on their Jurisdiction and on International Crimes', *BYIL*, 71 (2000), 259–315 ['Jurisprudence of the Yugoslav and Rwandan Criminal Tribunals']

Théorie du ius cogens international: Essai de relecture du concept (Paris: Presses Universitaires de France, 2001) [*Ius Cogens*]

'Nouvelle observation sur la détermination de la personnalité juridique internationale', *ZöR*, 57 (2002), 229–41 ['Nouvelle Observation']

Les Cours Généraux de Droit International Public de l'Académie de La Haye (Brussels: Bruylant, 2003) [*Les Cours Généraux*]

Réfléxions de Philosophie du Droit International: Problèmes Fondamentaux du Droit International Public, Théorie et Philosophie du Droit International (Brussels: Bruylant, 2003) [*Réfléxions*]

'Selected Problems in the Theory of Customary International Law', *NILR*, 50 (2003), 119–50 ['Customary International Law']

'Principles as Sources of International Law (With Special Reference to Good Faith)', *NILR*, 53 (2006), 1–36 ['Principles']

Koselleck, Reinhart, 'Begriffsgeschichte und Sozialgeschichte' in Reinhart Koselleck (ed.), *Historische Semantik und Begriffsgeschichte* (Stuttgart: Klett-Cotta, 1978), 19–36 ['Begriffsgeschichte']

Koskenniemi, Martti, *The Gentle Civilizer of Nations: The Rise and Fall of International Law 1870–1960* (Cambridge University Press, 2001) [*Gentle Civilizer*]

'Hersch Lauterpacht (1897–1960)' in Jack Beatson and Reinhard Zimmermann (eds.), *Jurists Uprooted: German-Speaking Émigré Lawyers in Twentieth-Century Britain* (Oxford University Press, 2004), 603–61 ['Lauterpacht']

'Why History of International Law Today?' *Rechtsgeschichte*, 4 (2004) 61–6 ['Why History of International Law?']

From Apology to Utopia: The Structure of International Legal Argument. Reissue with New Epilogue, 2nd edition (Cambridge University Press, 2005) (originally published 1989) [*Apology to Utopia*]

Krabbe, Hugo, *Die moderne Staatsidee*, 2nd edition (The Hague: Martinus Nijhoff, 1919) [*Moderne Staatsidee*]

Kunz, Josef L., *Die Anerkennung von Staaten und Regierungen im Völkerrecht* 'Handbuch des Völkerrechts' (Fritz Stier-Somlo, ed.) (Stuttgart: W. Kohlhammer, 1928) [*Anerkennung von Staaten*]

'The Status of the Holy See in International Law', *AJIL*, 46 (1952), 308–14 ['Status of the Holy See']

'The Nature of Customary International Law', *AJIL*, 47 (1953), 662–9 ['Customary International Law']

Laband, Paul, *Das Staatsrecht des deutschen Reiches*. 'Handbuch des öffentlichen Rechts der Gegenwart in Monographien' (Heinrich Marquardten, ed.) (Freiburg i.B. and Tübingen: J.C.B. Mohr (Paul Siebeck), 1883) [*Staatsrecht*]

Laborde, Cécile, 'Pluralism, Syndicalism and Corporatism: Léon Duguit and the Crisis of the State', *History of European Ideas*, 22 (1996), 227–44 ['Crisis of the State']

'The Concept of the State in British and French Political Thought', *Political Studies*, 48 (2000), 540–57 ['Concept of the State']

Lalive, Jean-Flavien, 'Un Grand Arbitrage Pétrolier Entre un Gouvernement et Deux Sociétés Privées Étrangères', *JDI*, 104 (1977), 319–49 ['Grand arbitrage pétrolier']

'Contrats entre états ou entreprises étatiques et personnes privées: développements récents', *RCADI*, 181 (1983-III), 13–283 ['Contrats']

Lapradelle, Albert de, 'Introduction' in James Brown Scott (ed.), *Le Droit des Gens, ou Principes de la Loi Naturelle, appliqués à la Conduite aux Affaires des Nations et des Souverains* (Washington: The Carnegie Institute of Washington, 1916), iii–lix ['Introduction']

Lauterpacht, Elihu, 'International Law and Private Foreign Investment', *Indiana Journal of Global Legal Studies*, 4 (1997), 259–76 ['Private Foreign Investment']

Lauterpacht, Hersch, 'Westlake and Present Day International Law', *Economica*, 15 (1925), 307–25 ['Westlake']

Private Law Sources and Analogies of International Law (London: Longmans, Green and Co., 1927) [*Analogies*]

The Function of Law in the International Community (Oxford: The Clarendon Press, 1933) [*Function of Law*]

The Development of International Law by the Permanent Court of International Justice (London: Longmans, Green and Co., 1934) [*Development*]

'Règles Générales du Droit de la Paix', *RCADI*, 62 (1937-IV), 95–422 ['Règles Générales']

'The Law of Nations and the Punishment of War Crimes', *BYIL*, 21 (1944), 58–95 ['Punishment of War Crimes']

Recognition in International Law (Cambridge University Press, 1947) [*Recognition*]

International Law and Human Rights (London: Stevens, 1950) [*Human Rights*]

Oppenheim's International Law: A Treatise, 8th edition (New York: David McKay Company, 1955) [*International Law*]

The Development of International Law by the International Court, revised edition of 'The Development of International Law by the Permanent Court of International Justice (1934)' (London: Stevens, 1958) [*Development* (II)]

'International Law – The General Part' in Elihu Lauterpacht (ed.), *International Law: Being the Collected Papers of Hersch Lauterpacht* (Cambridge University Press, 1975) (not previously published), 1–178 ['General Part']

'Westlake and Present Day International Law' in Elihu Lauterpacht (ed.), *International Law: Being the Collected Papers of Hersch Lauterpacht* (Cambridge University Press, 1975) (originally published 1925), 385–403 ['Westlake']

'Spinoza and International Law' in Elihu Lauterpacht (ed.), *International Law: Being the Collected Papers of Hersch Lauterpacht* (Cambridge University Press, 1975) (originally published 1927), 366–84 ['Spinoza']

'The so-called Anglo-American and Continental Schools of Thought in International Law' in Elihu Lauterpacht (ed.), *International Law: Being the Collected Papers of Hersch Lauterpacht* (Cambridge University Press, 1975) (originally published 1931), 452–83 ['Anglo-Amercian and Continental Schools of Thought']

'Kelsen's Pure Science of Law' in Elihu Lauterpacht (ed.), *International Law: Being the Collected Papers of Hersch Lauterpacht* (Cambridge University Press, 1975) (originally published 1933), 404–30 ['Pure Science of Law']

'The Grotian Tradition in International Law' in Elihu Lauterpacht (ed.), *International Law: Being the Collected Papers of Hersch Lauterpacht* (Cambridge University Press, 1975) (originally published 1946), 307–65 ['Grotian Tradition']

'The Subjects of the Law of Nations' in Elihu Lauterpacht (ed.), *International Law: Being the Collected Papers of Hersch Lauterpacht* (Cambridge University Press, 1975) (originally published 1947), 487–533 ['Subjects']

Le Fur, Louis, 'Règles Générales du Droit de la Paix', *RCADI*, 54 (1935-IV), 1–308 ['Règles Générales']

Leben, Charles, 'Hans Kelsen and the Advancement of International Law', *EJIL*, 9 (1998), 287–305 ['Kelsen']

'La Théorie du Contrat d'État et l'Évolution du Droit International des Investissements', *RCADI*, 302 (2003), 197–386 ['La Théorie du Contrat d'État']

Lesaffer, Randall, 'The Medieval Canon Law of Contract and Early Modern Treaty Law', *Journal of the History of International Law*, 2 (2000), 178–98 ['Medieval Canon Law of Contract']

'The Grotian Tradition Revisited: Change and Continuity in the History of International Law', *BYIL*, 73 (2002), 103–39 ['Grotian Tradition Revisited']

Link, Sandra, *Ein Realist mit Idealen – Der Völkerrechtler Karl Strupp (1886–1940)* (Baden-Baden: Nomos Verlagsgesellschaft, 2003) [*Realist mit Idealen*]

Llewellyn, Karl N., 'A Realistic Jurisprudence – The Next Step', *Columbia Law Review*, 30 (1930), 431–65 ['Realistic Jurisprudence']

'Some Realism about Realism: Responding to Dean Pound', *HLR*, 44 (1931), 1222–64 ['Realism about Realism']

Lovejoy, Arthur O., *The Great Chain of Being: A Study of the History of an Idea (The William James Lectures Delivered at Harvard University, 1933)*, 14th edition (Cambridge (Mass.): Harvard University Press, 1978) [*Chain of Being*]

Maitland, Frederic William, 'Moral Personality and Legal Personality (Sidgwick Lecture)', *Journal of the Society of Comparative Legislation*, 6 (1905), 192–200 ['Legal Personality']

Mälksoo, Lauri, 'The Science of International Law and the Concept of Politics: The Arguments and Lives of the International Law Professors at the University of Dorpat/Iur'ev/Tartu 1855–1985', *BYIL*, 76 (2005), 383–501 ['Concept of Politics']

Mann, F. A., 'The Proper Law of Contracts Concluded by International Persons', *BYIL*, 35 (1959), 34–57 ['Proper Law of Contracts']

'State Contracts and State Responsibility', *AJIL*, 54 (1960), 572–91 ['State Contracts']

Manner, George, 'The Legal Nature and Punishment of Criminal Acts of Violence Contrary to the Laws of War', *AJIL*, 37 (1943), 407–35 ['Criminal Acts of Violence']

Manning, William Oke, *Commentaries on the Law of Nations*, revised edition by Amos Sheldon (London: H. Sweet, 1875) (originally published 1839) [*Commentaries*]

Mantl, Wolfgang, 'Modernisierung und Dekadenz' in Jürgen Nautz and Richard Vahrenkamp (eds.), *Die Wiener Jahrhundertwende* (Vienna: Böhlau, 1993), 80–100 [*Modernisierung*]

Martens, Georg Friedrich von, *Précis du Droit des Gens Moderne de l'Europe (Tome 1–2)* (M. Ch. Vergé, ed.) (Paris: Guillaumin Libraires, 1858) (originally published 1788) [*Précis du droit des gens*]

Marvick, Dwane, 'The Work of Harold D. Lasswell: His Approach, Concerns, and Influence', *Political Behaviour*, 2 (1980), 219–29 ['Lasswell']

McCorquodale, Robert, 'The Individual and the International Legal System' in Malcolm D. Evans (ed.), *International Law*, 2nd edition (Oxford University Press, 2006), 307–32 ['Individual']

McDougal, Myers S., 'Fuller v. the American Legal Realists: An Intervention', *YLJ*, 50 (1941), 827–40 ['American Legal Realists']

'International Law, Power, and Policy: A Contemporary Conception', *RCADI*, 82 (1953-I), 133–259 ['Contemporary Conception']

McDougal, Myers S. and Harold D. Lasswell, 'Legal Education and Public Policy: Professional Training in the Public Interest', *YLJ*, 52 (1943), 203–95 ['Legal Education']

McDougal, Myers S., Harold D. Lasswell and Lung-chu Chen, *Human Rights and World Public Order: The Basic Policies of an International Law of Human Dignity* (New Haven and London: Yale University Press, 1980) [*World Public Order*]

McDougal, Myers S., Harold D. Lasswell and W. Michael Reisman, 'The World Constitutive Process of Authoritative Decision' in Richard A. Falk and Cyril E. Black (eds.), *The Future of the International Legal Order: Volume I: Trends and Patterns* (Princeton University Press, 1969), 73–154 ['World Constitutive Process']

McDougal, Myers S. and W. Michael Reisman. '"The Changing Structure of International Law": Unchanging Theory for Inquiry', *Columbia Law Review*, 65 (1965), 810–35 ['Unchanging Theory']

McFadden, Eric J., 'The Collapse of Tin: Restructuring a Failed Commodity Agreement', *AJIL*, 80 (1986), 811–30 ['Collapse of Tin']

McNair, Arnold, 'The General Principles of Law Recognized by Civilized Nations', *BYIL*, 33 (1957), 1–19 ['General Principles']

The Law of Treaties, 2nd edition (Oxford: The Clarendon Press, 1961) [*Law of Treaties*]

Mendelson, Maurice, 'The Subjective Element in Customary International Law', *BYIL*, 66 (1995), 177–208 ['Subjective Element']

Menon, P. K., 'The Subjects of Modern International Law', *Hague Yearbook of International Law*, 3 (1990), 30–86 ['Subjects']

Merelman, Richard M., 'Harold D. Lasswell's Political World: Weak Tea for Hard Times', *British Journal of Political Science*, 11 (1981), 471–97 ['Lasswell's Political World']

Métall, Rudolf Aladár, *Hans Kelsen: Leben und Werk* (Vienna: Franz Deuticke, 1969) [*Kelsen*]

Morgenthau, Hans J., *Die internationale Rechtspflege, ihr Wesen und ihre Grenzen* (Leipzig: Universitätsverlag von Robert Noske, 1929) [*Internationale Rechtspflege*]

La Réalité des Normes, en Particulier des Normes du Droit International: Fondements d'une Théorie des Normes (Paris: Librairie Felix Alcan, 1934) [*Réalité des normes*]

'Positivism, Functionalism, and International Law', *AJIL*, 34 (1940), 260–84 ['Functionalism']

Politics among Nations: The Struggle for Power and Peace, 5th edition (New York: Alfred Knopf, 1978) (originally published 1948) [*Politics among Nations*]

Mosler, Hermann, 'Die Erweiterung des Kreises der Völkerrechtssubjekte', *ZaöRV*, 22 (1962) 1–48 ['Völkerrechtssubjekte']

'Subjects of International Law', *EPIL*, 4 (2000), 710–27 ['Subjects']

Müller, Jörg Paul and Luzius Wildhaber, *Praxis des Völkerrechts*, 3rd edition (Berne: Stämpfli, 2001) [*Praxis*]

Neff, Stephen C., 'A Short History of International Law' in Malcolm D. Evans (ed.), *International Law*, 2nd edition (Oxford University Press, 2006), 29–55 ['Short History']

Nijman, Janne Elisabeth, *The Concept of International Legal Personality: An Inquiry Into the History and Theory of International Law* (The Hague: T.M.C. Asser Press, 2004) [*Concept of International Legal Personality*]

Nussbaum, Arthur, *A Concise History of the Law of Nations*, 2nd edition (New York: The Macmillan Company, 1954) [*Concise History*]

Nye, Joseph S. Jr., *Understanding International Conflicts: An Introduction to Theory and History*. 'Longman Classics in Political Science', 4th edition (New York: Longman, 2003) [*International Conflicts*]

O'Connell, D. P., 'La Personnalité en Droit International', *RGDIP*, 34 (1963), 5–43 ['Personnalité']

Oellers-Frahm, Karin, 'Die Entscheidung des IGH im Fall LaGrand - Eine Stärkung der internationalen Gerichtsbarkeit und der Rolle des Individuums im Völkerrecht', *Europäische Grundrechte-Zeitschrift*, 28 (2001), 265–72 ['Rolle des Individuums']

Oppenheim, Lassa. *International Law: A Treatise*, 1st edition (London: Longmans, Green, and Co., 1905) [*International Law (1st edn.)*]

'The Science of International Law', *AJIL*, 2 (1908), 313–56 ['Science of International Law']

International Law: A Treatise, 3rd edition (London: Longmans, Green, and Co., 1920) [*International Law (3rd edn.)*]

Orakhelashvili, Alexander, 'The Position of the Individual in International Law', *California Western International Law Journal*, 31 (2001), 241–76 ['Position of the Individual']

Palonen, Kari, 'The History of Concepts as a Style of Political Theorizing: Quentin Skinner's and Reinhart Koselleck's Subversion of Normative Political Theory', *European Journal of Political Theory*, 1 (2002), 91–106 ['History of Concepts']

Quentin Skinner: History, Politics, Rhetoric (Cambridge: Polity Press, 2003) [*History, Politics, Rhetoric*]

Paulson, Stanley L., 'The Neo-Kantian Dimension of Kelsen's Pure Theory of Law', *Oxford Journal of Legal Studies*, 12 (1992), 311–32 ['Neo-Kantian Dimension']

Pellet, Alain, 'Can a State Commit a Crime? Definitely, Yes!', *EJIL*, 10 (1999), 425–34 ['Can a State Commit a Crime?']

Phillimore, Robert, *Commentaries Upon International Law*, 3rd edition (London: Butterworths, 1879) [*International Law*]

Pisillo-Mazzeschi, Riccardo, 'International Obligations to Provide for Reparation Claims?' in Albrecht Randelzhofer and Christian Tomuschat (eds.), *State Responsibility and the Individual* (The Hague: Martinus Nijhoff Publishers, 1999), 149–72 ['Reparation Claims']

Pocock, J. G. A., 'Theory in History: Problems of Context and Narrative' in John S. Dryzek, Bonnie Honig and Anne Phillips (eds.), *The Oxford Handbook of Political Theory* (Oxford University Press, 2006), 163–74 ['Theory in History']

Politis, Nicolas, *Les Nouvelles Tendances du Droit International* (Paris: Librarie Hachette, 1927) [*Nouvelles Tendances*]

Pound, Roscoe, 'Mechanical Jurisprudence', *Columbia Law Review*, 8 (1908), 605–23 ['Mechanical Jurisprudence']

'The Call for a Realist Jurisprudence', *HLR*, 44 (1931), 697–711 ['Realist Jurisprudence']

Preiser, Wolfgang, *Die Völkerrechtsgeschichte: Ihre Aufgabe und ihre Methode* (Wiesbaden: Franz Steiner Verlag, 1964) [*Völkerrechtsgeschichte*]

Price, Roger, *A Concise History of France*, 2nd edition (Cambridge University Press, 2005) [*Concise History*]

Pufendorf, Samuel, *Über die Verfassung des deutschen Reiches* (Berlin: Reimar Hobbing, 1922) (originally published 1667) [*Verfassung des deutschen Reiches*]

De Jure Naturae et Gentium Libri Octo. 'The Classics of International Law' (James Brown Scott, ed.) (Oxford: The Clarendon Press, 1934) (originally published 1688) [*De Jure Naturae et Gentium*]

Quadri, Rolando, *Diritto Internazionale Pubblico*, 4th edition (Palermo: Priulla, 1963) [*Diritto Internazionale*]

'Cours Général de Droit International Public', *RCADI*, 113 (1964-III), 245–483 ['Cours Général']

Rama-Montaldo, Manuel, 'International Legal Personality and Implied Powers of International Organizations', *BYIL*, 44 (1970), 111–55 ['International Legal Personality']

Randelzhofer, Albrecht, *Völkerrechtliche Aspekte des Heiligen Römischen Reiches nach 1648* (Berlin: Duncker und Humblot, 1967) [*Völkerrechtliche Aspekte*]

Ratner, Stephen R., 'Corporations and Human Rights: A Theory of Legal Responsibility', *YLJ*, 111 (2001), 443–545 ['Corporations and Human Rights']

Rawls, John, *A Theory of Justice*, revised edition (Oxford University Press, 1999) [*Theory of Justice*]

Raymond, John M. and Barbara J. Frischholz, 'Lawyers who Established International Law in the United States, 1776–1914', *AJIL*, 76 (1982), 802–29 ['International Law in the United States 1776–1914']

Reisman, W. Michael, 'The View from the New Haven School of International Law', *ASIL Proc*, 86 (1992), 118–25 ['View from New Haven']

Remec, Peter Pavel, *The Position of the Individual in International Law according to Grotius and Vattel* (The Hague: Martinus Nijhoff, 1960) [*The Position of the Individual*]

Reuter, Paul, *Institutions Internationales* (Paris: Presses Universitaires, 1955) [*Institutions Internationales*]

'La personnalité juridique internationale du Comité international de la Croix-Rouge' in Christophe Swinarski (ed.), *Études et Essais sur le Droit International Humanitaire et sur les Principes de la Croix-Rouge en l'Honneur de Jean Pictet* (Geneva and The Hague: Martinus Nijhoff, 1984), 783–91 ['Comité international de la Croix-Rouge']

Richter, Melvin, 'Reconstructing the History of Political Languages: Pocock, Skinner, and Geschichtliche Grundbegriffe', *History and Theory*, 29 (1990), 38–70 ['History of Political Languages']

Rigaux, François, 'Des Dieux et des Héros: Réflexions sur une Sentence Arbitrale', *Revue Critique du Droit International Privé*, 67 (1978), 435–59 ['Sentence arbitrale']

Romano, Santi, *L'Ordinamento Giuridico* (Florence: Sansoni, 1951) (originally published 1918) [*Ordinamento Giuridico*]

Rosenne, Shabtai, *The World Court: What it is and how it Works*, 5th completely revised edition (Dordrecht: Martinus Nijhoff, 1995) [*World Court*]

Rosenthal, Bent, *Étude de l'Oeuvre de Myers Smith McDougal en Matière de Droit International Public* (Paris: Librarie Générale de Droit et de Jurisprudence, 1970) [*œuvre de McDougal*]

Rousseau, Charles, *Droit International Public (Tome II): Les Sujets de Droit* (Paris: Édition Sirey, 1974) [*Droit International Public*]

Rub, Alfred, *Hans Kelsens Völkerrechtslehre: Versuch einer Würdigung* (Zürich: Schulthess, 1995) [*Kelsens Völkerrechtslehre*]

Sadurska, Romana and C. M. Chinkin, 'The Collapse of the International Tin Council: A Case of State Responsibility?', *Virginia Journal of International Law*, 30 (1990), 845–90 ['International Tin Council']

Salvioli, Gabriele, 'Les Règles Générales de la Paix', *RCADI*, 46 (1933-IV), 1–164 ['Règles Générales']

Scelle, Georges, *Précis de Droit des Gens* (Paris: Recueil Sirey, 1932) [*Précis*]

'La Doctrine de L. Duguit et les Fondements du Droit des Gens', *Archives de Philosophie du droit et de sociologie juridique*, 2 (1932), 83–119 ['Duguit et droit des gens']

'Règles Générales du Droit de la Paix', *RCADI*, 46 (1933-IV), 327–703 ['Règles Générales']

Schermers, Henry G. and Niels M. Blokker, *International Institutional Law: Unity within Diversity*, 3rd revised edition (The Hague: Martinus Nijhoff, 1995) [*International Institutional Law*]

Schmoeckel, Mathias, 'The Internationalist as a Scientist and Herald: Lassa Oppenheim', *EJIL*, 11 (2000), 699–712 ['Internationalist as a Scientist']

'Lassa Oppenheim (1858–1919)' in Jack Beatson and Reinhard Zimmermann (eds.), *Jurists Uprooted: German-Speaking Emigré Lawyers in Twentieth Century Britain* (Oxford University Press, 2004), 583–99 ['Oppenheim']

Schorske, Carl E., *Fin-de-Siècle Vienna: Politics and Culture* (New York: Alfred A. Knopf, 1980) [*Fin-de-Siècle Vienna*]

Schulze, Hagen, *Staat und Nation in der europäischen Geschichte*, 2nd edition (Munich: C.H. Beck, 2004) [*Staat und Nation*]

Schwarzenberger, Georg, *Die internationalen Banken für Zahlungsausgleich und Agrarkredite*. 'Wirtschaftsprobleme der Gegenwart' (Adolf Weber, ed.) (Berlin: Junker und Dünnhaupt, 1932) [*Internationale Banken*]

A Manual of International Law, 1st edition (London: Stevens & Sons, 1947) [*Manual*]

'The Inductive Approach to International Law', *HLR*, 60 (1947) 539–70. ['Inductive Approach']

International Law Volume I: International Law as Applied by International Courts and Tribunals, 2nd edition (London: Stevens and Sons, 1949) [*International Law* (2nd edn.)]

Machtpolitik (Tübingen: J.C.B. Mohr, 1955) [*Machtpolitik*]

'The Fundamental Principles of International Law', *RCADI*, 87 (1955-I), 195–385 ['Fundamental Principles']

International Law Volume I: International Law as Applied by International Courts and Tribunals, 3rd edition (London: Stevens, 1957) [*International Law* (3rd edn.)]

Foreign Investments and International Law (London: Stevens and Sons, 1969) [*Foreign Investments*]

A Manual of International Law, 6th edition (London: Professional Books, 1976) [*Manual*]

Searl, John R., 'How to Derive "Ought" from "Is"', *Philosophical Review*, 73 (1964), 43–58 ['Ought from Is']

Seibert-Fohr, Anja and Rüdiger Wolfrum, 'Die einzelstaatliche Durchsetzung völkerrechtlicher Mindeststandards gegenüber transnationalen Unternehmen', *AVR*, 43 (2005), 153–86 ['Einzelstaatliche Durchsetzung']

Seidl-Hohenveldern, Ignaz, 'Die völkerrechtliche Haftung für Handlungen internationaler Organisationen im Verhältnis zu Nichtmitgliedstaaten', (Neue Folge) *Österreichische Zeitschrift für Öffentliches Recht*, XI (1961), 497–506 ['Handlungen internationaler Organisationen']

International Economic Law, 3rd revised edition (The Hague: Kluwer Law International, 1999) [*International Economic Law*]

Sereni, Angelo Piero, *The Italian Conception of International Law* (New York: Columbia University Press, 1943) [*Italian Conception*]

Diritto Internazionale (II/2) (Milan: Giuffré, 1960) [*Diritto Internazionale*]

Seyersted, Finn, 'United Nations Forces: Some Legal Problems', *BYIL*, 37 (1961), 351–475 ['United Nations Forces']

Objective International Personality of Intergovernmental Organisations: Do Their Capacities Really Depend upon Their Constitutions? (Copenhagen s.n.: 1963) [*Objective International Personality*]

Shaw, Malcolm N., *International Law*, 6th edition (Cambridge University Press, 2008) [*International Law*]

Shraga, Daphna and Ralph Zacklin, 'The International Criminal Tribunal for the Former Yugoslavia', *EJIL*, 5 (1994), 360–80 ['ICTY']

Simma, Bruno, 'The Contribution of Alfred Verdross to the Theory of International Law', *EJIL*, 6 (1995), 33–54 ['Contribution of Verdross']

Simmel, Georg, *Einleitung in die Moralwissenschaft: Eine Kritik der ethischen Grundbegriffe*, 2nd edition (Berlin und Stuttgart: Cotta, 1904) (originally published 1892–3) [*Moralwissenschaft*]

Simpson, Gerry, 'Duelling Agendas: International Relations and International Law (Again)', *Journal of International Law and International Relations*, 1 (2005), 61–74 ['Duelling Agendas']

Sinclair, Anthony C., 'The Origins of the Umbrella Clause in the International Law of Investment Protection', *Arbitration International*, 20 (2004), 411–34 ['Umbrella Clause']

Siotto-Pintor, Manfredi, 'Les Sujets du Droit International autres que les États', *RCADI*, 41 (1932-III), 245–360 ['Sujets autres que les États']

Skinner, Quentin, 'Meaning and Understanding in the History of Ideas', *History and Theory*, 8 (1969), 3–53 ['Meaning and Understanding']

'The state' in Terence Ball, James Farr and Russell L. Hanson (eds.), *Political Innovation and Conceptual Change* (Cambridge University Press, 1989), 90–131 ['State']

Visions of Politics I: Regarding Method (Cambridge University Press, 2002) [*Regarding Method*]

Slaughter, Anne-Marie, 'International Law in a World of Liberal States', *EJIL*, 6 (1995), 503–38 ['World of Liberal States']

Slaughter Burley, Anne-Marie, 'International Law and International Relations Theory: A Dual Agenda', *AJIL*, 87 (1993), 205–39 ['Dual Agenda']

Smend, Rudolf, *Verfassung und Verfassungsrecht* (Munich and Leipzig: Duncker und Humblot, 1928) [*Verfassungsrecht*]

Spiermann, Ole, 'The Other Side of the Story: An Unpopular Essay on the Making of the European Community Legal Order', *EJIL*, 10 (1999), 763–89 ['Other Side of the Story']

'"Who Attempts too Much does Nothing Well": The 1920 Advisory Committee of Jurists and the Statute of the Permanent Court of International Justice' *BYIL*, 73 (2002), 187–260 ['Statute of the Permament Court']

'The LaGrand Case and the Individual as a Subject of International Law', *ZöR*, 58 (2003), 197–221 ['LaGrand Case']

'Individual Rights, State Interests and the Power to Waive ICSID Jurisdiction under Bilateral Investment Treaties', *Arbitration International*, 20 (2004), 179–211 ['Individual Rights']

International Legal Argument in the Permanent Court of International Justice: The Rise of the International Judiciary (Cambridge University Press, 2005) [*International Legal Argument in the PCIJ*]

Stammler, Rudolf, *Theorie der Rechtswissenschaft* (Halle a.d. Saale: Buchhandlung des Waisenhauses, 1911) [*Theorie*]

Stein, Torsten, 'Kosovo and the International Community. The Attribution of Possible Internationally Wrongful Acts: Responsibility of NATO or of its Member States' in Christian Tomuschat (ed.), *Kosovo and the International Community: A Legal Assessment* (The Hague: Kluwer Law International, 2002), 181–92 ['Responsibility of NATO?']

Steinle, Stephanie, *Völkerrecht und Machtpolitik: Georg Schwarzenberger (1908–1991)*. 'Studien zur Geschichte des Völkerrechts' (Michael Stolleis, ed.) (Baden-Baden: Nomos, 2000) [*Völkerrecht und Machtpolitik*]

'Georg Schwarzenberger (1908–1991)' in Jack Beatson and Reinhard Zimmermann (eds.), *Jurists Uprooted: German-Speaking Emigré Lawyers in Twentieth-Century Britain* (Oxford University Press, 2004), 663–80 ['Schwarzenberger']

Stolleis, Michael, *Geschichte des öffentlichen Rechts in Deutschland 1. Band: Reichspublizistik und Policeywissenschaft 1600–1800* (Munich: C.H. Beck, 1988) [*Geschichte des öffentlichen Rechts (I)*]

Geschichte des öffentlichen Rechts in Deutschland 2. Band: Staatsrechtslehre und Verwaltungswissenschaft 1800–1914 (Munich: C.H. Beck, 1992) [*Geschichte des öffentlichen Rechts (II)*]

Geschichte des öffentlichen Rechts in Deutschland 3. Band: Staats- und Verwaltungsrechtswissenschaft in Republik und Diktatur 1914–1945 (Munich: C.H. Beck, 1999) [*Geschichte des öffentlichen Rechts (III)*]

Stone, Julius, *Social Dimensions of Law and Justice* (London: Stevens, 1966) [*Social Dimensions*]

Strauss, Leo, *What Is Political Philosophy*? (New York: The Free Press, 1968) [*Political Philosophy*]

Strupp, Karl, *Das völkerrechtliche Delikt*. 'Handbuch des Völkerrechts' (Fritz Stier-Somlo, ed.) (Berlin et al.: W. Kohlhammer, 1920) [*Delikt*]

'Das Ausnahmerecht der Länder nach Art. 48 IV der Reichsverfassung', *AöR*, 5 (1923), 182–205 ['Ausnahmerecht']

Grundzüge des positiven Völkerrechts, 4th edition (Bonn: Ludwig Röhrscheid, 1928) [*Grundzüge*]

'Les Règles Générales du Droit de la Paix', *RCADI*, 47 (1934-I), 263–593 ['Règles Générales']

Stumer, Andrew, 'Liability of Member States for Acts of International Organizations: Reconsidering the Policy Objections', *HILJ*, 48 (2007), 553–80 ['Liability of Member States']

Suarez, Francisco, *Selections from Three Works of Francisco Suarez*. 'The Classics of International Law' (James Brown Scott, ed.) (Oxford: The Clarendon Press, 1944) (originally published 1612–1621) [*Selections*]

Sylvest, Casper, 'International Law in Nineteenth-Century Britain', *BYIL*, 75 (2004), 9–70 ['International Law in Nineteenth-Century Britain']

Talmon, Stefan, *Kollektive Nichtanerkennung illegaler Staaten* (Tübingen: Mohr Siebeck, 2006) [*Kollektive Nichtanerkennung*]

Tams, Christian J., *Enforcing Obligations Erga Omnes in International Law* (Cambridge University Press, 2005) [*Obligations Erga Omnes*]

Tanca, Antonio, 'Dionisio Anzilotti (1867–1950): Biographical Note with Bibliography', *EJIL*, 3 (1992), 156–62 ['Dionisio Anzilotti']

Taylor, Charles, 'Hegel's Ambiguous Legacy for Modern Liberalism', *Cardozo Law Review*, 10 (1989), 857–70 ['Hegel's Ambiguous Legacy']

Thürer, Daniel, 'The Emergence of Non-Governmental Organizations and Transnational Enterprises in International Law and the Changing Role of the State' in Rainer Hofmann (ed.), *Non-State Actors as New Subjects of International Law* (Berlin: Duncker und Humblot, 1998), 37–58 ['Emergence']

Timms, Edward, 'Die Wiener Kreise: Schöpferische Interaktionen in der Wiener Moderne' in Jürgen Nautz and Richard Vahrenkamp (eds.), *Die Wiener Jahrhundertwende* (Vienna: Böhlau, 1993), 128–43 ['Wiener Kreise']

Tocqueville, Alexis de, *De la Démocratie en Amérique* (Paris: Gallimard, 1986) (originally published 1835) [*Démocratie en Amérique*]

Tomuschat, Christian, 'International Law: Ensuring the Survival of Mankind on the Eve of a New Century: General Course on Public International Law', *RCADI*, 281 (1999), 9–438 ['General Course']

Torrazza, Eugenio and Stefano Di Iorio, *Storia del Diritto Italiano* (Naples: Edizioni Simone, 1998) [*Diritto Italiano*]

Tribe, Laurence H., *American Constitutional Law: Volume One*, third edition (New York: Foundation Press, 2000) [*Constitutional Law*]

Triepel, Heinrich, *Droit International et Droit Interne*. 'Bibliothèque Française de Droit des Gens de la Fondation Carnegie' (A. de Lapradelle, ed.) (Paris: A. Pedone, 1920) [*Droit International et Interne*]

'Les Rapports entre le Droit Interne et le Droit International', *RCADI*, 1 (1923-I), 77–121 ['Rapports']

Truyol y Serra, Antonio, 'Doctrines Contemporaines du Droit des Gens', *RGDIP*, XXI–XXII (1950-1), 369–416, 23–40, 199–236 ['Doctrines du Droit des Gens']

Histoire du Droit International Public (Paris: Economica, 1995) [*Histoire*]

v. d. Heydte, Friedrich August Freiherr, 'Die Stellung und Funktion des Heiligen Stuhls im heutigen Völkerrecht', *Österreichische ZöR*, II (1950), 572–86 ['Stellung des Heiligen Stuhls']

Vaihinger, Hans, *Die Philosophie des Als Ob: System der theoretischen, praktischen und religiösen Fiktionen der Menschheit auf Grund eines idealistischen Positivismus*, 6th edition (Leipzig: Felix Meiner, 1920) [*Philosophie des Als Ob*]

Vattel, Emer de, *Le Droit des Gens, ou Principes de la Loi Naturelle, appliqués à la Conduite aux Affaires des Nations et des Souverains*. 'The Classics of International Law' (James Brown Scott, ed.) (Washington: The Carnegie Institution of Washington, 1916) (originally published 1758) [*Le Droit des Gens*]

Vazquez, Carlos M., 'Treaty-Based Rights and Remedies of Individuals', *Columbia Law Review*, 92 (1992), 1082–163 ['Treaty-Based Rights']

'Direct vs. Indirect Obligations of Corporations Under International Law', *Columbia Journal of Transnational Law*, 43 (2005), 927–59 ['Obligations of Corporations']

Veeder, V. V., 'The Lena Goldfields Arbitration: The Historical Roots of Three Ideas', *ICLQ*, 47 (1998), 747–92 ['Lena Goldfields Arbitration']

Verdirame, Guglielmo, 'The Divided West: International Lawyers in Europe and America', *EJIL*, 18 (2007), 553–80 ['Divided West']

Verdross, Alfred, *Die Einheit des rechtlichen Weltbildes auf Grundlage der Völkerrechtsverfassung* (Tübingen: J.C.B. Mohr, 1923) [*Einheit des rechtlichen Weltbildes*]

Die Verfassung der Völkerrechtsgemeinschaft (Vienna and Berlin: Julius Springer, 1926) [*Verfassung*]

Völkerrecht, 1st edition (Berlin: Julius Springer, 1937) [*Völkerrecht*]

'Forbidden Treaties in International Law', *AJIL*, 31 (1937), 571–77 ['Forbidden Treaties']

'Die Sicherung von ausländischen Privatrechten aus Abkommen zur wirtschaftlichen Entwicklung mit Schiedsklauseln', *ZaöRV*, 18 (1957), 635–51 ['Sicherung von ausländischen Privatrechten']

'Jus Dispositivum and Jus Cogens in International Law', *AJIL*, 60 (1966), 55–63 ['Jus Cogens']

'Entstehungsweisen und Geltungsgrund des universellen völkerrechtlichen Gewohnheitsrechts', *ZaöRV*, 29 (1969), 635–53 ['Gewohnheitsrecht']

Verdross, Alfred and Bruno Simma, *Universelles Völkerrecht: Theorie und Praxis*, 3rd edition (Berlin: Duncker und Humblot, 1984) [*Völkerrecht*]

Verhoeven, Joe, *Droit International Public*, (Brussels: Larcier, 2000) [*Droit International*]

Vermeer-Künzli, Annemarieke, 'As If: The Legal Fiction in Diplomatic Protection', *EJIL*, 18 (2007), 37–68 ['Legal Fiction']

Verzijl, Jan Hendrik Willem, *International Law in Historical Perspective Volume 2: International Persons* (Leyden: A. Sijthoff, 1969) [*International Law in Historical Perspective (II)*]

Villiger, Mark E., *Customary International Law and Treaties: A Manual on the Theory and Practice of the Interrelation of Sources*, 2nd edition (The Hague: Kluwer Law International, 1997) [*Customary International Law and Treaties*]

Vitoria, Francisco de, *Political Writings*. 'Cambridge History of Political Thought' (Anthony Pagden and Jeremy Lawrence, eds.) (Cambridge University Press, 1991) (originally published 1539) [*Political Writings*]

Von Mehren, Robert B. and Nicholas Kourides, 'International Arbitrations between States and Foreign Private Parties: The Libyan Nationalization Cases', *AJIL*, 75 (1981), 476–552 ['Libyan Nationalization Cases']

Voos, Sandra, *Die Schule von New Haven: Darstellung und Kritik einer amerikanischen Völkerrechtslehre* (Berlin: Duncker und Humblot, 2000) [*Schule von New Haven*]

Weber, Max, 'Politik als Beruf' in Horst Baier et al. (eds.), *Max Weber Gesamtausgabe* (Tübingen: J.C.B. Mohr, 1992) (originally published 1919), 156–252 ['Politik als Beruf']

Wehler, Hans-Ulrich, *Deutsche Gesellschaftsgeschichte 2. Band: Von der Reformära bis zur industriellen und politischen 'Deutschen Doppelrevolution' 1815–1845/49* (Munich: C.H. Beck, 1987) [*Deutsche Gesellschaftsgeschichte (II)*]

Deutsche Gesellschaftsgeschichte 3. Band: Von der deutschen Doppelrevolution bis zum Beginn des Ersten Weltkrieges 1849–1914 (Munich: C.H. Beck, 1995) [*Deutsche Gesellschaftsgeschichte (III)*]

Deutsche Gesellschaftsgeschichte 4. Band: Von Beginn des Ersten Weltkrieges bis zur Gründung der beiden deutschen Staaten 1914–1949 (Munich: C.H. Beck, 2003) [*Deutsche Gesellschaftsgeschichte (IV)*]

Weil, Prosper, 'Cours Général de Droit International Public: le Droit International en Quête de son Identité', *RCADI*, 237 (1992-VI), 9–370 ['Cours Général']

Weiler, J. H. H., 'The Transformation of Europe', *YLJ*, 100 (1991), 2403–483 ['Transformation']

Westphal, Kenneth, 'The basic context and structure of Hegel's Philosophy of Right' in Frederick C. Beiser (ed.), *The Cambridge Companion to Hegel* (Cambridge University Press, 1993), 234–69 ['Hegel's Philosophy of Right']

Wheaton, Henry, *Elements of International Law*. 'The Classics of International Law' (James Brown Scott, ed.) (Oxford: The Clarendon Press, 1936) (originally published 1836) [*Elements*]

White, Morton, *Social Thought in America: The Revolt against Formalism* (Oxford University Press, 1976) (originally published 1947) [*Social Thought in America*]

Wildhaber, Luzius, 'The European Convention on Human Rights and International Law', *ICLQ*, 56 (2007), 217–31 ['Human Rights and International Law']

Willard, Andrew R., 'Myers Smith McDougal: A Life of and about Human Dignity', *YLJ*, 108 (1999), 927–33 ['McDougal']

Willetts, Peter, 'Transnational Actors and International Organizations in Global Politics' in John Baylis and Steve Smith (eds.), *The Globalization of World Politics: An Introduction to International Relations*, 2nd edition (Oxford University Press, 2001), 356–83 ['Transnational Actors']

Williams, John Fischer, 'The Legal Character of the Bank for International Settlements', *AJIL*, 24 (1930), 665–73 ['Bank for International Settlements']

Winkler, Heinrich August, *Deutsche Geschichte vom Ende des Alten Reiches bis zum Untergang der Weimarer Republik* (Bonn: Bundeszentrale für politische Bildung, 2000) [*Deutsche Geschichte*]

Wolff, Christian, *Jus Gentium Methodo Scientifica Pertractatum*. 'The Classics of International Law' (James Brown Scott, ed.) (Oxford: The Clarendon Press, 1934) (originally published 1740–8) [*Jus Gentium*]

Wolff, Michael, 'Hegels staatstheoretischer Organizismus: Zum Begriff und zur Methode der Hegelschen Staatswissenschaft', *Hegel-Studien*, 19 (1984), 147–77 ['Hegels staatstheoretischer Organizismus']

Wright, Quincey, 'The Law of the Nuremburg Trial', *AJIL*, 41 (1947), 38–72 ['Nuremburg Trial']

Zoller, Elisabeth, 'International Criminal Responsibility of Individuals for International Crimes' in George Ginsburg and V. N. Kudriavtsev (eds.), *The Nuremberg Trial and International Law* (Dordrecht: Martinus Nijhoff, 1990), 99–120 ['Criminal Responsibility of Individuals']

INDEX

CAMBRIDGE STUDIES IN INTERNATIONAL AND COMPARATIVE LAW

Books in the series

Legal Personality in International Law
Roland Portmann

Vicarious Liability in Tort: A Comparative Perspective
Paula Giliker

Legitimacy and Legality in International Law: An Interactional Account
Jutta Brunnée and Stephen J. Toope

The Public International Law Theory of Hans Kelsen: Believing in Universal Law
Jochen von Bernstorff

The Concept of Non-International Armed Conflict in International Humanitarian Law
Anthony Cullen

The Challenge of Child Labour in International Law
Franziska Humbert

Shipping Interdiction and the Law of the Sea
Douglas Guilfoyle

International Courts and Environmental Protection
Tim Stephens

Legal Principles in WTO Disputes
Andrew D. Mitchell

War Crimes in Internal Armed Conflicts
Eve La Haye

Humanitarian Occupation
Gregory H. Fox

The International Law of Environmental Impact Assessment: Process, Substance and Integration
Neil Craik

The Law and Practice of International Territorial Administration: Versailles, Iraq and Beyond
Carsten Stahn

Cultural Products and the World Trade Organization
Tania Voon

United Nations Sanctions and the Rule of Law
Jeremy Farrall

National Law in WTO Law: Effectiveness and Good Governance in the World Trading System
Sharif Bhuiyan

The Threat of Force in International Law
Nikolas Stürchler

Indigenous Rights and United Nations Standards
Alexandra Xanthaki

International Refugee Law and Socio-Economic Rights
Michelle Foster

The Protection of Cultural Property in Armed Conflict
Roger O'Keefe

Interpretation and Revision of International Boundary Decisions
Kaiyan Homi Kaikobad

Multinationals and Corporate Social Responsibility: Limitations and Opportunities in International Law
Jennifer A. Zerk

Judiciaries within Europe: A Comparative Review
John Bell

Law in Times of Crisis: Emergency Powers in Theory and Practice
Oren Gross and Fionnuala Ní Aoláin

Vessel-Source Marine Pollution: The Law and Politics of International Regulation
Alan Tan

Enforcing Obligations Erga Omnes *in International Law*
Christian J. Tams

Non-Governmental Organisations in International Law
Anna-Karin Lindblom

Democracy, Minorities and International Law
Steven Wheatley

Prosecuting International Crimes: Selectivity and the International Law Regime
Robert Cryer

Compensation for Personal Injury in English, German and Italian Law: A Comparative Outline
Basil Markesinis, Michael Coester, Guido Alpa, Augustus Ullstein

Dispute Settlement in the UN Convention on the Law of the Sea
Natalie Klein

The International Protection of Internally Displaced Persons
Catherine Phuong

Imperialism, Sovereignty and the Making of International Law
Antony Anghie

Necessity, Proportionality and the Use of Force by States
Judith Gardam

International Legal Argument in the Permanent Court of International Justice: The Rise of the International Judiciary
Ole Spiermann

Great Powers and Outlaw States: Unequal Sovereigns in the International Legal Order
Gerry Simpson

Local Remedies in International Law
C. F. Amerasinghe

Reading Humanitarian Intervention: Human Rights and the Use of Force in International Law
Anne Orford

Conflict of Norms in Public International Law: How WTO Law Relates to Other Rules of Law
Joost Pauwelyn

Transboundary Damage in International Law
Hanqin Xue

European Criminal Procedures
Edited by Mireille Delmas-Marty and John Spencer

The Accountability of Armed Opposition Groups in International Law
Liesbeth Zegveld

Sharing Transboundary Resources International Law and Optimal Resource Use
Eyal Benvenisti

International Human Rights and Humanitarian Law
René Provost

Remedies Against International Organisations
Karel Wellens

Diversity and Self-Determination in International Law
Karen Knop

The Law of Internal Armed Conflict
Lindsay Moir

International Commercial Arbitration and African States Practice, Participation and Institutional Development
Amazu A. Asouzu

The Enforceability of Promises in European Contract Law
James Gordley

International Law in Antiquity
David J. Bederman

Money Laundering: A New International Law Enforcement Model
Guy Stessens

Good Faith in European Contract Law
Reinhard Zimmermann and Simon Whittaker

On Civil Procedure
J. A. Jolowicz

Trusts: A Comparative Study
Maurizio Lupoi

The Right to Property in Commonwealth Constitutions
Tom Allen

International Organizations Before National Courts
August Reinisch

The Changing International Law of High Seas Fisheries
Francisco Orrego Vicuña

Trade and the Environment: A Comparative Study of EC and US Law
Damien Geradin

Unjust Enrichment: A Study of Private Law and Public Values
Hanoch Dagan

Religious Liberty and International Law in Europe
Malcolm D. Evans

Ethics and Authority in International Law
Alfred P. Rubin

Sovereignty Over Natural Resources: Balancing Rights and Duties
Nico Schrijver

The Polar Regions and the Development of International Law
Donald R. Rothwell

Fragmentation and the International Relations of Micro-States: Self-determination and Statehood
Jorri Duursma

Principles of the Institutional Law of International Organizations
C. F. Amerasinghe

Lightning Source UK Ltd.
Milton Keynes UK
UKOW041411111112

201966UK00001B/81/P

9 780521 768450